Intimate
Domain

Studies in Violence, Mimesis, and Culture

Intimate Domain

DESIRE, TRAUMA, AND
MIMETIC THEORY

Martha J. Reineke

Michigan State University Press · *East Lansing*

Copyright © 2014 by Martha J. Reineke

⊛ The paper used in this publication meets the minimum requirements of ANSI/NISO
Z39.48-1992 (R 1997) (Permanence of Paper).

 Michigan State University Press
East Lansing, Michigan 48823-5245

Printed and bound in the United States of America.

20 19 18 17 16 15 14   1 2 3 4 5 6 7 8 9 10

LIBRARY OF CONGRESS CONTROL NUMBER: 2014931994
ISBN: 978-1-61186-128-0 (pbk.)
ISBN: 978-1-60917-415-6 (ebook: PDF)
ISBN: 978-1-62895-003-8 (ebook: ePub)
ISBN: 978-1-62896-003-7 (ebook: Mobi/prc)

Book design and composition by Charlie Sharp, Sharp Des!gns, Lansing, Michigan
Cover design by David Drummond, Salamander Design, www.salamanderhill.com
Cover art is *Oedipus and the Sphinx*, 1864, by Gustave Moreau, from the collection of The
Metropolitan Museum of Art, a bequest of William H. Herriman, 1920.

g green
press
INITIATIVE Michigan State University Press is a member of the Green Press Initiative
and is committed to developing and encouraging ecologically responsible
publishing practices. For more information about the Green Press Initiative and the use of
recycled paper in book publishing, please visit *www.greenpressinitiative.org*.

Visit Michigan State University Press at *www.msupress.org*

In Memoriam

Mary and Lester Reineke

Contents

Acknowledgments

The idea for this book emerged during a faculty seminar on *Antigone* at the University of Northern Iowa and crystallized when Rosemary Johnsen invited me to present a paper on *Antigone* at an annual meeting of the Colloquium on Violence and Religion (COV&R). I realized then that ideas I had explored in my book *Sacrificed Lives* merited further attention. Previously, I had reflected on how René Girard's mimetic theory enhances Kristeva's discussion of violence. In conversation with other feminist scholars, I realized that I should develop further the dialogue I had initiated between Kristeva and Girard. Just as I had found that Girard enhances and augments Kristeva's reflections on violence, I now saw that Kristeva offers key insights that helpfully extend the analytic powers of mimetic theory. *Intimate Domain* was born of this insight.

In multiple venues over many years, my colleagues in COV&R have been highly responsive to this project as I have shared drafts of chapters with them, and I thank them for their support. I also have been sustained in my efforts by the University of Northern Iowa, which granted me a professional development assignment and a summer fellowship to write several chapters of this book. I thank my graduate assistant, Chelsea DeLucenay, for her help, especially for the bibliographic support she provided for the chapters on

Proust. I offer thanks to reference librarian Jerilyn Marshall at the UNI Rod Library, who helped me track down elusive resources. Because a majority of the books and journal articles cited in this book were made available to me through interlibrary loans, I particularly appreciate the assistance of Rosemary Meany and Linda Berneking in the interlibrary loan department at the Rod Library. Their professionalism and commitment to outstanding service expedited my bibliographic research. That I was able to successfully complete this book I attribute also to my affiliation with the Academic Writing Club, a wonderful online community of scholars who held me accountable for daily writing during the two years I wrote the bulk of this book. Thanks goes to my colleague Susan Hill who, with unflagging optimism, always presented this project to me as "no different than writing a few journal articles." I express appreciation also to William Johnsen, editor of the Violence, Mimesis, and Culture series at Michigan State University Press, for his support and steadfast belief in my ability to complete this project. I would be remiss were I not to acknowledge that my own family has been indispensable to the success of this project. My husband, Bill, and my daughter, Beth, have been unwavering in their acceptance of my passion for scholarship. I am most grateful to them.

I began writing this book shortly after the death of my mother and wrote much of it during the years that my sister, Janalee, and I traveled together once a month to visit my father before he died. The death of one's parents is a unique rite of passage after which one takes up a new place on a multigenerational continuum. One's roles as a daughter, sibling, and parent are forever changed by the death of one's own parents, and one sees everything and feels everything differently afterwards. Reading *In Search of Lost Time*, *Antigone*, and *The Old Man and the Wolves* in the shadow of my parents' passing opened these works up in ways that I could not have imagined earlier. Demonstrating compassion for others throughout their lives, my parents remain models for me of relationships founded in acceptance rather than rivalry. Their example inspires the hope that pervades this book.

An earlier version of chapter 7 was published in *Kristeva's Fiction*, edited by Benigno Trigo, and sections of the prelude to part 3 and chapter 8 were published in *Philosophy Today*.[1]

The Family, Feminist Scholarship, and Mimetic Theory

I do not believe it is possible for a rational system, based on the data of consciousness, to respond to the evil and horror that exist in the world.

—Julia Kristeva, *Nations without Nationalism*

Great relationships sometimes never get off the ground because of a bad first date. With little knowledge of each other's backgrounds or personal styles, two individuals may interpret a communication snafu as a sign of fundamental incompatibility and never move on to a second date. Girard's rejection of psychoanalytic theory, developed from his reading of Freud early in his career, amounts to such a first-date miscue. A relationship that could have been beneficial to both psychoanalysis and mimetic theory remains largely undeveloped because of Girard's early dismissal of Freud. I want to revisit this failed relationship, especially in the interest of advancing our understanding of the role of the family in mimetic desire.

Girard uses the term "mimetic desire" to describe humanity's fundamental tendency to imitate others, which takes the specific form of a quest to acquire objects desired by our models. Because conflict over objects is endemic to our expressions of desire, Girard's mimetic theory not only accounts for the centrality of conflict to desire but also for ways in which culture emerges and functions to control that conflict. Although Girard has explored how mimetic desire functions in a variety of settings, the social institution that humans encounter first—the family—has received little attention from him or from scholars of his work. I trace Girard's inattention to the family to a specific reading by Girard of Freud's account of family dynamics, and I propose that an expanded understanding of psychoanalytic theory's perspective on the family will open mimetic theory to a number of productive insights. My goal is to augment the explanatory power of Girard's mimetic theory by drawing attention to themes that come to the fore in the examination of family life: sensory experience, trauma, and intimacy. These themes, which psychoanalytic theory illuminates, have been underrepresented in scholarship on mimetic theory.

Freud under Glass

Girard's perspective on Freud provides entrée to my discussion of family life. In *Violence and the Sacred*, Girard delineates his disagreement with Freud by distinguishing desire as understood by Freud from desire that Girard attributes to mimetic processes. Girard's criticism is pointed and succinct: "The mimetic process detaches desire from any predetermined object, whereas the Oedipus complex fixes desire on the maternal object."[1]

On Girard's understanding of family dynamics, a child is mimetically connected to his father and, in modeling himself on his father, *thereby* directs his desires toward his mother, as has his father before him. True, Freud does make a like observation: "A little boy will exhibit a special interest in his father; he would like to grow like and be like him, and take his place everywhere."[2] However, on Girard's reading, Freud replaces this account of a son's desire, which Girard would support, with a version that focuses on sexual cathexis. Freud subsequently argues that a boy's desire is directed immediately toward his mother. Moreover, Girard understands Freud to claim an adult perspective by the child toward his father: the child is purportedly aware that his competitive claim to his mother makes him a usurper of his father's position.[3]

Freud's description of family dynamics is wrong on several counts, according to Girard. Although Freud observes a child's primary identification with his father, "anterior to any choice of an object," Freud "deliberately" turns his back on this profound insight.[4] Moreover, Freud's account of desire is impossibly ambivalent: the human child's desire is linked at times to a "philosophy of consciousness" and at other times to a mute biologism.[5] Further, Freud attributes an adult mind-set to a child who actually is innocent of the "incest wish" attributed to him.[6] Finally, as a consequence of these initial mistakes, Freud errs in construing the family as a locus of conflict. Parents actually provide an environment for their child that consistently is safer than other environments because the parent/child relationship lacks acquisitive elements that mar other social relationships.[7]

In his criticism of Freud, Girard acts as a scientist does when preparing a sample for microscopic examination: he extracts and mounts on slides selected ideas from Freud's corpus and uses his fixative-like commentary to adhere these concepts permanently to glass. But the result of this experiment is problematic. I do not fault Girard for placing "Freud under glass"; rigorous science benefits when researchers capture on slides specific features of organisms, thereby making them available for close and repeated observation. Rather, I am concerned that Girard does not raise his eyes from his microscope, as it were, to examine how these concepts function *in a living system*. Viewed out of context and shorn of contested and developing features within Freud's corpus as well in psychoanalytic theory after Freud, the concepts preserved in "Freud under glass" are tainted by reductionism atypical in Girard's work. After all, Girard brings an expansive vision to his reading of Freud's *Totem and Taboo*. Most notably, when other scholars discount Freud's hypothesis of a founding murder by a primal horde, Girard fully engages that hypothesis.[8] However, Girard's challenge to Freud's depiction of the Oedipal dynamic is made to function as a comprehensive rather than discrete representation of family dynamics within psychoanalytic theory. Moreover, Girard treats these concepts as quasi-genetic phenomena. Throughout his career, Girard remains wary of psychoanalytic theory, as if its entire history is corrupted by the ideas he preserved early on in "Freud under glass." As a consequence, Girard is inattentive to diverse currents in the century-spanning, developmental trajectory of psychoanalytic theory.[9] Because some aspects of this theory have strong potential to contribute to mimetic theory, strengthening and refining it, that Girard's vision has remained fixed on "Freud under glass" has had deleterious consequences for Girard's thought and for the field of mimetic theory as well.

Mark Anspach well describes the perspective on Freud that I attribute to Girard. Introducing Girard to a novice reader of his work, Anspach explains that Freud and Girard are looking for universal mechanisms that account for desire. Girard recognizes that what he takes to be Freud's candidate—the Oedipal triangle—cannot actually account for the mechanism of desire. The Oedipal triangle "is not functional. One does not really know why it should go on generating substitute triangles."[10] Anspach helpfully captures Girard's reasoning "Freud's Oedipus is forever bound to a primordial object, the mother, and a primordial rival, the father; later relationships perpetually re-enact, for better or worse, this original triangle."[11] As understood by Girard, Freud makes every mimetic foe a stand-in for a father and every object of desire a stand-in for a mother. Anspach explains that Girard wants to free the mechanism of desire from these Freudian constraints so that desire can become "utterly open-ended" and characterized by "infinite variety."[12] Anspach quotes Girard as Girard draws on Proust to explain the process of mediation: "Beginning with Proust, the mediator may be literally *anyone at all* and he may pop up *anywhere*."[13]

But Girard's "Freud under glass," so well described by Anspach, miscon-strues Freud. Girard rightly acknowledges that Freud wants to understand the mechanism of desire; however, Girard does not attend closely to what motivates Freud in his quest. Freud aims to comprehend how desire is borne by the body. His attention is drawn, in particular, to wounded desire that is registered as trauma.[14] Freud's vision, as expansive as Girard's, hones in on early familial experiences not in order to conceive of adult relationships as replays of early encounters with mommy and daddy but in order to explore how early relationships persist in later life in the form of *embodied imprints*. For Freud, desire is open-ended and subject to infinite variety; neverthe-less, for better or worse, our bodies bear the legacy of early experiences of desire. Thus, if Girard teaches us that Proust introduces us to a mediator/model who can be "anyone at all," Freud would have us notice that Proust's narrator is not just "anyone at all." Rather, he is a man whose body attests to a specific history of sensuality and violence that, *woven through the richly colored tapestry of his life*, may include not only the delicious ecstasy of a madeleine but also acute suffering. Breaking through Girard's "Freud under glass," the Freud who enhances our awareness of Proustian sensation contributes to rather than detracts from Girard's own quest to understand the mechanism of mimetic desire. Girard, unparalleled in his mastery of key features of this mechanism, benefits from Freud's attention to embodied aspects of mimetic desire.

Several examples point to the utility of psychoanalytic theory for mimetic theory. Girard has a largely undeveloped explanation for how "mimesis that precedes representation" functions in early childhood. He claims that an "animal appetite" is the instigator of mimesis.[15] But infants are not nurtured and cared for by animal appetites. Psychoanalytic theorists have developed a nuanced portrait of infancy and early childhood that accounts for nascent mimeticism. In its prerepresentational world, an infant initially experiences mimesis within a maternal matrix rich with visual, tactile, acoustic, and kinesthetic meaning. Before a child longs to take its father's place "everywhere," the maternal world already is an "everywhere" in which the infant's initial mimetic interactions transpire. With their attention to the maternal matrix, psychoanalysts Melanie Klein and Julia Kristeva offer resources for incorporating into Girard's thought an enhanced understanding of mimesis in a prerepresentational environment.[16]

Psychoanalysis also can lend to mimetic theory clarity on a topic about which Girard has expressed ambivalent views: how humans exchange acquisitive for *positive mimesis*, a phrase that suggests relationships grounded in love, genuine intimacy, and compassion. Drawing on phenomenology in his early explorations of mimetic desire, Girard attributes to *sensory experience* the power to transform lives, so that humans can replace violence with compassion.[17] But, in Girard's later work, he turns away from sensory experience and the phenomenological method he previously employed to understand it. Visible also in his theory is a mounting uncertainty about humans' ability to demonstrate positive mimesis. Increasingly, individuals who engage in acquisitive mimesis are portrayed by Girard as *active agents* of conflict and aggression; however, those who display positive mimesis are portrayed as wholly *passive recipients* of grace. Exploring "the power that triumphs over mimetic violence," Girard asserts that "the Spirit of God possesses them and does not let them go."[18] With Girard unable to establish a propensity for an active aggressor to become a nonviolent agent of compassion, mimetic theory takes on a dualistic cast. Because Julia Kristeva offers psychoanalytic resources for addressing this issue in conjunction with existential phenomenology, her work can facilitate efforts to take up anew compelling insights from Girard's early work and incorporate them into his mature theory. Sensory experience can once again be treated as a vehicle for positive mimesis, and pathways for ongoing transformation from negative to positive mimesis can be identified, redressing concerns about dualism.

So too can psychoanalytic theory contribute to a more nuanced portrait of family dynamics in Girard's thought. After all, the family is the domain within which we practice our earliest mimetic relationships, and these relationships lay groundwork for mimeticism in later life. Infants and children exhibit desires that attest to their greater independence *and* dependence on mothers and fathers than is acknowledged by Girard. In his eagerness to disencumber children of the desires he believes Freud would impose on them, Girard overlooks important expressions of desire by children. Further, Girard bypasses the richly diverse valuing of mothers by their children, for he understands a mother's import for her child to exactly duplicate the significance the mother holds for the father, as if the child has no desire for its mother's company apart from the child's tutoring in that desire by its father. Girard also overlooks conflicts between young children and their parents. These struggles are as acutely virulent and traumatic as those Girard observes among adults even though young children's diminutive size and limited weaponry—usually their teeth and fists—limit their violence. Although Girard does acknowledge violent mimesis in families, especially in accounts recorded in literature of epic battles between older siblings and murderous aggression by grown children against their mothers or fathers, Girard casts the setting of early childhood in an idyllic light. Adults are the instigators of violence against children, and he imputes threats children may pose to their parents to adult projections.[19]

In multiple instances, psychoanalytic theory offers to mimetic theory important insights about family dynamics. For example, Julia Kristeva suggests that the breast of the maternal body, both present and absent, given and taken away, is the infant's first other in whom its own being arises.[20] Not truly an "object," the breast actually is a model; it offers itself as pattern—present and absent—that the infant itself assimilates when it incorporates the breast in its own body. Introduced within the maternal matrix to the loci of mimesis—a pattern of presence and absence, fulfillment and rejection—the human infant receives its first lesson in a body bounding that presages its emergence in the world as a relational being.[21] Indeed, this bounding is open and supportive. Infant tutoring in sameness and difference threatens neither to collapse into fusion nor to break apart in a conflict framed as alimentary threat: initial mimesis is positive mimesis.

So also do Luce Irigaray and Kristeva account for how a toddler's desire can be directed toward its mother in the absence of paternal tutoring. They choose as an example the *fort/da* game played by Freud's grandson, Ernst. Ernst is observed by Freud picking up a reel during his mother's absence. Throwing it away, Ernst says "*o-o-o-o*" (*fort*). Retrieving it, he says "*da*." Irigaray notes that Ernst desires his mother not with words, as would an older child, or even with his legs, as would a child who has fully mastered walking, but with his mouth. Ernst's world is bound by his gesture and by the sounds that vibrate in his mouth and resonate in his ears, forming a topos of desire. In magnifying what happens "in the mouth, between the lips, the tongue the palate, the teeth," Irigaray describes a rite of transition from the buccal space of undifferentiated being to a toddler's world. Kristeva concurs: in the very act of constituting the mother—now here, now there—within the space of his mouth, teeth, and tongue—the toddler experiences the birth of mimetic desire.[22]

Significantly, Girard expressly defends the *fort/da* game as an example of tutored desire.[23] Where Freud plays the puzzled grandfather who cannot decide whether to credit his clever grandson or Ernst's parents with the invention of the *fort/da* game, Girard asserts that "pure invention is not feasible." The child must have learned the game from an adult because interest in objects only emerges through imitation. Indeed, in order to preclude Ernst from being the creator of the game, Girard insists that, if Ernst is not imitating an adult, his play must be motivated by a "spirit of violence."[24] But a "spirit of violence," like the "animal appetite" described above, unnecessarily mystifies early mimetic behavior. As Irigaray and Kristeva demonstrate, the maternal matrix and the child's body comprise a divisible relation within which early mimeticism prospers. The mouth is the locus of infant and toddler relational being, and when Ernst divides his mother—"*o-o-o-o*" and "*da*"—the game he plays is very much his own. The "point" of the game also belongs to Ernst: he is experimenting with the risks and possibilities of desire. The reel is at Ernst's command only because it negativizes the force of desire to make that force in its very absence an object. With his play, Ernst experiments with the vicissitudes of desire that, even for a toddler, circle the lack of being that is our human condition.

Finally, in recognizing the existence of childhood aggression, psychoanalytic theory does not discount parental violence. However, children are not exempt from the lack of being that Girard understands feeds adult mimetic desire. Kristeva observes that the separation from the maternal matrix in which we have our initial being is "a violent, clumsy breaking away, with the constant risk of falling back under the sway of a power as securing as it is stifling."[25] Embattled and beset, nascent subjects demarcate space with their mouths. They bite, chew, and swallow sameness and difference. These somatic rites secure for the human subject its most basic boundaries. Moreover, the subject never rests easily; if its life experiences place it in the grip of trauma, the subject will recall these rites, repetitively confronting its lack of being, whenever the resources of language and culture prove insufficient to secure its standing in the world. Violence associated with the ontological illness of humankind thus has roots in childhood. In bypassing children's violence on which psychoanalytic theory offers nuanced commentary, Girard again misses out on the productive utility of psychoanalysis for mimetic theory.[26]

Despite shortcomings in Girard's reflections on the dynamics of interactions between parents and children, he demonstrates a finely tuned awareness of sibling relationships. The lateral deployment of rivalries among brothers and sisters garners his close attention. Girard's interest is shared by Juliet Mitchell, who cites Girard in her work. Mitchell contends that psychoanalysis, in theory and practice, neglects sibling relationships. She intends that her study of siblings rectify that oversight, thereby strengthening psychoanalytic theory. That Mitchell—a practicing psychoanalyst and theorist—shares common ground with Girard is significant. In acknowledging the importance of Girard's insights and in demonstrating that psychoanalysis is a living and open system, Mitchell establishes grounds for mutually productive dialogue with Girard and mimetic theorists whose scholarship is grounded in Girard's work.

However, to the extent that scholars of mimetic theory remain under the influence of Girard's "Freud under glass," such a dialogue is unlikely. To be sure, mimetic theorists apply Girard's theory to numerous facets of human experience—religious, cultural, economic, and political—in order to show that mimetic theory can illuminate conflict that remains inexplicable or misunderstood apart from this analysis. Working in disciplines that span the humanities and social sciences, they bring into critical purview all manner of acquisitive and violent behavior. They investigate life at its most encompassing—world wars and global economies—and at its most minute—mirror neurons. A rich and varied literature is the result of these efforts.[27] But, attentive to Girard's claim against Freud that the dynamics of desire within the family are effaced before an all-encompassing mimetic desire, mimetic theorists seldom make the family a focus for reflection. Nor do infancy and early childhood feature in their discussions.[28] In the wake of their inattention, an overworked idiom takes on new life: mimetic theorists risk "throwing the baby out with the Freudian bath water," thereby ceding examination of the family to other scholars, as if exploring familial patterns of mimetic desire from a Girardian perspective could not yield important knowledge about the family.[29] However, as I demonstrate with this book, critical inquiry about the family from a Girardian perspective not only sheds light on the family but also provides knowledge of utmost significance to mimetic theory.

Because "Freud under glass" discourages rather than encourages ongoing reflection on the family among mimetic theorists, it should no longer play a central role in their considerations. Nor should it be the measure by which mimetic theorists gauge psychoanalytic theory. "Freud under glass" fixes family relations in ways that render key features of psychoanalytic theory unrecognizable, and it presents as rigid and unchanging elements of this theory that are fluid and variable.[30] Mimetic theorists need to treat the concepts Girard has extracted from Freud as components of an open and dynamic system rather than as fixed ideas. When they do so, they will more readily appreciate ways in which psychoanalytic theory is a useful resource.

Ironically, the areas I have identified in Girard's thought that can benefit from insights of psychoanalytic theory are mirror images of concerns about Freud Girard has preserved in "Freud under glass." But now, neglect of a prerepresentational childhood, a problematic dualism, an unwarranted projection of an adult perspective onto a child's world, and a misconstrual of family dynamics appear as problematic features of Girard's thought, not Freud's. Finger-pointing is not a helpful exercise. In the interest of neutralizing mimetically charged disagreements among proponents of psychoanalytic

and mimetic theories, I emphasize my constructive intent in bringing psychoanalytic and mimetic theories into conversation. These theories are living
systems subject to change and development. Each faces challenges that moti-
vate its proponents in ongoing critical reflection. A constructive alternative
to "Freud under glass" and "Girard under glass" is available: conversation and
dialogue—undertaken separately as well as collaboratively—can strengthen
each theory's capacity to function as a vibrant and dynamic explanatory
framework.

Girard models such dialogue, for he backs a partnership between psychoanalytic theory and his own scholarship. He writes, for example, that
Freud's texts "support and validate mimetic theory."[31] In a discussion of
literature and psychoanalytic theory, Girard also offers a comment that is
especially pertinent, given my focus on literature in this book. He states that
"literature and psychoanalysis in the best sense need *each other*," and calls for
a dialogue "of equals" that will "reveal the relative power" of psychoanalytic
theory and literature.[32]

With *Intimate Domain*, I invite mimetic theorists to reflect more closely
than they have before about family dynamics. I submit that not only should
the family be discussed within mimetic theory, but also mimetic theory
should be critically analyzed in light of explorations of the family by psychoanalytic theory. Far from weakening mimetic theory, when aspects of it
are called into question, mimetic theory can only be strengthened by that
challenge. Attention to facets of human experience to which proponents of
mimetic theory previously have been inattentive can inspire elaborations
of mimetic theory that sustain and enhance its analytic force. I intend that
Intimate Domain further that goal.

Girard and Feminist Scholarship

I also offer this book as a contribution to feminist scholarship on Girard.[33]
Previous conversations by feminist scholars with Girard have resulted in a
varied body of scholarship; however, no feminist scholar has brought a sustained focus to the theme of mimetic desire and the family. With *Intimate
Domain*, I demonstrate the value for feminist scholars *and* mimetic theorists
of an extended conversation about shared concerns.

Luce Irigaray, Sarah Kofman, Julia Kristeva, and Toril Moi are among the first feminist theorists to write about mimetic theory.[34] For Irigaray and Kristeva, Girard's reticence to comment on the prevalence of female bodies among victims of sacrificial violence[35] and his articulation of a theory of mimetic desire that does not thematize the role of sexual difference in mimetic conflict become the occasion for their own groundbreaking work. Pursuing the implications of Girard's theory for instances of sexually differentiated violence and female sacrifice, they engage in a productive, creative extension of his thought.   By contrast, mimetic theory is not a productive resource for Kofman and Moi. Kofman challenges Girard for describing mimesis in ways that posit women as objects of conflictive male desire, never as agents of their own desire. Asserting against Girard the self-sufficiency of the woman Freud portrays in his essay "On Narcissism," she decries Girard's claim that this woman is "pretending" independence and his characterization of her as a "coquette" whose desire is strategically deployed between two men who compete for her.[36] For her part, Moi is critical of Girard's understanding of the maternal and child relationship. Because Girard wants to claim that all desire is mimetic *and* mediated, he cannot accept the unmediated desire of the child for its mother. Moi claims that Girard neglects the pre-Oedipal stage. Moreover, the mother and her desires are missing from Girard's portrait of mimetic rivalry.[37] Perceiving that their differences with Girard on specific points are indicative of larger problems with his theory, Moi and Kofman dismiss his theory.

Following the example set by Irigaray and Kristeva in the 1980s, a number of feminist scholars in the next two decades continue to locate constructive possibilities for feminist scholarship in Girard's theory. Girard is engaged by American and European scholars in the fields of literature, religion, and the social sciences.[38] But no extended discussion of the family and mimetic theory is undertaken. As a consequence, prospects for critical engagement with Girard's theory are incompletely mined by feminist scholars.

After thirty years of feminist reflection on mimetic theory, on what basis can feminist scholars engage Girard today? Surely, they will most productively move forward if they focus on aspects of feminist theorizing that have maintained the most saliency over time. Moreover, feminist scholars will most fruitfully engage Girard if they share with him the sense of urgency about the world he has conveyed in his most recent works, especially in

Battling to the End. On both counts, a recent observation by Julia Kristeva is most suggestive: Taking a retrospective measure of feminism and expressing fears that "we may have reached the point of no return" for a human community leaning toward destruction, Kristeva writes,

> I am convinced that after all the more or less reasonable and promising projects and slogans the feminist movement has promulgated over the past decades, the arrival of women at the forefront of the social and ethical scene has had the result of revalorizing the sensory experience. . . . The immense responsibility of women in regard to the survival of the species . . . goes hand in hand with this rehabilitation of the sensory.[39]

I take as my guidepost in this work Kristeva's assertion that close attention to sensory experience is among the most lasting legacies of feminism and one that offers important lessons for our time. I suggest that mimetic theory will be enhanced if, in dialogue with feminist theory, it finds the impetus to reestablish a central place within mimetic theory for sensory experience.

Girard invited an extended conversation with feminist scholars over a decade ago. In an interview with Richard Golsan, Girard comments on criticisms of his work by Kofman. He notes appreciatively that Kofman acknowledges some common ground with him, and he expresses regret that, in relegating her admission to a footnote, she forecloses on possibilities for further dialogue. Girard remains confident, he tells Golsan, that "some truly independent feminists, someday, will discover why mimetic desire should interest them," although he sets as a condition of that discovery that feminists "unload the 'pre-oedipal' stage."[40]

Decades after Kofman wrote her essay, the time is ideal for a renewed feminist engagement with Girard. A maturing field of feminist scholarship features a multiplicity of research methods, theories, and topics of inquiry that promote the independence of thought Girard has sought among feminist interlocutors of his work. A significant body of feminist scholarship on mimetic theory, grounded in attentive readings of Girard's works, establishes a solid foundation for further inquiry. In *Intimate Domain*, I build on this foundation in hopes that my observations may serve as an occasion for newly energized conversations by feminist scholars with Girard. I appreciate the opportunity *Intimate Domain* affords me to engage Girard in the thoughtful and comprehensive way his theory so clearly warrants.

Julia Kristeva and Mimetic Theory

I intend also that *Intimate Domain* constitute, by way of proxy, a dialogue between Kristeva and Girard. At one time, that Girard and Kristeva would directly engage each other's work seemed likely. In 1966, Girard heard Julia Kristeva give a presentation on Bahktin in Roland Barthes's seminar. Subsequently, he invited her to come to the United States to teach at Johns Hopkins University, where he was an associate professor. Recalling that invitation thirty years later, Kristeva writes that she did not accept it. Girard's invitation came up against Kristeva's negative views of the United States, offered as it was during the Vietnam War. Kristeva stayed in France.[41]

Although Kristeva and Girard's intellectual journeys took them in different directions, for her part, Kristeva has remained a student of Girard's work, citing him multiple times over the years. In Kristeva's early work, Kristeva joins Girard in tracing the origin of society to the revolt of the brothers against a father, grounding her insights in *Totem and Taboo*, as does Girard. As a consequence, as John Lechte and Mary Zournazi insightfully note, Kristeva understands that the human subject does not precede culture; rather, violence gives "rise to the individual, to subjectivity and to individuality."[42] In Kristeva's later work, similarly to Girard, Kristeva seeks alternatives in Proust to the violent dissolution of being. Arguing that *In Search of Lost Time* shows how memory is constitutive of the self, Kristeva suggests that, through his art, Proust restructures psychic space on the other side of violence and suffering. Thus, Kristeva's own work has moved forward in conversation with Girard's.[43] Girard's influence on Kristeva's work is attested to throughout *Intimate Domain*. By contrast, to my knowledge, Girard's theoretical reflections have not progressed in conversation with Kristeva. As a consequence, Girard and students of his work have not had an opportunity to consider how Kristeva's work illuminates Girard's and suggests an important augmentation of mimetic theory. *Intimate Domain* provides an opening for such reflection.

With *Intimate Domain*, I reflect on Girard's theory with the goal of enhancing its analytic power. Throughout, I maintain that Girard's theory is a vital resource for thinking about the family. I intend that my argument make his theory even more compelling. I seek also to promote among scholars of Girard greater attention to the family. Mimetic theory will be strengthened when we attend to the formative role family relations play in the history of desire, most particularly in respect to early sensory experience and its legacy in later life. I suggest also that the work I undertake can lead to an enhanced understanding of how feminist theory contributes to mimetic theory.

Family Matters

Thus the possibility that we can envision birth and death, that we can contemplate them within time and that we can speak about them with the Other by sharing with other people—in a word, the possibility that we can tell a story—is at the heart of the specific, nonanimalistic, and nonphysiological nature of human life.

—Julia Kristeva, *Hannah Arendt*

Oprah Winfrey, icon of popular culture, pens a monthly column titled "What I Know For Sure." Less bold than Oprah, who has been espousing sureties for years, I am certain of few things. However, beyond a doubt, I know that our early life experiences shape our lives in profound ways. My conviction has been tutored by psychoanalytic theory, which offers a compelling account of the lasting impact on us of our early experiences, especially within the family.

I frequently draw on my rural setting to explain to students the psychoanalytic perspective on early experience. The snow is dense and deep through much of the Iowa winter. In order to navigate the woods behind my home, I must break a path. "When I go out again," I ask students, "should I take a different route and struggle again through drifts of snow?" My students invariably suggest that I follow the path I previously have broken. My walk in the woods captures our life experiences as psychoanalysis understands it. Without regard for the possible benefits of breaking a new path—avoiding hidden tree stumps over which we have tripped repeatedly or ice on which we have slipped multiple times—in the woods that is our lives, we repetitively traverse the same course. *This I know for sure.*

In the long history of psychoanalytic theory, key proponents—Freud, Klein, Winnicott, and Lacan—take distinct approaches to "the walk in the woods." But three shared themes can be identified. Psychoanalytic theory proposes that our experiences are shaped by unconscious processes.[1] By this, psychoanalytic theory understands that *humans harbor a fundamental blindness* about the circumstances of our lives: we tread the same path through the woods of our lives oblivious to alternatives, even when another course might make our way easier. Psychoanalytic theory also takes a developmental perspective on human life: *early experience undergirds all that follows.* Indeed, throughout our lives, we retrace our steps, following paths cut in infancy and early childhood. Although some theorists observe enhanced proficiency among those who reconnoiter a trail traversed many times before, especially under the guidance of others,[2] others note ongoing difficulty. They emphasize that those who walk through the woods mourn what has been lost or never found along the trail. Finally, psychoanalytic theory suggests that *human life is dynamic but fraught.* Our initial posture in the world is one of curiosity: we are eager to see what is on the other side of the woods. But the comforts of home invite us, and the unknown may harbor dangers. Day after day, we arrive at the edge of the woods, inquisitive but wary. We push away recollections of bruises and bumps acquired on earlier walks, or we valorize the path we have cut previously, even though an objective bystander would find little along that way to applaud.[3]

Significantly, a metaphor often points to the most important elements of the phenomenon we wish to describe at the point when it begins to weaken, requiring that we modify it. As a consequence, I find myself needing to adjust my "walk in the woods" imagery in order to account for a fourth theme in psychoanalysis. Observing that we are not isolated subjects who walk alone through the woods of our lives, psychoanalytic theory asserts that, *at the most fundamental level, we are relational beings.* The "Forest of No

Return," referenced in the 1961 Disney film classic *Babes in Toyland*, offers a compelling scenario for a revision of my initial metaphor. The "Forest of No Return" is inhabited by trees that are sentient, living beings. Speaking and moving, the trees surround and capture a group of children.[4] So also, in the woods of our lives, those among and with whom we have our being are living presences. Not always benign, they sometimes appear as hulking, monstrous entities that thwart our journeys rather than support them.[5]

In *Intimate Domain*, I explore these four themes of psychoanalytic theory with special attention to family relationships. Girard's work features three of the four themes. For Girard, the *fundamental blindness* that affects human life is a *metaphysical disease or ontological illness brought on by mimetic desire.*[6] Only on a superficial level is mimetic desire oriented toward having things that another has or seeks to acquire. On a deeper level, Girard understands that desire arises in the subject because it lacks being. Looking to another to inform it of what it should desire in order to be, the subject finds its attention drawn not toward the object that the other recommends but toward the other who must surely be capable of conferring an even greater plentitude of being.[7] One's desire for the other is ontological: "Imitative desire is always a desire to be Another."[8] Desiring what the other desires because of a prior and more basic desire to be the other, the subject discovers that the closer he or she comes to acquiring the object of the model's desire and, through that acquisition, to the model, the greater the rejection or refusal of the subject by the model.[9] Thus, *human life is dynamic but fraught* because, in the grip of our desires, we are vulnerable to *acquisitive rivalry that devolves into violence.* Veneration and rejection structure the subject's experience until, in a shocking denouement of the dynamics of rivalry that sees difference between the subject and it model obliterated by a single, common desire, the model becomes a monstrous double by whom the subject is as much repulsed as she was earlier attracted.[10] The ontological illness of desire precipitates a mimetic crisis. Mimetic theory, our most comprehensive theory of *relational being*, describes these challenging circumstances, which are resolved in sacrifice.[11] But it also points the way to transforming alternatives. On these three points, the congruence of Girard's thought with psychoanalytic theory establishes a strong foundation for dialogue.

Initiating this discussion, I also augment Girard's theory in order to account for the one psychoanalytic theme missing from Girard's thought:

early experiences undergird all that follows. Girard's masterful explorations of mimetic phenomena in the ancient experiences of human societies, recorded especially in his studies of myth and tragedy, need to be matched by sustained attention to early experiences within our most intimate society, the family. For when our experience there is etched by *trauma* that closes us to time and encases us in repetition, we are precluded from experiencing a transformation that can heal us of our ontological illness. Psychoanalytic theory is a vital resource on which mimetic theory can and should draw to understand links between sensory experience, trauma, and intractable features of mimetic violence.

Why Literature?

Literature has special significance for Girard and Kristeva. Both claim that literature is *reflective and revelatory* of human experience in the world. But literature is especially important for my project because Girard and Kristeva assert that literature can *transform* human experience. Literature can expose the bankruptcy and violence of mimetic desire, play a role in redressing trauma, and open us to new experience.

In *Deceit, Desire, and the Novel*, Girard describes the characteristics of novelists who author great literature. They do not disguise and mask the truth of human experience, serving up "romantic" (*romantique*) illusions. To the contrary, their works are "novelistic" (*romanesque*) because they reveal and elucidate human circumstances.[12] Specifically, great literature invokes in microcosm the vicissitudes of mimesis that we struggle to comprehend in our larger world, bringing them into the uncomfortable light of day. Moreover, novels have the power not only to expose the bankruptcy of mimetic desire but also to show the way to a different existence in which "deception gives way to truth, anguish to remembrance, agitation to repose, and hatred to love.[13]

Acclaiming Girard's approach to literature, Eugene Webb places Girard in a lineage of "morally serious literary critics" inclusive of Dante, Samuel Johnson, and Sartre. Webb asserts also that Girard's interest in literature is out of step with his contemporaries who are disinclined to see in literature lessons in "moral truth." By contrast, Girard is committed to literature "not just for the sake of purely intellectual or aesthetic satisfaction but in order to find a way to deal with these problems in practice."[14] According to Webb, Girard contends that great works (*romanesque*) are their authors' testimony to "hard-won knowledge of how to live humanly well." Having experienced suffering and struggled, they also have been redeemed. A transformative truth emerges in their writing. Girard writes that the novelist is someone who "has overcome desire and who, remembering it, *can make a comparison*."[15] Moreover, Girard asserts that when we read great novels, we are tutored in the novelist's transforming experience. Novelists become models whose narratives invite imitation; "in reading, we relive the spiritual experience whose form is that of the novel itself."[16]

Kristeva attests to the power of the novel as well. A practicing psychoanalyst, she has discovered that the novel can put words "into contact with a whole dynamic of recollection that leads us at once to recall our traumas, the pains or the pleasures, and the most archaic sensations." Kristeva cites metaphor as a vehicle of translation whereby sensations, perceptions, and trauma are joined with the language of cognition.[17] Likening the novel to "lay analysis," she indicates that sometimes the novel is an even more powerful tool than psychoanalysis.[18] Indeed, storytelling enables subjects to access meaning previously inaccessible to them.

As has Girard, Kristeva attests to the transforming power of literature. Storytelling is a defining human activity, for only humans are aware that our lives are recountable. Drawing on Arendt, Kristeva makes storytelling a relational activity. Narration relies on two factors: we exist among others (*inter-esse*) and, through them, we are able to form memories and offer testimony.[19] That others are necessary for storytelling to be meaningful is not only a condition of creative exposition but also a condition of human life. Together, the narratable and exposable features of our lives make possible transformation. As philosopher Adriana Cavarero states most eloquently (also commenting on Arendt):

> Only in the improbable case of a life spent in perfect solitude could the autobiography of a human being tell the absurd story of an unexposed identity, without relations and without world. The existent is the exposable and the narratable: neither exposability nor narratability, which together constitute this peculiarly human uniqueness, can be taken away. The one

who is exposed generates and is generated by the life-story—this and not
another—which results from such an exposition.[20]

We exist because we share narratable lives. But even as Kristeva makes nar-
ratability a fundamental feature of relational being, Kristeva identifies acute
challenges that interrupt storytelling. Human suffering decouples what
should be joined: we have no memories to turn into stories or we are unable
to construct meaningful narratives. Active relationality is crucial to recovery from trauma that opens the door again to storytelling. As Colin Davis
observes in summarizing Kristeva's commentary on Arendt, when someone
hears another say, "Tell me a story," that other has mediated "what cannot
be called back to memory and what can be narrated."[21] Psychoanalysis and
literature thus share a common function: bridging the gaps and ruptures in
being brought on by trauma. One who issues an invitation to "tell a story"
sets in motion processes that re-create our humanity and effect healing.

Kristeva writes that narrative is "the most elaborate kind of attempt, on
the part of the speaking subject, after syntactic competence, to situate his or
her self among his or her desires and their taboos that is at the interior of the
oedipal triangle."[22] Not encapsulated by a narrow interpretation of the Oedipal complex, this triangle provides a frame for a broad and dynamic reading of the lack of being that sends us down the road of metaphysical desire.
Attesting to that lack, narratives record the distortions of desire: maladaptive
social interactions, repetitive and compulsive behaviors, and deep-seated
conflicts. But narratives also feature imaginative openings to new being.

Guillemette Bolens offers a theory of narrative that illuminates how narratives can transform our being, as Girard and Kristeva both claim. In *The
Style of Gestures: Embodiment and Cognition in Literary Narrative*, Bolens
explains that, for an artist and those who encounter his or her work (e.g.,
readers of novels, viewers of dramatic performances), narratives are linked
through *kinesis* to sensory experiences. As defined by Bolens, kinesis is distinguished from kinesthesia. The latter refers to motor sensations and to how
the brain senses bodily movement; the former refers to the "interactional
perception of movements performed by oneself or another person" in relation to factors such as extension, speed of a gesture, and relation of limbs to
the rest of the body.[23] Crucial to the reception of meaning by an artist and
her reader or audience are patterns of bodily gesture and sensory experience

evoked in narrative descriptions. Linguistic meaning is grounded in kinesic activity.[24] Memory figures prominently in kinesis, facilitating responses to others' gestures (actual or described).[25] We create and respond to texts that describe sensory experience because we can summon through kinesis a past experience like those to which a narrative attests. For example, when we follow a character in a novel such as *In Search of Lost Time*—reacting to his gestures, taking note of his responses to another's smile, sharing his discomfort when he stumbles on a path—we know his experience kinesically because of our own corporal memories. In this way, Bolens suggests, novelists activate their own kinesic capacity and ours.[26]

In support of her theory of corporeal narrativity, Bolens cites researchers and philosophers who study motor cognition and link verbal signification with perceptual and motor actions. She references recent research on mirror neurons in support of her theory.[27] Although early research on mirror neurons suggested that they activate when an individual observes someone else performing a similar action, more recent research has shown that mirror neurons are not specific to visual observation. Mirror neurons fire also when someone listens to action-related sound. Indeed, Kemmerer and Gonzalez-Castillo are representative of a number of neuroscientists who argue that mirror neurons "should be defined by functional rather than anatomical criteria."[28] Such functional criteria support connections Bolens forges between embodied cognition and narratives. Bolens cites research by Pulvermüller and colleagues that shows how the silent reading of verbs such as "lick," "pick," and "kick" is correlated with increases in brain activity in areas activated by actual movement of the tongue, fingers, or feet.[29] In their research, Beilock and Lyons label as "motor resonance" the process by which the same neural substrates are recruited whether one is reading about another's actions or modeling action on another's actual performance.[30]

Bolens's theory has strong similarities with Vittorio Gallese's notion of intercorporeity. Defining "intercorporeity" as "the mutual resonance of intentionally meaningful sensor-motor behaviors," Gallese grounds intercorporeity in mirroring neural mechanisms. Significantly, he claims, as does Bolens for kinesis, that intercorporeity is crucial for our knowledge of and capacity to interact with others.[31] As a consequence, intercorporeity can be likened to the active relationality to which Kristeva points when she talks about the crucial role others play in establishing conditions for a narratable

life. In turn, Levinas offers helpful insights that describe how such a narratable life is grounded in embodied processes. When Levinas describes how
thinking happens, his words could also apply to the storytelling. Thought,
he writes, "does not start with an antecedent representation, or with those
significations, or with phrases to be articulated. Hence one might say thought
operates in the 'I can' of the body. It operates in it before representing this
body to itself or constituting it. Signification surprises the very thought that
thought it. . . . What is it to have a meaning? . . . [I]t is not the mediation
of the sign that forms signification, but signification (whose primordial
event is the face to face) that makes the sign function possible."[32] Whether
scholars describe processes by which human experiences take on meaning
and are shared as kinesis, motor resonance, intercorporeity, or the "I can" of
the body, they enable us to understand that our thoughts about the world,
which we express by way of written or spoken narratives, are run through
with kinesic meaning. Narrative meaning is embodied and shared.

    In the descriptions of kinesis summarized here, Bolens and other
researchers account for the transformative potential of narrative. Playing a
key role is the fundamental relationality of kinesis. More complex than a
mere indexing of gesture and movement that would assign specific meanings
to a smile or a wave of the hand, kinesic responsiveness founds our capacity to experience the presence of another. When we see someone smile, we
do not code that smile as "happiness." Gestures are not meaningful to us
because we "translate" them into signs. Rather, when we look at someone
smiling, somatosensory images that correspond to what it would feel like to
be the locus of the same emotional expression that prompted the smile are
generated. Another's smile takes on meaning for us based on somatosensory
images that are formed when we put ourselves in another's place "affectively,
kinesthetically, introceptively, olfactorily, aurally, and so forth." Kinesis is
"multimodal."[33] Thus, Bolens argues, quoting Giorgio Agamben, "the gesture
is . . . communication of communicability."[34] Kinesis does not give us the
meaning of a thing; rather, it gives us the being of another.

    As modes of active relationality, our kinesic connections are at work
when someone says "Tell me a story." Re-creating our humanity, these connections effect healing. However, as the narratives I explore also show, kinesic communicability is not always transformative. Kinesis can be distorted
or interrupted by trauma that blocks or contorts somatosensory images that

otherwise would be put into play when someone "tells a story." As a consequence, a corporeal narratology must account for the interruptions of kinesis by trauma and not only for healing that restores us, by means of kinesis, to meaningful relations with others.[35]

Bolens's analysis of kinesis illuminates the transformative power of metaphor in narrative, a power cited by Girard and Kristeva, especially in their studies of Proust. Girard acknowledges the transformational "I can" of the novelist and his reader when he asserts "in reading, we relive the spiritual experience whose form is that of the novel itself."[36] For example, in highlighting the spiritual impact of the madeleine, Girard writes that it is an "exception" to the rule of metaphysical desire. Asserting that "there is no mediator in the case of the 'madeleine,'" Girard labels it a "privileged moment" and an "annunciation" that leads forward to the revelation of *Finding Time Again.*[37] Kristeva's perspective is similar. For her, metaphorical meaning does not consist only of the substitution of a complex or abstract idea for one rooted in the imagery of everyday experience, thereby bridging the unfamiliar and familiar. Instead, metaphors link sensation and idea, resulting in an "image made incarnate."[38] Writes Kristeva of this lived image: "Since bringing things together is a *metaphor*, and sensation implies a *body*, Proustian time, which brings together the sensations imprinted in signs, is a *metamorphosis*."[39] Similar to Girard, Kristeva points to the restorative outcomes of the final volume of *In Search of Lost Time*, when truth is grafted onto the actual body of the narrator and made available to his readers as well.[40] That Girard and Kristeva describe kinesis, albeit without using the term, demonstrates that research Bolens cites sustains Girard's and Kristeva's insights while establishing links between literary analysis and empirical research.

Attentive to the analytic potential of Bolens' explorations of narrative kinesis, I find inspiration in her approach for the texts I explore in *Intimate Domain.* Proceeding by way of a *corporeal hermeneutics*,[41] I demonstrate how the evocation of bodily expressiveness through kinesis is a fundamental condition of narrative meaning.[42] As I examine how traumatic narratives, especially those associated with the family, attest to the disruption of an "I can" of the body, I consider too how narratives enable author and reader to recollect and retrieve an "I can." As I employ a corporeal hermeneutics to study three exemplary narratives, I explain precisely how retrieval happens. I give new life to notions of affective memory and sensory experience that

Girard finds important in his early work but sets aside in the later development of his theory. I return these concepts to the center of mimetic theory, thereby strengthening its capacity to account not only for violence that stems from mimetic rivalries and its associated trauma but also for healing and transformation—the positive mimesis that mimetic theory has not fleshed out in full.

As I reflect on the power of narratives to illuminate and transform the lives of artists and their readers or audiences, I hold these narratives always in the light of psychoanalytic theory and mimetic theory. Nevertheless, I do not suggest that these theories "explain" the literature I discuss. They are not grids that I affix to the works I discuss in order that they conform to preset reference points. Instead, following Peter Brooks, I see in theories and literature "an interference of two systems." Juxtaposing literature and theoretical processes, I can "see what happens when they start to contaminate one another."[43] Most important, because psychoanalytic theory and mimetic theory enable me to cross boundaries that typically separate personal from literary narratives, they contribute to an understanding of how we "construct necessary fictions by which we dream, desire, interpret, indeed by which we constitute ourselves as human subjects."[44] The family romance is one of these "necessary fictions."

A Family Romance and an Intimate Domain

The family in the throes of mimetic desire is a family caught up in a "family romance." Freud coined this phrase in order to describe a young child's fantasy that its current parents are not its real parents. But, following Marianne Hirsch, I reframe the term.[45] By "family romance" I mean *fundamental patterns of mimetic desire among family members*. As I explore mimetic desire within the family, I examine also how trauma is foundational in human experience, making our desire a metaphysical illness. The vicissitudes of desire, whirling around the subject and its models, devolve into rivalry. Lacking being, we seek it in our models; however, woundedness is the sole outcome of our quest. Trauma marks our lack and its intractability. Yet we persist in our desires, intending that acquisitive mimesis remedy lack and mitigate the effects of trauma; nevertheless, because desire is concomitant with our existing in want of being, desire's powers are multivalent. Acquisitive mimesis is the bandage we wrap around our suffering *and* its originating cause. As a consequence, it has no restorative powers; indeed, acquisitive mimesis aggravates trauma. In desiring, we remain vulnerable to the ongoing replication of trauma. As I attend to trauma in mimesis, I break new ground not only for mimetic theory but also for the developing field of trauma studies.

I take my definition of "trauma" from Juliet Mitchell, who distinguishes "weak" from "strong" trauma. "Weak trauma" has many synonyms: a shock, a disturbance, or a difficulty. Weak trauma can be integrated into my life story. When I say, "That was traumatic; however, I've come to terms with it," I am describing weak trauma. Whether I experience a tornado or an earthquake, lose my job, or fail in my marriage, if I am able to recount these experiences and incorporate them into my life, I have experienced weak trauma. By contrast, "Strong trauma refers to something that does not change or develop."[46] Always there, strong trauma can "emerge again and be 'reused.'" Mitchell explains that physical and psychic strong trauma share in common an excessive strength that breaks through the surface. Strong physical trauma penetrates skin or muscle. But strong psychological trauma ruptures the very structures of psychic life.[47] As a child develops and embarks on what I have called "a walk in the woods," establishing initial pathways for being, difficult relationships with parents and siblings cause disturbances to which the child responds. The child typically integrates these challenges, which may be labeled "weak trauma," into its ongoing development. But familial relationships also can be an occasion for strong trauma. In these cases, trauma is psychogenic. Breaching the very foundations of being, strong trauma results in repetitive suffering. In that repetition, future instances of suffering can feature the intensity of the originating violation, replicating the preexisting trauma. In the midst of strong trauma, one enacts and repeats suffering but cannot understand it. For those in the throes of strong trauma, there is no "going on" or "learning from experience."[48] The "walk in the woods" becomes an exercise in blind, repetitive suffering.

In this book, I focus on strong trauma. Strong trauma takes us deep into the family romance and to our earliest experiences of conflict and desire. I am especially attentive to the life history of trauma. Trauma may present as a continuous history of pain; however, similar to a cancer cell that lies dormant in the bone for years, trauma may remain buried until, like a suddenly fast-replicating malignancy, it unexpectedly breaks through at the center of our existence, throwing us into acute suffering.

My emphasis is uncommon among mimetic theorists. Notwithstanding Girard's close attention to the cyclical aspects of violence, neither he nor students of his work have given trauma close attention. I offer mimetic theorists an opportunity to enhance their awareness of the affective and bodily nature of repetitive violence. Intending that the role trauma plays in mimetic desire and acquisitive rivalry be better understood by mimetic theorists, I examine the place of trauma in the family romance. As a result of my explorations, I hope that the analytical promise of mimetic theory may be more fully realized.

In support of that goal, I do not only focus on the family romance. Assuredly, the family is a site for problematic desires that issue in trauma-laden, acquisitive rivalries. However, the family also is an intimate domain, *a space for healing from trauma and for positive mimesis.* My definition of intimacy is shared by Girard. In *Battling to the End*, Girard links intimacy with positive mimesis, describing as "intimate mediation" processes that "transform mimeticism and open the door to the other side of violence."[49] He associates this innermost mediation with Augustinian theology (*Deos interior intimo meo*). Asserting that in Christ alone intimate mediation is possible, Girard observes an identification with the other that "supposes a special aptitude for empathy." But Girard does not offer a fully developed theory of intimate mediation. We do not learn from him how we may replace acquisitive rivalry with intimacy. Nor in discussing identification does he make a case for our embodied access to intimacy. As a consequence, intimacy is insufficiently represented in Girard's work and in the writings of mimetic theorists.

Julia Kristeva facilitates my efforts to see the family not only as the locus of a family romance but also as an intimate domain. Kristeva distinguishes intimacy (*l'intimité*) from expressions of privacy within close, personal relationships. As Cecilia Sjöholm suggests, for Kristeva, "Intimacy is a function of subjectivity that always appears to touch the truth of ourselves."[50] Linked with affect—sensation, mood, feeling—the intimate is not so much a function of a psychic interior as it is a "discourse of corporeality" that joins language with sensibility.[51] For Kristeva, intimacy also is associated with revolt. Rehabilitating revolt from its current confinement within the narrow constraints of political action, Kristeva returns to the etymological roots of "revolt" in the Latin *volvere*.[52] She identifies "revolt" as "unveiling and returning." Associating revolt with Proust and Augustine, she suggests that the theologian's fundamental questioning (*questo mihi factus sum*) finds expression in a "remembrance of things past."[53] Characterizing "re-volt" as a "gestation of psychic space," Kristeva finds exemplary Mallarmé's expression of revolt. Mallarmé targets previous investments by a unitary subject who, advancing through a "musicalization of meaning," interrelates differences through which the subject and Being are reconstituted.[54]

Kristeva's revolt is not that of the slave against its master, a battle Girard would typify as acquisitive rivalry. For Kristeva, revolt contrasts with violence, foregrounding instead renewal and regeneration. Specifically, in intimate revolt, the subject opposes distortions in human relationships through love it experiences as sensory activity of the body. As such, revolt does not *transgress* the law that, from Girard's perspective in *Battling to the End*, is the law of war; rather, revolt *displaces* the authority of violent mimesis within the psychic economy.[55] *Intimacy structures desire as cause rather than as goal.*[56]

As I interrogate the family romance, I draw on Kristeva. I assert not only that ongoing trauma is an attribute of mimetic violence, but also that the body plays a central role in facilitating healing from trauma. Just as mimetic rivalry is not only a linguistic and social phenomenon but also tactile and affective, so also is intimacy. In attending to intimacy as a practice of corporeality, I emphasize that humans are not released from the grip of violent mimesis when we acquire the *idea* of nonviolence. Positive mimesis requires the conversion of our entire being, not only cognitive realignment. At its core, conversion is a sensory experience grounded in kinesis that restores and protects intimacy.[57]

As I place the family romance (*romantique*) and an intimate domain (*romanesque*) at the center of my reflections, I explore three exemplary narratives: Proust's *In Search of Lost Time*, Sophocles's *Antigone*, and Julia Kristeva's *The Old Man and the Wolves*. Employing a corporeal hermeneutics, I treat these works as traumatic texts within which healing subtexts may be found as well. In each, traumatic memory, closed in upon itself, becomes open to narrative memory with potential to create community out of embodied recognition and forgiveness. Proust shows us with Marcel that humans can break with trauma. He enables us to glimpse healing in the form of *aesthetic promise*. Sophocles reveals with Antigone how this promise takes the form of an *ethical possibility*. Kristeva, invoking suffering fathers in a world beset by malaise, attests that, at the very end of the world, persons can yet embrace transformative possibilities of a *posttraumatic future*.

Outline of an Intimate Domain

A "psychic chronology" suggested in *Totem and Taboo* by Freud and highlighted by Juliet Mitchell establishes my frame for inquiry. When Freud explores the origins of human society, describing a gang of brothers who slay the primal father, he notices that the subject of the story is one brother who tells the tale. Freud muses, "The lie of the heroic myth culminates in the deification of the hero. Perhaps the deified hero may have been earlier than the Father God.... The series of gods, then, would run chronologically: Mother Goddess—Hero—Father God." Applying Freud's insight, Mitchell highlights a like sequence in her analysis of infancy and early childhood: maternally marked experiences, sibling encounters, and paternal relations.[58] Taking my cue from Mitchell, in Part 1, as I explore Proust's *In Search of Lost Time*, I attend to the *maternal function*. In Part 2, Sophocles's *Antigone* becomes my focus for exploring *sibling relationships*. In Part 3, I reflect on the *paternal function* as I examine Julia Kristeva's *The Old Man and the Wolves*. Unlike the other two works, this contemporary novel is not a literary classic about which Girard has written. Nevertheless, far from creating problematic discontinuities in the dialogue between Girard and Kristeva that I promote in this book, *The Old Man and the Wolves* enables me to bring focused attention to concerns Girard and Kristeva share. Both offer trenchant observations on a contemporary world bent on destruction in which the paternal function is in decline.

That I delineate what I mean by familial functions is essential. After all, psychoanalytic theory is criticized for reifying family relations, treating as timeless and universal roles of mothers, fathers, and children that are historically and culturally specific. In this book, I follow Kristeva, Mitchell, and Lacan in describing three functions that comprise a psychic chronology for family life. According to these theorists, psychoanalytic theory is not sociology.[59] Familial functions are distinct from historically and culturally diverse social relations within families. As Teresa Brennan confirms, psychoanalytic theory does not attend to processes of socialization that enable individuals to assume different types of roles within the social institution of the family; rather, it attests to a *process of becoming* that must occur if there are *to be* subjects in a social world.[60]

The *maternal function*, as depicted by Kristeva, references the maternal body as a thoroughfare, threshold, or filter not directly accessible in language. It is associated with the buccal space of human infancy. When Lacan describes how mothers help their infants experience identification through face-to-face play, which is an ego-founding activity that he names the "mirror stage," he is not depicting the maternal function. Instead, the maternal function, as Ewa Ziarek observes, is the "tain" in the Lacanian mirror, the silver lining that produces the specular representation without appearing in it.[61] But even this lining has a back and a front, as it were, for the pre-representational maternal matrix is already a mimetic structure oriented toward plenitude and loss. There is pleasure in warmth, nourishment, and loving care; however, there is also abjection—as the infant turns away from an embrace that seems suffocating and from nourishment that has begun to sour. For the not-yet-a-subject, separation is deeply unsettling because, on its way to language, the emerging subject renounces and divides what has been its undifferentiated union with being.[62] Writes Kristeva: "Matricide is our vital necessity, the sine-qua-non of our individuation."[63] Mimesis is born in this space of division within the maternal body.

But these rites of nascent mimesis—negation and identification—need not even be associated with the "maternal." Following Lacan, Kristeva describes the center of attraction and repulsion from which subjects are disinherited in order to become creatures of language as "the Thing."[64] Invoking multiple terms for aspects of the maternal function that predate language acquisition, Kristeva helpfully reminds us that we have no direct access to the ridge in being—the tain in the mirror—we seek to explore. Words point to but cannot capture processes through which an embodied being becomes an expressive organism and is constituted as a subject in the very opposition between presence and absence.[65]

Likewise, Mitchell's notion of the *sibling function* does not primarily reference the actual social configuration of families with two or more children. As a consequence, a child who has no siblings is not at risk of failing tasks critical to its development. Mitchell states that "everyone has a potential sibling."[66] The child who has no siblings uses fantasy to carry out its sibling work. For both the child with a sibling and the child who imaginatively creates a sibling, the sibling is always first "a replication of oneself who has to become other than oneself." Whether negotiated in the presence of an actual sibling or in reaction to a fantasy about a sibling, a young child's encounter with its sibling displaces the grandiose self. In the wake of this encounter, the child achieves singularity. Indeed, singularity— the potential for recognition of a specific other as oneself—is the decisive feature of sibling relationships.[67]

The *paternal function* likewise points to a process of subject creation rather than to a specific social context (e.g., contemporary Western societies) in which men take up parenting. Lacan offers the definitive contemporary statement of this function with his notion "Name-of-the-Father." Lacan incorporates homophony into his description: the name (*nom*) of the father is also the "no" (*non*) of the father that underscores its legislative and prohibitive function. The paternal function is associated with a Symbolic order. This order is the location for the exchange of words among persons who speak to each other. Within this system, no words have positive existence; rather, their meaning is entirely a function of their relational difference. Thus, the father is not an empirical father but a law-giving function around which specific human societies of exchange are constructed

Kristeva focuses much of her attention on a paternal function active prior to the acquisition of language, which is shaped by affect and sensory experience. To describe this function, associated with the work of primary identification in early childhood, she takes from Freud terminology with which to describe a paternal role that predates the child's acquisition of language: the father of individual prehistory. Typified also as the Imaginary father, which reflects Kristeva's attunement to Lacan's division between a Symbolic order of language and that which precedes it,[68] this father is not linked with the history of fatherhood, empirically speaking. Indeed, because this father predates language, "he" emerges prior to any awareness of sexual difference. As a consequence, Kristeva suggests that the father of individual prehistory is the same as "both parents" or even "X and Y."[69]

These three functions—oriented toward maternity, siblings, and paternity—name primary "GPS coordinates" for our walk through the woods of our lives. *They establish in the human subject initial pathways for mimetic desire as well as for acquisitive rivalries that emerge from that desire and devolve into violence.* However, these functions also establish patterns of embodied being that are susceptible to healing. In the wake of violence and its attendant trauma, they can open us to relationships shaped by loving mimesis. In Proust's *In Search of Lost Time*, a break with maternally marked trauma, always tentative, makes healing possible, but only as aesthetic promise. In Sophocles's *Antigone*, healing takes the form of an ethical praxis, when, at the grave of Polyneices, Antigone assumes a stance toward her sibling that is oriented toward love, not sacrifice. In Kristeva's *Old Man and the Wolves*, the old men of Santa Varvara create a healing praxis accessible through a narrative that celebrates intimacy. Engaging these narratives, we pass by way of a corporeal hermeneutics from a *maternal promise* that interrupts the violent trajectory of mimetic desire into a space shared with our siblings that is shaped by *an ethics of intimacy.* Emerging from that space, we at last encounter paternal figures—fathers past and future—whose loving compassion may inspire us to *build a posttraumatic future.*

Part 1: Mothers and *In Search of Lost Time*

Girard and Kristeva share a passion for Proust: Girard has written extensively about Proust, and Kristeva has made Proust the focus of two books.[70] Why is Proust compelling? Girard claims that *In Search of Lost Time* attests to mimetic desire and its correlate, an "ontological sickness" or "metaphysical illness." Contending that this sickness infects *all* humans in the modern era, Girard likens us to the characters of the novel. All too aware of their radical insufficiency, they attempt to fill the void of their being via mimesis. Seeking being in others, they would become "gods in the eyes of each other."[71] Girard perceives an awakening by the protagonist of *In Search of Lost Time* to illusory and problematic aspects of mimetic desire. Not only does the novel expose his ontological sickness, but also, the novel's concluding volume, *Time Regained*, records an awakening of the protagonist to the truth of his illness. Proust and the novel's readers move toward recognizing that a life built on the illusion of mimetic desire and rivalry is fundamentally wrongheaded. Although redemption glimpsed in *In Search of Lost Time* exists only on the aesthetic plane, Girard applauds its existential truth.

Similar to Girard, Kristeva recognizes mimesis in the novel and its critique. Even more than Girard, she attends to aesthetic features of the text in order to explore how Proust exposes the fragmentation of being, notwithstanding efforts the characters in the novel make to possess being. Significantly, Kristeva emphasizes two features of the novel's aesthetic and psychological contours to which Girard does not closely attend. She looks intently at the *material* dialectic to which the novel grants access: a visceral and sensual imprint of meaning, which Bolens would typify as kinesis, disrupts desire recorded in the text. Kristeva writes that, when readers become caught up in *In Search of Lost Time*, "they are not uniquely in the words, but in the narrator's body."[72] Second, Kristeva uncovers the *maternal* cast of the novel. Kristeva glimpses an original plenitude of being that has been sacrificed, resulting in ongoing trauma for the novel's narrator. The redemptive aspect of the text, for Kristeva as for Girard, is confined to the aesthetic moment. However, the discourse she describes re-creates a forgotten link to the maternal body that is revelatory of healing.

Kristeva's reflections on trauma, the maternal body, and embodied pathways to healing highlight the potential for productive augmentation of Girard's theory and the importance of that effort. Kristeva and Girard concur that mimetic desires that first emerge with nascent subjectivity factor in decisive ways in all subsequent conflicts. Violence original to the microcosm of interpersonal relations is replayed in the macrocosm of society. But Girard emphasizes the significance of sensory experience to mimetic transformation only in his early work. Kristeva's reading of Proust shows what Girard loses when he sets aside sensory experience and no longer attends to how it facilitates healing from mimetic illness. I argue that augmentation of his theory along lines suggested by a corporeal hermeneutics informed by Kristeva is necessary if Girard is to take full purchase on the ontological sickness he describes and identify its cure. Returning to aspects of Girard's early theorizing that he later sets aside, I establish that his theory remains an extraordinary resource for all who seek to understand our ontological illness and its solution. In tracing ontological sickness to the maternal matrix at the very threshold of human subject formation, I show also how Kristeva secures Girard's theory on firmer ground, thereby making it more compelling.

<h1 style="text-align:center">Part 2: Siblings and Antigone</h1>

Psychoanalyst Juliet Mitchell inspires my reflections on siblings, mimetic rivalries, and Sophocles's *Antigone*. Mitchell typifies interactions among siblings in terms of an "Antigone complex."[73] She explains that she is prompted to develop this paradigm because psychoanalysis has neglected lateral relations among brothers and sisters. Vertical relations between parents and their children have dominated, as has the complex that bears the name of Antigone's father and brother: Oedipus. But Mitchell points to the importance of a new paradigm named after Antigone. Although parents play a crucial role in the lives of their children, siblings also establish vital relationships with each other. These interactions feature powerful emotions: a child anxiously imagines that its sibling will replace it in parental affections; this child's brother or sister fears that its sibling harbors feelings of violent jealousy that pose a threat. Coming to terms with their anxieties and fears, siblings introduce each other to the social dimension of human existence.

Lateral relationships also are paradigmatic for Girard. When a subject's attention is focused on an object that the model desires, as both the subject and the model approach that object, the symmetry of their desires causes the object to disappear from view. They see only each other and become more and more undifferentiated from each other. Their rivalry escalates, leading to violence. Twins offer especially compelling evidence of mimetic conflict, for as rivalry intensifies, their physical likeness to each other exacerbates the threat each poses for the other.[74] Girard recognizes that siblings need not be twins to experience reciprocal anxiety and fear. He cites fraternal relationships in myth and history—Cain and Abel, Jacob and Esau, Eteocles and Polyneices, Romulus and Remus—that demonstrate the proliferation of enemy brothers whose fraternal violence presages cultural violence.[75]

Mitchell expressly cites the influence of Girard's theory of mimetic rivalry on her theory of sibling relationships. Where most theorists of violence attribute hatred to the *difference* others pose for us, similar to Girard, Mitchell understands that the animosity she observes among siblings is linked to *sameness*.[76] In particular, when a new baby joins a family, the toddler who is the older sibling believes that the baby is another version of itself: this baby, "seeming to stand in my place, has killed me." As Mitchell perspicaciously observes, "The sibling is par excellence someone who threatens the subject's uniqueness."[77] But even when several years separate siblings, a new brother or sister represents love (as mirrored in their sibling likeness) for the older child as well as the threat of annihilation (the new sibling could replace the older child). Rage *and* adoration flood forward.[78] An ecstatic encounter of a young child with another so like oneself is juxtaposed with the trauma of having been annihilated by someone who has taken one's place.

Three features of Mitchell's reflections are especially relevant to the corporeal hermeneutics that informs my project. Mitchell explains how anxieties associated *with the maternal body* are joined with those that ascribe fears of annihilation and fantasies of destruction to siblings. She observes too that the instability and fragility that attend founding moments in social being are tactile and affective and not only linguistic and social. Mitchell's insights about the role of *embodied affectivity* in mimesis are especially illuminating in respect to trauma. Mitchell submits that trauma in early childhood cannot be healed unless the *deep trauma* that ushers in emptiness—parental absence, suffocating annihilation, replacement by a sibling—is redressed.[79] Because Girard does not address these features of sibling relationships, Mitchell's work points to how mimetic theory may be augmented, enhancing its explanatory power.

Applying Mitchell's insights to Sophocles's *Antigone* in ways that link the Antigone complex with this Greek tragedy, I explore *Antigone* as a story of trauma and healing. My discussion is inspired by Girard's brief comments on *Antigone* in *Things Hidden since the Foundation of the World*. Here he recalls the words of Simone Weil and typifies Antigone as one whose gesture of love places her outside a sacrificial orbit: Antigone breaks with the victimage mechanism endemic to human mimetic rivalry to become a *figura Christi*. But Girard's comments are tantalizingly and frustratingly brief. When Girard states that Antigone makes cause with the scapegoat and exposes the victimage mechanism, Girard appears to exempt *Antigone* from his long-standing view that Greek tragedy falls short of revelatory insights contained in biblical narratives.[80] But Girard does not explicitly grant *Antigone* exceptional status. Indeed, in his recent *Evolution and Conversion*, Girard seems to belie his assertion in *Things Hidden since the Foundation of the World* that Sophocles offers us a *figura Christi* in Antigone. Girard asserts that were Sophocles to "do away with the lynching of the victim, he himself would be lynched."[81] But if Antigone is *figura Christi*, Sophocles does precisely what Girard has said he cannot do; moreover, Sophocles is not "lynched."

The argument I make for *Antigone* could have been Girard's, were he to have explicated the argument at which he hints in *Things Hidden since the Foundation of the World*. I link Girard's comments on *Antigone* with his reflections on *Oedipus the King* and *Oedipus at Colonus* in order to explore how, within the larger context of the Theban cycle, *Antigone* shows Sophocles exposing the victimage mechanism. Advancing a corporeal narratology sensitive to kinesis, I examine *Antigone* for connections between lateral and vertical family relationships, affective values in these relationships, and the role of trauma in mimetic illness.

The outcome of this effort constructively augments Girard's theory. Drawing on Mitchell as well as on Kristeva, I suggest that intimacy comprises the distinctive feature of Antigone's love for her brother, a love that is an alternative to sacrifice. Intimacy, a form of positive mimesis grounded in intercorporeity, contrasts with mimetic rivalry that creates monsters out of siblings. In the wake of trauma, which is an affective and bodily expression of the lack that haunts human being, skewing human relationships, intimacy alone promises healing from ontological illness. Employing a corporeal narratology oriented around kinesis, I emphasize the centrality of ritual, her brother's burial, to Antigone's journey toward intimacy. My focus on ritual highlights the role of affective memory and sensory experience in opening up human experience to transformation. Amplifying Girard's theory of mimetic desire in this way, I establish that Antigone is an exemplar of lateral relationships to which we are first acclimated as young siblings. Explaining how we build on these relationships, creating human society, I show how Antigone accesses an ethics of intimacy that opens onto an alternative space. When Antigone performs rituals on behalf of her brother, reaching down into the depths of human woundedness—even death—to effect healing, Antigone, like Christ, acts outside an economy of sacrifice.

Part 3: Fathers and *The Old Man and the Wolves*

I turn my attention last to the fate of the father in contemporary society. Reflecting on Kristeva's novel *The Old Man and the Wolves*, I move forward from the ethics of promise glimpsed in *Antigone*. My goal is to more fully flesh out ways in which a posttraumatic future may be accessed. My inquiry, which is grounded not only in Kristeva's novel but also in her theoretical work, promises to amplify in helpful ways Girard's own reflections on the future of desire.

Already, in Part 2, Antigone has cast into question a psychoanalytic narrative that would underwrite Oedipal subjectivity as law. Antigone, emerging as an anti-Oedipus,[82] opens the door for a no-holds-barred exploration of the paternal function, for Antigone already challenges Oedipus as a marker of psychoanalytic normativity. Indeed, in tracing the history of the house of Labdacus, I highlight strangeness endemic to that house. No clear light stemming from a fatherly source illuminates it; instead, the house is haunted by the uncanny. This strangeness, which makes not only Oedipus but also Antigone riddles to themselves, suggests the significance of social and familial alliances within the house of Labdacus that are pre-and trans-Oedipal, which Lacan and Kristeva associate with the Imaginary order. In contrast to relationships forged through language in the Symbolic order, these alliances feature "direct and immediate identification" that is "prior to sexual differentiation."[83] As a consequence, even as I turn to a discussion of the paternal function in Part 3, I already have broken with a psychoanalytic claim on Oedipal identification with a prohibitive father.[84]

I follow Kristeva, who turns to literature, especially in her novel *The Old Man and the Wolves*, to trace the fortunes of the father in the contemporary world. In her commentary on the novel, Maria Margaroni insightfully suggests that *The Old Man and the Wolves* restages for our time the parricide of *Totem and Taboo*.[85] However, even as Kristeva believes that a weakening of paternal authority has resulted in paternal death, Margaroni observes that Kristeva recasts conflict. The battle in the novel is not between a father and his sons; rather, conflict turns on a scission *within* the paternal function between the dead father of a Symbolic and sacrificial economy and a loving father encountered outside that economy.[86]

When the narrator of the novel describes herself as a "disciple of dead fathers," we are invited to join with her in reflecting on paternity in a post-Oedipal world.[87] In the absence of the father of the Law, Kristeva locates another paternal function in the novel that, in her theoretical work, she associates with "the father of individual prehistory." Kristeva states that she takes this term from Freud, who develops this concept in his 1923 *Ego and the Id*.[88] Distinct from the Oedipal father who has underwritten social order, this father is associated with nascent development of the subject within the Imaginary order. The father of prehistory makes his mark outside relations of power; instead, as Stacey Keltner observes, he is associated with "primary relations to otherness."[89] Kristeva's distinctions enable me to delineate within the family romance important differences between acquisitive rivalries and dynamics of otherness that, if constitutive of our being, nevertheless open onto transformative processes of subject creation. These processes, attuned to love rather than to conflict, are akin to positive mimesis described by mimetic theory.

My discussion is especially important for mimetic theory, I argue, because when the young Girard abandons a phenomenology of sensory experience, he sets mimetic theory on a course that causes it to lose touch with positive mimesis. As Kristeva introduces us to fathers who do not succumb to excesses of internal mediation that threaten to destroy contemporary society, she also points out a way forward to positive mimesis. Grounded in a hope that emerges in the poetry of ancient Rome and is also visible in Orthodox Christianity, Kristeva's transformative vision, to which we are introduced by the old men in her novel, is an alternative to the apocalyptic vision that dominates Girard's most recent work.

In *The Old Man and the Wolves*, Kristeva assesses the "fragile threshold" along which transformative processes may be glimpsed, notwithstanding a widespread crisis of meaning to which the novel's narrative attests. She does so as *The Old Man and the Wolves* moves between two temporal registers: a violent and troubling present visible in the city of Santa Varvara[90] and a past perfectly balanced between light and shadow to which the Roman poets Ovid and Tibullus attest.[91] Although Santa Varvara seems at first encounter to be an eastern European resort city, readers of Kristeva's novel gradually experience it as a "global village" impossible to locate on a map: "Santa Varvara is in Paris, New York, Moscow, Sofia, London, Plovdiv and in Santa Varvara too, of course."[92] Wolves lurk in Santa Varvara, signaling an invasion of banality and meaninglessness that leads to "all pervasive violence" and "barbarity.[93] In hearkening to an earlier era, the poetry of the Roman poets fragments the narrative in a "multiplicity of codes and voices." Although Ovid and Tibullus bring to the fore "a modern Christ-like sensitivity that echoes our own anguish," they also point beyond crisis toward "another culture, another mentality."[94] The dual registers of the novel function in a mirror-like way, illuminating mimetic conflict and pointing to potential resolutions of that conflict.

Woven throughout the narrative of *The Old Man and the Wolves* is testimony to the transformative work undertaken by those whom Kristeva associates with the father of individual prehistory. The old men in the novel are a focus not only of anguish but also of hope. Not the fathers of the law, each "orphaned, suffering, uprooted father" of the novel is an embodied man "present with the full weight of his psychology, his affects, his fears. A rebel, if you wish, and at the same time a man of sorrows, in a certain way a Christ-like figure." This man—multiplied in the mirror-like pages of the novel—points beyond "the situation we are experiencing, at the end of the world" toward intimacy and love.[95]

In the pages of the novel, kinesis is fundamental to the suffering of old men caught in the sacrificial world of Santa Varvara; so also is kinesis a powerful antidote to that suffering as the old men offer *iconic* witness to healing. Kristeva invokes key tenets of a theological anthropology informed by Orthodox Christianity to demonstrate via a corporeal hermeneutics how affective memory and sensory experience enable the paternal function to yet function, even as fathers all about us succumb to rivalries that replace meaning with emptiness, hope with despair.[96] Offering compassion, the Christlike witness of Kristeva's old men breaks with debilitating mimetic rivalry. Where Girard would see the Son and Father withdraw from the world in the face of escalating violence, Kristeva would see that a God of love yet offers relationship on the far side of a symbolic and sacrificial economy. In this way, kinesis opens onto kenosis: passage through death is offered where "eyes of the flesh . . . may yet regard the spirit."[97] Thus, Kristeva's novel points beyond itself to the incarnational theology of the Eastern Church. Promising participation in the life of God, this theology brings to expression the intimate mediation to which Girard alludes but which he does not develop. Checking Girard's apocalyptic vision, this theology can be drawn on to magnify Girard's allusions to positive mimesis and strengthen a tenuous thread of hope that is woven through Girard's work.

PART 1

In Search of Lost Time

Mothers

Marcel wearily dips the cake into the tea and, as the soaked crumb touches his tongue, he feels miraculously delivered from his wretchedness. . . . The renewed sensory impression provides a material bridge between the past and the present; the world of Combray springs back to life in all its original freshness.

—René Girard, "Introduction," *Proust: A Collection of Critical Essays*

In Proust's world, the child is an adult who recalls loving people and places with his mouth—people and places that his grown-up desires claim are harmless. . . . The hope of reviving our past is tentatively suggested, for if our past can hide itself "in some material object (in the sensation which that material object will give us)," chance alone should be enough to bring it into our world.

—Julia Kristeva, *Time and Sense: Proust and the Experience of Literature*

Marcel Proust's *In Search of Lost Time* is a powerful account of mimetic desire. Proust confronts us with the bankruptcy of the narrator's desires as well as with our own; so also does he enable us to participate in the narrator's release from the strictures of desire and his transformation. Chronicling hope and not only despair, the narrator of *In Search of Lost Time* attests to salvation that is threaded through life trauma.

Tracking the narrator's story across the pages of the novel, Girard offers a profound reading of *In Search of Lost Time*. I appeal to that reading here, for Girard is exceptionally adept at describing the vicissitudes of metaphysical desire in the novel. Building on Girard, I advance a corporeal hermeneutics as I attend to Proust's evocation of sensory experience and its attendant affective memory. His insights illuminate the family romance—those fundamental patterns of mimetic desire among family members. With my reading of Proust informed by Kristeva, I explore how, within the family romance, our earliest expressions of mimetic desire have a maternal referent. Highlighting also themes from *In Search of Lost Time* that attest to trauma, I bring forward phenomenological elements in Girard's early work that fall out of view in his later work, notwithstanding that they play a vital role in a comprehensive theory of desire. Attending to embodied experience on behalf of mimetic theory, I show how a theory of kinesis—intercorporeal perception—augments mimetic theory in two crucial ways. It is critical for understanding functions of metaphysical desire that lead to debilitating ontological illness, and it is vital for understanding how humans can access an intimate domain that is transforming rather than traumatic. I argue that, if we are to understand how metaphysical desire can be overcome, we must return to sensory experience and affective memory—the "I can" of the body—highlighted by Girard in his early work. That experience, I contend, is our sole means of access to an intimate domain; moreover, *In Search of Lost Time* is our road map.

Sensory experience is central to René Girard's encounters as a young scholar with Proust. His reflections on *In Search of Lost Time* begin with the madeleine. As the scene is described by Girard, the narrator[1] of the novel arrives home after a long day, and his mother serves him tea and a little cake. Marcel dips the cake in the tea and, as the cake crumbs touch his tongue, he is transported back in time to a moment in his childhood when he joined his bed-ridden aunt for tea and ate a madeleine. Through what Girard calls "the curious phenomenon of *affective memory*,"[2] Marcel bridges past and present to resurrect a memory of a life and a town like no other: his childhood in Combray.[3] Late in the novel, long after Marcel has left Combray, drawn away

from the town by promises and desires, affective memory again plays a decisive role in the novel's narrative. Invited to visit the Guermantes clan, Marcel
crosses their courtyard, only to feel that the uneven cobblestones beneath
his feet have suddenly become stones in the Baptistery of St. Mark's Basilica
in Venice he visited years before. For a moment, Marcel is standing in that
open square rather than in the courtyard of the Guermantes. Experiencing
another "sudden and extraordinary blossoming of affective memory," the
present and the past are bridged by Marcel. In what Girard describes as a
moment of complete conversion, everything shifts—"the outer and inner
world, future and past, dispersion and unity, desire and attachment, possession and contemplation, disintegration and aesthetic creation." Affective
memory, Girard notes, is "only one aspect" of this "spiritual conversion." But
it is one aspect that "will not fail to provide the energy needed for the great
work of art which is to come." As the reader concludes the novel that the
narrator describes as now ready to be written, the reader "cannot doubt that
the promise has been fulfilled."[4]

Girard's comments, dating to 1962, follow a longer commentary on Proust
in Girard's first book, *Mensonge romantique et vérité Romanesque*,[5] published
in 1961. Affective memory is a central concept in both works. Drawing on a
compelling example—the young Marcel's visit to the theater—Girard begins
Mensonge with a groundbreaking sketch of the dynamics of triangular desire.
Marcel has a passionate desire to see a performance of the great actress La
Berma, who has been an object of admiration by Bergotte, a popular novelist
idolized by Marcel. When Marcel eventually attends a performance, he is
profoundly disappointed. La Berma's performance is unremarkable. Following the event, Marcel confesses his disillusionment with the great La Berma
to Norpois, a former ambassador and friend of Marcel's father. Norpois
responds with favorable commentary on La Berma, and Marcel adopts Norpois's views as his own.[6] Labeling this scene an "essential Proustian" moment,
Girard affirms that Marcel's desire is a borrowed desire.[7]

Girard attributes to Proust's use of metaphor Proust's ability to show
us imitative desire. Indeed, Girard suggests that Proustian art "reaches its
culmination in the creation of metaphors."[8] Metaphors offer testimony to
the metaphysical nature of desire, establish the sacred relationship between a
subject and his model-mediator, and demonstrate that the subject seeks the
fullness of being in that model. Because little on the surface distinguishes

the worlds of the subject and model-mediator—they occupy the same objective space—metaphors establish boundaries that transform a walk into a pilgrimage and the home of a model-mediator into a cathedral.[9] The powers of metaphor are visible in Marcel's visit to the theater. When Proust offers up a marine kingdom as a metaphor of the social elite, nymphs, Nereids, and Tritons "are not simply a decoration." Everything in the scene is false and theatrical except the "immense hunger for the sacred."[10] Proust evokes these memories of his youth but is no longer poisoned by them, Girard claims, because "affective memory carries with it condemnation of the original desire."[11]

Recalling in 2008 his early work on Proust, Girard states that *In Search of Lost Time* "is one of the novels which was fundamental to my literary education but also to all of my ideas."[12] So also does Girard attribute to Proust, along with Stendhal, Flaubert, Cervantes, and Dostoevsky, the "intellectual breakthrough" that puts him "on my way to the mimetic theory."[13] Even so, if Girard attributes to Proust a founding role in the development of his mimetic theory, key words associated with Girard's analysis of Proust do not persist in his later work. Terms such as "perception," "sensory impression," "material bridge," and "affective memory" comprise a constellation of expressions that disappear from Girard's vocabulary. On his way to the theory of mimetic desire, Girard leaves these concepts behind. Moreover, when Girard has discussed Proust in recent years, although many of his comments echo themes first addressed in his early work on Proust, references to sensory impressions are missing. That affective memory would play a role in an individual's conversion—enabling that individual to experience healing from ontological illness—is not an idea that Girard revisits or claims in later work. Even though affect and sensation are central to Girard's formative encounter with *In Search of Lost Time*, playing a key role in his theory of how the narrator is freed from the grip of metaphysical desire, these terms disappear from Girard's lexicon. Why?

In a 2007 interview with Pierpaolo Antonello, published as *Evolution and Conversion*, Girard recalls his early philosophical interests: "from Sartre I went to Merleau-Ponty and all the authors related to phenomenology, which fascinated me and for a while I wanted to write in the phenomenological style."[14] Antonello suggests to Girard that "your intellectual interests were not clearly defined," and Girard concurs. Girard comments that his "intellectual breakthrough" awaited his encounter with novelists (Proust, Stendhal, Flaubert, Cervantes, and Dostoevsky).[15]

Without a doubt, when Girard writes about Proust in 1961 and 1962, the vocabulary of phenomenology persists. Understanding that mimetic desire runs through the body, Girard finds in sensory experience the mechanism of spiritual conversion. Moreover, in *Deceit, Desire and the Novel*, Girard suggests that Proust's references to "*habit, sensation, idea*, or *feelings*" allude to an incipient phenomenology within the pages of *In Search of Lost Time*.[16] Indeed, Girard asserts that "the most fruitful intuitions of phenomenological and structural analysis are already present in Proust."[17] Nevertheless, as Girard breaks through to mimetic theory with Proust, he breaks away from phenomenology.[18] As he begins to exercise the distinctive scholarly voice with which he will articulate essential features of mimetic theory, Girard is increasingly inattentive to the role affective memory and sensory experience play in human life. In *Violence and the Sacred* and *Things Hidden since the Foundation of the World*[19] as well as in more recent works,[20] sensory experience and associated terminology figure not at all.

That Girard no longer attends to sensory experience in his later work on Proust, bypassing even Proust's indigenous phenomenological insights, is most apparent in Girard's discussions of conversion. In 1961–62 and in 1999, Girard's remarks on conversion converge on the courtyard of the Guermantes in Proust's *In Search of Lost Time*.[21] In 1962, Girard uses the phrases "spiritual conversion" and "an extraordinary blossoming of affective memory" to describe what happens to Marcel as he walks through the cobblestoned courtyard leading to the Guermantes's door. But in 1999, Girard maintains from his original description only the concept of conversion. Sensory experiences that are critical to Marcel's conversion in 1962 are treated in 1999 as "trivial incidents . . . like walking on the uneven pavement of the Guermantes' courtyard." In 1962, feet on flagstones resituate Marcel in the past and "take him back" to Venice; in 1999, similar recollections leave Marcel wholly in the present.[22] A transformation that in 1962 "will not fail to provide the energy needed" to create his novel is, in 1999, a purposeful avowal. Writes Girard in 1999:

> This kind of remembrance triggers in him an aesthetic and spiritual illumination that transforms him completely. This tiny event provides him with his whole subject matter, the dedication needed to write the book and,

above all, the right perspective, a perspective totally free for the first time of the compulsion of desire, of the hope of fulfilling himself through desire.[23]

Change is triggered in Marcel and, possessed of a new outlook on life, he moves forward with determination.

But what elicits the illumination that supplies Proust with the substance of *In Search of Lost Time*? How does he attain the viewpoint that lifts him free of mimetic desire and empowers him to expose its mechanism? In 1999, Girard does not say. But in 1962, Girard names what has sparked Proust's aesthetic and spiritual illumination. The "outward and downward movement of pride" that is Proust's preconversion state is succeeded by an "inward and upward movement," and "affective memory" features in this transformation.[24] True, Girard credits affective memory with being responsible for only a single element of conversion; however, in 1999, Girard is altogether silent. He is intent to situate Proust's "great surge of creativity" within traditions of Christian conversion, likening the cork-lined bedroom in which Proust writes his novel to a monastic enclosure. He notes, for example, that Proust expresses some interest in learning more about Christianity during his post-conversion years in order that he may understand his transformation better.[25] But Girard does not speak to the larger anthropological question: *What are the initiating factors in Proust's conversion?*

If Girard had elaborated in 1999 on Proust's transformation, what would he have said? Is Proust filled with the grace of the Holy Spirit as he walks through the Guermantes's courtyard? Girard implies as much when he states that the conversion is "comparable in most aspects" to Christian conversion and "functions as such."[26] But what makes Proust capable of this change? In 1962, Girard claims that affective memory is "the Last Judgment of Proustian existence and "the salvation of the writer and of the man Marcel Proust."[27] He addresses a central question of theological anthropology—what undergirds the human capacity for conversion—with the notion of affective memory, claiming that "affective memory is the nucleus of all Proust's work" and "the source of the truth and the sacred."[28] Girard's silence on this question in 1999 is telling.

In Stephen Duffy's study of theological anthropology, he explains why it is important for theological anthropologies to address the human capacity for transformation. The vulnerability and fragility of human existence needs to be named, but so also should "the inherent goodness of human finitude" be addressed.[29] Theological anthropologies rightly emphasize that humans are incapable of their own accord of a full expression of human possibility within the order of creation. The human capacity for self-constituting agency *is* marred by violence toward one's self and others. Nevertheless, these anthropologies attest inadequately to such failures in human life when they attribute human evil to willful acts against God or to nature in respect to which humans are wholly passive. As Paul Ricoeur observes, "Finitude is neither evil or sinful, but a creative limit meant to orient and protect freedom rather than repress it."[30] Finitude is a dimension of the self that is part of the goodness of creation, and anthropologies that speak about Christian grace should account for structures of finitude—such as human sensory experience—out of which that goodness can be brought to expression. When anthropologies attend to these structures, grace can be seen to focus on that which is estranged from God, not on that which is alien to God.[31] In doing so, they speak to *potential* for the graceful recreation of human lives.

Girard's inattention to critical features of a theological anthropology points to a lacunae in his theory of conversion. On the one hand, Girard wants to claim that humans can exchange conflictual mimetic desire for positive mimesis that leads to empathy for others and love of God.[32] On the other hand, as Rebecca Adams observes, when Girard describes this positive desire, he does not explain *how* humans come to demonstrate it.[33] As Adams remarks, Girard does "*tell us* that we can take on this new perspective"; however, Girard does not *show us* how humans relinquish roles of victim and persecutor in a system of acquisitive mimesis and assume new roles.[34] We do not learn from Girard how humans become graceful.

Did Girard's attention in the early 1960s to affective memory and sensory experience point the way to a more complete anthropology? When Girard dropped this line of reflection, attributing it to a phenomenological style of inquiry extrinsic to his mimetic theory, did he sustain no loss to his interpretation of Proust or to the development of his theory? Or, in setting aside foundational insights he traces even to this day to his encounter with *In Search of Lost Time*, did Girard abandon a crucial element of his theory: an account of *how* humans are able to move from a past characterized by mimetic conflict to a future in which they express new forms of being, grounded in nonacquisitive mimesis? I suggest that Girard's theory did incur a loss when he turned away from his early explorations of affective memory. If we are to have a full and robust mimetic theory, we should reclaim Girard's early insights and reestablish a strong connection between the human capacity for positive transformation and sensory experience. *We should develop a corporeal hermeneutics oriented toward kinesis.*

Julia Kristeva offers Girard a pathway. In common with the early Girard, Kristeva begins her inquiry into Proust with the madeleine. So too is her reading of Proust and his concept of involuntary memory influenced by phenomenology. Kristeva associates Proust's exploration of society with mimetic processes; further, Kristeva is similar to Girard in finding Proust's use of metaphor decisive to the transformative power of the novel.[35] Kristeva also locates points of resonance between Proust's experience of writing the novel and the Christian experience of conversion. She joins Girard in likening the transformative experiences of *Finding Time Again* to Christian grace.[36] However, in staying with affective memory and sensation in her efforts to understand, when Girard does not, Kristeva assists us in reclaiming sensory experience for mimetic theory. Her approach, rooted in what Bolens describes as a corporeal hermeneutics and informed by psychoanalysis as well as by the work of philosophers such as Maurice Merleau-Ponty, is of decisive value. It sustains our efforts to find in Proust fundamental insights for mimetic theory and to bring to full expression a comprehensive theory of metaphysical desire. Kristeva augments Girard in ways that are important for a mimetic theory that would aim to account not only for humanity's vulnerability to metaphysical desire but also for the human capacity for transformation. She offers a sustained account of how affective memory and sensory experience play a vital role in the transformation of the narrator, a transformation that she and Girard typify as conversion. As Kristeva reflects on the narrator's struggles with metaphysical desire and his transformation, she attends also to the critical role of *maternal referents* in that sensory experience.

To be specific, Kristeva adds to Girard's perspective on *In Search of Lost Time* a distinct awareness of how Proustian time functions in relation to involuntary memories that link past and present in a *metaphor*. Girard understands the significance of metaphor to the work of memory and concurs with Kristeva that the emblematic expression of that work is the madeleine. The madeleine is an "exception" to the rule of metaphysical desire. Writing that "there is no mediator in the case of the 'madeleine,'" Girard labels it a "privileged moment." Preparing the way for the insights of *Finding Time Again*, the madeleine is "in a sense its annunciation."[37] For Kristeva also, an intense experience in the *present* awakens a *past* experience of childhood. The joining of these two moments becomes a third moment in time: *the time of the literary or analytic work that gives expression to the moment of remembering*. It is, as Proust says, *le temps retrouvé*.[38] But as Kristeva celebrates Proust for "inaugurating a new conception of temporality,"[39] she develops a more nuanced theory of metaphor than does Girard.

Central to Kristeva's insights is Proust's description of the narrator/author as an X-ray operator.[40] The narrator suggests that the "visible charm" of persons escapes him, for he is like the X-ray operator who is able to see "beneath the sleek surface of a woman's belly, the internal disease which is gnawing at it." Others may think that the narrator is "looking at them"; however, he is "radiographing" them. Radiography enables Proust to express how memories are accessed. Our memories, painful or pleasant, have previously resided in our bodies. We have had a sensory connection to them (as does a woman to the painful symptoms of disease), but we have not been able to create exteriorized signs of these symptoms. Time creates the association between sensations, enabling their imprinting (as in a radiographic image) and subsequent diagnosis. This associative labor is the work of metaphor. Indeed, "Proustian time X-rays memories."[41]

Within the context of a literary work, *metaphor* is like an electromagnetic wave that closes the gap between past and present in *le temps retrouvé*, enabling the narrator to move from trauma toward transformation. As understood by Kristeva, metaphors do not create meaning by substituting a complex or abstract idea for one rooted in everyday experience, thereby bridging the unfamiliar and familiar. Nor do metaphors function primarily to awaken us to new possibilities in habitual speech, enlivening the ordinary or hackneyed.[42] Instead, metaphors link by analogy sensation and idea, resulting in an "image made incarnate."[43] Writes Kristeva of this lived image: "Time is this bringing together of two sensations which gush out from the signs and signal themselves to me. But since bringing things together is a *metaphor*, and sensation implies a *body*, Proustian time, which brings together the sensations imprinted in signs, is a *metamorphosis*."[44]

In this work of metamorphosis, which can be likened to the radiography Proust has described, Kristeva observes that the reader experiences a sensory identification that is "the place of sacred communion."[45] This metamorphosis is what Bolens names kinesis and Gallese typifies as intercorporeity.[46]

Admittedly, Girard too recognizes this metamorphosis, labeling it a sacred transformation. However, Kristeva's keen attention to sensory experience amplifies Girard's account. Kristeva observes the child narrator's efforts to understand his pleasure in the madeleine: "Where could it have come to me from—this powerful joy?" In subsequent mouthfuls, as the magic fades and the narrator sees that the source of joy lies elsewhere, he laments, "I put down the cup and turn to my mind. It is up to my mind to find the truth. But how?"[47] The narrator describes as a "difficult task" his efforts to determine what has happened, for as he tries to represent what he has tasted, connections that must be held together—perception *and* meaning, taste *and* vision, that which is perceived *and* that which is signified—begin to separate. The work of the novel will be to join what, already in the first pages of the novel, begins to drift.[48] Indeed, if the novel is to be an occasion for conversion, for healing, the joining of sensory perception with signification must be among its primary achievements. As a consequence, the reader will participate also in the transformative kinesis reported by the novel's narrator.

Sensory experiences play a vital role in the transformation of the narrator, proving instrumental to his attaining empathetic lucidity. However, Proust's account of the X-ray operator points to another significant aspect of sensory experience. The narrator's distress, powerfully evoked by his disturbing reference to a hidden growth that is buried in a woman's belly and gnaws at her insides, becomes a second point of focus for Kristeva, leading her to explore maternal relationships in the text. When Kristeva establishes the importance of these relationships to metaphysical desire and its healing alternative, she insightfully augments Girard's analysis of mimetic desire. In the novel, the child narrator's anxiety is directed initially toward his mother and centers on his intense feelings for her. In the throes of a family romance, caught up in patterns of mimetic desire that shape interactions among family members, he wants to be united with her; however, he also fears a threatening, consuming connection with the maternal body.

In its most basic form, mimetic desire features a subject, a model, and an object of desire. The subject emulates the model and adopts her desire for an object from the model. *In Search of Lost Time* introduces us to a child narrator, more of a proto-subject than a subject, and to the object of his intense and highly ambivalent adulation: his mother. However, the dynamics of the child narrator's desire are misread if we attribute his desire solely to an Oedipal scenario that would install the child's father in the role of model. Yes, a triangulating vector of desire connects the child and his father, as the child seeks the mother's regard. However, as I will demonstrate in what follows, the primary dynamic of desire and trauma in the text turns on an earlier, triangulated desire that links the proto-subject with the maternal body. This body, not the father, is an infant's first other; moreover, it also is an infant's first model. The infant negotiates standing in the world in assimilation to and separation from the maternal body, experiencing all the dynamics of desire—ecstatic connection and monstrous threat—in relation to this body. In its divisibility, turned toward or away from the infant, the maternal body tutors the infant in patterns of mimetic desire that are foundational for all later patterns of desire.[49] It proffers wholeness of being at the very same time that it also introduces the infant to its own lack of being. In this way, the division in being that is the maternal body—model *and* other—engages the infant in dynamic play among points of an original triangle. In the life of the narrator of *In Search of Lost Time*, this original triad has issued in a problematic and traumatic legacy. *In Search of Lost Time* tells the story of the narrator's quest for healing from this trauma.

Central to his quest are sensory experiences. The child narrator replicates his encounters with his mother kinesically, drawing on his sensory experience, especially the world offered up through his mouth. When an infant, not-yet-a-subject, begins to separate from the maternal body, the division in being that culminates in a discrete "I" is both pleasurable and a source of anxiety. Most significantly, the accession of the subject to standing in the world is not accomplished once and for all. Under stress, the subject will revisit its initial boundary work: the allure of reuniting with the maternal body as well as the threat of not surviving that rejoining. Thus, the narrator's anxiety about the maternal body transposes into suffering when he becomes an adult, especially when his desires are expressed in sadomasochistic ways. The anguish of his failed desires, in which mimetic conflict replaces a hoped for reciprocity of desire, is lived out by his body.

Kristeva writes of the central role that all literature plays in recording this crisis: "Far from being a marginal activity in our culture," literature actually "represents the ultimate coding of our crises."[50] Only as Proust's narrator moves through and out of this trauma will the narrator be able to attest to transformation and exchange mimetic desire within the constraints of the family romance for love within an intimate domain. Proust chronicles how a young child's early history with the maternal body establishes an initial pathway for mimetic desire as well as for acquisitive rivalries that emerge from that desire and devolve into violence. Akin to GPS coordinates to which we appeal on our "life-walk through the woods," the maternal function, like the sibling and paternal functions, establishes a key parameter for mimetic rivalry within the context of the family romance. Most significantly, Proust records in his novel how the child narrator's relationship to the maternal body of his infancy also establishes patterns of embodied being that are susceptible to healing. In the wake of violence and its attendant trauma, Proust's narrator will summon these and attest to the potential for transformation.

If we are to follow Proust on his journey, we need to address the substance of affective memory and sensory experience in the novel. A corporeal hermeneutics supports that effort. That we also give close attention to Proust's allusions to and struggles with the maternal body is essential; for, just as this battle is critical to Proust's incarceration within the prison of mimetic desire, so too is its outcome decisive for his conversion. The maternal relationship—one of three familial functions that establish in infancy and early childhood initial pathways for mimetic desire as well as for the acquisitive rivalries that emerge from that desire and devolve into violence—plays a critical role in establishing for the narrator a pathway forward to positive mimesis. Highlighting these themes by way of a dialogue with Kristeva, my inquiry advances our understanding of the human experience and enhances the capacity of mimetic theory to illuminate it.

In chapter 1, I explore a newspaper essay by Proust titled "Filial Sentiments of a Parricide." Girard argues that this essay prepares Proust for the revelatory work of *In Search of Lost Time*. I concur with Girard's assessment of Proust's essay. Even so, I suggest that Girard is insufficiently attentive to ways in which affect and sensory experience play a critical role in Proust's break with metaphysical desire, which has begun with his essay "Filial Sentiments of a Parricide." In chapter 2, I offer a reading of *In Search of Lost Time*. Drawing on Kristeva's analysis of this novel, I explain that the narrator of *In Search of Lost Time* does not easily escape the ontological illness that besets him. The narrator's anxiety about the maternal body is registered as ongoing trauma, replicating the suffering already depicted in Proust's essay on the parricide. In chapter 3, as I demonstrate how the narrator of *In Search of Lost Time* and its author are freed from the strictures of metaphysical desire and experience healing, I facilitate a dialogue between Girard and Kristeva that confirms the significant potential in Kristeva's corporeal hermeneutics for constructive amplification of Girard's theory.

CHAPTER 1

The Eyes of a Parricide

At bottom, we make old, we kill all those who love us, by the anxiety we cause them.

—Marcel Proust, *Filial Sentiments of a Parricide*

Accoording to Girard, an exploration of Proust's *In Search of Lost Time* should not begin with the novel; rather, it should commence with reflection on a newspaper essay by Proust titled "Filial Sentiments of a Parricide."[1] Girard argues that this essay constitutes a transformative moment for Proust, providing an occasion for him to break through the strictures of metaphysical desire that have mired him in ontological illness. Girard contends that, in the aftermath of writing this essay, Proust is newly able to identify with others in a nonrivalrous way. Further, Girard submits that insights Proust attains from the essay provide him with the impetus to write *In Search of Lost Time*. The novel attests in fuller detail to a transformative process begun with Proust's composition of the *Le Figaro* essay.

I concur with Girard that "Filial Sentiments of a Parricide" lays the groundwork for *In Search of Lost Time*; however, I suggest that Girard underplays important features of this essay. As I focus on how "Filial Sentiments

17

of a Parricide" depicts the human body and references maternal death, I
establish a basis for exploring *In Search of Lost Time* in ways attuned to roles
affective memory and sensory experience play in transforming the trajectory
of mimetic desire. Both function to free the narrator of the novel from the
painful confines of a family romance and to open him to an intimate domain
of positive mimesis.

Proust's Copernican Revolution

Late in *Deceit, Desire, and the Novel*, Girard focuses his attention on "Filial
Sentiments of a Parricide." The article, Girard asserts, sheds "brilliant light"
on the miracle of novelistic insight that will subsequently prove crucial for
Proust's writing of *In Search of Lost Time*.[2] Written and published in *Le Figaro*
in 1907, "Filial Sentiments of a Parricide" describes a young man, Henri van
Blarenberghe, who kills himself after murdering his mother.[3] Proust begins
the article by referencing correspondence he has had with Henri, which has
established Henri in Proust's memory as a pleasant and distinguished young
man. Subsequently, Proust turns his attention to the sensational details of
the murder. As Henri's mother lay dying, she is said to have cried out, "What
have you done to me! What have you done to me!"[4] Girard observes that,
with a telescoping effect, Proust focuses on relations between mothers and
sons in general even as his comments increasingly display a more personal
tone.[5] Writes Proust:

> If we think about it, perhaps there is no truly loving mother who would
> not be able, on her last day and often long before, to reproach her son with
> these words. At bottom, we make old, we kill all those who love us, by the
> anxiety we cause them, by that kind of uneasy tenderness we inspire and
> ceaselessly put in a state of alarm.[6]

Proust's remorseful identification with Henri becomes revelatory when
Proust muses about other mothers' sons. Perhaps these sons, reflecting on
their mothers' aging and the trouble they have caused their mothers, could
yet have a "*belated moment of lucidity which may occur even in lives completely
obsessed by illusions, since it happened even to Don Quixote*" (*dans ce moment*

tardif de lucidité que les vies les plus ensorcelées de chimère peuvent bien avoir,
puisque celle même de don Quichotte eut le sien).[7] Empathically connected
with others, the parricide who "recovers his lucidity in the course of expiating the crime and expiates his crime in the course of recovering his lucidity"
offers a point of entrée to the miracle of Proust's own novel.[8]

Girard proposes that the *Le Figaro* article captures Proust, a struggling
writer who has demonstrated little capacity for memorable prose, in the
moment of discovery that starts him on a path to literary immortality. As
Proust speaks of the lucidity of a son and Don Quixote, he lays out what
alone has the power to break apart the mimetic rivalry that characterizes
metaphysical desire. When we are able to identify with others, we establish a
transforming distance from desire and open ourselves to truth. Empathy with
another, exemplified by the son who recognizes near the end of his mother's
life that he has made her life difficult and painful, ushers in transformation.
Sustained over time, empathy frees us from the strictures of desire. According to Girard, Proust offers direct and indirect testimony to the significance
of his discovery. By way of direct acknowledgment, Proust gives *Le Figaro*
permission to edit and cut his text, with the exception of the paragraph that
mentions Don Quixote, which he asks the editor not to cut. Moreover, and
subsequent to the publication of this article, an enlightened Proust begins
writing *In Search of Lost Time*.[9]

In a 1965 essay, "From the Novelistic Experience to the Oedipal Myth,"
Girard comments further on the van Blarenberghe case and its influence
on Proust.[10] He argues that "Filial Sentiments of a Parricide" constitutes a
"Copernican revolution" for Proust[11] and asserts that Proust's evocation
of a newly self-aware and empathetic son demonstrates "the unity of novelistic genius."[12] Proust joins other novelists who discover "their delusion
and wretchedness" at the point of "death," break free of the constraints of
metaphysical desire, experience rebirth, and subsequently write of their
life-altering transformation, exposing their readers to the truth they have
discovered about desire. Indeed, for Girard, Proust's enlightened reflections
on the parricide suggest that other individuals can experience transformation and break away from the strictures of metaphysical desire. For that to
happen, one must recognize that one is like Henri, a bad son. The "signs of
the other must become signs of the self" so that "the double is revealed to be
a double."[13] The revelation or revolution in existence that follows dismantles

oppositions that have structured the psyche and created mimetic rivalry. A new creative life unconstrained by acquisitive desire will follow.

Earlier, in *Deceit, Desire, and the Novel*, Girard describes how Proust takes purchase on such a life. The narrator of *In Search of Lost Time* attests to his transformation with particular eloquence near the end of *Finding Time Again* when the hero "dies" and is "reborn" as the writer of *In Search of Lost Time*. On Girard's reading of these passages in *Finding Time Again*, which feature a disturbing spectacle of aging, Proust contrasts the death of persons who will pass from this world without possibility of resurrection with the novelist's own transformation. Thanks to the powers of "affective memory," the novelist attains hard-won clarity about his own confrontation with death."[14] He comes to know that "the ultimate meaning of desire is death but death is not the ultimate meaning of the novel." He "clings by his finger-tips to the edge of a cliff," expecting to fall into the abyss; instead, he finds himself supported by air.[15] Absolute loss is surpassed in a moment of conversion, from which a capacity for relationships outside the prison of metaphysical desire is born.

For Girard, the key feature of transformation or conversion is the novelist's renunciation of a self-centeredness that had set him on the path to imitation.[16] The novelist who once disdained others emerges from the pain of failed desires able to identify with others and recognize them as persons like himself. What is true for others is true for the novelist; what has made others snobs has made the novelist a snob also.[17] Recognizing within his own life the sins of which he has accused others,[18] Proust's moment of unifying recognition comes to expression "in the miracle of the novel."[19] Its hero, who has been separated from the novel's creator, is now joined as one with the author: Proust at last attains a breadth and depth of vision that presages the renunciation of desire.[20] The absence of desire in the present opens up memory, enabling past desires to be recaptured, but in a transformed form.

The temporal context for Proust's momentous transformation at the end of *In Search of Lost Time* is set by Bergotte. In *Swann's Way*, Bergotte is the model who the young Marcel seeks to emulate, before he is distracted by the mimetic turbulence of Parisian salon society. Reappearing in *Finding Time Again*, Bergotte prefigures the work of the novel. Bergotte enables readers to perceive that the narrator is having a revelatory vision and experiencing a metamorphosis that will prepare him to compose the very novel whose concluding pages they are now reading. Bergotte has died; however, his books "keep watch like angels." In anticipating the death and resurrection of the narrator-Proust, Girard suggests that Bergotte signals readers that *In Search of Lost Time* is born from the transformation that has occurred in its author's life.[21] Proust's hero will not kill himself; he will write a novel.[22] Readers share in Proust's spiritual transformation when they see through ruses of metaphysical desire as these are exposed by Proust and witness the miraculous descent of novelistic grace.[23]

Girard offers a compelling account of revelatory alternatives to metaphysical desire discovered by Proust in "Filial Sentiments of a Parricide" and further attested to by *In Search of Lost Time*. But has Girard fully mined the article that he says explains Proust's "rebirth"? One moment the novelist is losing his grip on the cliff of life experience and at risk of plummeting to his death; the next, he is supported in a graceful existence. What happens in the interval? Girard states early in *Deceit, Desire, and the Novel* that *affective memory* plays a key role in the upward movement of transformation. A source of truth, affective memory founds graceful existence. Moreover, in his essay on Proust, Girard asserts that *sensory impressions provide a material bridge* between past and present, making transformation possible.[24] As Girard concludes *Deceit, Desire, and the Novel*, celebrating the novelist and his lifesaving conversion, does Girard continue to give sensory experience and affective memory roles in Proust's transformation?

Let's consider sensory experiences depicted in "Filial Sentiments of a Parricide." Past and present are joined for Proust as maternal and filial memories come together.[25] Further, multiple references to bodies in "Filial Sentiments of a Parricide" alert us to the significance of corporeal memories to Proust. Proust writes about the bodies of the living, and he writes in graphic detail about the corpses of Mme van Blarenberghe and her son. He comments also on the bodies of Ajax and Oedipus, describing Oedipus's blinding in particularly gruesome terms. Journalistic sensationalism cannot be Proust's aim. After all, in this same essay, Proust excoriates readers of *Le Figaro* who wish to begin their day with "that abominable and voluptuous act called 'reading the newspapers.'"[26] That Proust self-consciously aims to avoid melodrama suggests that we should seek another rationale in order to account for bodies that are strewn across the pages of "Filial Sentiments of a Parricide." Only as we account for these unsettling aspects of the essay can we arrive at a comprehensive account of its transformative impact on Proust.

But writing of the article at the conclusion of *Deceit, Desire, and the Novel*, no rationale is provided by Girard. Graphic depictions of the dead in "Filial Sentiments of a Parricide" must be without importance to the life-changing impact of the essay on Proust, for Girard takes no notice of them. As a consequence, testimony to affective memory is shorn by Girard of the most compelling instances of affect and sensation. In writing of Proust's transformation, Girard does explain that Proust embarks on a path to self-critical lucidity and empathy that breaks away from mimetic rivalry. But Girard does not show how sensory experience figures in that journey. Girard does point to themes of death and transfiguration, which are key features of the end game in the journey of metaphysical desire. However, Girard largely bypasses the body work that lies between these two points, to which Proust alludes in "Filial Sentiments of a Parricide" in near lurid detail. Missing are full explanations of the relationship between affective memory, sensory experiences of the body, and the transformation of metaphysical desire. Drawing only on Girard for support, readers are uncertain how to follow Proust as he moves, in the aftermath of "Filial Sentiments of a Parricide," through the hills and valleys of daily life to the transformed life to which *In Search of Lost Time* attests. In "Filial Sentiments of a Parricide," Proust identifies strongly with the bodily travails experienced by the persons he describes. But as Girard reflects on Proust's passage from "Filial Sentiments of a Parricide" to the cathedral of the novel,[27] that trauma might feature in Proust's journey is left largely unexplored by Girard. He does not take its measure. Indeed, having discovered the key to mimetic transformation in Proust's life-changing moment of lucidity, Girard seems already to be putting a distance between himself and the phenomenological insights on sensory experience that have featured elsewhere in his early studies of Proust.

As I take a second look at aspects of "Filial Sentiments of a Parricide" to which Girard gives insufficient attention, I find inspiration in Proust's image of the narrator as X-ray operator. The operator knows that affective memory is also bodily memory. As Kristeva points out, Proustian time, so critical to emancipation from metaphysical desire, "brings together sensations imprinted in signs."[28] The empathy that accrues to one who escapes the prison of metaphysical desire is *a lived expression of caring by an embodied individual*. A critical "radiography" inspired by Proust's metaphor enables me to advance a corporeal hermeneutics that reveals new insights about "Filial Sentiments of a Parricide."

The Eyes Have It

References to bodies are abundant in "Filial Sentiments of a Parricide." Among all features of the human body depicted in the article, eyes are the most pervasive. Proust describes eyes that see falsely—as happens to Ajax when Athena veils his vision so that he will slaughter shepherds and flocks in the Greek camp without knowing what he has done.[29] But Proust writes too that when we perceive with the eyes of memory, even though our actual eyes "go suddenly blind to surrounding objects," we actually "see" with great clarity. Our eyes become machines, "telescopes of the invisible."[30] Recalling his visits to the salon of Princess Mathilde, Proust describes the Princess's eyes when she is engrossed in recollecting past experiences. Although the Princess's eyes cease to engage things around her, her eyes yet "resurrect" experience. Connecting sensation with signs, the invisible with the visible, when the Princess gazes in memory she joins the present and past together.[31] With Proust's references to the work of memory attested to by the eyes of the Princess, he offers a first sketch of a theory of time to which the lived metaphor of sensations imprinted with signs is critical. Eyes that have been veiled by trauma cannot see; sensory changes are needed if these eyes are to be released from trauma to see again.

Proust's reflections on eyesight and memory comprise the background for a comparison he draws between the eyes of Henri van Blarenberghe and Oedipus. Proust's account is gruesome. After killing his mother, Henri not only slashed his face with a dagger but also pointed a gun at his head, blasting open "the whole left side of his face" so that his left eye *"lay on the pillow."*[32] Describing the scene as if he is a direct witness, Proust's eyes turn toward the invisible. The eye on the pillow is that of the "miserable Oedipus, torn out in the most terrible act in the history of human suffering." Intent that he "no longer see the evil he has suffered and the disaster he has caused," Oedipus strikes his eyes and "black blood flows down his cheeks" as he demands to be driven from the land.[33] Summoning powers that join sensation and sign in a metaphor, Proust links past and present disasters, making them one in the body of the parricide.

Although the eyes of Henri and Oedipus are striking images in "Filial Sentiments," of primary significance in the essay is a passage that immediately precedes the commentary on sons and Don Quixote that Girard cites as confirmation of Proust's revelatory moment of lucidity. Describing the aging maternal body, Proust catalogs physical alterations—faded eyes, white-streaked hair, hardened arteries, choked kidneys, a strained heart—and attests to the emotional changes that transpire for mothers when their "invisible hopes" are at last exhausted.[34] Proust's words allude to a complex sensory experience. Bringing to view "the slow work of destruction" that results finally in maternal death, Proust elicits from his reader a visceral response to his unsettling account.[35]

That Proust associates physical *and* psychic trauma with aging is not surprising. Consumed by suffering following the death of his mother, when Proust picks up his pen to write "Filial Sentiments of a Parricide," he has not written for over a year.[36] In his 1961 *Mensonge romantique et vérité romanesque,* Girard acknowledges this sad time and surmises that the "death which Proust is in the process of living in 1907" is doubtlessly "reflected in all his writing of this period."[37] So also does Girard recognize that aspects of the article have an "'Oedipal' atmosphere [that] is quite striking."[38] But in his 1965 comments on "Filial Sentiments of a Parricide," Girard understands Proust's encounter with death differently. Excluding Proust's mother and her agonizing death from his analysis, Girard states that the one who "dies" and is reborn in 1907 is Proust.[39] Girard asserts that neither an "external biographical link" nor a connection to a "mundane tragedy" plays a role as Proust moves from the *Le Figaro* article to take up the work of the novel.[40]

But the maternal figures that shadow "Filial Sentiments" should not be summarily dismissed. Key features of the essay are rendered inexplicable in their absence; moreover, similar aspects of *In Search of Lost Time* that I examine in the next chapter are incomprehensible in the absence of an analysis attuned to maternal references in the text. In both instances, a corporeal hermeneutics oriented toward the maternal is critical to our efforts to understand how Proust exposes the structure of metaphysical desire and points to a metamorphosis in being.

That Girard has not sufficiently acknowledged the significance of references to our most intimate society—the family and especially the mother—in "Filial Sentiments" is underscored when we look closely at the article's final words that Proust cited as critical to the full interpretation of the article and which he exhorted Gaston Calmette, the editor of *Le Figaro*, not to cut. As noted above, Girard has found special significance in Proust's request, arguing that it attests to Proust's own awareness that a few lines, "written in a hurry for a daily newspaper," are actually of momentous significance.[41] But the editorial secretary at *Le Figaro* proved unresponsive to Proust's request. Girard has built his case on the concluding passage of the *published* article that speaks of the lucidity of sons and Don Quixote. But Proust's request was directed toward another paragraph *that was never published*.[42] The suppressed paragraph that Proust urged Calmette not to delete reads:

> Let us remember that for the ancients there was no altar more sacred, surrounded with more profound superstition and veneration, betokening more grandeur and glory for the land that possessed them and had dearly disputed them, than the tomb of Oedipus, at Colonus, and the tomb of Orestes at Sparta, that same Orestes whom the Furies had pursued to the feet of Apollo himself and Athene, saying: "We drive from the altar the parricidal son."[43]

Proust's comments, coming after his troubling depiction of the blinding of Henri and Oedipus, suggest that Girard's assertion that the parricide "recovers his lucidity in the course of expiating the crime and expiates the crime in the course of recovering his lucidity" needs a nuanced interpretation, for the paragraph that Proust insists must be kept in the article alludes to persisting trauma. Proust does not focus on a graceful transformation; rather, he casts his discerning gaze on a parricide who must undertake an arduous journey if he is to be freed from the anguish of maternal death.

I concur with Girard that a paragraph in "Filial Sentiments of a Parricide" Proust singled out as essential should have a special significance for our interpretations of the article and the novel that follows. However, because the paragraph to which Proust has asked that we attend is the one cited above rather than the one on which Girard has focused his attention, Proust's evocation in the article of bodily trauma is not incidental. Moreover, because

Proust evokes Orestes—the mythic prototype of maternal murder—the tragedy of maternal death about which Proust writes is not "mundane." If Proust is transformed by insights he achieves in the writing of "Filial Sentiments of a Parricide," the unpublished conclusion of the article suggests that Proust makes a difficult passage to the cathedral of *In Search of Lost Time*. After all, Proust is ineluctably linked with a son who has been driven from an altar by the Erinyes.[44] The Erinyes, ancient Greek entities especially associated with interfamilial strife, often appear when blood or natal bonds are at issue or in the wake of threats to a mother-child bond.[45] Named by Proust in this key paragraph, these Furies cast shadows along the path he walks from the essay to the novel.

Acknowledging with Girard that, in the aftermath of his reflections on parricide in the *Le Figaro* article, Proust appears newly possessed by a revelatory lucidity on which he takes purchase as he writes *In Search of Lost Time*, I assert that we understand that lucidity best if we examine closely themes of the unpublished paragraph from "Filial Sentiments of a Parricide" that are referenced also in the novel.[46] Threats to the maternal-child bond described on the pages of *In Search of Lost Time* suggest that Proust's transformation is not sudden. His lucidity is hard-won, for he must confront his own Furies in remorse over the death of his mother. Only after exile will the parricide enter the cathedral of the novel to rest finally at the foot of its altar. As Kristeva observes, confronted with a world in disarray, Proust must still search for "the lost, invisible temple of the sensory time of our subjective memories." But the time for which he searches entails "pretense, betrayal, sensory excess, and erotic extravagance." Attuned always to the "violence of marginality" that has marked his life and that of his characters, Proust must come to grips with trauma if he is to experience grace and communion.[47] Trauma, constitutive of a gap in space and in time, precludes Proust from immediately surmounting his past after the brief moment of empathic identification with another to which he attests in "Filial Sentiments of a Parricide." This gap will close only as lived metaphors, like radiographic images created by the X-ray technician to whom Proust has likened himself, gradually bridge the space and time of trauma. Rendering Proust's gaze newly expansive and inclusive, these metaphors swirl through the pages of *In Search of Lost Time*. Making the invisible visible, these metaphors at last release the author-narrator from the painful repetition of suffering and open him to transformative healing.

With Kristeva as a guide, I examine how sensory experiences shape mimetic processes, presaging fear of others and conflict as well as empathy toward others and joy. The characters of *In Search of Lost Time*, especially its narrator, bring these experiences to light and enable us to experience them through kinesis. For the narrator, an initial experience of an Other/Model, a maternal body that is a source of anxiety and pleasure, threat and security, is decisive. Encounters with maternally marked bodies later in life, as pleasurable as they are unsettling to the narrator, feature in the novel as well. My analysis, grounded in a corporeal hermeneutics, demonstrates how the narrator's anxiety about the maternal body is registered in trauma. Most important, my discussion shows how the narrator's transformation occurs only after the narrator has been healed of this trauma. Traumatic sensory experiences depicted throughout *In Search of Lost Time* are transposed to a different register by the author-narrator who describes them, resulting in healing and transformation. Charting with Kristeva Proust's metamorphosis from a past characterized by mimetic conflict and death to new forms of existence grounded in nonacquisitive mimesis, I amplify Girard's account of Proust. My aim is to enhance mimetic theory's capacity to offer a more comprehensive analysis of the most significant aspects of human experience.

CHAPTER 2

Of Madeleines, Mothers, and Montjouvain

A book is the product of another self than the one we manifest in society, by our habits, by our flaws. If we want to understand that other self, we can succeed in doing so by recreating it within ourselves, in our own depths.

—Marcel Proust, *Contre Sainte-Beuve*

My route forward with Proust begins with the madeleine. Girard cites the madeleine as a preliminary revelation for Proust—a "first glimmer of novelistic grace" for the novel that is to come—and Kristeva also begins her reflections on Proust with the madeleine.[1] However, because Kristeva draws out elements of this metaphor of which Girard takes no notice after he sets aside his early interest in affective memory and sensory experience, her observations can enhance Girard's mimetic theory. Reflecting on the madeleine from a perspective grounded in Kristeva's corporeal hermeneutics, I demonstrate how an augmented mimetic theory can offer a comprehensive analysis of the most significant aspects of human experience. In support of that objective, as I explore the madeleine, I address themes of affective memory and sensory experience, maternal presence and absence, death, trauma, and erotic excess.

Of Madeleines and a *Petite Madeleine*

Kristeva wants to begin her discussion of *In Search of Lost Time* with the madeleine, but she pauses. The madeleine is a cliché. Potentially deadening us to the richness of Proust's text and getting in the way of our consideration of *In Search of Lost Time*, the madeleine might best be avoided. Nevertheless, Kristeva invites us to consider this small cake anew: the madeleine, she asserts, delivers us into a magic circle (or spiral) of the metamorphosis in being that occurs in the novel. There we meet a child who is "an adult who recalls having loved with his mouth persons and places that his adult desires regard as merely anodyne."[2] Describing *In Search of Lost Time* as if it is a musical composition, Kristeva alerts us to "eight movements" that comprise our initiation into this magic circle.

With the narrator of *In Search of Lost Time*, we arrive at the first movement of this composition in the grip of voluntary memory.[3] Indeed, seeking to recall his childhood in Combray, the narrator asserts that if anyone were to ask him about Combray, he would be able to offer only a few recollections summoned by "the memory of the intelligence." "The rest of Combray," he declares, "was really quite dead for me."[4] Having resolutely closed the door on the past, the narrator nevertheless continues to reflect (second movement).[5] He cites the belief that souls of the dead can become captives of "inferior creatures": animals, plants, and inanimate objects. He wonders, could humans experience a similar transformation? If we were to encounter our past, captive to a material object, would it not depend on chance? As it were, luck is with the narrator (third movement).[6] It is a winter's day in Combray and the narrator is bemoaning that everything about Combray has ceased to exist for him. His mother suggests tea and sends for a little cake: "And soon, mechanically, oppressed by the gloomy day and the prospect of another sad day to follow, I carried to my lips a spoonful of the tea in which I had let soften a bit of *madeleine*."[7] Invaded by a "delicious pleasure," the narrator speaks of a metamorphosis; for the essence of this pleasure has proved transformative. It was "not merely inside me, it was me."[8] The reader wants to share this pleasure with the narrator; however, Kristeva would have the reader pause: why is the cake a madeleine?

Kristeva notices that, in the first version of the text, the reference in the tea scene is to a "dry rusk."[9] Observing that Proust chooses names for characters in the novel with care, Kristeva suggests that when Proust names the cake, he does not do so casually. He must know that the cake, which he calls a "*Petite Madeleine*," capitalizing the name, refers to Mary Magdalene.[10] Mary Magdalene, around whom the Christian tradition has conflated three Marys of the Bible—the sinning woman who anoints Jesus, the sister of Lazarus and Martha, and the Mary who is the first to see the risen Christ—is metamorphosed in the text and in the narrator's mouth. The madeleine, now a small cake, is a complex mix of saintliness and sin.[11] But is this all?

Kristeva observes the power of names to evoke sensation: just saying the name of a well-known geographical location can take us there, releasing "through the oxygen of memory, a plethora of sensations, impressions and delights."[12] To whom or to where might the "madeleine" take us, if not to the Bible? Kristeva locates a madeleine in the "geography" of pages in the novel that immediately precede the madeleine scene. Marcel's mother has been reading to him a novel by George Sand: *François le champi*. Sand's story is about a foundling who is taken in by a miller's wife: Madeleine Blanchet. The child is loved by her; eventually, as an adult, he becomes her lover and husband.[13] So also does a Madeleine appear in Proust's life: as a character in a novella by Proust titled *L'Indifférent*. In this short work, Madeleine de Gouvres is a noblewoman in love with a man named Lepré who is unresponsive to her. Readers recognize this Madeleine from her description. Wearing a blouse of yellow tissue covered with cattleyas, she is an early version of Odette. But when Madeleine moves to *In Search of Lost Time*, becoming Odette, she loses her name; moreover, female and male roles are inverted.[14] Kristeva draws together Madeleine Blanchet and Madeleine de Gouvres, suggesting that they constitute the fourth movement in the "musical" composition of *In Search of Lost Time*. Once joined, these women comprise a maternal motif: a beloved mother whom a son wishes to marry is also indifferent and unattainable.[15] For Kristeva, these Madeleines appear in the novel in metamorphosed form: they are captive to an "inferior object," the *petite madeleine*. We read of the delicious pleasure of madeleine/Madeleine in the mouth of the narrator. They fill him "the same way that love acts."[16] For the briefest of moments, he experiences "the most infantile and archaic" of human contacts: oral connection with the maternal body.[17]

The narrator moves on, bringing a self-conscious awareness to his act of eating (fifth movement).[18] He ponders the source and meaning of his extraordinary experience. But, as he takes another bite of the cake, the sensations diminish. The narrator surmises that "the truth I am seeking lies not in the cup but in myself."[19] Insulating himself from sensation, stopping his ears, and concentrating, he seeks an image, a representation of his experience (sixth movement).[20] The narrator labels his task "difficult," for he is asking that memory create a bond between perception and signification. A fortunate substitution eases his task. The narrator's memories alight on Aunt Léonie rather than on his mother (seventh movement).[21] Kristeva traces this substitution: actual experience (the mother's madeleine) is displaced in all of its vertiginous intensity. Not only does this displacement make possible the joining of perception and image, but also it establishes stability and place for the narrator.[22] Everything is now solid, recognizable, and safe (eighth movement).[23] Oral proximity to a mother who holds one close while reading *François le champi* but who often withholds the kisses one desperately desires is replaced by the recollection of Aunt Léonie—bourgeois, sometimes sickly, always a fixture of Combray.

The narrator directs our attention still further away from the Madeleine/madeleine when he recalls a Japanese game played with a porcelain bowl in which little scraps of colorful paper have been steeped, "as if it were necessary," Kristeva observes, "to set up a maximum distance, a foreign country, to enable us to see, again to the maximum extent, how evanescent is the object of desire which the little madeleine offers to be sensed."[24] Thanks to the anchoring role of Aunt Léonie, the narrator can safely apprise us that a lurking threat has been domesticated and tamed by an act of signification.[25] Sensation is now aligned with chaste memories rather than with secrets of a family romance. "Divested of female sexuality, of its female corporeality, leaving behind nothing but the tender, loving care," the madeleine, "the nodal point of a childhood memory," has done its work. The madeleine has brought to life the house of Proust's birth.[26]

The composition of the madeleine, a work in eight movements, is a first glimpse at the wonder that is the Proustian metaphor. Times—past and present—are evoked. Spaces—an intimate and archaic maternal space and a stable, provincial space of an aunt's home—are experienced. Cake that crumbles on the tongue becomes a sensation that, imprinted in signs, creates a metamorphosis. But the composition is not yet fully described. The narrator's eye scans Aunt Léonie's bedroom and recalls the madeleine and the porcelain bowl filled with colorful paper. He contends that everything comes forward to his mind "like a stage set." If so, Aunt Léonie's sofa is in his purview. He does not mention the sofa here; however, when he writes of the sofa later in the novel, he recalls how the soul of one who is dead becomes the captive of an inanimate object. Aunt Léonie's sofa speaks to her nephew. The narrator has inherited the sofa (along with other pieces) from Aunt Léonie and has consigned it to a brothel where it now resides, "defiled by brutal dealings" to which he has condemned it. Passing the sofa as he walks through the brothel, the narrator hears Aunt Léonie "cry out silently to me": a soul "imprisoned, subjected to constant torture, and begging forever to be freed."[27] He stops frequenting the brothel; he cannot bear to look at the sofa, for he responds as if "the dead woman herself was being violated." Only later does he recall his direct participation in an early profanation of the sofa: his first sexual experience occurred with a cousin on that sofa when it resided in Aunt Léonie's bedroom.

For Kristeva, the metonymy that makes possible a transposition from a mother who is uncomfortably proximate to an aunt who embodies staid safety is fundamentally unstable. The sweet taste of the madeleine gives way to an ignoble erotic secret.[28] Distance is followed by *desecration*. Before we enter the cathedral of the text, we will walk through a brothel. The Proustian metaphor, a powerful instance of kinesis, will embrace the body sadomasochistically. A son will seek revenge against the mother. Transubstantiation will be preceded by suffering and death.

But we should not be surprised. Already in "Filial Sentiments of a Parricide" the essential features of this journey, intrinsically embodied and corporeal, are in play. Proust observes that others see only madness in Henri's murder of his mother; however, Proust asks readers to "re-see" (*revois*) Henri with him.[29] Sharing with readers Henri's letter to Proust a year before, Proust asks that readers notice Henri's deep filial love. Concerned that readers not consume "Filial Sentiments of a Parricide" as "a fine little morning treat,"[30] to digest along with their café au lait, Proust directs readers to Greek tragedy.[31] Proust wants to "open the room of crime to the air of heaven, to show that this commonplace event was exactly one of those Greek dramas, their presentation of which was almost a religious ceremony." Henri is not a brute but "a noble example of humanity."[32] Henri doesn't differ from readers of *Le Figaro* because he has murdered his mother; rather, he is distinguished from them by the transformation he undergoes *after* he has "dispatched his mother" (*achevé sa mère à coups de poignard*).[33] Society gossip sees in Henri only a debauched life. But the ancients, for whom the tombs of Oedipus and Orestes were the most sacred of sites, teach that redemption follows upon degeneration and death. The narrator of *In Search of Lost Time*, also a parricide, prepares to follow *in the footsteps* of these Greek heroes in order that he may discern, on the other side of pain and suffering, the "joy of living."[34]

"The Mother Is at the Heart of Primal Sado-Masochism"

Caught up in a metaphysical desire that features debilitating mimetic conflict, Proust makes writing *In Search of Lost Time* a passage from grief and suffering to healing and joy.[35] Accompanying Proust, we discover that maternal bonds feature at every moment of this journey. Proust's evocation of maternal relationships enables him (and the readers of his novel) to come face-to-face with motifs of suffering, violence, death, and eventual redemption that he has delineated previously in "Filial Sentiments of a Parricide." These motifs are visible in key scenes of the novel: the drama of a young child's goodnight kiss, the Montjouvain episode with Mlle Vinteuil and her lesbian lover, the grandmother's death, and echoes of the Montjouvain scene in later volumes of the novel. Each event features the narrator's complex reactions to death. Indeed, as Kristeva suggests, "death makes it possible for violence and remorse to be inserted into the very heart" of the narrator's sensibility.[36] Moreover, each scene demonstrates that cruelty is manifest in human life—even in childhood. Testimonials to trauma, each vignette aligns also around a single theme: "Time will be truly regained only if [the narrator] rediscovers the particular form of violence that marked his initial experience of loss." Thematically expressed, each of these episodes asserts that "that which delights me and abandons me also kills me; but I am capable of putting to death that which is my delight."[37] Throughout, sensory experiences maintain a powerful hold on the narrator.

Maternal and sensory features of mimetic desire within the frame of a family romance are visible from the first pages of *In Search of Lost Time* as the young narrator seeks a goodnight kiss from his mother. Contrasting images of light and darkness frame this scene, positioning the narrator in a visual order "mediated by an embodied subject."[38] These images are portents of instability and loss in the narrator's life. He recalls many past occasions when he awakened from sleep unable to identify his whereabouts. Beset by a mounting anxiety, he sought comfort in the familiar walls and furnishings of his bedroom; however, they were strange and uncanny. When his mother and grandmother noticed his disquiet, they gave him a magic lantern to ease his transition to the night. But instead of soothing him, the lantern exacerbated his unease. Casting everything in an alien light, the lantern transformed even the doorknob on the bedroom door into a threat. Previously a predictable fixture the narrator could take for granted, it became a strange spiritual presence that served as the "astral body of Golo."[39] But the darkness that inevitably followed eventide brought with it something even more terrifying: death. Recalling the night of the goodnight kiss, the narrator speaks of his room as a mausoleum and describes his bed as a tomb. Referring to his bed garments as a shroud, the narrator surrounds himself with emphatic testimony to a childhood cause: he avowed that a kiss alone could save him from death.[40] In making his mother's presence or absence a drama of life or death, the narrator suggests that life itself is at stake. The mother is a prime source of protection—her kiss is salvific—but she also is abject menace. When she withholds her kiss, leaving the young child to lie alone in the iron bed he imagines to be his grave, she becomes the deadly mother.

Writing of the scene of the goodnight kiss, Angela Moorjani insightfully observes that the child's alternating senses of love and hate are subtly intertwined but nonetheless extraordinary in what they evoke.[41] Playing his own version of the *fort/da* game,[42] the narrator wants the mother close *and* far away. Closeness promises comforting unity but also poses a threat of consumption or suffocation by the maternal body.[43] Distance creates a like anxiety: if the source of one's being is too far away, one will cease to exist. Therefore, when the child actually attains his wish—his mother not only comes to his room to kiss him but also stays the night—the narrator does not experience the bliss he has so eagerly anticipated:

> I ought to have been happy: I was not. It seemed to me that my mother had just made a first concession which must have been painful to her, that this was a first abdication on her part from the ideal she had conceived for

me; and that for the first time she, who was so courageous, had to confess
herself beaten. It seemed to me that, if I had just gained a victory, it was
over her that I had succeeded, as illness, affliction, or age might have done,
in relaxing her will, in weakening her judgment, and that this evening was
the beginning of a new era, would remain as a sad date.[44]

At its most primal, this passage alludes to oral deprivation that threatens an
infant with the dissolution of being. The maternal body is gratifying *and*
frustrating; it is comforting *and* provocative of anxiety and anger.[45] The
episode also offers mirror images of threat: a mother incarcerates her child in
a hostile room to protect herself from its voracious attacks; reaching out to
that child, she appears ready to attack it. Maternal and paternal interdictions
that would have the child acknowledge the primacy of the parental relationship also cloud the fantasy.

Writing of the overriding emotion of guilt in the scene of the good-night
kiss, Kristeva observes its precursors and successors. That an assertion of
one's own desires kills the other is prefigured in Proust's "A Girl's Confession"
(1896) when the assertive eroticism of its heroine causes her mother to die.
It features also in "Filial Sentiments of a Parricide." But guilt and maternity
are most substantively addressed in "Intermittences of the Heart," one of the
most haunting sections of *In Search of Lost Time*. Here, the theme of death is
transposed from the body of the mother to that of the grandmother. At one
remove from his mother, the narrator can more safely track guilt's contours.
As a consequence, "Intermittences of the Heart" brings to view the powerful
roles of sensation and affective memory in the experience of guilt; so also is
the important work of mimesis and its transformative potential made visible.

The setting of the story is Balbec, and the initial tone of the scene is light
and even crude, for the narrator is anticipating an encounter with the maid of
Madame Putbus, who, by virtue of her class, should be willing to meet every
demand of his inflamed desire.[46] But the tone of the story changes dramatically when the narrator experiences "a convulsion" of his entire being. He has
bent over to remove his boots for the night and, as he touches the first but-
ton, his chest suddenly swells, "filled with an unknown, divine presence."[47]
Sobbing, tears streaming, he perceives that his grandmother is rescuing him
from the "aridity of [the] soul," distress, and loneliness. More than a year after
her funeral, in a "complete and involuntary memory," she appears to him in

"living reality," leaning over to assist him with removing his boots as she had done when she was alive.

The narrator ponders these "disturbances of memory" and how they are linked to "the intermittences of the heart." He observes that, even though we imagine that all our past goods and sorrows are "perpetually in our possession," most of the time they are in an "unknown domain."[48] The narrator believes that his grandmother has appeared because the "self that I was then and which had vanished all that time ago" has returned, making him again "nothing more than the being who had sought refuge in his grandmother's arms."[49] But what has precipitated his transformation? The narrator says that, for the first time, he perceives his grandmother's death as a grave loss. Moreover, he also is newly aware of the suffering he has caused his grandmother, especially as he recalls that he wounded her when he callously dismissed a photo of her that had been taken by Saint-Loup.[50]

But, just as the narrator is reporting on the miracle of finding his grandmother again "as if in a mirror," he discovers that she has turned into a stranger who does not know him.[51] What has happened? The narrator's newfound empathy for his grandmother recalls Proust's evocation of the newly lucid son in "Filial Sentiments of a Parricide." In this moment of empathetic connection with his grandmother, acquisitive mimesis, with its contours of threat and mistrust, is replaced by mutual recognition. Indeed, the narrator's empathetic connection with his grandmother suggests transformative, positive mimesis. But the moment does not last. Brought to the door of the cathedral, the narrator can glimpse through its opening the fruits of spiritual transformation. But he loses his footing, stumbles, and steps back. Empathetic connection devolves into fatal difference, "for the dead exist only in us."[52]

The narrator professes that he will take on his grandmother's suffering as his own: blows he has directed against her he will direct against himself. The narrator is transparent in describing his situation: he wishes for "the nails to be driven yet more firmly home that had riveted her memory inside me." Not seeking to make the suffering "any easier" or pretending that he can rejoin his grandmother in "an indissoluble harmony" if he gazes at her photo, the narrator asserts:

> I was anxious not to suffer only, but to respect the originality of my suffering, such as I had suddenly endured it against my will, and I wanted

to continue to endure it, in accordance with its own laws, each time this strange contradiction between survival and oblivion, intersecting within me, returned. I knew not, certainly, whether I might one day isolate some element of truth in this painful and at present incomprehensible impression, but that, if I were ever able to extract that element of truth, it could only be from this same impression, so particular, so spontaneous, which had been neither traced by my intellect nor inflected or attenuated by my pusillanimity, but which death itself, the abrupt revelation of death, had hollowed out in me, like a thunderbolt, in accordance with some inhuman, supernatural diagram, like a double and mysterious furrow.[53]

Ongoing empathy and compassion, elicited in the narrator by the involuntary memory of his grandmother, proves elusive. Just as references to Orestes in "Filial Sentiments of a Parricide" have previously forecast, the narrator will make an anguished journey in exile. He will take in death, and trauma will hollow him out.[54]

A dream sequence is now inserted in the text.[55] In this dream, the narrator laments that he has not written to his grandmother in six months. The grandmother is entombed in a small, rented room, for she is paralyzed and cannot leave. The dream features mirror-like transpositions. At the beginning of the scene, when the narrator has stooped to remove his boots, his grandmother has appeared, as if in a mirror. Later, the dream mirrors the good-night kiss sequence of *Swann's Way* but reverses images of entombment (as mirrors do). In the episode of the goodnight kiss, the narrator is in the tomb of his iron bed and his mother comes to him. In this dream, the grandmother is entombed and the narrator must come to her. Notably, the instrument that connects the narrator and the grandmother/mother remains the same in both scenes, cutting through each in identical fashion. In *Swann's Way*, the young narrator sends a letter to his mother, which leads his mother to his tomb; in the dream, the narrator's father conveys a message from the grandmother's "tomb" to the narrator. She is happy to hear that the narrator is going to write a book.[56] In each instance, writing opens a tomb and promises to unite the living with the dead. Thus, as the narrator moves to embrace pain and suffering, he understands that the internalization of the mother/grandmother's pain, which he is about to endure, will not end in his death. He will not be entombed; rather, he will emerge from his burial chamber to become transformed by writing. But as the narrator rises from the dream, he has not yet broken free of his deathly existence. All contact with his grandmother is blocked. The miracle of affective memory cannot be summoned at will to bring back his grandmother. He turns toward the wall of his room but hears nothing, for the partition across which they used to communicate by tapping is silent.[57]

Important to the dream sequence is the odd sequence of words with which it ends: "stags, stags, Francis Jammes, fork."[58] Let us consider each of these words in turn. Commentators typically associate the reference to "stags" with the medieval legend of Saint Julien. In the legend, a stag predicts a parricide.[59] "Francis Jammes" is the name of a poet held in high esteem by Proust who sent Proust an adulatory letter after the publication of *Swann's Way*.[60] However, in his letter, Jammes also disapproves of the Montjouvain episode between Mlle Vinteuil and her lesbian friend and tells Proust that he should delete it. Taking up Jammes's concern in a letter to François Mauriac, Proust explains that he cannot comply with Jammes's advice, notwithstanding his high regard for the poet, because "I had constructed this work so carefully that this episode in the first volume explains the jealousy of my young man in the fourth and fifth volumes, so that by ripping out the column with the obscene capital, I would have brought down the arch."[61] The cathedral of the novel is founded on sadism and erotic excess. Finally, Proust's reference to "fork" is to an involuntary memory of the sound a fork makes when it hits the edge of a plate. An early draft of *Swann's Way* does include a scene in which the sound of a fork generates an involuntary memory;[62] however, in the published novel, this reference has been deleted.

Elucidating the disjointed words—"stags, stags, Francis Jammes, fork"— with which the narrator's dream concludes, I extract a narrative run through with powerful kinesic activity: "I must confront the death of my mother for which I am responsible; truly I must confront her death; and I must also come to terms with a troubling scene that Francis Jammes tells me I should not mention in my novel; only then will I be freed from intimations of parricide and sadism; such healing, entering through my senses as an involuntary memory (perhaps the sound of a fork tapping a plate), will enable me to 'extract something spiritual' from my life."[63] Thus, the dream sequence joins a passionate love for and aggression against a parental figure, guilt felt toward a parent whose death one has caused, and a need for healing, to which the work of affective memory illuminated by Kristeva's corporeal hermeneutics will point the way.

The complex nuances of the narrator's mourning of maternal death are refracted through the location in the novel of "Intermittences of the Heart." Although the death of the grandmother is described in *The Guermantes Way*, with ironic details that mix scenes of familial distress with descriptions of insensitive and awkward gestures by others,[64] only much later in *Sodom and Gomorrah* does the narrator experience the depths of that loss when, unlacing his shoes in preparation for bed, he encounters his grandmother in an involuntary memory. But the narrator's poignant reunion, made painful when he loses his grandmother once again, is juxtaposed in *Sodom and Gomorrah* with scenes of sadomasochistic eroticism and diverse explorations of sexual inversion.

Why is a moving recollection of an intimate family experience put side by side with images of violent eroticism that Proust warned his editor readers would find shocking and indecent?[65] For Kristeva, the scene in *Sodom and Gomorrah* captures essential revelations by Proust about temporal existence. Identity is constructed only through a succession of selves. Sensations, including violent ones, play a critical role in memory.[66] Reminding us that a child psyche has been forged in a specific relationship with a mother, Kristeva suggests that "Intermittences of the Heart" attests to continuities between sadomasochism within adult relationships and the sensitivities of a child to that violence. Thus, principle themes of the novel are joined when the death of the grandmother is inserted in this volume. The underside of a blissful experience of passionate communion with another is a "putting-to-death."[67] Moreover, the "faculty of memory that makes us aware of this duality" is grounded in "'the full-fledged existence of our bodies.'"[68] These two themes, already visible in the good-night kiss scene in *Swann's Way*, are expressed again in the narrative structure of *Sodom and Gomorrah*.[69]

What is more, these themes are part of a cluster of images that, threaded through and around *Sodom and Gomorrah*, link a child's ambivalent and violent relation to maternity with the possibilities of mutual recognition (or its denial). As a consequence, these themes attest to compelling links between a maternal body and the work of mimesis that a comprehensive mimetic theory should track. The narrator has talked about the mimetic relationship that he had with his grandmother; he even has found himself in the mirror of her face; but, in rejecting her after she has made an effort to preserve that relationship with a photo, she has become a stranger to him.[70]

Maternal profanation that is associated with mirror work appears also in Proust's notebook of 1908. Reversing the source of affirmation, Proust writes of "the maternal face in that of a debauched grandson."[71] Echoes of the same appear in *Against Saint Beuve* when "the face of the son who lives on, like a monstrance in which a sublime mother, now dead, places all her faith, is like the profanation of a sacred memory."[72] This mirroring, deathly maternal face appears too in *Sodom and Gomorrah*. As the narrator compares the likenesses of sons with their parents, he observes that "sons consummate in their faces the profanation of their mothers."[73] Mirror work points here only to mimetic conflict and death. But can a mother and a son who gaze at each other experience joyful recognition within an intimate domain? We do not yet know.

The profanation of the mother is signaled especially in *Swann's Way* in the scene at Montjouvain. The name "Francis Jammes," part of the metonymic chain of words in the dream sequence, "stags, stags, Francis Jammes, fork," alerts us to the centrality of the Montjouvain episode for Proust. After all, in Proust's correspondence with Paul Souday he emphatically asserts that the cathedral he is erecting would "come tumbling down on the reader's head" but for the "cornerstone" set in the first volume by a scene between Mlle Vinteuil and her friend.[74] Mlle Vinteuil is dressed in mourning clothes, for her father has died. Observed through an open window by the narrator, the young women are engaged in erotic foreplay and seem aware that they are being watched by unknown others. Mlle Vinteuil's friend spits on M. Vinteuil's photograph. Complicit in this scene, Mlle Vinteuil is the cruel rather than adoring child. But how can this scene be about the profanation of a mother when the object of disrespect is a father? Importantly, M. Vinteuil is given a maternal characterization in the text. A longtime widower who has been utterly devoted to his daughter, his maternal credentials are impeccable. Writes the narrator, "My mother recalled the sad end of M. Vinteuil's life, completely absorbed as it was first in giving his daughter *the care of a mother or a nursemaid*, then in the suffering his daughter had caused him."[75]

Echoes of the Montjouvain scene and its theme of maternal profanation are heard too in later volumes of *In Search of Lost Time*. Each time, as loss and guilt are accompanied by violence, cruelty, and disavowal of relationship, Proust sheds light on how sadomasochism and bodily suffering shape human lives, framing that which is deadly *and* that which is spiritually transformative.

A Strange Changeability of Loved Ones: Permutations of Metaphysical Desire in Sadism and Masochism

Building on the cornerstone that is the Montjouvain episode, Proust explores themes of death and transfiguration. He invokes a faculty of memory that is grounded in the traumatic suffering of bodies in order that he may be set free of their effects. Scattered through the later volumes of *In Search of Lost Time* is diverse testimony to Proust's preoccupations: reflections on sadism, attestations to masochism, excurses on male homosexuality and puzzled musings about lesbian eroticism. Proust's interest in these themes is not especially personal or sociological. Though his thoughts are informed by incidents in his own life as well as by fictional and nonfictional explorations of these themes by his contemporaries, Proust has not written a treatise on the sexual mores of La Belle Époque. Rather, Proust turns to these themes because they offer entrée for substantive reflection on his deepest concerns. Appealing to these topics, Proust can make sense of "the strange changeability of loved ones." Exploring how some of the most significant revelations of the novel emerge from narratives that depict sadomasochism and lesbian eroticism, with Proust we gain insight into the structure of metaphysical desire and its alternatives; for, as Girard too has recognized, "Sexual activity mirrors the whole of existence."[76]

In making the case for the illuminative potential of Proust's uncomfortable and discomforting forays into painful sadomasochism as well as his musings about homosexuality, I focus, initially, on Girard's account of sadomasochism in order that I may subsequently augment it. Girard offers a story that well summarizes the dynamics of masochism:

> A man sets out to discover a treasure he believes is hiding under a stone; he turns over stone after stone but finds nothing. He grows tired of such a futile undertaking but the treasure is too precious for him to give up. So he begins to look for a stone which is too heavy to lift—he places all his hopes in that stone and he will waste all his remaining strength on it.[77]

Girard understands that continual disappointment makes the man in search of treasure "desire his own failure." He sees that "only that failure will indicate an authentic deity."[78] As a form of metaphysical desire, masochism gathers into one whole previously distinct phases of the metaphysical process. In internal mediation, that the mediator-model might harbor hostile intentions against the imitator is entertained, as a matter of course, by the imitator. After all, the imitator feels inferior to the one whose desire he or she is copying. Therefore, when the imitator perceives that access to the source of fulfilled desire is being denied, the imitator will focus blame on the mediator-model, who, after all, is superior and must therefore exert more control over desire and its aims than does the imitator.[79] But, in masochism, the phases of desire are experienced in compact form: the imitator chooses the mediator because of the obstruction that the mediator provides, not because of positive qualities. Acute sensitivity to the mediator leads the imitator to focus on what he or she perceives to be a necessary relation between unhappiness and shame in the work of metaphysical desire. A masochist is born when, confronted with a mediator whose actions are increasingly characterized by poor treatment and hostility, the imitator claims that experience as revelatory of being. Rather than disavow the entire project of metaphysical desire, the masochist sees failure, pain, and suffering as "signs of divinity and the preliminary condition of all metaphysical success."[80] From this moment, whenever the imitator enters the field of desire, he or she will consistently look only for those stones that are too heavy to lift and will see in them the fulfillment of his or her desire.

Girard observes the lucidity of the masochist. Because he or she sees connections along the pathway of metaphysical desire that others miss, the masochist is a more perceptive consumer of desire. But the masochist does not take full purchase on lucidity. Instead of abandoning the entire enterprise of metaphysical desire, the masochist embraces it all the more.[81] Writes Girard of this harmful stage in the history of metaphysical desire: "When the desiring subject perceives the abyss that desire has hollowed out beneath his feet, he voluntarily hurls himself into it, hoping against hope to discover in it what the less acute stages of metaphysical sickness have not brought him."[82] When the narrator of *In Search of Lost Time* talks about "the abrupt revelation of death" that has hollowed out in him a "double and mysterious furrow," he is attesting to the masochistic stages of metaphysical desire.[83] Experts misunderstand masochism when they focus solely on masochists' supposed desire for shame, humiliation, and suffering. Humans do not seek out shame and suffering. What they seek is the fullness of being that eludes them. In order to obtain access to this divine being, they will do whatever they perceive to be necessary.[84]

Having explored the general contours of "existential" masochism, Girard considers more specifically masochism and sadism within sexual relationships. Although the ideal partner in a sexual relationship would be the mediator-model with whom one could attain a unity of being, such bliss always eludes humans. Indeed, to the extent that one moves closer in a sexual relationship to what one imagines will be a moment of shared communion, one begins to notice flaws in one's partner that chip away at desire, eventually rendering the beloved undesirable.[85] For the masochist, sexual desire focuses on the gap between the ideal object of desire and the masochist's own inadequacy. The masochist feels closest to that ideal when he or she is being subjected to brutalities he or she imagines would issue from that perfect being. The masochist does not want or "enjoy" suffering per se; rather, the masochist wants to be connected to the model-mediator, and the masochist imagines that brutal or humiliating experiences will evoke that connection.[86] Sadism reverses these dynamics. The sadist determines that unity with being has been achieved. But to effect this transformation, albeit a counterfeit one, the sadist must double with the victim, transforming the victim "into a replica of himself." In that gesture may be found what Girard identifies as a "strange 'communion' between the victim and his tormentor."[87]

Kristeva shares with Girard a similar perspective on the dynamics of sadism and masochism. She notes that desire is vulnerable to time's changes. It will culminate in death unless it becomes destructive desire, as in the instances of sadomasochism in the text of *In Search of Lost Time*. However, Kristeva emphasizes *the centrality of sensation* to that destructive work. Her account of the devolution of desire is forthright: "Desire consists of drawing loved ones toward yourself, dissolving them in your own perceptions until they become contaminated, unattainable, confused with objects, external, woven in the same fabric, neither inside nor outside, but a continuous chain of sensations."[88] As masochism and sadism work from opposite ends of the spectrum of desire, they eventually meet a common end: the dissipation of being. The loved one with whom one sought the fulfillment of desire fades, leaving behind "sensations as well as the flesh of my memory."[89]

Kristeva's comments on sensation and Girard's exposition of the dynamics of sadism and masochism are helpful preparation for a consideration of the place of emotional cruelty and sexual violence in *In Search of Lost Time*. Do scenes of sadism and masochism, especially those that feature homo-eroticized cruelty and violence, underscore in some essential way failures of metaphysical desire to which Proust already has devoted countless pages of the novel? Are these scenes uniquely enlightening of the novel? That we mobilize a corporeal hermeneutics in order to answer these questions is crucial, for they are of profound importance not only to an enhanced understanding of the achievement of the novel but also to a fuller appreciation of the significance of Girard's and Kristeva's interpretations of this work.

Filial Sentiments of a Parricide as well as the scene of the goodnight kiss and the scene depicting the narrator's grief over his grandmother's death in *In Search of Lost Time* have alerted us already to the importance of this inquiry. When Proust links the failures of metaphysical desire with matricidal aggression and the death of the subject, he establishes that *the essential structure of that failure is profanation*. Observes Kristeva, "A son who is one with his mother punishes himself by profaning her, and he punishes her by profaning himself."[90] Proust's explorations of sadism and masochism, which follow on the founding theme of maternal profanation, augment his insights into a destructive maternal desire, and for two reasons. As Kristeva points out, when the narrator holds himself responsible for the deaths of his mother and grandmother, Proust "enables violence and remorse to be introduced into the child-narrator's sensibilities while simultaneously suggesting that cruelty is omnipresent."[91] Time can only be regained if this violence can be recuperated. And, as Girard rightly claims, sadism and masochism play a key role in that recuperation because one attuned to their dynamics is able to attest with enhanced lucidity to the dynamics of metaphysical desire even though this lucidity is not ultimately freeing. When the narrator, caught in the throes of metaphysical illness, explores this uncomfortable terrain, Proust advances the critical work of the novel. He sets the narrator on a path that will gradually expose the bankruptcy of metaphysical desire. Because sadism and masochism press the edges of that desire, collapsing their end points in on each other in an intimate agony that skirts the death of the subject and its other, they expose the true costs of metaphysical desire that are glossed over in its less acute stages.

But this subject matter is especially enlightening in a respect not yet addressed. Scenes of sadism and masochism in *Sodom and Gomorrah* are also often scenes of homosexual relations. Proust does not forge this connection to show that homosexuals take special purchase on sadism and masochism. Rather, when homoerotic scenes incorporate sadomasochism, Proust is able to address problems associated with metaphysical desire in a uniquely revelatory way.[92] These scenes are fundamental to the novel because they take place *on a field of bodily intimacy and sensation*. Knowledge of this field is necessary for understanding metaphysical desire and transformative alternatives to it. For example, sadism as well as masochism are associated with Baron de Charlus. In subjecting himself to beatings, Charlus's self-consuming desire, expressed in sadomasochistic sex, literally becomes a consumption of the skin, the flesh. Charlus writes on his very body Proust's words: "Love drives us not only to the greatest sacrifices on behalf of the person we love, but sometimes even to the sacrifice of our desire itself."[93] Observes Kristeva, Charlus "kills Morel inside his own lacerated body, incorporating the one he can no longer possess or desire." Graphically testifying to the traumatic devolution of metaphysical desire, sadism and masochism thus are "fundamentally autoerotic."[94]

Most important, Proust turns to scenes of homoerotic desire in the novel because they offer him sufficient distance from a sea of threatening *maternal* intimacy such that he is able to engage the transgressive threat and transformative potential of that intimacy from a position of relative safety. Proust struggles in the novel to navigate these treacherous shoals, for the narrator is caught between a desire to differentiate from the maternal body and to remain undifferentiated from it. Failure entails death of self *or* maternal death. Yet he must persevere because the maternal body is a point of origin for lack and for the quest for being that fuels metaphysical desire. While scenes of profanation dramatize his dilemma as a high-stakes battle, homoerotic relations afford him a less fraught opportunity to explore a domain of bodily intimacy. The residents of Sodom and Gomorrah choreograph sameness and difference, joyous ecstasy and threatening aggression, in ways that, for Proust, suggest a replication of the maternal landscape of his childhood.

In exploring homoerotic relations, I do not suggest that Proust's extended attention to them is a symptomatic acting out of aggression against his mother. Nor is Proust's consideration of homosexuality a confessional exercise. Were I to assert that Proust writes about liaisons with men of which his mother would disapprove so that he can precipitate the anger he imagines she would have, amplify the suffering he imagines she would endure, and magnify his own guilt, I would misrepresent one of the most notable achievements of the novel. After all, Proust's depictions of homoerotic relationships are distinguished by thoughtful, even meticulous, attention to patterns of sameness and difference in these liaisons, not by high-pitched, self-condemning drama.[95]

Furthermore, one need not be a slavish proponent of Freudian analysis to understand that Proust finds nothing compelling in an Oedipalized solution to the problem of a mother whose mimeticized proximity and distance from her son is simultaneously life-taking and life-giving. As Proust's concerns are refracted through the anxieties of the child narrator in the novel, the paternal function is all but absent from the text; indeed, instead of a father's "no" that would signal clear boundaries to the child narrator, he experiences a father's "yes."[96] But, in his observations of homoerotic relationships, Proust locates clues with which to decipher the puzzle of maternal sameness and difference in another register: one that is oriented toward the maternal body.

Proust's reflections can be typified as thought experiments grounded in kinesis. The narrative lines of the Sodom and Gomorrah accounts are linked with corporeal memories on which Proust draws in search of meaning. In the first, which I will call "the Sodom experiment," Proust expresses disdain for a theory of male homosexuality that asserts that men are attracted as men to other men. Men who express desire for sexual contact and relationship with members of the same sex do not want contact with the same, as would be implied by the prefix "homo." Arguing instead for a theory that maintains sexual difference, Proust understands that male inverts embrace the feminine and desire their opposite (a masculine man) in a sexual partner.[97] Indeed, the effeminate man most desires the most manly of men: a viral, heterosexual male who will not return his love. Just as the quest for undifferentiated unity with a maternal body is lost to its essential difference, so also does homosexual desire founder on a difference that precludes the one who desires from experiencing reciprocal desire. In the Sodom experiment, homosexual desire is not based on reciprocated sameness; rather, the experiment testifies to disunity and difference in relationships of desire among men, and in ways reminiscent of Proust's own problematic relationship to maternal difference.

In rehearsing maternal loss without relief, the Sodom experiment is fundamentally unsatisfying.

The second experiment, focused on Sapphic desire, proves far more instructive. Charting in "the Gomorrah experiment" the dynamics of sameness—source of absolute threat and unconditional salvation—Proust undertakes the most important work of the novel. On behalf of his narrator, Proust explores an emancipatory path away from a family romance that saw the child narrator's desire develop into a metaphysical illness that threatened him with extinction. Albertine becomes the instrument of this emancipation. As Proust continues to track "the strange changeability of loved ones" in his relationship with Albertine, his explorations necessarily take on a maternal cast. The revelatory features of this encounter, drawing out the transformative potential of kinesis, will bring Proust freedom from traumatic suffering and death as he comes at last to the heart of the cathedral that is the novel.

Gomorrah Is Not Sodom: The Transformative Power of Albertine

As the focal point of "the Gomorrah experiment," Albertine does profound work in the narrative of *In Search of Lost Time*.[98] However, she also poses a challenge, for Gomorrah is not the transposed shadow of Sodom. Offering the narrator a unique template for his fantasy of reciprocated desire, Albertine and her sisters in Gomorrah display an erotic sensibility that is grounded in sameness; yet the narrator cannot even begin to comprehend their stance.[99] Male rivals for the attention of a female, the narrator claims, are a known quantity—they play by recognizable competitive rules. And male inverts abide by these same rules, even though the role of aggressor is inverted for the female-like, male subject. But how can one understand a woman such as Albertine when the weapons of competition in Gomorrah are invisible to one not a native of those environs?[100] Proust is wholly baffled.

His descriptions attest to the indecipherable mystery that is Albertine. Whenever she appears among a group and the narrator seeks her out, he cannot be certain that his eyes have lighted on Albertine. Her body is depicted dissolved into small pieces, as if she were an impressionist painting.[101] Albertine's manners are not predictable. Sometimes she appears well-bred; at other times, she seems crude. Lacking a parental heritage, she is an orphan.[102] Her sexual identity—a boyish androgyny—is a puzzle. When Dr. Cottard offers his expertise, informing the narrator that women "derive excitement through the breasts," the narrator finds the pleasure of which the scientist speaks incomprehensible.[103] The narrator's description of a kiss, a gesture whose intimacy is suggestive of communion with Albertine, results only in ten Albertines and a collision of flesh and senses that risks devolving from desire into disgust.[104] Even in Albertine's imagined illicit love scenes, the narrator is nonplussed by a Gomorrah that has nothing in common with Sodom.

Often, the narrator attests to the mystery of Albertine using images that link her with the sea.[105] Her nose is like a little wave. Her cheeks and eyes are fluid like the ocean. When the narrator hears her breathing, it reminds him of the sound of waves or the sea breeze. Her hair becomes waves. The narrator's complete inability to grasp hold of Albertine is well conveyed by the sea imagery.[106] Moreover, because the sea conveys a sense of irrecuperable mystery that a less substantive body of water would not, Albertine is shown to have depths wholly unknowable to the narrator. When he touches Albertine and likens this act to holding a stone that contains the salt of the oceans, he feels he is touching "no more than the sealed envelope of a person who inwardly reached infinity."[107] The narrator senses that *Albertine cannot be captured.*

Nevertheless, apart from the narrator, Albertine is the most omnipresent character of *In Search of Lost Time*. In a 1915 letter, Proust describes Albertine as "the one who plays the biggest role and brings about the *peripeteia*."[108] Albertine, the narrator says, has "fertilized me through grief and even, at the beginning, through the simple effort which I had had to make to imagine something different from myself."[109] As the Gomorrah experiment concludes with the narrator likening himself to Orestes,[110] Albertine becomes the elucidating exception to narrator's explorations of an otherwise violent and tragic history of metaphysical desire. How does the enigmatic Albertine take on this transformative role, enabling the narrator to overcome guilt and rage, end his exile as a parricidal son, and prepare to enter the cathedral of the novel? The final scene in *Sodom and Gomorrah* offers an answer.

Titled "Intermittences of the Heart II," this scene opens with Albertine and the narrator on a train. Unbeknownst to Albertine, the narrator is intending to sever their relationship the following day. As Albertine prepares to disembark, the narrator mentions only that he is planning to contact Mme

Verdurin, from whom he hopes to obtain information about M. Vinteuil's music. While Albertine makes her way down the aisle toward the train's exit, she blithely calls back to the narrator that she can readily procure any musical pieces he would like thanks to her friendship with Vinteuil's daughter and that daughter's best friend. When Albertine's declaration registers on the narrator, the scene of profanation at Montjouvain that the narrator had supposed was buried deep inside him surfaces. He sees laid out before him full confirmation of his previous suspicions: Albertine's desire *is* Sapphic. Now, as the "fateful consequences" of his wicked actions "explode before his eyes," the narrator identifies with Orestes and understands that he has met his punishment for having allowed his grandmother to die.[111] The narrator is beside himself: "This was a terrible *terra incognita* on which I had just set foot, a new phase of unsuspected suffering that was opening."[112]

But even as the narrator falls into new depths of pain, he also speaks of the "joy of a beautiful discovery."[113] A series of rapidly changing scenes follow. In a panic, the narrator calls out to Albertine in order that she remain in Balbec. Anguished over what he believes he has learned about Albertine, he worries that his mother will hear him sobbing through the thin partition that separates their rooms, and he tries to stifle his sobs. Suddenly, the door to his room opens and a woman wearing his grandmother's dressing gown enters. Startled, he takes a moment to perceive that the woman who has entered his room is not his grandmother but his mother, who "for a long time has resembled my grandmother far more than the young and laughing momma" of childhood. He hears his mother ask him why he is crying.[114]

As the narrator begins to speak to his mother about Albertine, she looks toward the window and directs his attention toward the rising sun, "so that I should not lose the benefit of a spectacle my grandmother regretted that I never watched." But the narrator does not see the scene that his mother sees. When he looks where his mother is pointing, he sees Mlle Vinteuil at Montjouvain. Only now, Albertine has become a stand-in for Mlle Vinteuil's friend, and she has joined Mlle Vinteuil in the ritual desecration of M. Vinteuil's photo. Bearing "an extraordinary resemblance to his grandmother," the narrator's mother continues to look toward the window, and suddenly, the entire scene becomes a tableau. Mother, grandmother, and profaning child are gathered together on either side of a window: those who have died and the ones who have caused their deaths are joined in a single frame.[115]

Exacerbating the deadly atmosphere of this scene is the narrator's jarring announcement that, notwithstanding the pain he knows he will cause his mother, he will marry Albertine.[116]

At this moment, Albertine becomes the *peripeteia* of the text. And she does so precisely as she serves to connect the narrator to his most fundamental concern: the profanation of the mother. Albertine who cannot be captured, whom the narrator will and will not marry, whose desire remains incomprehensible to the narrator because no lexicon defines it and no scientific investigation has been able to expose its substance, becomes for the narrator *a screen for his own being*. Later, in *The Fugitive*, the narrator expresses with great clarity his own understanding of what has transpired. In the midst of a scene otherwise encased within the strictures of mimetic desire, as the narrator alternately professes not to love Albertine in order that she be persuaded to love him *and* professes to love her in order to free himself from her desire, the narrator speaks truthfully of the bankruptcy of his desire. He asserts, "Man is a being who cannot move beyond his own boundaries, who knows others only in himself, and if he alleges the contrary, he is lying."[117] Albertine *is* the narrator.

Thus, as he observes mother and grandmother gathered together before the unholy altar of Montjouvain and sees Albertine preparing to spit on the photo, the narrator becomes the profaning child. But the familial tableau in which he is participating soon becomes layered:

> This was the scene I could see behind that spread out in the window, which was nothing more than a mournful veil, superimposed on the other like a reflection. It seemed indeed almost unreal, like a painted view. Facing us, where the Parville cliffs jutted out, the leafy tableau of the little wood where we had played hunt-the-ring sloped all the way down to the sea.[118]

The transformed landscape promises to unlock the deathly painfulness of metaphysical desire so that it may give way to joyful transformation:[119] But how do suffering and death that are framed all round by deadly mimeticism become revelatory? Let's look more closely at the details of this scene from a family romance.

That Albertine takes the place of Mlle Vinteuil's friend is significant. After all, Mlle Vinteuil's friend is the custodian of M. Vinteuil's musical genius, and Vinteuil's artistic legacy will be critical to the transforming vision the narrator ultimately attains, enabling him to write the novel. That the narrator is beholden to this unnamed friend of Mlle Vinteuil integrally links the aesthetic transformation that is to come with pain and suffering. After all, Vinteuil wrote in a type of script decipherable only by this unknown woman. Her desecration of M. Vinteuil's memory is thus overlaid by her gift: not only is M. Vinteuil's music made available to others posthumously, but also the transcribed sonata becomes for Proust one of the most powerful metaphors of his novel. When Albertine replaces the unnamed friend, she opens the narrator to the transcription of the tableau into healing art.[120]

The profaning scene, coalescing around the women, also is significant: Mlle Vinteuil and Albertine stand on the far side of the window; the narrator's mother and grandmother stand before it. But, in identifying with Albertine, the narrator exposes us to aspects of this grouping whose full significance becomes apparent only gradually. Eventually, the narrator will hold himself responsible for a double murder: Albertine and his grandmother.[121] Indeed, the tableau foreshadows destruction; for, caught up in this house of mirrors, the narrator appears trapped by the deadly devolution of desire. Nevertheless, the roles of the mother and grandmother within the tableau create a dynamic that suggests hope rather than failure.

In the days leading up to this scene, the narrator repeatedly has attested to the presence of his mother and grandmother at Balbec. As a consequence, we readily accept that there are two maternal figures in the tableau. Indeed, throughout "Intermittences of the Heart II," the narrator's doubling of mother and grandmother has become ever more insistent. Deliberately and repetitively evoking both women, Proust is adamant that we see with him two maternal figures.[122] Nevertheless, the narrator also documents their closeness: mother and grandmother have resided in a room separated from the narrator only by a thin partition; one wears the other's clothes; over time, they have come to physically resemble each other.[123] Carefully and self-consciously, Proust paints *the very image of maternal splitting* in order that readers not efface that splitting by treating the grandmother as "only" a projective image of Proust's mother. The author insists on a mother *and* a "Grand Mother"[124] even as he also suggests they are one. As a consequence of this maternal splitting *and* reunification of two beings *in one body*, the narrator no longer need divide a nurturing mother from a threatening mother as he did in *Swann's Way*. There, a stable Aunt Leonie countered an unsettling mother who kissed the narrator and read him stories about prohibited desires. By conceiving of an aging grandmother free of her own desires and making her one with the desiring mother who has been the source of his anxiety, Proust at last enables the narrator to hold together as one a mother who is both good and bad, a maternal body that embraces him and one that is experienced as a suffocating threat.

Elisabeth Ladenson traces Proust's rapprochement with maternal splitting to the function of Mme de Sévigné in the novel.[125] After the death of the grandmother, the narrator's mother devotes herself to her memory. The vehicle for this mother-daughter bond is Mme de Sévigné's correspondence, which the narrator's mother regularly quotes. Attesting to a mother's devotion to her daughter; the letters speak also of a son whose troublesome "side" causes the mother great woe. When the narrator's mother writes him a letter, the narrator perceives that he is excluded as an addressee of this correspondence: "In each of the three letters I received from Mamma . . . she quoted Mme de Sévigné at me, as if these three letters had been, not addressed by her to me, but addressed by my grandmother to her."[126] Even so, instead of being enraged by his exclusion, in "Intermittences of the Heart II" the narrator accepts it. The very mirroring for him of a maternal desire that is directed elsewhere—that acknowledges both suffering and anger toward a wayward son—neutralizes the threat he has experienced in maternal difference and indifference.[127]

A comprehensive interpretation of "Intermittances of the Heart II" now can be advanced. Proust does not view the maternal desire he depicts through an Oedipal lens. Maternal desire is decidedly nonphallic. Moreover, the resolution of "the Gomorrah experiment" in the revelation of Albertine's desire, which Proust has the narrator comprehend as part of the same tableau in which he confronts the dynamics of maternal desire, is ultimately not threatening to the narrator. Holding in one frame a tranquil landscape and a disturbing scene of erotic intimacy, the translucent, painted view proves revelatory. Although there are intimations of death—the tableau circumscribes all parties in a reciprocal knowledge that will be fatal to each—rather than suggesting a storm-tossed ocean in which the narrator might lose himself and drown, the sea of Sapphic desire becomes an unexpected portent as ships traverse it "through mists still hung in blue and pink shreds over waters littered with the pearly debris of the dawn. . . . smiling at the oblique light that had turned their sails and the tips of their bowsprits yellow."[128] *One could paint this desire*. Indeed, that the narrator will do as much will become evident in the concluding volumes of the novel.

Let's look one last time at the tableau on which the final curtain comes down in *Sodom and Gomorrah*. We observe pairings of intimate relationships whose reciprocity revolves around sameness. Mother and grandmother, Mlle Vinteuil and Albertine, are gathered together around the profaning altar of Montjouvain, mirroring each other in a fantasy of reciprocated desire from which the narrator is wholly excluded. Indeed, when the painted view overlays the window scene, the narrator's exclusion is sustained. Having exposed his mother to the lethal truth of his life—Albertine has enabled the narrator to also play the role of the profaning child in this scene—the narrator should die. Instead, he hints of hope. A metaphysical miracle happens despite the narrator-author's efforts to know sameness and difference, to domesticate the threat posed by the bad mother and threatening maternal body of the family romance, and to control the full spectrum of mimetic desire, which entails both longing and fear. Although this closing scene in Sodom and Gomorrah ostensibly rehearses the Montjouvain scene and amplifies the matricidal guilt that has been Proust's preoccupation since writing "*Filial Sentiments of a Parricide*," the distinctive profile of Gomorran sexuality in this tableau opens up the family romance in a new way. Trauma no longer overwhelms, for the kinesic power of metaphor has done its work. In bringing together sensations in signs, the lived image of the seascape overlays traumatic repetition—suffered by those in the throes of metaphysical illness—with promise. Embodied expressiveness at last "communicates communicability."[129]

Albertine is instrumental to this change. In writing of the seascape, the narrator recalls that he has watched sunsets with her at this very site. He observes the coming of the dawn and the boats that pass by him on their way out to the sea only to return again at sunset. Through a succession of hours— day to night to day—he sees arrayed before him a scene that, if insubstantial, has not been canceled out or concealed by the nightmarish Montjouvain scene.[130] The past is not erased; however, a way forward opens as the view through the window onto Montjouvain becomes a screen and the narrator's imagination crosses time. The tableau, which has mirrored the author's maternal trauma and taunted the narrator with the impossible fulfillment of mimetic desire represented by Sapphic sameness, has not disappeared; however, it is veiled. And the alternative the narrator glimpses, now only a wisp, will gain substance as Proust paints with words the vision he has just witnessed. In the interim, Albertine will die, but the artist will live.[131]

In *Sodom and Gomorrah*, the narrator has confronted the end point of metaphysical desire when he has come face-to-face with its bankruptcy, thanks to the window scene at Balbec. The narrator has seen laid out before him the fully embodied threat of mimetic rivalry and annihilation. But also he has experienced a capacity for being that previously has eluded him. Excluded from the circle of maternal desire in which his mother and grandmother express devotion to each other and excluded as well from a circle of erotic desire to which Albertine and Mlle Vinteuil alone have access, the narrator has experienced what, from one perspective, is the tragic incomprehensibility and indifference of desire within a family romance. Others have turned away from him, and his mother's gaze has taken in only the sea—not her profaning child. But this scene has not been interpreted by the narrator as potentially lethal to his own being. He has not attempted to violently insert himself into the tableau so as to demand the others' attention, nor has he withdrawn from in despair. Now, proceeding haltingly, with many a false start and detour,[132] the narrator builds on this experience. Thanks to Albertine, he experiences healing from ontological illness through the lived metaphor of art.

A master of narrative kinesis, in *Sodom and Gomorrah*, Proust has shown the interplay between the "body" of a text and human bodies depicted in that text by its author. Confirming what Maurice Merleau-Ponty has written of the relationship between these bodies, Proust makes of each "a knot of living meanings, not the law for a certain number of covariant terms."[133] True, on some level, Proust's descriptions, preserved on the pages of his novel, are abstractions from experience; for example, a "rosy face" and "arched eye brows" are visually and tactilely specific features of Albertine's face.[134] Still, the Proustian narrative can be said to bring forth the lived experience of embodied meaning in a manner attested to by Merleau-Ponty when he writes that any "conceptual significance is extracted from a wider one, as the description of a person is extracted from the actual appearance of his face."[135] As a consequence, when we read Proust, we are able to take purchase on one of Merleau-Ponty's most important claims about narrative meaning. Just as in an encounter with another person we respond to a facial expression or performed gesture and not to isolated features of a face or segments of an arm, so also do we not extract the meaning of a novel we are reading from ideas depicted on its pages; rather, in both instances we participate in "an inter-human event" that "ripens and bursts forth" upon us.[136] As I discuss in more detail in the chapter that follows, when Merleau-Ponty characterizes kinesic perception in ways that mesh so eloquently with Proust's mode of expression, Merleau-Ponty enables us to understand how new sensory experiences enable Proust to reverse long-standing effects of trauma and access a future from which he previously has been excluded.

CHAPTER 3

The Journey Home
Is through the World

But sometimes it is just when everything seems to be lost that we experience a presentiment that may save us; one has knocked on all the doors which lead nowhere, and then, unwittingly, one pushes against the only one through which one may enter and for which one would have searched in vain for a hundred years, and it opens.

—Marcel Proust, *Finding Time Again*

The narrator of *In Search of Lost Time* is beset by trauma. By his own admission, he locates suffering in two maternally marked experiences in his past. The event he cites first is that fateful evening when his "mother abdicated her authority," in the young Marcel's bedroom at Combray; the second encompasses the many months during which the narrator observed the slow death of his grandmother.[1] The narrator is anguished: not only did he inflict pain on his mother when he "traced in her soul a first wrinkle and caused a first white hair to appear," but also he wounded his grandmother with hurtful words.[2] The narrator speaks also of distress that he cannot grasp or commit to rational understanding. He describes as "incomprehensible" a spontaneous "revelation of death" that has hollowed out in him a wound, a "double and mysterious furrow."[3] The narrator's trauma, we have come to see, is linked to his separation from the maternal body, a separation painfully but largely unconsciously negotiated by young children but one that is distinctively preserved in Proust's novel, where it becomes a focus for the narrator's journey to spiritual transformation. How does Proust heal the wound in his being and experience grace?

Cathy Caruth's analysis of trauma informs my examination of how Proust overcomes trauma. According to Caruth, at the heart of trauma is an experience that "repeats itself, exactly and unremittingly, through the unknowing acts of the survivor and against his very will." On Caruth's understanding, trauma is characterized also by a wound. Most significant, she writes that the painful repetition of trauma is broken when *a voice is released through the wound*. The voice that cries out from the wound witnesses to a truth that the victim of trauma cannot fully know.[4]

Following Caruth, I suggest that, through much of the novel, the narrator of *In Search of Lost Time* seeks to speak to a truth he does not know and cannot fully comprehend: the traumatic engraving of mimetic desire on the body. But how can his woundedness be understood? Caruth draws attention to Freud's efforts to understand trauma nondualistically. Freud observes that physical trauma—a crushed limb—is typically comprehended at the moment of injury; by contrast, one who is psychically wounded may be wholly unaware of harm on the occasion of the causing event. Indeed, traumatic events typically happen too soon and unexpectedly to be known at all and may not register on the victim until that individual has been wounded for a second time.[5] Caruth reminds us too that Freud does not rigidly distinguish physical from psychic trauma: both reside on a common continuum. Just as a living substance can be saved from external threats if it erects a protective shield, so also is consciousness able to raise "a barrier of sensation and knowledge that protects the organism by placing stimulation within an ordered experience of time."[6] We are shielded from psychic trauma by a break in the mind's experience of time that we name "fright." When we are frightened, our minds recognize a threat to our being one moment too late. *Not experienced in time, trauma is not fully known.*[7] Repetition ensues; for, in the absence of knowing what has endangered our life, we return again and again to the task, necessary and impossible, of grasping the threat that we have been unable to know in time.[8]

Distinctive to Caruth's account of trauma is her attention to features of the failure in time that perpetuate the trauma. She points out that, in studying dreams of traumatic events, Freud discovers that the fright we experience is not so much associated with the violence we have endured as with its aftermath: we are frightened because we have survived an event without knowing how, for trauma has blocked access to the event through memory. If we apply Caruth's insights about the twin failures of time and knowledge to the narrator's revisitation of his grandmother's death in *In Search of Lost Time*, we can understand how her demise has hollowed out a deep furrow in his being. Even as the narrator describes his wound as double, as if to mark an injury from/to his mother *and* grandmother, he finds incomprehensible that he has lived even as he has harmed others. What the narrator repeatedly fails to grasp and what prevents the wound in his being from healing is that he has survived, *without knowing how*. In the narrator's traumatic dreams, illustrated by the sequence of words that concludes one dream—"stags, stags, Frances Jammes, fork"—the narrator does not obsessively rehearse the threat to his existence represented by his parricidal wishes. Rather, of concern to the narrator is his inexplicable survival, which he must attempt to achieve again and again, because he has not been able to claim that survival in time. By analogy, in the wake of an accident, what one finds traumatic is not one's brush with death but one's brush with life: one has gotten away and *does not know why*. Thus, Caruth shows us that *trauma circles a future that cannot be claimed.*[9]

Caruth's insights illuminate the narrator's experience, but leave unaddressed how the narrator's voice in *In Search of Lost Time*, constrained by the ongoing repetition of trauma, is at last able to break free. Melanie Klein offers an insightful augmentation of Caruth's theory, for Klein typifies the aftermath of parricide as "mourning." Mourning permits the reliving and reworking of loss associated with parental violence. Thus, Klein helps us to understand how the young Marcel experiences parental aggression. Not only does he fear suffocating aggression against him by a maternal entity from whom, mired as he is in the throes of mimetic desire, he is unable to separate, but also he resents her when she is absent, for he fears that he cannot survive her absence. Mimetic desire initiates a metaphysical illness that threatens to prove lethal to him. But Klein shows us too how, in splitting the maternal object, Marcel is able to mourn the loss of a maternal presence that he damaged in his own aggressive efforts to carve out a space in the world independent of his body of origin. His mourning enables him to revisit that loss in order to rework it and repair his being. Eventually, his mourning merges with a creative process.[10]

Serene Jones offers a further account of this process. For traumatized persons, the imagination is truncated. Trauma results in fractured speech and gestures that delineate "spaces marked by fear and constructed for protection." As a consequence, open narratives are missing from the lives of the traumatized. So too do they have little sense of agency: their capacity to plan and move forward unravels. Holes and gaps in the lives of the traumatized are filled with fear and silence; time is frozen and all sense of meaningful action is curtailed.[11] However, Jones locates "graceful possibilities of imagination" that emerge in the wake of trauma when mourning opens up onto acts of creativity. Crucially, gestural meaning rather than words often announces the opening of the creative imagination onto the "landscape of grace," where those whose lives have been fractured by violence can experience healing.[12] Thus, sensory experience offers a vital bridge to healing from trauma.

In their attention to the role of the imagination and sensory experience in healing trauma, Caruth, Klein, and Jones offer insights that cohere with Girard's early views. In *Deceit, Desire, and the Novel*, Girard states that affective memory unlocks trauma, making possible the artistic achievements that constitute "the salvation of the writer and of the man Marcel Proust." Girard says that affective memory "carries with it condemnation of the original desire" and replaces mimetic rivalries with "communion."[13] However, Girard is inattentive in his later work to the role affective memory and sensory experience play in transforming a deadly metaphysical desire into positive mimesis and communion. Amplification of Girard's mimetic theory by way of a corporeal hermeneutics is needed in order that we may focus on the intimate domain in which metaphysical desire is tutored and account for *how* sensory experience provides for healing from trauma originating in that intimate domain. Significant to this effort should be attention to maternal referents that figure prominently in traumatic kinesis.

Joining the theories of trauma, maternal mourning, and graceful imagination sketched here, I employ a corporeal hermeneutics to account for the narrator's transformation recorded in the final volumes of *In Search of Lost Time*. The trauma the narrator has rehearsed, which he has traced to the bedroom of the young Marcel and observed circling Montjouvain again and again in the form of maternal profanation, is a trauma that the narrator did not know and could not know because a protective shield had been put in place, rendering the young child incapable of experiencing *in time* his differentiation from his mother.[14] Because his trauma was not experienced in time, the narrator has remained wounded. He mourns, reliving and reworking loss, until he is able, in what becomes a creative process of healing, to give voice to his wound. Art, which crosses the barrier of sensation and knowledge that has shielded the narrator from full exposure to trauma, becomes the instrument of healing. Employing sensation to reverse trauma's effects, the narrator will access a future from which he previously has been excluded. The knowledge that has eluded the narrator previously, miring him in traumatic repetition, will now come to expression in his novel. As the narrator takes his first, halting steps forward on this healing journey, architecture features prominently in his discoveries.

Venetian Architecture: Strawberry Ices and the Flagstones of St. Mark's

Insights garnered in *Sodom and Gomorrah* position the narrator outside the space of trauma. No longer one who can only mourn, he can create new meaning and find time again. Nevertheless, because of Albertine's continued presence in the novel, the narrator takes ironic purchase on his fragile achievement. His halting progress is exemplified by a scene in *The Prisoner* in which Albertine likens relishing frozen desserts to engaging in oral erotic play. Putting to the test the staying power of the narrator's newfound awareness, Albertine plays sacrilegiously with a central Proustian metaphor. She requests ices "molded into every kind of improbable architecture" including "temples, churches, obelisks"[15] and proposes to melt these sacred images in the back of her throat so that "all the monuments will leave their stony sites and travel into my chest."[16] Lest her allusion be missed, after proclaiming her intention to "use my lips to demolish, pillar by pillar, those Venetian porphyry churches that are made of strawberry ice-cream," Albertine muses that, when she was with Mlle Vinteuil at Montjouvain, they resorted to drinking sparkling mineral water because ices were not available. Albertine's audacious and lascivious commentary, albeit blunted in its offensiveness by association with a frosty confection, nevertheless is an affront to the novel's author and narrator for whom the cathedral is a sacred metaphor.[17] As Albertine's desires elude, confound, and challenge the narrator, the reader wonders if Albertine rather than the narrator is in charge. Will the narrator's transformation be derailed by, of all things, raspberry ice?

Initially, in *The Prisoner*, the power of mimesis is accentuated rather minimized. Thus, even as the narrator moves to physically constrain Albertine, she frees herself from his grip, turning the tables of mimesis on him. As Stephen G. Brown suggests, Albertine's mouth is the source not only of illicit desires and physical appetites but also of subversive discourse.[18] All the while, the narrator seems unaware that he is being played and profaned. Albertine, who cannot be captured, who is always a mystery, threatens to demaster the narrator, absorbing him into the now icy waters of the sea that is Albertine. But this disconcerting turn of events is not as threatening to the narrator as may initially appear.

Brown argues persuasively that, in *The Prisoner* and *The Fugitive*, Proust challenges rather than sustains the mimetic struggles that have typified the narrative in its early volumes. Indeed, that *The Prisoner* and *The Fugitive* are Albertine's stories, more than the narrator's, underscores rather than undercuts the discovery that the narrator has made standing with his mother at the window in Balbec. In an especially lucid moment, the narrator is explicit on this point. He writes, "The more desire advances, the more true possession recedes. So that if it is possible to obtain happiness, or at least freedom from suffering, what we should seek is not the satisfaction, but the gradual reduction and final elimination of desire." The narrator goes on to say that if an author who is writing a book about the vagaries of desire wants to "express this kind of truth," he will approach the woman who has been the object of desire and say to her "This is your book."[19] Thus, as Albertine naughtily taunts the narrator, he distances himself from her story. His actions demonstrate that all attempts to master desire founder; and suffering is the legacy of that failure. The mystifying signs of mimetic desire cannot be outthought with words, nor can desire's allure be outmaneuvered through actions. Only the transformative power of art will enable the narrator to access meaning outside the strictures of metaphysical desire.

Late in the novel, when the narrator visits Venice with his mother, art becomes a revelatory counterpoint to Albertine's desire. Change is announced by the city itself, which comes to life in unexpected ways. At first, the narrator comments on a prosaically scenic Venice. Describing elegant women who recline on cushions in gondolas, the narrator's words bring to mind images in an impressionist painting. But the water begins to roil, the gondola bucks and rocks, and Venice surges forth toward the narrator.[20] The power of involuntary memory is awakened, and sensations rush in, as if they "had been waiting in their place."[21] Notes Kristeva of this transformation:

> Once Venice has infiltrated the book, the text partakes of sensation. As an imaginary presence that for Proust is immediately sensual, Venice vibrates in the air that surrounds the book, which is transformed into a deep blue, into pink columns. Just as the city of Venice shows that manmade beauty may coexist with nature, so, inversely, a book can become nature itself. A book, then, is life.[22]

As images of Venice mingle with the narrator's own flesh, the seascape at Balbec, bathed in pink and blue, melds with the watercolor shades of Venice: "here, the pink reflection of the evening on the flower-covered wall of a country restaurant, a feeling of hunger, the desire for women, the pleasure of luxury—there, the blue scrolls of the morning sea enveloping the musical phrases which partially emerge from them like the shoulders of mermaids."[23] The narrator is reconciled to and reconnected with the past as he experiences the apotheosis of desire in the pure color of sensation.

Kristeva suggests how the narrator's mother is central to the transformation that ensues in Venice. Prior to their visit, the two have shared a special connection to the city through Ruskin's descriptions of it, which the narrator's mother has read to him.[24] Building on that bond, the narrator imagines his mother's body uniting with Venice's. Moreover, as sensations experienced by the narrator enable him to merge also with Venice, unity with his maternal origins is achieved.[25] The scene at St. Mark's baptistery represents a turning point, for the narrator is able to write from the viewpoint of "the absolute present."[26] Lucid at last, he merges with time's trajectory, no longer encased within the strictures of repetitive trauma or beset by metaphysical illness. How is this change precipitated?

Kristeva proposes that flesh becomes stone as the artist is made one with the very substance of Venice that has surged forth into his body. When the narrator places his mother within Venetian architecture and art, she at last is incorporated permanently in a world where she cannot be lost; but she is also incorporated into his body, absent the threat that she previously has posed to him.[27] The initial structure of this transformation is sketched early in the visit to Venice when the narrator, returning by gondola to his hotel, glimpses his mother standing in a window, beneath the hotel's vaulted arches. Attempting to "form her lips into a smile," she gazes intensely in his direction. With her face illuminated by the midday sun, she leans forward as if to embrace him. From that moment on, through the powers of access granted by kinesic connection, when the narrator happens on a cast of this stone arch in a museum, he hears it call to him, "I remember your mother well."[28]

This scene parallels a depiction by Ruskin in *The Stones of Venice* of the tomb of Doge Dandolo, in St. Mark's baptistery. Dandolo's tomb, which is topped by a life-size image of the body of the Doge, as if asleep with a "sweet smile" on his lips, is positioned beside a window so that sunlight streams across his face.[29] When light falls on the narrator's mother under the hotel window arch, she also is made one with the stone. She lives on, as has Dandolo, first in the stone of the Venetian hotel and shortly thereafter in St. Mark's baptistery.

The spiritual "baptism" that takes place as the narrator traverses the stones of St. Mark's is redemptive. Desire and loss—framed always for the narrator as maternal promise and trauma—is transported from the body of the narrator's mother into the body of Venice itself. The narrator draws on Carpaccio's *Martyrdom of the Pilgrims and the Burial of St. Ursula* for his description. Noting the elderly woman in the foreground of the painting, dressed in mourning black with a shawl over her head (exactly as his mother is wearing black and a shawl), the narrator observes that Carpaccio has portrayed her as if she is a stone column, at one with the cathedral rock. Now he finds that his mother who stands beside him in St. Mark's is likewise a permanent feature of its sanctuary. Just as the mourning woman in the Carpaccio painting melds with the steps of the cathedral, the narrator's mother merges into the tiles of St. Mark's, for "nothing can ever again remove this red-cheeked, sad-eyed woman, in her black veils." He knows that he will be "certain to find her because I have reserved a place there in perpetuity, alongside the mosaics, for her, for my mother."[30]

In the wake of this momentous experience, the narrator sets out in search of other artistic masterpieces. He seeks a painting in which Albertine is memorialized, just as his mother has been by the Carpaccio painting. As if playing a game of "Where's Albertine?," the narrator considers works by Carpaccio, Whistler, and a handful of other artists.[31] At last, he finds in one of the Companions of la Calza evidence of Albertine. The guild member's coat depicted in the painting reminds him of one of her dresses. But, instead of reassuring the narrator, the painting the narrator had sought as a reliquary for Albertine disturbs him. His powers of kinesis in disarray, the narrator feels "invaded with indistinct, impermanent feelings of desire and melancholy."[32] He goes in search of Mme Putbus's maid, anticipating the pleasures of erotic conquest. The transporting experience of St. Mark's baptistery fades, for the metaphysical desire that has plagued the narrator throughout the novel still lurks; indeed, as the narrator's mother boards a train, leaving behind Venice and her son, the narrator is in despair. As if contravening the scene at St. Mark's and making a mockery of the narrator's desolation, the air around him is suddenly polluted by the sound of an all too prosaic "O sole mio." Looking toward the water, the narrator sees that the "soul of Venice has drained away from the canal." With the city crumbling around him, the narrator's visit to Venice draws to an inauspicious end. Only the astute observer can look positively on what has transpired there; for this observer will recall that, when the narrator set out to visit St. Mark's, he paused to collect notebooks in which to record his observations.[33] Venice may crumble; however, the narrator will eternally preserve his experience with his words.[34] A traumatic narrative will give way to healing.

Trauma, Conversion, and Time

Having committed his experiences in Venice to his notebook, in *Finding Time Again*, the narrator prepares to write the novel that is coming to a close for its readers. But what will the narrator write? In the throes of metaphysical illness, he has been in exile with Orestes; now, after a long journey, he has reached St. Mark's cathedral. Traveling with the narrator, we have identified the role the maternal body plays in initiating anxiety about being out of which the narrator's metaphysical desire has been forged. We have seen also that suffering has played a critical role in the exposure of metaphysical desire. Exploring the structure of trauma, we have determined too that only as the narrator is able to come to terms with trauma will metaphysical desire be engaged and challenged. But does the artistic insight that makes possible the writing of *In Search of Lost Time* leave the narrator where he began: a guilty parricide? Stephen G. Brown suggests that the narrator conquers matricide by entombing his mother in the novel. She is sacrificed for her son's art, purchasing for him a kind of immortality. Suffering is his penance for matricide, the precondition and force behind his art.[35] Angela Moorjani submits that the narrator-novelist remains caught in the repetition of loss. Indeed, where Brown suggests that the narrator purchases a measure of freedom at the expense of his mother, Moorjani insists that *In Search of Lost Time* is not a redemptive work. Moorjani leaves the narrator suspended in an Orestean moment, asserting that Proust's novel is "a funeral monument marking, that is, both revealing and screening, the secret wound of cryptic interiority that is the wellspring of his art."[36] Do Brown and Moorjani offer an accurate depiction of the outcome of the narrator's quest to become freed from trauma? Does the novel testify only to unending suffering?

Those who consign the narrator of *In Search of Lost Time* to ongoing traumatic repetition belie the lucidity Proust already displayed in *Filial Sentiments of a Parricide*. Instead of concluding our reading of the novel in despair, we are ready to appreciate the key role that sensation—initially painful but eventually joyful—plays in the transformation of mimetic desire. Sensory identification *is* the place of "sacred communion."[37] Art, the kinesic instrument of transformative sensory identification, makes possible a rebirth of the narrator that is not also an ongoing iteration of maternal violence. As *In Search of Lost Time* draws to a close, the narrator is set free from trauma to find time again.

The narrator's own account of his situation is explicit. Reflecting at a distance in *Finding Time Again* on the young Marcel's desire, he promises to exchange the impatience of life lived according to desire for that "which normally remains invisible to us, the form of time."[38] He will wait for time, and then he will compose a "transcription of the universe" that is loyal to its source, so that he can depict "a place in time that grows ever larger."[39] No longer separated from the past by the traumatic severing of thought and experience, the narrator will advance a "notion of embodied time" and make it a "prominent feature of my work."⁴⁰ Thus, he will enter what Kristeva calls a "timeless time"—the spatial eternity of literature that Proust likens to a cathedral.⁴¹

But the narrator wants to take one final look at "errors of the senses" that he now recognizes falsify our perceptions. He describes how we add features to the faces of others that actually are "empty spaces" on which we superimpose a "reflection of our desires." He speaks of a prior dislocation of experience, when he was forced to confront a "hundred masks" and struggled to "block out the sound of the conversations which the masks were holding all around me."⁴² Speaking as one who has been released from the grip of mimetic rivalry, the narrator perspicaciously describes how humans' fascination with imitation accounts for our enthrallment to desire.

Kristeva argues that Proust's commentary in *Finding Time Again* on the problematic role of imitation in human lives is influenced by the work of Gabriel Tarde.⁴³ Tarde considered society to be governed by imitative interactions. In his writings, he stresses how social groups behave in crowd-like ways as we try to resemble others in our group. As a consequence, Tarde writes that "the universality of imitation is at the essence of social life."⁴⁴ Kristeva suggests that, because Proust already is an outsider to the dominant social currents of his day as a Jew and a writer, he is drawn to Tarde's sociological theory as a way to make sense of the artificiality he sees in the wider society.

But Kristeva suggests that Proust's rich analysis of human experience is indebted also to Schopenhauer. Although Proust wants to subject the social bonds of his day to an X-ray in order to expose the underlying disease of imitation, Proust also is attracted to a different reflective impulse. In Schopenhauer, he finds an attention to Being that counters the society of spectacle.⁴⁵ Kristeva suggests that what Proust finds compelling in Schopenhauer is the link between will and human suffering, which leaves as a sole recourse for the human spirit "to be engulfed" in the nonself, in nothingness, in "the absolute cessation of will." Proust focuses, in particular, on art as consolation. When Proust writes that "ideas come to us as the successors to our griefs," Kristeva believes that he has Schopenhauer in mind.⁴⁶

Kristeva suggests that when Proust brings Tarde and Schopenhauer together, they do not join but "collide." As a result, Proust takes most seriously the power of the group over the individual, but he also sees that art has its own power: art can "shred the social order into tiny pieces." Imaginative experience, notes Kristeva, can stabilize and sublimate social life, enabling us to keep "lucid and even ironic in the face of Opinion while leaving us immersed in the surging forth of Being."[47] But even as Kristeva is appreciative of how Proust's informants shape his aesthetic theory and practice, she argues that his literary works "go much further" than is suggested by Tarde's and Schopenhauer's influence. Proust's appeal to sensation and embodied experience, especially the experience of suffering, marks the originality of his art.[48]

Bringing to expression in prose Proust's ideas, the narrator of *In Search of Lost Time* turns from the masks that surround him, declaring that he will "go down into myself" in order to find sounds that have always been there but that "I did not know that I was carrying."[49] Attesting to how he has borne trauma with his body, the narrator writes of the power of bodies that contain the past: "Bodies can do so much damage to those who live them, because they contain so many memories of joys and desires already effaced form their minds, but cruel indeed for anyone who contemplates and projects back through the array of time the cherished body of which he is jealous, so jealous as to wish for its destruction."[50] Even so, the body is not captured by mimetic desires; rather, the body, opening up onto metaphor, becomes an instrument for rebuilding of the world.

The truth of metaphor cannot be grasped, for example, in a manner similar to cinematographic film, which relies on an audience to certify it as real.[51] Metaphorical truth is not out there, to be viewed at a distance; it "already exists within each of us" fueled by our kinesic capabilities. The writer's task is to translate embodied truth into art. The work of desire—"our vanity, our passion, our imitative faculties, our abstract intelligence, our habits"—is "undone by art" in order that we may arrive at what lies in the depths of each of us.[52] The narrator understands that this work entails suffering; however, it also entails joy when we attain access to people's "divine form."[53] Ideas that tap a greater reality substitute for sorrow and transform suffering into joy.[54]

Swann's experience of the Vinteuil septet offers Kristeva an example of the narrator's notion of metaphorical truth. The "little phrase" is described as a "liquid rippling of sound." Subsequently, Swann falls in love with the music and with Odette. As Swann's love for the woman and the music mingle, "the little phrase," their "national anthem," comes into its own. More powerful than an *analogy*, the phrase that links Odette with music establishes a *relationship of contiguity*. Whenever Swann hears the music, he is with Odette in the Verdurin salon, and they are listening to the Vinteuil sonata together. Time is this bringing together of two sensations that gush out from the signs. The *analogical* work of music, keyed to the narration of one's story—a sonata becomes a couple's special song—takes place in time. Indeed, with its analogical powers, the imagination enables the narrator of a story to span time. But the imprinting of sensation in music—the sounds and form of the sonata—establishes this contiguity of relationship.[55] Spanning time, a drama of love and loss is experienced not only by the couple who listens to this sonata together, but also by a maternal-infant duo whose initial soundings found nascent codes, deathly and erotic, in a drama of love and loss.[56] Because it is the function of a metaphor to bring things together and sensation implies a *body*, Proustian time, which brings together the sensations imprinted in signs, is a *metamorphosis*.[57] For Proust, the artist reproduces with metaphors connections that he discovers already present in the world. Drawing these connections together and condensing them, the artist can "guide the surface of signs toward depth."[58]

As a consequence, Kristeva writes that the embodied experience attested to by Proust's narrator is an "opening up to the other" that has its roots in the primary object, the maternal body, which is the "archaic focal point for needs, desire, love, and repulsion."[59] It is associated with a process of individuation that includes "depression, hallucination, longing, and all the graces and joys procured by compensation, reunion, or independence." Contingent on "inaccessible" memories, this process also is directed toward work that "radiates my culture with the most hidden traumas, which it inscribes on my psyche and my body."[60] The metaphor, joining sensation and perception, creates a bridge between the body and the idea that results in the transubstantiation of words into flesh.[61] As kinesis anchors this bridge, metaphors are made meaningful.

Attesting to his own discovery of the centrality of sensation to the work of memory and transformation, the narrator of *Finding Time Again* observes that, when he attempts to capture Venice in memory, with "so-called snapshots" of his visit, he is unable to bring the city to life again. But when the narrator's feet touch the cobblestones in the Guermantes' courtyard, the stones communicate immediately to him his visit to St. Mark's, as if these sensations had been there all along, merely waiting to be summoned.[62] The narrator expresses his surprise that sensations—his feet touching cobblestones, the sound of a fork, the feel of a napkin against his lips—violate the law that separates existence from imagination. Yet, when involuntary memories are summoned by sensation, his past experiences do exist, if only for a moment. He is able to apprehend what previously has alluded him: "time in its pure state."[63] Moreover, the miracle that brings the past forward also removes the anxiety of death in ways that "leafing through a picture-book" does not.[64]

The narrator writes that what is experienced in involuntary memories is not a duplicate of sensation but sensation itself;[65] indeed, but for the brevity of the sensation, we would lose all consciousness of the present. After all, these sensations "force our nostrils to breathe the air of places that are actually far away." Admitting to a disjunction between his present and past, the narrator asserts that he has been unable to recover the beauty of Balbec picture-book style. Therefore, rather than focus on signs that have proved irrecoverable, he will attend to what might be called "hieroglyphs." Not available to the intellect, these are "material impressions" from which may be extracted something spiritual.[66] They are given to him "just as they are"— he can't force them. These are what counts as true experience. The material traces of impressions *made on us* are the warrants for their truth. Aligning these impressions with art, the narrator asserts that art cannot be created, for it preexists us and can only be discovered.[67]

In order to emphasize that impressions truly are material, the narrator draws on an example. He describes entering a library and pulling books at random from the shelves; "absent-mindedly opening one," he finds himself gazing at the pages of *François le champi*, the volume by George Sand read to him by his mother during that fateful night at his childhood home in Combray. The book, he discovers, summons "the child I was then," evoking "all the wonder of that night." The book asks to be "looked at only by his eyes, loved only by his heart."[68] The narrator suggests that, when we encounter an object that is associated with features of our life long past, all of the experiences of our initial encounter with it return. When any of us pick up a book from a long time ago, along with words on a page that come back to us as we read, we also experience a mix of accompanying images, perhaps its binding or the "strong wind and bright sunlight of the day when we were reading it."[69] Indeed, the texture of the paper and the way the book opens along its spine may evoke much more vividly than the text itself our past experience with the book. The narrator is insistent that the one who reexperiences the book *is the person we were in the past.* When he pulls *François le champi* from the shelf and sees its red binding and title, the narrator asserts that "a child immediately rises up within me and takes my place." That child is the one who reads it, with the same dreams from the past and the same anxieties. He likens his character to an "abandoned quarry," from which countless statues can be hued.[70] Arriving at his oft-quoted definition of a metaphor, the narrator states that what we call "reality" is a relationship between sensations and memories that is simultaneous. Truth begins, he says, "at the moment when, by bringing together a quality shared by two sensations, he draws out their common essence by uniting them with each other, in order to protect them from the contingencies of time, in a metaphor."[71]

Involuntary memories that metaphors solicit are not acts of "remembering." As Thomas Lennon points out, "to remember" describes a task like "to seek"; by contrast, the work of involuntary memory is "to find." Lennon observes that this distinction is replayed in the contrast between the titles of early English translations of the concluding volume of Proust's novel—*The Past Recaptured*—and the newer title: *Time Regained.* The earlier title implies that the narrator has taken on a project of remembering his past and grasping hold of it. The newer title shows that involuntary memory, which is the narrator's concern in the novel, does not document where we were and who we were with when key events happened. Instead, involuntary memory announces *a self rooted in time who at last finds his way.* Appropriately, *moment bienheureux*, a phrase Proust also uses to describe incidents of involuntary memory, recalls a theological appellation: those who have received the grace of salvation are the *bienheureux.*[72]

Proust reveals the power of metaphysical desire as well as how it can be surpassed. In our efforts to experience being, we initially are blocked, for our lack of being and immersion in a world of desire precludes us from even imagining what is absent. Moreover, we hide our lack from ourselves by living in spaces we perceive to be crowded with others: the salons of a Faubourg Saint-Germain, hotel dining rooms, or street cafes. But Proust's art exposes the truth: we have been swept up in a mimetic desire that is fueled by a lack of being. The faces around us mask emptiness, for we are living devoid of affective connection.[73] Nevertheless, a mimetic desire that separates us from each other is countered by sensation that exists "at the interface of the world and the self." Not oriented by a lack of being, as are our desires, sensation accesses what is "nourished by the essence of things."[74]

Being, experienced as metaphor rather than as lack, is not exempt from powerful mimetic processes. But metaphor does offer what Kristeva calls an "exemplary form of witness." Although being remains shadowed by violence, metaphor creates openings for being.[75] Past and present sensations are magnetized by the same desire. Within this network, sensation is fixed as an impression. As such, it has something of the generality of an idea; but, as incarnate idea, it is anchored in sense, in the world.[76] Those we love, as the narrator loves his mother, are the occasion for suffering; desire is the pursuit of suffering. But impressions—hieroglyphs or figured truths—enable us to depart from that pain.[77] By depriving people of their identity within the play of desire, impressions annihilate them. But by restoring persons to places and time through affective memory, a new truth is transcribed on sensations of long ago. In the final volume of *In Search of Lost Time*, that truth is grafted *onto the actual body of the narrator.*[78]

Why is Proust determined to explore sensation as a form of language? Drawing on Bolens, I suggest that Proust's determination is undergirded by his acute sensitivity to the work of kinesis. He demonstrates a capacity for kinesis that establishes him as an exemplar among artists. Utilizing Caruth's insights, I suggest also that Proust must explore sensation as a form of language in order to release a voice from a wound. He draws on sensation that has been brought to expression in a metaphor in order to overcome a trauma that he has not experienced in time and therefore has not fully known. Caruth's insights are affirmed by Kristeva, who asserts that the imperative to capture lost time that we see in Proust is due to "another time and another experience in which time-thought-language had not taken place." In this other time, a child is locked in struggle with a maternal presence, as nourishing as it is threatening. For the narrator to regain time, that he be reconciled to desires and objects associated with his early life is not enough. Rather, he can only regain time by also "causing it to return, extracting what is felt out of its dark dwelling, snatching it from the inexpressible in 'granting a sign.'"[79] With art, the narrator can forge a connection with being that inscribes divisions and boundaries in being that demarcate a subject in the world without sacrifice. Erotic excess, violence, and jealousy are not consigned to the margins of the narrator's text or the author's life. Instead, the narrator-author holds in balance the contradictions of human experience and does so by threading through the text suffering *and* joy, profanation *and* redemption.

Kristeva suggests that Proust views the human journey in a manner similar to Maurice Merleau-Ponty.[80] Indeed, Merleau-Ponty acknowledges his debt to Proust when he writes: "No one has gone further than Proust in fixing the relations between the visible and the invisible, in describing an idea that is not the contrary of the sensible, that is its lining and its depth."[81] Similar to the Proustian impression, Merleau-Ponty's "perceptual faith" does not expose humans to a fullness of Being that would transport humans out of the world; instead, meaning moves through things themselves.[82] Transformed *in* Being, we "sing the world."[83] Drawing on Merleau-Ponty to illuminate the central insights of *Finding Time Again*, Kristeva shows how Proustian experience becomes graceful and transformative, opening the narrator to a new type of being, no longer constrained by violence and mimetic conflict.

Merleau-Ponty makes "flesh" a central image of such transformation and uses this term, Kristeva reminds us, with reference to Proust.[84] According to Merleau-Ponty, always already there is kinship between my sight or touch and things. Because I am of the same universe as things, I am not a foreigner in the world. I do not win it by taking possession of it like an explorer from abroad. Rather, I am possessed by the world: I am of it.[85] I am in touch with the flesh of things because I too am flesh. "To be of the flesh" reminds us that the foundational experience of the world is not achieved by a consciousness that interrogates objects at a distance; rather, at my foundation, I am in bodily dialogue with things. My body is not a screen obstructing my access to things, but is my only means of access to the world. The thickness of my flesh is matched by a thickness of things. My flesh "concentrates the mystery of its scattered visibility."[86]

Merleau-Ponty asserts that there is no name in traditional philosophical reflection that designates flesh, for it is not matter or psychic material. Flesh is an "element" in the sense of being "a general thing, midway between the spatiotemporal individual and the idea, a sort of incarnate principle."[87] Flesh brings the presence of Being where there is a fragment of being. Adhering to location, flesh offers facticity; it sustains Being's presence with things. Being is not out there in front of me but surrounds and traverses me: my being is formed in the midst of Being. As a consequence, the fleshly exchange that give me things, gives me the other. The fission of the sentient and the sensible that makes my body capable of communicating with things also founds transitivity between my body and that of another. Speech does not break with the flesh but accomplishes the intentionality of being-in-the-flesh by other means.[88]

I am formed in the midst of Being. Moreover, as a consequence, I share a connection with others. Writes Merleau-Ponty:

> It is said that the colors, the tactile reliefs given to the other, are for me an absolute mystery, forever inaccessible. This is not completely true; for me to have not an idea, an image, nor a presentation, but as it were the imminent experience of them, it suffices that I look at a landscape, that I speak of it with someone. Then, through the concordant operation of his body and my own, what I see passes into him, this individual green of the meadow under my eyes invades his vision without quitting my own, I recognize in my green his green, as the customs officer recognizes suddenly in a traveler the man whose description he had been given. There is here no problem of the alter ego because it is not I who sees, not he who sees, because an anonymous visibility inhabits both of us, a vision in general, in virtue of that primordial property that belongs to the flesh, being here and now, of radiating everywhere and forever, being an individual, of being also a dimension and a universal.[89]

In describing how the flesh connects us with others, as two persons bring to the world a common vision, nurtured by the sensation of color, Merleau-Ponty could be recording the thoughts of the narrator's mother on the occasion of her visit to Venice with her son. For Venice, a vision in pink marble and blue canals inhabits the narrator and his mother, joining them as one flesh.

Merleau-Ponty's ontology of the flesh, depicting the terrain Proust traverses in *In Search of Lost Time*, offers tantalizing glimpses of a transformation in Being. This transformation does not float above violence that mars our being, constraining us within mimetic rivalries, but moves through it to its other side. Kristeva acknowledges that "violence and evil remain the inescapable reverse side of the inconsistency of Being."[90] Proust's acute awareness of bodily suffering is testimony to this truth. But Proust shows that desire need not end in suffering. Yes, we are always only intermittently in the presence of Being, incapable of capturing it; nevertheless, we experience Being.[91]

Merleau-Ponty describes that experience by drawing on an example from *In Search of Lost Time*: "the little phrase" in Vinteuil's sonata. He states that the ideas Proust sees summoned in music and art would not be better known to us "if we had no body and no sensibility"; rather, in the absence of our bodies, these ideas would be wholly inaccessible. Writes Merleau-Ponty: "It is not only that we would find in that carnal experience the occasion to think them; it is that they owe their authority, their fascinating, indestructible power, precisely to the fact that they are in transparency behind the sensible, or in its heart."[92]

When a musician performing Vinteuil's sonata reaches "the little phrase," he does not latch on to the musical idea, notwithstanding that he could point to specific notes associated with "the little phrase" if asked to identify these notes on a sheet of music. Rather, the musician is possessed by the music: he "feels himself to be at the service of the sonata; the sonata sings through him or cries out so suddenly that he must 'dash on his bow' to follow it."[93] Creating "open vortexes in the sonorous world," the moments of the sonata are part of the Being of being.[94]

With her appeal to Merleau-Ponty's ontology, Kristeva sheds light on a critical distinction between her analysis of Proust and Girard's. For both Kristeva and Girard, Proust's story is about conversion—one who is lost experiences grace. But, as I have argued, Girard announces the experience of grace but does not show us what about humans makes us capable of escaping the throes of acquisitive mimesis. Girard's grace is a thunderbolt that confers lucidity wholly and immediately on one who is thus emancipated from the strictures of metaphysical desire. When Girard depicts conversion, "The Spirit takes charge of everything." Its recipients are passive, for "it is the Spirit of God that possesses them and does not let them go."[95] With her appeal to Merleau-Ponty, Kristeva employs a corporeal hermeneutics that shows the way to grace: processes of affective memory and sensory experience make persons capable of transformed existence. Further, she is able to forge links between the person Proust was—caught in the traumatic reenactment of a maternal loss he perpetually mourned—and the person he becomes through the experience of grace, and to do so in ways that show continuities between loss—an inevitable silence in Being—and transformed existence. The veiling of Being to which Kristeva draws our attention is a crucial insight because, in its absence, *grace bears its own kind of violence.*

Writing about trauma and grace, Serene Jones sheds light on how grace may be experienced as violence. Jones writes that, for most of her life, she subscribed to a story about grace with a clear plotline: "Sin is met by grace, and grace conquers." When humans become mired in wrongdoing, God dramatically intervenes, and something new and good emerges in the world. But as Jones worked with victims of traumatic experiences in a counseling capacity, she came to perceive the intractable grip of trauma and to wonder about the adequacy of the classic rendering of the "before and after grace" story to lives caught up in traumatic repetition. The "grace that shocks us and turns us around," promising a "radical discontinuity between the past and a divinely established new relation," can be psychically overwhelming to someone who has experienced a traumatic blow that has shattered her being. For victims of violence, whose fragile stand in being threatens to fail under even slight winds of change, a world-shattering grace can be a new form of violence.[96] Jones writes that she began seeking another model of grace when she realized that "most survivors are never completely made new" and that "the old gouges of violence in the brain and body are carried forward with them."[97]

Jones's explorations of grace, homing in on depths of the traumatic experience, offer a better match for Proustian grace than Girard has provided. For Girard, Proust's *Le Figaro* article signals a transforming moment—a sudden moment of lucidity—when a son recognizes that he has caused his mother pain. Freed by that identification from the constraints of metaphysical desire, he testifies to his transformation by writing *In Search of Lost Time*. But the narrator of *In Search of Lost Time* does not tell a dramatic, turn-around story. To the contrary, he writes trauma, dwells in trauma, and mourns for most of the three thousand pages of the novel, offering his readers a profound attestation to trauma's intractable nature. Grace and conversion are not sudden and are not marked in the narrator's life by a linear pathway of recovery from acquisitive rivalries by which he has been beset. The narrator's lucidity is uneven; he must surmount chasms and overcome backslidings. Fear and the repetition of past violence shadow him.

Jones's theology of grace is a match for Proust's artistic rendering of grace: both attest to how graceful conversion is experienced in the wake of trauma. For Proust, grace does not announce itself with a clarion call. It is not experienced as a "before and after" story that knocks him off his feet and overwhelms him: *that* is what the trauma that has locked Proust out of time has done. Instead, Proust reminds us with acute sensitivity of the fragility of grace. Even more significant, Jones identifies two factors that are visible in Proust's artistic rendering of graceful conversion and are critical also for a theology of grace that is attuned to the challenges trauma poses to those who would hope for transformation. She observes that grace for the traumatized cannot work by violence, and it must work through the body. Traditional approaches to grace are characterized by discontinuity between past and present: one who is a recipient of grace is psychically overwhelmed by love and epistemologically undone. Swept off one's feet by grace, one feels that one's world has been wholly dismantled. But this depiction of grace replicates what happens during a violent experience: the recipient is overwhelmed, undone, and rendered helpless in the grasp of a more powerful force.[98] Why, Jones asks, would anyone who has been ravaged by violence want, trust, or be open to grace that advances in this way?[99] Grace for the traumatized needs to be gentle and yet sturdy enough to persist in a world that veers again and again back into violence. Seeking a less naive and more ambiguous portrait of grace, Jones also realizes that grace can happen only through practices that replace the physical traces of trauma—quick startle responses, headaches, exhaustion, depression. Grace must tap into that affective memory and change it.[100]

Jones's "trauma-wise" approach to grace emphasizes experiences that invoke tactile memories of prior wounds while at the same time supporting one and holding one steady, preparing one to move out of the pain. When one experiences this support, one is not magically healed. Rather, one's wounds, at last, can be borne. One can finally attain a space in the present for mourning and for wonder: such grace does not only look forward; it looks backward and forward at the same time. Whereas trauma has been relentless in its backward movement, in grace that invites mourning and wonder, we are at last able to carry on with traumatic loss but also become open and new. We are always both broken and beloved. We are these two things. That is grace.

This grace, which Jones has sketched with great sensitivity, is attested to by Proust as well. Proust's stance in the world is that of one who is constantly on the move, reconnoitering the aisles of the cathedral that is the novel even as he walks again in the footsteps of the exiled sons. Always wary of the pretenses of Being deployed within the interstices of metaphysical desire, by virtue of his acute kinesic activity, Proust also is afforded tantalizing glimpses of a transformation in being evocative of grace. As a consequence, the narrator's transformation in *In Search of Lost Time* does not float above the world, safe from its violence and suffering. Indeed, as Kristeva's corporeal hermeneutics so eloquently demonstrates, Proust's unique contribution to the history of desire is this: the unity of the Proustian experience—sensual, artful, and blasphemous—always escapes us. The impossible of which he writes holds to the fragmentation and polyphony in being *within* human existence. We are always only intermittently in the presence of Being, incapable of capturing it.[101] In such a circumstance, Proust's narrator, Kristeva muses, is neither in the *status corruptionis* of sin, nor the *status integratatis* of conceptual understanding, but remains in the intermediate stage of *status gratiae*.[102] The "polymorphism" of the novel leaves room for regression—not only the narrator but all of us can find ourselves caught up in the throes of metaphysical desire. Every profanation and deceit of the narrator's mimetic desires can be ours, in spades. We can live again and again a trauma because we cannot know, because we do not have time to do otherwise.

But the novel also offers glimpses of uncommon kinesic lucidity and invites us to transcend rather than succumb to desire in order to participate in a new relationship to Being. Kristeva calls this intimacy. Intimacy does not unite us with the oneness of Being; rather, it incorporates otherness into Being, enabling us to embrace the dislocating strangeness of Being as familiar rather than divisive. Intimacy, supported by our memory work, witnesses to the flesh of Being—connection *and* suffering. Always intercorporeal, intimacy is sustained by a chiasmus, a porosity in Being that precludes fusion with Being as well as violent dispossession from Being. Restoring to us the involuntary memory of a lost time by soliciting our intimate regard, *In Search of Lost Time* offers something to our present century. Alternately caught in a society of spectacle, in which what counts as sight is what appears on the screens of our TVs, computers, and phones and lost to the passion of bodies that leaves us empty of meaning, the reader of Proust today, Kristeva suggests, wanders off, becomes increasingly lost, and then is found. This is grace. Suspended within the space of Proust's novel, this experience is as much for our time as it was for Proust's.[103]

PART 2

Antigone

Siblings

Children, where are you?
Here, come quickly—Come to these hands of mine,
your brother's hands, your own father's hands
that served his once bright eyes so well—
that made them blind.

     —Sophocles, *Oedipus the King* (1480–81)

Siblings play a critical role in mimetic rivalries that characterize the family romance. As a consequence, our relations with siblings anticipate, for better or worse, later adult relationships. As we grow and our world expands beyond the immediate family to encompass other relationships, we may remain caught in rivalries that have characterized our initial relationship with our siblings. Or, diverging from that scenario, we may experience with our siblings and with others a supportive intimacy that enables us to overcome the effects of trauma and violence in our lives.

 Antigone is a timeless story about the vicissitudes of sibling relationships. With *Antigone*, Sophocles explores with great acuity the violence that attends sibling rivalries. So also does his tragic art open onto transformative possibilities of an intimate domain that, opposed to an economy of sacrifice in which those around Antigone are caught, offers possibilities for healing and transformation. In what follows, I link Juliet Mitchell's psychoanalytic explorations of the embodied and affective aspects of mimeticism in sibling relationships with René Girard's commentaries on Sophocles's plays about Oedipus and his siblings. My goal is to strengthen the explanatory power of mimetic theory. When I draw also on a corporeal hermeneutics informed by the work of Julia Kristeva, I am able to address the role of trauma in onto-logical illness and illuminate a space for intimacy modeled by Antigone in her love for her brother, thereby expanding on Girard's own insights. Girard glimpses this space when he refers to Antigone as *figura Christi*, but he does not elaborate on his observations, valorizing instead biblical narratives to which he compares *Antigone*. In what follows, I advance an argument that could have been Girard's were he to have pressed forward with a full com-mentary on *Antigone* and linked that commentary with his extensive analyses of *Oedipus the King* and *Oedipus at Colonus*.

Mitchell offers entrée to my project in her provocative study *Siblings*. She writes that, when she began research on a psychoanalytic theory of sib-ling relationships, she cornered colleagues with a question, "Did Oedipus have a sister?" In response, she received only blank stares. Eventually she determined that she would need to answer her own question: "Yes, Oedipus *did* have a sister. In fact, he had two. Ismene and Antigone were his daugh-ters *and* his sisters (he also had two sons/brothers)."[1] Mitchell suggests that her colleagues' silence can be explained, in part, by the paucity of references Oedipus makes to his siblings in Sophocles's *Oedipus the King*. Only once does Oedipus refer to Ismene and Antigone as his sisters, when he asks them to touch his hands.[2] But Mitchell also finds reason to believe that her col-leagues were flummoxed by her question because, as fellow psychoanalysts, they regularly undervalue lateral relations among siblings, preferring to emphasize children's relations with their parents.[3] She is troubled that, as a consequence of their neglect, psychoanalysts have developed a portrait of desire that bypasses some of its most significant currents.[4]

Mitchell writes that the displacement of a child by the birth or arrival of a sibling evokes a powerful desire to eliminate the sibling. Because this desire is not tethered to the Oedipal complex, siblings confront a taboo that is both weaker and stronger than the prohibition on parricide. On the one hand, because violent desire a child directs toward its sibling is not shrouded in the complexities of the Freudian unconscious or a Lacanian lack, the child confronts a weaker "no." On the other hand, prohibitions against the lateral violence that siblings represent are ensconced in social codes: "You must not kill your bother Abel; you must instead love your brother (neighbour) *as yourself*."[5] Injunctions against sibling violence mandate that a child's violence turn into love; crucially, this love is already present as love one has for oneself. These injunctions form the foundation not only for relations among siblings but also for society itself, the fraternity of humankind.

Mitchell offers an example from her clinical practice. She has observed in the waiting room of her clinic a baby who is disturbed because another baby in the room is being nursed by its mother. So also has she watched as small children compete for toys. Mitchell concurs with Klein that these actions suggest jealousy. But Mitchell observes that, not only will young children crawl faster to reach and grab objects before their competing peers capture them, but also they will pass objects back and forth between each other in rudimentary, collaborative play. In both instances, lateral interactions are central to the children's experiences–the breast is no different than the toy in this regard.[6]

Mitchell suggests that a subject's capacity to love a sibling as it loves itself is not an attribute of narcissism or object-love. Rather, it is a desire born of *the transmutation of hatred*.[7] This transmutation is especially associated with siblings. It begins with an initial adoration by a child for a younger sibling. Because this child previously has occupied a privileged place in its relationship with its mother, the child expects the new baby in the home to be an extension of itself, a replication: "There will be more of me."[8] But the sibling also is confronted with a potential loss of place: how can there be two in the place I share with mother? This loss is experienced as trauma.[9] As Mitchell states, "The crucial absence here, then, is not the absent phallus (the castration complex) but the absent self."[10] The older child feels that its sibling has usurped its place; the sibling's desire has annihilated it. This loss and attendant threat are subsequently expressed as hatred.[11]

Mitchell suggests that the child must acclimate to "the law of the mother" in order to be freed of hatred. Whereas Lacan describes the Oedipus complex in terms of a child's accommodation to the law of the father, Mitchell associates the "law of the mother" with the "Antigone complex."[12]

Just as the father's law describes how children accede to a Symbolic order by which language is oriented around *lack and difference* (which deploys its own patterns of desire), so also does the law of the mother ready children for human society by introducing children to *seriality and sameness*.[13] As the law of the mother solicits siblings' attention, each child learns that his or her place is marked by similarity and serial division. The law of the mother enables children to "form a social group in which one loves because one is the same." Siblings who accommodate that law interact positively with each other. Because siblings introduce each other to the social dimensions of human existence, Mitchell suggests that the sibling relationship founds human community.

Mitchell grounds her insights on the Antigone complex with remarks on Antigone and the Sphinx in Greek tragedy. Reading Sophocles in light of Hesiod, Mitchell offers the provocative observation that the Sphinx who engages Oedipus is his sister. The Sphinx has been depicted as a mother by others because she devours those who fail to guess her riddles. But if she is a sister, as Mitchell surmises, the Sphinx points to a different threat: a confusion of sameness and difference among those who share a common space. For Mitchell, the Sphinx, a "more primitive version of Antigone," sets the tone for everything that follows in the Greek tragedy.[14] She is the older sister who wants to kill Oedipus; she is also the younger sister-daughter whose proximity to Oedipus proves unsettling.

Girard highlights this aspect of the Sphinx in his own depiction of her. When Girard states that the Sphinx "dogs Oedipus's tracks and he dogs hers,"[15] Girard could be describing Moreau's painting of *Oedipus and the Sphinx*. Possessing the facial features of a beautiful young woman, Moreau's Sphinx gazes seductively into Oedipus's eyes. Although similarities in the faces of the Sphinx and Oedipus hint of kinship, with uncomfortable intimations of incest, the Sphinx's animal form contrasts markedly with Oedipus's body. As the Sphinx grips Oedipus's thighs with her back paws and claws at his chest with her front paws, the viewer cannot help but notice severed limbs at the base of Moreau's painting that mark the threat the Sphinx poses to Oedipus. Fascinating and repelling, cloying and dangerous, the Sphinx truly is Oedipus's monstrous female sibling.[16]

Indeed, Moreau paints what Mitchell describes: adverse powers of sameness and difference whirl around the Sphinx, threatening to destroy the house of Labdacus.[17] Above all, the Sphinx's desire sets the stage for the tragic quandary of Sophocles's *Antigone*: *How are differences that fade into an annihilating sameness and a sameness that transforms into threatening differences negotiated in a family, in a society?* This question frames my discussion of Sophocles's *Antigone*.

In an insightful commentary on *Antigone*, Mary Beth Mader underscores the link Mitchell would draw between the mythic context of the "Antigone complex" and its psychoanalytic counterpart, thereby assisting me in addressing the quandary of *Antigone*. With critical acuity, Mader reflects on commentaries on *Antigone* that explain Antigone's assertion that she would not have violated Creon's command against burial for anyone but her brother. Mader notices that when commentators puzzle over Antigone's claim, they invariably bypass the fundamental complication of Polyneices's irreplaceability: the criminal confusion of kinship within the house of Labdacus. Although commentators are attentive to the pollution that hangs like a cloud over Oedipus in *Oedipus the King* and *Oedipus at Colonus*, they frequently assume that Antigone stands in clear light in *Antigone*. Mader calls attention to the miasma that envelops Antigone as well, pointing out that Antigone has not only to figure out how to negotiate a relationship to a brother in order to bury him but also determine *what a brother is and is not*. Antigone must struggle with how to make Polyneices "only her brother," whereas family precedent is "namely that of *generating one's own siblings*."[18] For Mader, Antigone's "insistence on performing the burial rites for her brother as a brother consecrates not just a dead beloved sibling but a certain precarious version of siblinghood or brotherhood itself."[19]

The task that Mader sees as Antigone's is the task of early childhood highlighted by Mitchell: the child who views the arrival of a new sibling as an opportunity for there to be "more of me" must discover the rudiments of generational order. Some relations are those one cannot generate oneself (father, mother) and some are relations that one can (child, husband, wife). The young child accomplishes the Antigone complex when the child achieves what Antigone does in her burial of Polyneices: the child articulates lines of seriality and sameness in ways that enable the child to love rather than loathe its sibling, replacing traumatizing threat with openness to the other.[20]

Girard would not be surprised that Mitchell turns to Greek tragedy in order to name the complex she associates with sibling conflict. Like

Mitchell, Girard understands that tragedy exposes how fraternal relationships are central to social violence. Writing of myth's relation to tragedy,
he observes, "The transition from the myth to tragedy must be defined,
we said, as a transition from the paternal to the fraternal relationship."[21] In
Violence and the Sacred, Girard discusses the pairing of brothers in Greek
myth and notes that the presence of enemy brothers signals a sacrificial crisis
in society.[22] Rivalry among brothers is emblematic of mimetic rivalry, for
similarities among brothers evoke a threatening loss of difference that presages any sacrificial crisis.

But Girard and Mitchell share even more in common. He concurs with
her that lateral relations exemplified by sibling conflict, rather than vertical
relations associated with parental prohibitions, are the initiating force in
humans' acclimation to a social order. Challenging Freud for his account of
the child's competition with his father to possess an object (mother), Girard
emphasizes that rivalry is about being, not having.[23] Only as conflicts on a
lateral axis are resolved can humans live with each other, loving the other
as they love themselves. Thus, when Mitchell frames the family romance—
fundamental patterns of mimetic desire among family members—differently
than do other psychoanalysts, turning away from vertical relations oriented
toward a parent and toward lateral relations among children who must come
to terms with the fear that a sibling will take their place, annihilating their
very being, she moves in a direction with which Girard has sympathy.

The alignment between Mitchell and Girard is especially well illustrated in a recent essay by mimetic theorist Mark Anspach. Anspach cites
Sybil Hart's research on young children. Hart conducted an experiment in
which a twelve-month-old child observed its mother cooing at and strok-
ing an infant-size doll. In Hart's study, the infant demonstrates increasing
interest in its mother as the mother focuses her attention more and more
on the doll. Rather than model its desire on its mother and compete for
the doll with its mother, the infant challenges the doll for the attention
of its mother. So also are increasing expressions of anxiety by the infant
focused on the doll—the rival for the mother's attention—rather than on
the mother. Writes Anspach: "the child longs to be where the doll is, happily
ensconced in the mother's lap and basking in her positive vocal affect. In
short, the child takes the doll as its model. One might even say that, at that
precise moment, the child wants to be the doll; it wants to be the one on the

receiving end of the mother's positive vocalizations."[24] Thus, Anspach shows that a mimetic analysis of relationships between a mother and child focuses on a horizontal axis, to which Mitchell also draws attention, rather than on a vertical axis oriented toward parental desire, to which psychoanalysis traditionally has attended.

Anspach's reflections on Hart's empirical data correspond also with a central hypothesis of mimetic theory: human conflict originates in an "intersubjective nexus."[25] Whereas rivalry has traditionally been understood to focus on objects—societies go to war over land, oil, or other valued property—Girard places imitation at the heart of rivalry. An object becomes valuable when another person or society of persons values it. Hart's empirical research, according to Anspach, assists mimetic theorists in understanding processes that undergird as well as threaten human community.[26]

Most significant for my own effort to align Mitchell and Girard in their espousal of theories oriented toward a common understanding of childhood desire and rivalry is that both Mitchell and Girard cite the Cain and Abel story as a narrative about the *founding of human community*. Girard writes, "The murder of Abel goes back to the origins of humanity and the foundation of the first cultural order."[27] But Girard also offers helpful insights to Mitchell when he notes how tutelage for participation in human community is recorded differently in myth, tragedy, and biblical narratives. *Myth*, according to Girard, justifies the killing of a brother in order to secure one's place. *Tragedy* problematizes that killing by tracking the loss of difference in fraternal relationships. The Bible condemns the killing of a brother and replaces myth and tragedy with a call to ethical responsibility.[28] In delineating distinct moments in human acculturation to social justice, Girard strengthens bonds between microcosmic dynamics of lateral relations within the family that initiate human society, on which Mitchell focuses, and their macrocosmic counterparts in society, to which those society's narratives attest.

Girard's observations on how biblical narratives differ from tragedy in their exposition of lateral violence are especially important. According to Girard, tragedy problematizes the killing of siblings, which is an advance over its justification in myth. However, when tragedy tracks the loss of difference in fraternal relationships that culminates in reciprocal violence, tragedy does not subject the ultimate ramifications of that violence to critical exposition.[29] By contrast, biblical narratives expose violence and describe the permutation of sibling hatred into love of the other. The community that hears Yahweh's question to Cain, "Where is your brother Abel?" and Yahweh's exhortation, "Listen to the sound of your brother's blood, crying out to me from the ground," is summoned by God to a biblical ethic of just care for one's "brothers."[30] Thus, the Bible replaces myth and tragedy with an "enormous ethical demand." Humans are called to treat each other not as "rival brothers but as real brothers."[31]

Most significantly, Girard joins Mitchell in taking special notice of Antigone when, in *Things Hidden since the Foundation of the World*, he observes intimations of a biblical ethic in Antigone's actions. Antigone comes into view as Girard considers the biblical story of the two harlots (1 Kings 3:16–28). Two prostitutes share a house. Each has borne a child. One of the women alleges that the other lay on her own child, killed him, and then substituted the accuser's child for the dead child. But the accused woman contests this charge. She claims that the sole remaining child is hers. Solomon is called on to resolve the conflict. He suggests dividing the child in two and distributing its body between the two women. One of the prostitutes refuses this solution. Dropping her claim to the child in order that the child may live, she reveals herself to Solomon as the child's true mother.

Girard frames this tale along familiar and unfamiliar lines. Initially, the story suggests a mimetic crisis precipitated by a rivalry among doubles. The women are both prostitutes, share a house, and make identical assertions.[32] Each woman, fascinated and repelled by her rival, loses sight of the child whose possession she contests. Challenging readers of the story who would typify the actions of the good prostitute as gesture of self-sacrifice, Girard asserts that a sacrificial analysis misconstrues the story. In renouncing her claim on her son, the good prostitute's / good mother's actions fall within the orbit of life, rather than death. Transforming the sacrificial landscape, she anticipates the passion of Christ. Indeed, the good prostitute is a *figura Christi*. She dies so that someone will live. The actions of the good prostitute and those of Christ disrupt the symmetry of a sacrificial economy: kill or be killed. Breaking free from an orbit of mimetic desire and vengeance, Christ and the good prostitute break through to an orbit of love typified by self-giving, not sacrifice.[33]

Guy Lefort, Girard's interlocutor in *Things Hidden since the Foundation of the World*, suggests to Girard that the acts of the good prostitute are reminiscent of Antigone's. Concurring with Lefort, Girard notes that a sacrificial crisis forms the background for each story. In Antigone's case, a crisis arises when her brother Polyneices leads an army against Thebes in order to assert his rights of inheritance against his brother, Eteocles. Consumed in paroxysms of reciprocal violence, Polyneices and Eteocles die.[34] Creon, ruler of Thebes, denies Polyneices rights to burial. Girard secures the sacrificial portent of the story when he suggests that Creon offers Polyneices as a scapegoat whose death will return the community to stasis. A sacrificial scenario accounts also, Girard suggests, for Creon's emphatic call for the Thebans to be "unanimous in their execration of Polyneices."[35] Absent that, Polyneices's powers as a scapegoat will be insufficient to restore the community to wholeness. But the sacrificial scheme is interrupted when Antigone rejects Creon's edict, claims her brother's body, and buries it. With her actions, Antigone repeats Polyneices's defiance of the state, commencing a tragic trajectory of violence that concludes with multiple suicides: Antigone, Haemon (her betrothed), and Eurydice (Haemon's mother and Creon's wife) die.

Antigone's actions are supposed to mirror those of her brother. He was to have been a scapegoat for Thebes, and Antigone should replace him; however, Antigone does not become a scapegoat in her brother's stead. Subverting that agenda, Antigone transforms a sacrificial landscape. Reflecting on Antigone's challenge to Creon, Girard recalls the words of Simone Weil, who typifies Antigone as the most perfect *figura Christi* of the ancient world. Like the good prostitute, like Christ, Antigone's gesture of love for her brother, which results in her own death, is not self-sacrifice. Antigone's gesture falls outside the sacrificial orbit because she chooses love rather than death. Girard recalls Antigone's words: "I was not born to share hatred but love."[36]

Acknowledging that Antigone exemplifies a nonsacrificial ethic, Girard's affirmation of her actions is muted. He states that *Antigone* is a great work of literature; however, he avers that *Antigone* is not on the same level as the "Judgment of Solomon." After all, Antigone takes her stand over a dead body; but the good prostitute's love extends to a living child. Therefore the nonsacrificial message of Antigone is "less spectacular" than that of 1 Kings. Girard concludes that Weil would more productively have directed her astute powers of observation to the Old Testament rather than to Sophocles. There she would have located multiple instances of *figurae Christi*, among them the good prostitute of 1 Kings.[37]

Girard's comments on Antigone are important. On the one hand, Girard's claim that Antigone is not a scapegoat positions her in proximity to the ethical demand of the scriptures that calls for nonrivalrous relations among siblings and, by extension, all humans. When Girard invites the reader to release Antigone from a sacrificial orbit, he opens *Antigone* to a fresh reading. I concur with Girard that Antigone's story situates her at the border of a sacrificial economy. She is not a creature of it. On the other hand, that Girard's affirmation of Antigone is understated concerns me. On my reading, Sophocles's *Antigone* offers a compelling challenge to the conventions of acquisitive mimesis. Not disavowing the Bible's own critique of rivalrous violence, I assert that Antigone's stance against mimetic rivalry and sacrificial violence is vibrantly embodied and exceptionally instructive. Drawing on a psychoanalytic analysis indebted to Mitchell's theory of the Antigone complex as well as on a corporeal hermeneutics suggested by Kristeva, I argue that a Girardian critique of mimetic violence can be enriched by renewed attention to *Antigone*. Mitchell's and Kristeva's views of key aspects of desire, illuminated by my exposition of *Antigone*, shed new light on Girard's theory, enhancing our appreciation for its importance while suggesting avenues for augmentation that promise to make mimetic theory even more compelling.

With my argument illuminated by Girard's discussion of *Oedipus the King* and *Oedipus at Colonus*, I explore *Antigone*. Confronting a loss of boundaries and its attendant mimetic contagion, Oedipus and Antigone embody contrasting responses to differences that fade into annihilating sameness and sameness that transforms into threatening differences. My discussion is in accord with what Girard might have written about *Antigone* were he to have reassessed earlier commentaries on *Oedipus the King* and *Oedipus at Colonus* in light of his professed acknowledgment in *Things Hidden since the Foundation of the World* that Antigone breaks with an economy of sacrifice in which Girard believes Oedipus remains caught. In chapter 4, I focus on the Theban outsider and the mimetic rivalry that drives the tragic action in *Antigone*. In chapter 5, I augment Girard's theory, addressing themes and issues to which he has not attended. I explore the alternative to sacrifice glimpsed in *Antigone* by attending to the theme of trauma in the text as well as to sensory experience. Just as sensory experience plays a critical role in Proust's *In Search of Lost Time* in opening persons in the throes of ontological illness to a healing alternative, so also does it play a like role in *Antigone*. But Girard's essays on

Oedipus the King and *Oedipus at Colonus* show ongoing problems for mimetic theory in the wake of his inattention to sensory experience in his later work.[38] Girard no longer accounts for transitions from sacrifice to transformation, trauma to healing, by appeal to a phenomenology of sensory experience; however, Girard does not offer an alternative explanation. *How* alternatives to ontological illness *are to be secured by those who suffer* remains unfounded in Girard's work. Aiming to redress this lacuna in Girard's thought in order to strengthen mimetic theory, I found my discussion of *Antigone* in chapter 6 on a corporeal hermeneutics that draws out ways in which this tragedy's antisacrificial trajectory is driven forward by kinesis.

CHAPTER 4

The House of Labdacus: On Kinship and Sacrifice

Outside the ancient city, outside every closed city, the only road is the one that *follows the scapegoat*.

—René Girard, *Oedipus Unbound*

Sophocles's three Theban plays—*Antigone, Oedipus the King, Oedipus at Colonus*—are not formally a trilogy. Sophocles wrote the plays across the span of his career and *Antigone*, whose dramatic action comes late in the chronology of Oedipus's family, was likely written and performed a decade before *Oedipus the King* and over three decades before *Oedipus at Colonus*.[1] As a consequence, the plays that comprise the Theban cycle are most often understood to share a familial narrative drawn from myths rather than a single artistic frame of reference. In *Oedipus the King*, Oedipus fulfills an oracle when he kills his father and marries his mother. In *Oedipus at Colonus*, a formerly disgraced Oedipus is rehabilitated; the gift of his body to Athens positions him within the cult of the hero. In *Antigone*, the story of Oedipus concludes with the death of Antigone, who has stood by her father but around whom coalesces a deadly violence that always besets the house of Labdacus.

I do acknowledge the reluctance of some scholars to view these three plays as a trilogy. Not only were they not composed in chronological order but also there are inconsistencies among the three tragedies in the portrayal of the main figures as well as in the narrative sequencing of events. At the same time, scholars frequently discuss these tragedies in relation to each other: Oedipus's life and legacy feature in all three, and all exhibit overlapping themes and patterns important to Sophocles. In my discussion, "Theban cycle" functions as a *critical heuristic*, which facilitates an enhanced understanding of *Antigone* while also shedding light on the other plays, particularly *Oedipus at Colonus*.

Common to the three tragedies is Thebes, a city born of autochthony and fratricide in the aftermath of the battle of the Sown Men who, according to myth, originated in the earth and emerged from it already fighting each other.[2] Not only is Oedipus closely associated with Thebes but so also are his children/siblings: Eteocles, Polyneices, Antigone, and Ismene. In these plays, Thebes is more than the physical setting for dramatic action: it provides a *topos* for tragedy. As a consequence, when we encounter Thebes with Sophocles, we are caught up in fundamental questions of existence that revolve around individuals, families, cities, and the cosmos.[3] But Thebes invites these questions not as a model for Athens but as the "anti-Athens."[4] Writes Zeitlin:

> Thebes, *the other*, provides Athens, the self, with a place where it can play with and discharge both terror of and attraction to the irreconcilable, the inexpiable, and the unredeemable, where it can experiment with the dangerous heights of self-assertion that transgression of fixed boundaries inevitably entails, where the city's political claims to primacy may be exposed and held up to question.[5]

Thebes—fascinating and repelling at once—is a closed system defined by its secure boundaries.[6] As a consequence, Athens should be safe from any dangers Thebes poses, and the audience that gathers on the southern slope of the acropolis in the theater of Dionysus should have no reason to fear that a dangerous contagion might rise from the *skene* to envelop them. Any malaise born of misdirected desire in Thebes should stay safely within that troubled city's walls.

But Oedipus is emblematic of the problematizing of Athenian security. Oedipus is an outsider to Thebes. Yearning for a place where he might be an "insider" and at home, Oedipus looks to Thebes. However, to his horror, Oedipus discovers that he has been too much "at home" in Thebes.[7] What he perceives to be his first acquaintance with Thebes is, in fact, his second, for Thebes is the city of his birth. Oedipus's exile from the city signals a key role that outsiders play in times of unrest: he is paradigmatically a scapegoat. As one who has caused a contagion to descend upon Thebes, destroying the safety of home that its inhabitants would find in it, he must be banished.[8] However, banishment does not repair fault lines that have emerged in the topos of Thebes. Throughout the tragic plays that tell the story of Oedipus, Oedipus's relation to Thebes is fraught. Even in *Oedipus at Colonus*, which revolves around the question of a home for Oedipus, Thebes remains a site of ambiguity and confusion. Were Oedipus to return to Thebes he would not reside within its midst; instead, he would be left at the perimeter, "home and not home, returned and not returned."[9] A liminal figure, ever associated with threat as well as promise, Oedipus shows Thebes not to be a closed system—a discrete other to Athens. Rather Thebes and the man whose body is emblematic of it *are others without clear boundaries*. When boundaries—of bodies or of cities—are not securely demarcated, pollution can multiply and contagion spread. Oedipus brings the problem of the outsider to the fore within Athens.[10] As a consequence, Thebes cannot offer the Athenians who contemplate it in the theater of Dionysus ready assurance about their own standing in the world. Rather than insulate Athenians from division and uncertainty, Oedipus and the house of Labdacus that shares in his pollution confront Athens with irresolvable challenges.

Nevertheless, recent interpretations of fifth-century BCE Greek tragedies, including *Antigone*, suggest that Athenian audiences did meet the challenges posed to them by these works. Christian Meier asserts that tragic drama enabled Athen's citizens to come to terms with extraordinary changes in their political and social institutions. In the face of a mismatch between institutional innovation and perspectives rooted in custom, tragedy enabled the population to affirm past traditions while also conforming to the principles and order of early democracy. Because tragedy "rehearsed contemporary questions" at a safe distance, it insulated the populace from direct confrontations with their fears and insecurities. Assisting Athenians in calibrating a "precise balance" in their social and political life, tragedy bound citizens together with a common purpose.[11]

Other scholars echo Meier. Charles Segal argues that fifth-century tragedies staged "contemporary debates on large moral and political issues" while "forging solidarity within the civic framework" that supported cooperation within a democratic society."[12] Discussing *Antigone*, William Blake Tyrrell, Larry Bennett, and Helen Foley give focused attention to one particular moral and political issue: changes in practices of public and private burial and women's roles in lamentation for the dead.[13] In the two decades preceding the writing of *Antigone*, tensions associated with shifting social norms about burial practices festered. Funerary legislation was intended to regulate conflicting loyalties between kin and the city-state.[14] But ongoing funerary legislation throughout the sixth and fifth centuries BCE suggests that repeated interventions were required to counter regression by a populace who regularly returned to earlier customs.[15] With these controversies forming the cultural backdrop to Sophocles's *Antigone*, the play reproduced Athenian concerns and reconciled the community to new ways.[16] Because Creon's denial of burial to Polyneices's corpse portrays an intrusion on the family and its rituals similar to that experienced by Athenians in the development of public funerals, Tyrrell and Bennett assert that the play resonated with its Athenian audience. They suggest that Sophocles drew on his influence as a leading figure in the political life of Athens and used the play as a vehicle to teach Athenians "how to live piously."[17] Under Sophocles's tutelage, the audience for *Antigone* could acknowledge past error and set out on a path for future unity. Foley asserts that tragedy responded to a need "to bolster the democratic ideology of the public funeral" with its emphasis on "muting public displays of grief."[18]

In familiarizing readers of *Antigone* with the historical context out of which the play emerges and highlighting themes that would have resonated with a fifth-century Athenian audience, recent interpretations of *Antigone* enable readers to look at the tragedy with fresh eyes.[19] However, these interpretations are inattentive to some striking features of this tragedy. Most notably, audiences and readers today, for whom the pressing social issues of Sophocles's time no longer figure, still respond to *Antigone* with profound emotions, suggesting that *Antigone* taps disquiet pervasive in human experience. That Sophocles's story is compelling for audiences and readers *in any era* suggests the need for additional analysis. Surely, Sophocles must not only be viewed as a political leader or a pedagogue but also as an artist attentive to divisions in human lives and society that are deeper and broader than those visible in the political and social conflicts of fifth-century Athens.

Rush Rehm draws attention to powerful currents running beneath the surface of tragedy. He submits that marriages and deaths, weddings and funerals, in tragedies such as *Antigone* do not create order but measure disorder. Shifting boundaries of *oikos* and *polis* are dislocated rather than secured by tragedy. Making its audience uncomfortable, tragedy confronts them with "what is hard to glimpse in the everyday world, glossed over by patterns of habit and custom."[20] When tragedy catches up its audience and sets its members down in unfamiliar and unnerving territory, tragedy forces its audience—then and now—not only to see the social world differently but to see themselves differently.[21]

As Stacy Keltner reminds us and as Jean-Pierre Vernant perspicaciously affirms, tragedy displaces certainty in any era. A logic of "ambiguity and reversal" shapes the Theban cycle. Oedipus is king and *pharmakos*, stranger and native, clairvoyant and blind, a dispenser of justices and a criminal, a savior and threat. The question that permeates the cycle—Who is Oedipus?—also permeates every audience for tragedy. Tragedy problematizes human existence, rendering its narrative always fresh *and* perennial. Thus, as Keltner observes, in attending to the story of Oedipus and his kin in Sophocles's tragedies, every audience confronts a riddle of existence. This riddle is attested to by tragedy; however, its power to confound is not confined to the Greek world.[22]

Girard and Mitchell describe this tragic effect well: Girard associates the threatening features of tragedy with ontological illness, Mitchell with strong trauma. Psychogenic in nature, strong trauma breaches the very foundations of being, resulting in repetitive suffering. For Girard, Sophocles is not expressing political opinions but exhibiting revelatory insight.[23] When radically destabilizing themes of pollution, sacrifice, and death undermine the thresholds of *oikos* and *polis* in *Antigone*, audiences—then and now—confront a *metaphysical* threshold.[24] Mitchell would typify changes in the cultural institutions of Sophocles's day, cited in recent scholarly criticism, as traumatic, but in the "weak" sense of the term. Indeed, scholars use the language of weak trauma when they expressly note that the citizens of Athens, supported by instructive lessons they received from watching tragic drama, were able to come to terms with social and political changes of their day. Weak trauma is amenable to solutions associated with the development of an ancient democracy. But Mitchell understands that tragedy is about strong trauma. Indeed, she specifically mentions the deaths of Polyneices and Eteocles in *Antigone* as examples of strong trauma.[25] Attesting to repetitive suffering that emerges in the wake of fractures at the very foundation of being, strong trauma evoked by tragedy is profoundly unsettling to every audience, now as in the past.

With Girard and Mitchell, I examine *Antigone* from a perspective attuned to Girard's notion of a metaphysical threshold and to Mitchell's theory of strong trauma. I continue also to draw on Foley, Tyrrell, and Bennett. Although the functional frameworks they employ draw their readers' attention to weak trauma—cultural concerns about burial practices—their rich and complex commentaries on *Antigone* exceed those frameworks, thereby opening up Antigone for an analysis attuned to strong trauma. Applying these scholars' insights, drawing on mimetic and psychoanalytic theory, and advancing a corporeal hermeneutics, I offer an enhanced reading of *Antigone*.

In a recent essay on *Antigone*, Charles Shepherdson establishes parameters for my approach when he challenges interpretations of the play that translate its language directly into the "discourse of the city." Cautioning against efforts to remove Sophocles from his home in fifth-century Athens in order to isolate him in a literary domain, Shepherdson asks also that we not assign Sophocles's *Antigone* only to the public sphere.[26] He suggests that we observe how tragic poetry inherits myth that it remembers and "reconstitutes." To tear tragedy from "the womb in which it was conceived" is to force on it "a different tongue."[27] By contrast, when we approach Antigone from the standpoint of tragedy, we hear in Creon's and Antigone's voices an opposition to myth that is grounded in their being and not only in debates of the fifth century BCE polis.

Critical to Sophocles's tragic vision is the tension between Creon and Antigone that is signaled early in the play by the word *amēchanon*. Creon proclaims that it is "no easy matter (*amēchanon*) to discern the temper of a man, his mind and will, till he be proved by exercise of power."[28] Ismene uses the same word in the opening scene of the play to declare impossible Antigone's intended actions on behalf of her brother (*amēchanon erais*).[29]

Amēchanōn, like a binary star, defines the relationship between Creon and Antigone in the Theban universe. Creon says, "I hold all the power," and the audience knows immediately that he holds none; Antigone says of her brother, "I am his own and I shall lie with him who is my own," and the audience knows that her words position her to inherit the mantle of the tragic hero. She will do what she says.[30] In their respective singularity, Creon and Antigone offer two different ways of being a human subject and raise compelling questions about the scope and limits of human life, that which is no easy matter, the impossible—*amēchanōn*.[31]

True, the *words* that Antigone and Creon use are common to legal, social, religious, and economic discourse of fifth-century Athens; however, their *meaning* is tethered to a more substantial register. Thus, when Creon proclaims that, if one places *philia* before *polis*, he will "count him nowhere," the audience of tragedy does not hear in these words only themes from social and political debates in Athens. Drawn forward with Creon to a different space, the audience is there when Creon, felled by his own blindness, becomes lost to life itself. Mirroring the one he has condemned, Creon will say in the end of himself "me who am no more than nothing."[32] And Antigone? She who has been typified by her sister as in love with the impossible (*amēchanōn erais*), takes her audience to a metaphysical threshold where we too will find ourselves poised, to perish or to live.

Girard prepares us to explore this threshold with Antigone because he closely attends to oppositions and reversals in tragedy. Girard is aware that Sophocles's Thebes is generally taken by scholars to be an anti-Athens; however, like Shepherdson, Girard illuminates fundamental aspects of the Thebes-Athens relation. Extending Shepherdson's argument, Girard writes, "tragedy is interested in reversal as such; it cares little for the domains these reversals happen to affect."[33] Girard observes that the *content* of a reversal is irrelevant when we look at its most significant aspects: the *alternation* between two entities that constitutes their relationship. When interpreters say that Sophocles is making Thebes the counterexample of values he is espousing, they neglect what is most essential: the *dynamics* of reversal. Everything that is significant to tragedy is caught up in tragic action; as a consequence, this action, rather than its specific content, is central. Figures who oppose each other—Creon or Antigone, Ismene or Antigone, Eteocles or Polyneices, Athens or Thebes—are not the focus of tragedy. Instead, tragedy homes in on volatile, reciprocal relationships: Oedipus *and* Creon, Creon *and* Antigone, Ismene *and* Antigone, Eteocles *and* Polyneices, Athens *and* Thebes. True, "the antagonists never occupy the same positions at the same time." Thebes is never Athens. But as the rhythm of tragedy quickens, each protagonist assumes in quick succession the position of the other. "Cyclothymia" abounds.[34] Girard observes that those who populate the landscape of tragedy are oblivious to its shifting contours, in which everything ultimately reverses: "There is not a moment when those involved in the action do not see themselves separated from their rivals by formidable differences."[35] Each party to conflict believes that he or she is taking in the whole picture; yet each represents only one feature of it. Oedipus, Creon, and Antigone are each, in turn, outsiders. Each stands opposed to whatever contagion and violence besets Thebes. But each, eventually, is drawn into a conflict that reduces difference to sameness, and generates difference out of sameness. Each is caught up in lateral relationships that found and confound humankind.

As I follow Girard in examining these lateral relationships, central to my analysis are themes of mimetic desire and conflict. The Theban plays bring us to the threshold of a sacrificial crisis, there to see that a metaphysical disease, an ontological sickness, and not only changing cultural norms, infects Thebes. A monstrous doubling among the characters leads to escalating violence, scapegoating, and death. Moreover, even as I look at Thebes with Girard, I also attend to two features of the Theban cycle that he neglects. *Antigone* is largely missing from Girard's work. Furthermore, notwithstanding Girard's fondness for depicting mimetic desire with metaphors of ill health, Girard does not closely examine a spreading contagion of violence that is *written on the bodies of the plays' protagonists*. As a consequence, he misses an important opportunity to develop insights on *Antigone* that he proffers in his remarks on the prostitute in 1 Kings and to link those insights with his extensive commentaries on *Oedipus the King* and *Oedipus at Colonus*. Attending to that which Girard neglects, I uncover a critique of ontological illness in *Antigone* that, at the very threshold of metaphysical desire, points to a healing alternative. My focus is on the evocation of sensory experience through kinesis that is evident especially in gestural movement in the tragedy.

In the Shadow of Death: Mimetic Rivalries in *Antigone*

Early episodes of *Antigone* offer evidence that the dramatic narrative does not lend itself solely to a functional calculus favored by some contemporary critics. Antigone and Ismene's relationship, sketched from the first lines of the play, shows how the multifaceted dynamics of the play, resonating at deep levels with its audience, invite an analysis rooted in mimetic theory. Ismene and Antigone initially appear different from each other: Ismene emphasizes her deference to men; Antigone directly challenges Creon. But their actions increasingly feature mimetic doubling. Both live in the shadow of the curse-laden house of Labdacus. When Antigone describes Ismene as *autodelphon*, "of the same womb,"[36] because Antigone and Ismene are daughters *and* sisters of Oedipus, Antigone's words attest to excessive closeness—a family romance gone wrong. As Tyrrell and Bennett note, that Homer uses similar words to portray the "double maternal field" of Oedipus's family and Aeschylus describes the births of Oedipus and his children as "from the same sowing" makes Sophocles's words all the more incisive.[37] As a consequence, there are intimations of a threatening contagion in Antigone's summoning of Ismene even as Antigone seeks to conform to cultural traditions that will protect the community from pollution and secure for the deceased a good death.[38]

As Tyrrell and Bennett remind us, Antigone and Ismene's doubling points to dangers at both ends of human life: as womb mates they enter life under peril; but as sisters who are to look over their brother's burial, they need to act in concert.[39] Because antiphonal keening requires at least two voices,[40] in the absence of Ismene, Antigone will have no one to answer her cries, and she will subject her brother to a bad death. At risk are not only *oikos* and *polis*, but life itself. If Antigone is not assisted by Ismene, a spreading pollution will threaten all of Thebes with the consequences of a bad death.

In refusing Antigone's request, Ismene introduces additional tensions into her conversation with her sister. Challenging Ismene to prove she is wellborn,[41] Antigone couches her argument in terms of patriliny, rather than filial responsibility. Antigone's words are harsh; yet commentators on Antigone have been reluctant to ascribe conflict to Antigone and Ismene's relationship. Although both sisters are the product of incest, which necessarily inscribes their relationship with an improper sameness, a number of commentators are at pains to establish stabilizing, proper differences between them, even as that effort compromises their readings of *Antigone*. As Tyrrell and Bennett masterfully demonstrate in an essay on Antigone and Ismene, when commentators force sisterliness between Antigone and Ismene where none exists, their efforts rebound, and the sisters' mimetic conflict stands out in bold relief.[42]

Ismene's confrontation with Creon during which she pleads for Antigone's life is critically revelatory, according to Tyrrell and Bennett. In response to Ismene's challenge, Creon responds with a crude dismissal. Antigone is a fully dispensable bride to Haemon, "for the furrows of others can be plowed."[43] Ismene persists, suggesting to Creon that Antigone and Haemon are especially fit for each other. But Creon is contemptuous: "I hate evil wives for my son."[44] In response, Ismene apparently directs her words to Haemon: "Dearest Haemon (*O philtath' Haimon*), how your father dishonors you!"[45] But should not Antigone be calling her fiancé "Dearest," rather than Ismene? Seeking to inscribe proper boundaries between Antigone and Ismene, in order that misplaced affection of Ismene for Haemon not exacerbate a rivalry between the sisters, a number of commentators assign this passage to Antigone.

Tyrrell and Bennett describe how this passage flummoxes commentators.[46] Kamerbeek cannot conceive that Ismene could refer to her sister's intended as "*philtath*" in the presence of Antigone. Kitto asserts that the term would "sound not quite natural coming from Ismene."[47] So also does Jebb assign line 572 to Antigone, crafting an elaborate explanation of why Antigone, who has been silent since line 560, suddenly inserts herself into the exchange between Creon and her sister. For Jebb, Antigone finds herself unable to remain silent in the face of Creon's polemic against "bad wives." Lifting herself out of the muddy field into which she has been thrown by Creon's words, Jebb finds Antigone taking the high road. He writes that Antigone's "solitary reference to her love heightens in a wonderful degree our sense of her unselfish devotion to a sacred duty." But Jebb's efforts to assign the line to Antigone place him in a bind when he arrives at the next line. Someone asks Creon if he intends to rob his son of his bride. Jebb realizes that Antigone cannot be the speaker because the question would have her plead for her own life; Ismene cannot ask the question because she already has pleaded for Antigone's life, and Jebb finds that she can do so only once.

Jebb assigns the line to the chorus, Tyrrell and Bennett point out, but ends up "corrupting the stichomythia into a polyphonic free-for-all."[48]

Commentators maintain fidelity to the text when they acknowledge mimetic rivalry between Antigone and Ismene, argue Tyrrell and Bennett. When Ismene refers to Haemon as "most dear Haemon," she *is* "too affectionate, too intimate, too sexual for a sister" who is speaking of Antigone's intended.[49] Girard's mimetic theory enables Tyrrell and Bennett to come to terms with a passage that nonplusses other commentators. Antigone and Ismene are caught up in a monstrous doubling, a rivalrous family romance born of their incestuous origins. As a consequence, that they would each desire Haemon and that Ismene would bring that desire to expression in a heated exchange with Creon is understandable. In the mimetic universe they occupy, a contagion of impropriety infects both. No devoted and mutually supportive sisters occupy this tragic space.[50]

Conflict in Ismene and Antigone's relationship is a counterpoint to the raw violence that characterizes Creon's relationships with others. Caught up in the excesses of rivalrous action, Creon exemplifies the entire pattern of mimetic desire at its most extreme. As ruler of Thebes, Creon mouths worthy principles of leadership: He expresses concern for the citizens of the polis and professes loyalty to the city.[51] But when Creon asserts that the polis belongs to the one with power, displays disinterest in his subjects' approval, and doubts their loyalty, he reveals his mimetic investments.[52] As Mary Whitlock Blundell argues, Creon treats the *polis as a personal possession*.[53] Haemon's critique is telling: he suggests that his father would be a good ruler of a desert, for a polis that is the possession of a single person is not truly a polis.[54] Creon's stance is illuminated by mimetic analysis: Creon seeks from others—his son, Antigone, the citizens of Thebes, the gods—the being he lacks. But, when others respond to him, Creon treats them as competitors for a *polis* that is his alone to possess. Indeed, the more that others acknowledge his rule and respond to the demands he makes for loyalty, the more Creon perceives them as competitors.

As storm clouds gather around Creon, a widening violence, endemic in mimetic conflict, is visible. Confronted with the deaths of Eteocles and Polyneices, Creon attempts to distinguish the two from each other. If Eteocles were still alive, Creon suggests, he would take Creon's part against

Polyneices and deny his brother burial. But the brothers are more like than unlike each other: both have called violence on themselves and have been fatally wounded; both have been misguided because of their desire for power and wealth; and both have put Thebes at risk. Creon's own actions advance the symmetry of disorder. Preparing to properly bury Eteocles and to deny burial to Polyneices, Creon will fail. In a mimetic universe, the distinctions Creon wishes to uphold are unsupportable.

Portents of disaster in Antigone and Ismene's interactions and of violence in the doubling of Eteocles and Polyneices are prime testimony that Sophocles intends with *Antigone* to contribute to what Girard calls the "art of tragedy" and not primarily to instruct his Athenian audience about changing cultural norms. Girard points out that tragic dialogue and violence turn on symmetry, and he emphasizes tragedians' sustained efforts to deprive their audience of "any means of taking sides." The enveloping violence is "too impersonal in its workings, too brutal in its results" to permit distinctions among characters that assign "good" or "wicked" to them. Thus, the tragedians faithfully sketch the trajectory of mimetic violence, which always ends in a paroxysm of monstrous sameness. The dramatic action of a tragedy moves in ever expanding waves of symmetry; as a contagion of violence engulfs all, the action topples over in a sacrificial crisis.[55]

Central to the expanding violence in *Antigone* is the tragic notion of disaster: *atē*. As Ruth Padel notes, on the one hand, *atē* refers outward—to calamities and difficult situations that are part of the dramatic action of the play. In *Antigone*, the chorus sings that nothing comes to human life "without *atē*."[56] But *atē* also turns inward when Sophocles depicts suffering as *atē*. Moreover, both elements merge in the form of embodied disaster when Ismene and Antigone are described as "two *atē*'s" to their father or uncle. Most powerfully, in *Antigone*'s "*atē* hymn,"[57] Sophocles links the multiple valences of *atē* that tragedy incarnates: god (*theos*) "drives mind (*phrenes*) to disaster (*atē*)."[58] This hymn, described as the "spiritual heart of the play" by Padel, attests to the divine infliction of disaster as well as to the generativity of violence.[59] The house of Labdacus will fall victim to *atē*: "For those whose house is shaken by the gods, no part of ruin is wanting." Likened to darkness that runs beneath the sea and rolls up onto the shore as a black sand,[60] *atē* offers no deliverance to the house of Labdacus. Indeed, the house will be "mown down": by the gods who will invoke the Erinyes as instruments of destruction.[61]

As the dramatic action of the play intensifies, Creon is caught up in spiraling violence: *Atē* is upon him, for "evil seems good to him whose mind the gods is driving towards disaster."[62] Sophocles cites words familiar to the Athenian audience from Homer. In his quarrel with Achilles, Agamemnon asserts, "I am not responsible, but Zeus and Destiny and an Erinyes walking in the mist who in assembly put savage *atē* in my mind."[63] Creon will be destroyed: not only does he misapprehend the circumstances associated with Polyneices's burial, but also his mind is beset by madness that contaminates his interactions with Antigone, Ismene, and Haemon.[64]

In *Antigone*, intersecting themes of *atē*, mind, and madness attest to a metaphysical illness that results in a sacrificial crisis. According to Padel, Greek tragedy perceives harm to have multiple causes and to issue in a chain of consequences. As harm's effects spread out and burrow down into Greek society, minds are damaged, resulting in madness.[65] Greek tragedy is imbued, Padel asserts, with Homer's concept of *atē*. For Homer, *atē* references damage to mind, life, or fortune. *Atē* suggests something done to someone by another, including a god, and also damage that one does to oneself. Padel acclaims Homer's rich insight: he refuses to see *atē* as a limited choice, an either-or. For Homer, harm cannot be attributed to god *or* human, others *or* oneself; instead, harm is always double. Accordingly, "Violent foolishness provokes violent response" and "Inner violence calls out world violence." Homer's perspicacity makes him an astute student of mimetic rivalry. Indeed, Homer attests to reciprocal violence, which is a definitive feature of developing mimetic rivalry.[66]

As Padel testifies to Homer's cognizance of the *reciprocity of violence*, she suggests the tragic poets share this awareness with him. True, the multivalent aspects of *atē* are "thinned" by the tragic poets. *Atē* has a more straightforward meaning for them than it does for Homer: *atē* is "disaster" or "death." But even as they no longer focus intently on the dynamic interplay between outer and inner harm, as does Homer, the tragic poets implement his insights, drawing on the entire genre of tragedy to enact *atē*'s sequence. Writes Padel: "To keep the word's epic range in a tragic play would overload things. It would sing too loud: a Wagnerian soprano in a madrigal chorus. . . .

In Homer, it is all over in one or two lines. You cannot have one word for the link between a harmed mind and harm in the world in a genre that exists to explore that very link."[67] Making *links* between inward and outward violence the focus of tragedy, tragedy engages *atē*. The process *is* the play.

Significant to this process is "madness." Not only does tragedy enact *atē*, but also tragedy replaces *atē* "with the personifications or the experience of madness."[68] With the notion of madness, the tragic poets explore "the world damage that damaged minds do." Specifically, in fifth-century tragedy, madness is a mark of *generative violence*.[69] Proper to the meaning of *atē* is the notion that violence builds on itself. Although madness begins with one who is damaged, it spreads. In Homeric myth, madness is neatly deployed: it is either a cause (leading a person into error) or a consequence (punishing one who has erred).[70] In tragedy, madness observes no boundaries: the divine is outside (*theos*) and inside (*daimōn*);[71] the mind is passive and active; external and internal explanations of desire, disease, suffering, and violence mix and proliferate.[72]

This *generative violence*, a feature of advanced mimetic conflict, is displayed to powerful effect in tragedy. Because madness in tragedy is, in fact, a product of divine *and* human scission, it often is portrayed *around* figures and narrative themes rather than ascribed *to* individuals as something that is *in* them.[73] The figures of tragedy are marked by a "relation to madness, which is out there in the world." An external menace that threatens to reverse itself, madness that was once outside moves inside, as boundaries shatter and pollution spreads. Erinyes and Lyssa abound in a tragic environment where madness proliferates.[74]

When scission in the divine world melds with conflict in the human world, the madness that ensues places humans in what Padel describes as a double bind.[75] Ensnared by contradictory demands, humans are "God-trapped." Prohibitions are set forth, but humans are unable to comply; instead, humans find themselves in situations where they must violate these prohibitions, and then they are punished. In recognizing that human and divine relationships in tragedy mirror each other, Padel's comments on the double bind that shapes tragic madness echo Girard's own thinking on mimetic rivalry; for he too understands that contradictory imperatives "form the basis of all human relationships" and account for the prevalence of violence in these relationships.[76]

As the dramatic action of *Antigone* moves forward, contradictory imperatives abound. Creon, Haemon, Antigone, and Ismene are caught in wave upon wave of violence that signals a loss of difference between and among them, prefiguring death. Creon and Haemon, for example, engage in reciprocal accusations. Haemon challenges Creon's decision to punish Antigone's actions on behalf of her brother with death, an act that will take his fiancée from him. Creon accuses Haemon of mindless behavior (*phrēn-*) and Haemon counters, "If you were not my father, I would say you were mad (*phron-*)."[77] As they hurl charges of disloyalty to *oikos* and *polis* at each other, their interactions attest to generative violence. On a superficial level, they truly appear to be at odds. As a father, Creon expects respect from Haemon; as a ruler, Creon assumes that Haemon will be an obedient subject.[78] From Creon's perspective, Haemon's anger is unfilial, and his challenge to Creon's judgment against Antigone is disloyal. But Haemon understands himself to be a good son acting out of concern for his father; moreover, Haemon thinks that he is a loyal subject. He likens himself to a scout who aims only to conscientiously report to his superior what he has heard "under cover." When Haemon tells Creon that "the city is lamenting for this girl, saying that no woman ever deserved it less," he believes that he is sharing information that will enable Creon to take immediate steps to avert disaster.[79] But Creon and Haemon's differences, attested to by their contradictory perceptions of each other's filial and political stances, quickly efface. In tragedy, as Girard asserts, everything turns on relationships, and Creon and Haemon's differences collapse before a threatening sameness that is characteristic of intensifying mimetic rivalry.

As Tyrrell and Bennett note, Creon and Haemon engage in a competition for Antigone that is played out before the Theban people.[80] For his part, Creon perceives that he cannot back down in his contest with Haemon without losing standing before Thebes. He attempts to undermine Haemon by accusing Haemon of being inferior to a woman.[81] Creon taunts Haemon, shouting "You shall never marry this woman while she is alive!"[82] In turn, Haemon speaks of Antigone, throwing her, like a weapon, in Creon's face: "Then she will die and by her death she will destroy another."[83] Enraged, Creon moves to end the competition by eliminating the object—Antigone—over which Haemon and he have struggled: "Bring the hateful creature, so that she may die at once close at hand, in the sight of her bridegroom!"[84]

Disaster looms, for the gods punish those who break the sacred laws. If Antigone dies at Creon's hand, he will have violated a law against killing one's kin, breaching the sacred order and generating pollution (*miasma*). Creon is aware of the consequences of his actions. He attempts to appease the gods, promising to put out "enough food to escape pollution (*miasma*) so that the whole city may avoid contagion."[85] The gods do not *cause* pollution when laws are broken; rather, pollution is an *effect* of the violation of the sacred.[86] For her part, Antigone cannot be the *pharmakos* that will protect Thebes against a deadly contagion. As Tyrrell and Bennett cogently observe, because Antigone has not been deemed impious by the gods, she cannot bear the miasma and free the community from it.[87] Creon will expel her from the city and entomb her outside its walls; however, she will not take with her the pollution that threatens the city. She is not the sacrifice that will bring peace and stability to Thebes. Creon has called Antigone a source of pollution; but, in the end, he will become the *miasma* that destroys the city. Once the confident pilot of the ship of state, Creon now is likened to the harbor of Hades and lost to the city on the "wild roads."[88] There Creon, not Antigone, will be the scapegoat/*pharmakos*. As the last of the archaic Thebans—the dragon men—Creon embodies the Theban other who will be vanquished by the Athenians. Indeed, as his mythic genos defines him as monstrous, Creon is an exemplary scapegoat.

Exiled and entombed in a rocky cave, Antigone enters a liminal state that lifts her out of the sacrificial economy in which she has been bound by her interactions with Creon, Haemon, and Ismene. Antigone's liminality, powerfully attested to by the funeral and wedding imagery of the tragic text,[89] suspends her in an indeterminate relationship to life and death. "Living neither among mortals nor as a shade among the shades, neither with the living nor with the dead," Antigone is a *metoikos*.[90] Antigone's liminal status also aligns her with Niobe. Sings Antigone: "I have heard that the Phrygian stranger, Tantalus' daughter, died the saddest death, near the lofty Sipylus . . . very like her am I."[91] Niobe returned to her father in that rock, just as Antigone returns to hers. As Antigone cries out that she is caught between life and death, "living neither among mortals nor as a shade among the shades," the chorus is blunt in their description of her situation: "You stumbled against the lofty altar of Justice, my child! And you are paying for some crime of your fathers."[92] The chorus does not see that Antigone is about to exchange the perverted ritual Creon has planned for her into a transformative alternative to sacrifice. For them, Antigone is a scapegoat who must take the pollution of her family to her tomb in order to save Thebes. But even as the chorus speaks, the path of *atē* divides; it cannot subsume Antigone. Antigone sees her responsibility differently. Thus, Antigone's speech about Niobe announces a division in the forward movement of the tragedy. Speaking only once more, Antigone remains caught in a kind of freeze frame as the dramatic action of the play swirls around her. We will return later to Antigone and Niobe; for now, we follow Creon down the path of *atē*.

As Creon's way diverges from Antigone's, he continues to play out sacrificial themes and to demonstrate how disaster (*atē*) is the inevitable outcome of mimetic rivalry and generative violence. The seer Tiresias arrives to report the spread of contagion in Thebes. Birds are in a frenzy, goaded by madness.[93] As Charles Segal notes, the sounds of shrieking (*klazontas*) birds place the threat to Thebes at the very boundaries of human order. The cries of the birds link animal madness with the loss of intelligible speech (*bebarbarōmenos*). With the failure of language, the formation of a peaceful society is not possible. Just as the birds attest to the breakdown of human community, so also do they "disrupt the voices that tell humans of the purposes of the gods."[94] As the birds carry carrion from the corpse of Polyneices to the altars within the city, the gods no longer accept the prayers of those who would gather at these altars.[95] Tiresias implores Creon to step back from rage so that the city may return to order. But Creon, caught up in the throes of mimetic rivalry, has no ears for this messenger of the gods. Comparing himself to a target at which an archer is shooting arrows, Creon views Tiresias as a deadly competitor.[96] Waging yet another battle of words characterized by stichomythia, Creon trades word-blows with Tiresias. Each aims to deliver a final word that will prove lethal to his foe.[97] Creon's violence knows no bounds; for, in defending his mistreatment of Polyneices, he challenges even the gods. Creon avows, "even if Zeus' eagles should snatch the body and bear the carrion up to their master's throne! Not even then shall I take fright at this pollution and allow him to be buried."[98] Leveraging his prophetic acumen, Tiresias finally breaks free from Creon's efforts to ensnare him. He departs, but not before he has warned Creon again of the consequences of his acts against Polyneices and Antigone. Tiresias proclaims that the arrows Creon has shot at others will turn back on him, and Creon will not be able to escape their sting: "All the cities are stirred up by enmity," and the Erinyes of Hades and the gods now lie in wait for Creon. But a human cannot win a mimetic battle with gods.[99]

For a moment, Creon holds his wrath, realizing that his desires are leading him straight into the "net of disaster" (*atē*).[100] He asks the chorus what he should do, and they recommend that he act quickly before the gods destroy him.[101] But the violence generated by Creon's mimetic rivalries is about to consume his family. As Creon approaches the cave where Antigone is entombed, evidence abounds of chaotic reversals that his actions have caused. The wedding chamber is now a tomb; the funeral lament that reaches his ears is sung by a man (Haemon) rather than by a woman (as Antigone would have sung to Polyneices). Further, Creon and Haemon's rivalry intensifies as each becomes a monster before the other. Spitting into his father's face,[102] Haemon glares at his father with "savage eyes" (*agrion*).[103] When Creon engages Haemon, Haemon draws his sword against his father but misses. Turning his aggression back on himself, Haemon falls on his sword, reaching out to clasp Antigone as he dies.[104]

In the next scene, Creon enters the city carrying the body of Haemon. Hoping that his actions have borne final fruit, he asks, "What is there that is yet more evil, coming after evils?"[105] As if in response, Eurydice bursts through the door of the palace at center stage in an "eruption from inside" that demonstrates the profound damage that has been done to the cloistered confines of the household by Creon's actions.[106] Eurydice has been on her way to propitiate the gods in the wake of the failed sacrifices described by Tiresias moments before; however, just as she releases the bolt on the gate of the palace, she overhears the messenger and is drawn forth as the description of disaster reaches her ears. When Eurydice hears that her child is dead, she remains silent and returns to the interior of the home. In a final mimetic reversal, Creon is left to take up traditional mourning song. He sings with great agitation about Haemon's death, as Haemon's body is brought on stage. The messenger interrupts to report that Eurydice is dead. The palace door opens, and her body is brought on stage. Not only is Creon flanked by the corpses, but also by Megareus, the son who was sacrificed to save the city. His name is brought forth by the messenger who, reporting on Eurydice's last words, announces that she has labeled Creon a "child murderer."[107] Creon cries, "Ah! Attendants, led me off at once, lead me out of the way, me who am no more than nothing!"[108]

The path of desire, along which Creon strode in his effort to find in others the being he lacked, ends in catastrophe with a mass stilling of life, including Creon's. Haemon forecast his father's demise much earlier when he reminded his father that "whoever think that they themselves alone have sense, or have a power of speech or an intelligence that no other has, these people when they are laid open are found to be empty."[109] Creon has been laid open and he is empty. In this most deadly outcome of a family romance, a mother and her sons, also brothers to each other, are dead, and a father has become a child-killer. Mimeticized violence has run rampant, overturning all human order.

"In the Eyes of the Wise": From Conflict to Conversion

But what has become of Antigone's desire as it has moved away from Creon's during her journey to the cave of her death? When she is "laid open," is she too found empty? Creon's story is steeped in traditions of sacrifice; can Antigone's story be different? Can her family romance be transformed by an intimacy that will exchange acquisitive rivalry for love? Significantly, Antigone does not follow a straight course away from sacrifice, as if Sophocles somehow recognizes the inability of his audience to easily embark with Antigone on a nonsacrificial journey.[110] Instead, the audience is schooled by Sophocles in the ways of ontological illness as he invites the audience to explore three distinct paths with Antigone.

The first of these paths, the most archaic, leads directly to sacrifice. Along this route, which tragedy enables the Greek imagination to closely track, Antigone walks hand in hand with a long line of virgins whose lives have ended in sacrifice. Of course, in the theater, no actual sacrifice is portrayed. Instead, as Loraux explains, words convey the *parthenos* in her passage from life into death. Evoking the most archaic of mysteries, powers beyond this world look favorably on humans if a virgin is offered up to them. As her blood flows, a city is saved. Moreover, the words of tragedy typically support a transition from life to death that disguises its sacrificial import: the dead virgin becomes the bride of Hades, and she does so with nobility, reclaiming *what has happened to her* as her own.[111] But Antigone's death is not noble in this way. Instead, the chorus states that Antigone is the only human to enter Hades of her own free will (*autonomos*).[112] Moreover, they are brutally direct in their assessment: "The respect you showed is a noble kind of respect; but power in the hands of him to whom it belongs, is in no way to be flouted, and you were destroyed by your self-willed passion."[113] Antigone may not be counted among the virgins sacrificed for their city. The chorus's strong words are meant to dissuade all but the most foolhardy from pressing forward with Antigone along a path of sacrifice.

A second path now opens up for Antigone. Having been labeled "self-willed," Antigone appears to act in accord with the Greek ethic of "helping friends and harming enemies." According to Mary Whitlock Blundell, beginning with Homer and surviving into the Roman period, Greek popular thought is pervaded by the notion that humans desire and derive satisfaction and pleasure from helping their friends and harming their enemies.[114] Linked with this norm is justice of the talion: repayment in kind for harm done to oneself as well for favors directed toward oneself.[115] The Greek *philos* (friend) and *philia* (friendship) have a broader context of meaning than do "friend" and "friendship" within contemporary society. *Philos* and *philia* apply to a broad nexus of personal, political, business, and family relationships.[116] Friends are "a refuge in misfortune, indispensable in daily life, and the essential base for political ambition."[117] Friendship is grounded in notions of reciprocity and mutual benefit. Within the family, kinship ties are based on affection. Devoted to those with whom one shares blood ties, members of a family express philia when they reciprocate favors. But philia is not restricted to the family; it is applicable to the polis as well. Patterns of family loyalty are replicated in the public sphere, including acts of generosity that are reciprocated in kind by their recipients.[118]

Antigone's claim to value philia above hatred and Creon's assertion that an "enemy is never a *philos*" appear to show Antigone subscribing to the code of "helping friends and harming enemies."[119] She aligns herself with philia when she ignores the conflict that has divided her brothers and commits herself to the proper burial of Polyneices. Further, Antigone wishes suffering on Creon, and she threatens Ismene with hatred if Ismene refuses to support her.[120] Moreover, Antigone's use of monetary metaphors conforms to the "help friends and harm enemies" lexicon. She calculates that her brother's body is a "sweet treasure" (*glykyn thēsauron*) and that her own death will be a gain (*kerdos*).[121]

Although differing from Antigone in his interpretation of the code of "help friends and harm enemies," Creon stands firmly within the social nexus of that code. He too relies on metaphors of monetary exchange, most memorably when he responds with angry disdain to Tiresias's warning about the pollution that is threatening Thebes. Asserting that "long since I have been sold and exported by your tribe," Creon accuses Tiresias of pursuing only personal gain.[122] In his final response to Tiresias, Creon is defiantly dismissive: "Know that you will never be able to trade on my judgment!"[123] Creon also cites his commitments to philia; however, for him the polis is the primary context for the expression of friendship. Likening the polis to a ship at sea, Creon asserts that if he saw a threat approaching, he would never "make a friend of the enemy of my country, knowing that this is the ship that preserves us, and that this is the ship on which we sail and only while she prospers can we make our friends."[124]

Girard would call the "help friends and harm enemies" code a "closed system." It brings to expression mimetic rivalry and generative violence because it regularly devolves into sacrifice and scapegoating. People caught up in such a system blame violence on others, believing that they never initiate conflict. But because violence is mimetic, even though an opponent is always deemed the instigator, violence leaves no one innocent. The code of "help friends and harm enemies" is such a system.[125]

But even as Antigone's and Creon's comments mirror each other, suggesting that both are committed to "helping friends and harming enemies," the mimeticism to which their shared vocabulary attests breaks apart as Antigone's actions belie her commitment to that code.[126] Antigone's curt and dismissive response to Ismene, in which Antigone asserts that, even were Ismene to change her mind about assisting Antigone with the burial of her brother, Antigone would not want Ismene to help her, points to initial fractures in Antigone's adherence to the code.[127] Further, even when Antigone's exchanges with Creon feature currency metaphors, Antigone uses these metaphors differently than Creon. As Robert Goheen insightfully argues, Antigone's *motivations* for using monetary metaphors and her *evaluation* of them must be analyzed. At first glance, these metaphors situate Creon and Antigone in a common ethical nexus; on closer analysis, they split Antigone from Creon. When Creon uses currency metaphors, his words attest to his investment in the code of "help friends and harm enemies" as a governing principle for the polis. When Antigone uses currency metaphors while simultaneously acting in ways that move her to the margins of Thebes and toward death, her words expose as bankrupt principles of exchange upheld by those who help friends and harm enemies.[128] Antigone is not a party to generative violence; instead, standing outside the "help friends and harm enemies" nexus, she is accountable to the gods rather than to her kin. Because Antigone challenges rather than emulates the values of "help friends and harm enemies," the second path proves a dead end for those who would follow Antigone away from mimetic rivalry and sacrifice.[129]

But a third path now opens up: the way of the gods. Along this path, Antigone is an exemplar of unwavering devotion. And truly, the chthonic gods—Zeus, Hades, Acheron—live for Antigone with an intensity not recognized by anyone else in the tragedy.[130] From her perspective, the ordinances of the gods "have life, not simply today and yesterday, but forever."[131] Antigone confidently speaks of her last journey that will culminate in her becoming the bride of Acheron.[132] When she talks of entering the "caverns of the dead," she attests to the deep feeling she has for those she will find there.[133] Is Antigone's way of devotion a path forward to a nonsacrificial economy? Features of this path invite especially close attention.

Of immediate note are differences between Antigone's and Creon's religious orientations.[134] Where Antigone is oriented toward the chthonic gods, Creon is shown to turn a deaf ear to these gods. But religious motives cannot be assigned only to Antigone. That Creon is loyal to the polis does not mean that he cedes loyalty to the gods wholly to Antigone. Creon's loyalty to the polis is in accord with religious belief. Creon summons the gods of the city in his first speech and appeals to Zeus in committing himself to the welfare of Thebes.[135] Creon's reverence for the gods is not a perfunctory expression of his political leadership. In defending his refusal of burial to Polyneices, Creon makes a genuinely impassioned appeal to the gods.[136] Thus, Creon adheres also to the sacred and embodies the norms he professes; however, for him the domain of lived devotional practice is associated with the city. His worship is public and punctuated by festivals and pageantry.[137]

The conflict between Antigone and Creon moves to a new register as the *contrast* between Antigone's and Creon's religious practices transitions into *a competition* between their gods. As Tiresias reminds Creon, in condemning Antigone to death, Creon has "hurled below one of those above, blasphemously lodging a living person in a tomb" even as he has also prevented the burial of Polyneices, thereby keeping here "something belonging to the gods below, a corpse deprived, unburied, unholy." Creon's gods of the city have no rightful claim to Antigone or Polyneices, as the Erinyes will soon remind him.[138] As conflict breaks out along the path of devotion, how are we to understand what is happening? Was not this path, the last one Sophocles would have us explore, supposed to lead away from violence and sacrifice?

Although Girard is writing specifically of *The Bacchae* when he describes the turn to the religious in Greek tragedy, his comments apply equally well to *Antigone* and alert us to the significance of key developments in this tragedy. Girard observes that religion comes to the fore at a particular juncture in a tragic narrative. Human mastery of events, typified by appeals to the polis and to the power of its statesmen, has been challenged. Distinctions between polis and *oikos* subsequently have disappeared; ritual sacrifices have become corrupted. No one can distinguish any longer between statesmanship and "unbridled ambition" or between piety and blasphemy. Now, "men set to quarreling about the gods." In the midst of that struggle, a new sacrificial crisis emerges. From the perspective of those who have been beset by violence, this sacrificial crisis presents itself as divine intervention and revenge.[139]

No wonder then that Antigone and Creon's conflict is mirrored in divine disorder as the dramatic action of Antigone moves toward a denouement. Their mimetic conflict results not only in their doubling, but also in the blurring of distinctions between the gods of the earth and those of the city. Both Creon and Antigone participate in this confusion when differences in religious practice that have defined them break down. Creon, whose devotion most often is typified as civic and directed toward the gods of the city, actually is shown to have a profound connection to the chthonic gods. After all, he is a "dragon man," the last of the archaic Thebans. These beings emerged from an autochthonous line sown by Cadmus from dragon's teeth. The chorus has alluded to these origins when they have told of Polyneices being routed by "his dragon-foe." But with the death of his sons, Megareus and Haemon, Creon is the sole remaining male member of "the Sown Men."[140] Thus, as *Antigone* moves toward its tragic conclusion, Creon is

linked ever more closely to the chthonic gods. And Antigone, whose personal and familial devotion has always been oriented toward the gods of the
earth, nevertheless is linked definitively with the gods of Olympus. Indeed,
these gods are at the fore in the dust storm that covers the body of Polyneices
after the guards have undone the work of the first burial.[141] This dust is of the
earth (*chthōn*); however, the Olympian gods stir that dust, in an expression
of "celestial grief" (*ouranion achos*).[142]

The actions of these Olympian gods, not those of Antigone, are decisive in the burial of Polyneices. The Watchman does report that he has seen
the corpse of Polyneices covered lightly with dust. However, as Tyrrell and
Bennett invite us to observe, evidence of human actions on behalf of Polyneices is missing: no tracks move forward or away from the body; no liquid
offerings protect the body from pollution; indeed, the ground has not been
broken. The Watchman's report points to actions of the gods, for which there
is precedent in traditions of ancient Greece.[143] When circumstances prevent
early burial of a corpse, gods are known to intervene, providing a protective
dusting of the corpse. So also when humans refuse to bury a corpse, gods may
step in, as in the case of Hector in the *Iliad*.[144] In *Antigone*, the gods intervene
twice as the corpse of Polyneices lies unburied on a field. After the Watchman
removes the dust that has protectively covered the corpse, it is exposed to the
elements; in response, the gods create a whirlwind, momentarily blinding the
Watchman and providing cover for Antigone to approach her brother's body.
As the storm weakens, Antigone is seen pouring a libation over the body of
her brother and heard making the sound of a bird cry.[145] Birds are multivalent
symbols in Greek tragedy: they announce impending disaster but also are
revelatory of a god's will.[146]

Has Antigone's journey away from violence toward transformation
reached a dead end? Has she moved forward only to become hopelessly
mired in accentuated mimetic conflict that has drawn the gods into the fray?
To the contrary, whereas the confusion of divine and human boundaries in
the heightening of a sacrificial crisis does destroy Creon, Antigone experiences affirmation.[147] Her journey will follow a heroic pattern with regular
allusions to *a quest into the unknown*. Departing from all paths taken previously by heroines of Greek tragedy, Antigone will break new ground when
she is "laid open" and confronts directly the prospect of her own death.

Antigone's distinctive stance is foreshadowed when she is arrested and interrogated by Creon. She does not claim that the gods have done the work that Creon attributes to her. Far from denying that she is responsible for the events that have transpired on the field where Polyneices's corpse rests, Antigone avows: "I say I did these things, and I do not deny them."[148] That Antigone assumes responsibility for acts on behalf of her brother that *the text would attribute to the gods* shows generative violence in action. From the perspective of those who have been beset by the widening violence that is threatening all of Thebes, the emerging sacrificial crisis presents itself as divine intervention and revenge.[149] The loss of differences multiplies: the work of the gods of the city and the earth, human and divine powers can no longer be distinguished, mirroring a similar loss of difference between Antigone and Creon. But Antigone stands apart from this troubled scene to speak in her own voice and claim acts as her own.

Antigone's novel stance, which lifts her above the morass of the sacrificial crisis, becomes fully visible when she speaks to her tomb, at once her bridal chamber. In that liminal moment that presages her transition and final departure from the stage, Antigone addresses her mother and her brothers—Eteocles and then Polyneices.[150] Recalling that she has engaged in funeral rituals for all, Antigone asserts that she would not have defied Creon and Thebes to bury "the children of whom I was the mother or had my husband perished"; no, only for her brother—this dead brother Polyneices—has she performed the burial rites, in defiance of all who would oppose her actions.[151] Antigone's words are surprising, for they attest to a uniqueness of Antigone's relationship with her brother for which the audience has not been prepared. The narrative has not hinted that Antigone might express such a perspective, nor do cultural mores suggest that Antigone's speech is typical of women of her day.[152] Most notably, Antigone's words do not reflect the mimetic conflict that has shaped the narrative. Instead, as Antigone speaks from within the isolation and pathos of her liminal stance, her words distance her from generative violence.

Habituated to conflict, the audience expects to hear Antigone attest to the mimetic rivalries that have beset her up to this moment. Her words should mirror her monstrous doubling with Creon. Having manned and unmanned each other throughout the play, they should copy each other to the end—Antigone to be buried alive and Creon to become a living corpse.[153] Or Antigone should make one final, desperate move to help friends and harm enemies.[154] Or Antigone should summon the gods in order to speak within a sacrificial register that now is as evocative of Olympus as of Hades.[155] Or maddened by all that has transpired, Antigone should make only incomprehensible sounds. But the words that Antigone does utter when she is laid open are clear and spoken from a different register entirely. At the end of her journey, she abandons all claims—to gods, to family, to social codes. As Knox so insightfully observes, Antigone's courageous spirit turns, in the end, on that which is "purely personal."[156] What commends Antigone to all who encounter her, then as now, is the *singular* nature of her love. With all mimetic rivalries peeled away, Antigone stands alone with her brother.

The audience arrives with Antigone at this juncture after following her along three paths. Each, were Antigone to have followed it to its end, would have resulted in sacrifice or would have taken the form of mimetic competition that eventually would have culminated in sacrifice. As a consequence, when Antigone reaches her end, stepping away from all previously traveled paths to move forward along an unknown way, the specificity of Antigone's voice and her actions, as she reaches out to Polyneices, are of critical import. When Antigone is "laid open," she speaks of him with words that take Antigone outside of the sacrificial economy in all its manifestations. Polyneices has always lived up to his name: "full of discord."[157] But, outside the institutions and relationships that would circumscribe Antigone's words and actions within a framework of generative violence, Polyneices is, at last, no competitor and no rival. Hovering over the body of Polyneices, Antigone's libations cleanse her brother of his violent history as a warrior and offspring of a criminal act. Differences that have always faded into an annihilating sameness and a sameness that has transformed always into threatening differences in the trauma-filled house of Labdacus are at last laid to rest. Antigone's revelatory insights and gestures enable her to assume a new stance. Refusing sibling hatred, she will love her brother as herself.

Having traced a narrative of metaphysical crisis in *Antigone*, we are at last able to affirm Juliet Mitchell's trenchant insights, with which we began our reflections on *Antigone*. Antigone does exemplify the "Antigone complex." Drawing on Girard's mimetic theory, we have shown how generative violence can be countered along a lateral axis represented by love between siblings. But if humans are to encode this love as law within human communities, they must become capable of turning away from violence as has Antigone. In summoning love of a brother, Antigone shows us that we learn to love first as brothers and sisters, long before we become immersed in institutional nexuses of violence—polis, *oikos*, Hades, and Olympus—that are as much a part of our time as of Sophocles's. At the threshold of socialization, one learns to love a singular other as one loves oneself. One who loves one's sibling has learned the "law of the mother": one loves because one is the same. Only as one learns to negotiate a sameness that is not threat, which does not lead one to fight over a space that cannot be shared, does human experience open up on mutual existence with another that establishes preconditions for human community that will not be governed by reciprocal violence.

In his own search for that which in human experience attests to forms of community not shaped by mimetic rivalry, Girard has invoked the Joseph story of the Hebrew Bible. He has cited the "enormous ethical demand" placed on us when this story calls us to replace rivalry with reciprocal care and regard.[158] Girard has stated that he has glimpsed this same possibility with Antigone. The argument of this chapter, expanding on these themes, has aimed to show the potential of mimetic theory to more fully illuminate how Antigone's story, like Joseph's, offers us an opportunity to embrace this ethical demand.[159]

But *how* does Antigone embrace a nonsacrificial ethic? How is her conversion from a sacrificial to nonsacrificial stance achieved? Having traveled with Antigone along three pathways of sacrifice sketched by Sophocles, when Antigone veered from those paths to undertake a novel quest, we were so focused on not tripping as we followed her that we looked only at our feet, lest we stumble on unfamiliar terrain. We need to retrace our steps and take up our journey with Antigone for a second time. But now, we need to lift our eyes as we walk. Surveying our surroundings, we need to assess how and when the landscape changes from one marked by sacrifice to one in which love can thrive.

Undertaking this journey with Antigone, I continue my efforts to augment Girard's mimetic theory, attending, as he does not, to the critical role sensory experience plays in facilitating nonsacrificial engagement with others. Key to my interpretation of *Antigone* is an examination of intimacy that I ground in a corporeal hermeneutics. Intimacy offers a way to understand the singularity of Antigone's love for her brother and to comprehend how such love becomes an alternative to sacrifice. Intimacy is what is blocked in the face of trauma, and "intimate domain" is the name I give to the space we enter with Antigone when, having been healed of trauma, we are able to imagine and to claim forms of human community that are not bound by sacrifice. In the absence of intimacy, humans remain rooted in structures of mimetic rivalry, caught in an ongoing replication of trauma. Their family romances and social affairs are distorted, devolving into conflict. Trauma is the affective and bodily expression of the lack that haunts human being, distorting our relationships and condemning humans to circle a future we cannot name. Mimetic desire is the name we give to the false quest to name this future; however, because desire bandages the wound in human being rather than heals it, mimetic desire is ineffective as a salve; indeed, desire actually deepens the wound. Only intimacy heals.

Antigone's display of intimacy, reported by the guard, is wholly embodied:

> She cried out bitterly with a sound like the piercing note of a bird when she sees her empty nest robbed of her young, just so did she cry out, weeping, when she saw the corpse laid bare and called down curses on those who had done the deed. At once she brought in her hands thirsty dust, and from the well-wrought brazen urn that she was carrying she poured over the corpse a threefold libation.[160]

In making her offering, Antigone acts in ways that have what Bolens would recognize as profound kinesic meaning. One need not translate Antigone's gestures into signs in order to comprehend what Antigone accomplishes with them. For Antigone's actions immediately are shown to give her the very being of her brother, pointing to a restoration of relationship for her and for those who participate in her gesture. The healing that results is my focus, as I continue to reflect on *Antigone*.

CHAPTER 5

Trauma and
the Theban Cycle

Many are things are formidable [*deina*], and none more formidable than man.

—Sophocles, *Antigone*

How can intimacy become a subject for critical reflection?[1] Intimacy is typically understood to focus on emotions of love and supportive family bonds. But if family life is the beginning point for reflection on intimacy, it is not the only terrain we can explore in an effort to understand it. Helpfully, Julia Kristeva both broadens and narrows the field for critical reflection on intimacy. She broadens it when she links intimacy to art, religion, and psychoanalysis and cites the unique capacity of these forms of cultural expression to *protect the singularity of human life.*[2] Kristeva narrows the context for critical reflection on intimacy when she specifies that art, religion, and psychoanalysis home in on intimacy when they focus on the *sensory experience of the body.* Sensory experience often plays a role in the expression of intimacy; however, for Kristeva that which is most significant about connections between sensory experience and intimacy is that sensory experience is *the way that intimacy in human life is protected from threats that would destroy it.* Just as mimetic rivalry is not only a linguistic and social phenomenon but also tactile and affective, so also is intimacy a healing alternative to rivalry and sacrificial scapegoating, expressed in bodily form. The intimate domain is characterized by affect, sensation, mood, and feeling. Intimacy is a practice of corporeality. As a consequence, mimetic violence is not resolved when one subscribes to the *idea* of nonviolence, for nonviolence requires the conversion of one's entire *being.* Central to this conversion is a sensory experience that restores and protects the vitality and the singularity of human intimacy against trauma that makes intimacy impossible.[3] But how do the life practices oriented toward sensory experience advance human intimacy?

Addressing this question, I employ a corporeal hermeneutics in order to look closely at *how* Antigone came to embrace the singularity of Polyneices's life, love him, and thereby witness to an intimacy that opens out on nonsacrificial modes of human community. I track sensory experiences to which Antigone attests, giving special attention to trauma associated with sibling conflict. This paradigmatic social relationship is foundational for human society, and the healing of sibling relationships that have been riven by mimetic violence is a precondition for establishing an ethical existence oriented toward the others—an intimate domain. As a consequence, I explore *Antigone* as a traumatic text within which also may be found a healing subtext, a text in which traumatic memory, closed in on itself, is finally opened to a narrative memory that creates community out of recognition and forgiveness.

Previously, in my exploration of Proust's *In Search of Lost Time,* I considered how trauma references a primordial separation from the maternal body that initiates the family romance. I attended to a *vertical* axis along which the nascent subject passes in separation from the maternal body in order to assume a place in the world. Now, with *Antigone,* I explore the family romance again; however, this time, I focus on a *lateral axis* along which a subject's first relations with others emerge. In *Antigone,* trauma is played out in this new register, in which confused sibling relationships, skewed by generational disorder within the house of Labdacus, are especially significant. In keeping with the approach I took to Proust's *In Search of Lost Time,* I draw here too on Caruth's insights about trauma, which are about a form of suffering Mitchell calls "strong trauma." I recall that, for Caruth, traumatic experiences are characterized by repetition in which the survivor is caught up unknowingly and against her will.[4] Caruth states that one who is traumatized suffers from a pain that cannot be grasped or committed to rational understanding. Such suffering hollows one out, forming a kind of wound. Caruth suggests that the agonizing repetition of trauma is broken when *a voice is released through the wound*. The voice that cries from the wound witnesses to a truth that the victim of trauma cannot fully know.

Following Caruth, I suggest that Antigone possesses a voice that cries out from a wound. She speaks to a truth that initially she does not know and cannot fully comprehend. But what is this wound? Caruth's observations about Freud's reflections on trauma point to an answer. Freud has observed that, in contrast to physical trauma associated with an injury, one who is psychically wounded may be wholly unaware of any harm on the occasion of the causing event. Indeed, traumatic events typically happen too soon and unexpectedly to be known at all.[5] We are shielded from trauma by a break in the mind's experience of time. This breach is not caused by a pure quantity of stimulus (as is the case for a physical assault on the body); rather, a threat is recognized by the mind one moment too late. *Not experienced in time, the trauma is not fully known.*[6] In the breach, repetition ensues. Unaware of what has endangered one's life, one returns to the moment of trauma to confront again and again the necessity and the impossibility of grasping the threat.

Caruth writes that an aspect of the "impossible history" of trauma that is most unsettling is that one who is traumatized is *caught inside an event for which there is no witness*. The person who is harmed is not able to offer testimony to his or her own experience. Moreover, because latency defines the traumatic event, there can be no external witness. Indeed, the contaminating power of trauma captures anyone who would occupy the space of a witness and speak the truth about violence. A witness emerges, suggests Caruth, only as we find ourselves able to home in on a victim's departure from the trauma and *bear witness to that leave-taking*.[7]

Invited by Caruth to examine *Antigone* from a perspective attuned to time and that which has been lost to time, I seek an expansive vision that can account for the impossible history of trauma. I observe Antigone for evidence that she can bear witness to another's departure from suffering, breaking with a contagion that crosses time. My perspective opens out on the Theban cycle; after all, Antigone's time encompasses not only *Antigone* but also *Oedipus the King* and *Oedipus at Colonus*. Trauma has beset the entire house of Labdacus and has spread across generations. Attentive to the traumatic profiles of all three tragedies, I may better explore what, within the frame of the Theban cycle, constitutes a threat that, neither experienced nor witnessed in time, is subject to painful repetition.

Trauma and the Theban Cycle

Charles Segal's trenchant comments on *Oedipus the King* locate psychic and physical trauma within this tragedy. Distinguishing between the myth of Oedipus and Sophocles's recasting of that myth in tragedy, Segal observes that *Oedipus the King* calls into question "one of the most fundamental elements of mythic narration, the representation of time."[8] Although Oedipus seemingly is driven forward along a linear path—as if he is advancing *in* time—his path regularly is exposed as circular. Caught up in a past he cannot transcend, Oedipus seeks closure and certain answers to questions of the past that will launch him forward, enabling him to claim a life at last. But gaps and fissures in time widen, casting him deep into the past. Chronological time is not wholly in abeyance: the plot appears to track a forward-moving Oedipus.

Nevertheless, far from bridging the past to the future, each new episode in *Oedipus the King* opens on a yawning chasm, leaving Oedipus outside of time. The birth of a child also is the occasion to discover a prior threat against a child's life; an encounter with a father leads to a discovery of an earlier parricide; an encounter with a mother becomes also an occasion that exposes long-buried incest. Writes Segal: "The remote past, with the blood ties that should assure him an intimate place in both house and city, cancels out the present, in which he possess wife and kingdom after fulfilling the role of the young conquering hero (like Perseus or Theseus) who arrives from a distant land."[9] Each discovery closes rather than opens time. As a consequence, Oedipus's life story remains untold and unwitnessed. Oedipus's blinding functions as a powerful symbol of the trauma by which he remains beset.

Girard places the traumatic repetition described by Segal within the context of reciprocal violence. Patricide establishes "violent reciprocity between father and son." Moreover, patricide strikes at fundamental distinctions within a group, creating entanglements along previously well-defined boundaries. All are caught up in the confusion: fathers and sons, fathers and daughters, and brothers and sisters. That the focus of violence is incest underscores how Oedipus becomes "the slayer of distinctions."[10] Moreover, in the ensuing contagion of violence, conflict consumes Thebes as each member of the community becomes a double of another. Converging in their undifferentiated unity on an isolated figure—Oedipus—Thebes "hurls itself blindly into the search for a scapegoat."[11]

Two features of Girard's portrait of reciprocal violence in *Oedipus the King* cohere with a traumatic reading of this tragedy. Writing of Oedipus, Girard asserts that the mechanism of reciprocal violence is *circular*, and he attests to a *failure of memory* that prevents resolution of that conflict. The cyclical nature of violence is attested to in Oedipus's fraught relationship with Laius: "Each seeing in the Other a real or potential rival, each takes refuge in the same violence."[12] Recalling the injury to the infant Oedipus's foot on the occasion of his exile, Girard uses the language of physical trauma to name this violence: "What is perpetuated from father to son is the injury and the distancing, it is the violence and the usurpation, it is that wound to the foot that runs from father to son in the family of Labdacus." Always, "Flight from the father is an ironic return to the father."[13] After the community is caught in a contagion of violence, acts of vengeance and reprisal persist: Each person stands ready to preemptively strike out against every other person, for no act can be considered anything but groundwork for further aggression. As a consequence, violence cycles on, unable to "burn itself out."[14]

This repetition of violence is momentarily interrupted by the emergence of a surrogate victim, on whom the entire community can focus its anger. But the expulsion of the scapegoat Oedipus ushers in only temporary calm. The community, once hypervigilant in its search for threats and possessed of a "baleful knowledge," is caught up in "all inclusive" ignorance. Their collective violence *erases all memory of the past*. Girard writes, "Men cannot confront the naked truth of their own violence without the risk of abandoning themselves to it entirely."[15] To confront violence in all its nakedness is to touch woundedness; however, that cannot be done without becoming lost to/in the wound entirely. In this way, Girard's evocation of the erasure of memory by violence in *Oedipus the King* attests to an unspeakable trauma.

Caruth's depiction of trauma has similarities with Girard's account of reciprocal violence. Caruth writes that trauma "is always the story of a wound that cries out, that addresses us in the attempt to tell us of a reality or truth that is not otherwise available." This truth, characterized by a delayed appearance and arriving in the form of a belated address, is linked to "what remains unknown in our very actions and our language."[16] Caruth locates a "double telling" in stories of trauma, for they feature a crisis of death and a correlative crisis of life. The double telling of which Caruth writes recalls Girard's description of a sacrificial crisis, of which the story of Oedipus is a most striking example. The community that is beset by pollution and a spiraling violence and the community that rises up against a scapegoat, experiencing a sudden restoration of peace, are one. That community's story is a "double telling" in which the truth that would link the crisis of death with the restoration of life is subject to delayed appearance. The community has no memory on which it could draw to join these stories.[17]

If *Oedipus the King* lends itself to a traumatic reading, what of *Oedipus at Colonus*? As Oedipus ascends to the cult of hero,[18] some would argue that Oedipus breaks free of traumatic repetition in which he is mired in *Oedipus the King* and experiences healing. Knox, Segal, and Zeitlin offer key evidence. Writing of the conclusion to *Oedipus at Colonus*, Knox observes that Oedipus becomes a seer and that Theseus recognizes him as a prophet.[19] Previously Oedipus has been mired in the past, his body hopelessly polluted. But Knox records that Oedipus is saved by divine intervention and invited into a future with the gods. Perceiving that Oedipus is their peer, the gods speak to him directly, welcome him, and grant him divine powers and immortality.[20] Segal, citing Otfried Becker, argues the Oedipus's end is an "apotheosis not only of the tragic hero but of tragedy itself."[21] Indeed, *Oedipus at Colonus* marks the "passing of the tragic age of Greece," for its hero no longer attests to a fragile existence, riven by divine and human paradox, but to the *transfiguration of suffering by a savior*. Oedipus becomes the "ultimate resolution": his heroization is "totally unambiguous" and his blessings transmute pollution of an accursed past into "timeless healing and civilizing power," which he bestows on Athens.[22] Zeitlin suggests that Oedipus, alone of the tragic heroes, rises above the repetition of time in which he has been caught. Becoming a "master of time," he is a truly prophetic presence.[23]

Although Knox, Segal, and Zeitlin suggest that Oedipus, freed from a multigenerational continuum of suffering besetting the house of Labdacus, is able to bless his fellow citizens with healing, we can affirm their perspective only if we neglect the volatile standing of the hero in ancient Greece. In emphasizing Oedipus's capacity to work for the good of Athens, these scholars shed light on one side of the heroic profile, leaving its other side in shadows. Oedipus's powers, which result in his veneration as a benefactor of the city-state, are dangerously active. A lifelong bearer of pollution, Oedipus's *daimōn* regularly is associated with the Erinyes, whose invasion of the house of Labdacus can be traced to the familial murders. Thus, if Oedipus has led an extraordinary life that ends with an equally extraordinary death—his body a salvific presence for Athens—we err if we forget that "extraordinary" in the Greek context is fraught with danger.[24] As Sarah Iles Johnston points out, Oedipus could yet send disease and madness against Athens just as surely as he could offer protection under the seal of the Olympian gods. Indeed, the hero narratives of ancient Greece regularly emphasize as vitally important that a hero's remains rest comfortably in the ground of his native home. If the hero is buried elsewhere, his ghostly presence may harm his hosts.[25] Ismene and Antigone attest to peril when they despair over their father's death in a foreign land and entreat Theseus to take them to Oedipus's grave.[26] That "home" for Oedipus has always featured disordered familial relationships exacerbates their anxiety. Although Theseus attempts to appease the sisters, telling them that he promised Oedipus he would inform no one the location of the burial site, the play ends without offering evidence that Oedipus is at rest. Oedipus remains among the "restless dead," as Johnston argues. Furthermore, the chorus's prurient interest in rehearsing details of Oedipus's life inserts a persistent dissonance into the tragic text, pointing toward ongoing traumatic repetition. Casting an additional pall over the text is the hero's declaration that his "polluting daemon will live on forever in Thebes."[27] Moreover, as even Knox must acknowledge, Oedipus remains constrained to the very end by the ethics of helping friends and harming enemies,[28] evincing a commitment to a normative system that, as analyzed in the previous chapter, remains rooted in structures of mimetic rivalry, thereby promising ongoing replication of trauma.

But the most compelling evidence against locating transformational healing in *Oedipus at Colonus* is the curse he directs against his sons and brothers, Polyneices and Eteocles. Near the end of the play, Ismene initiates a conversation with Oedipus about Polyneices and Eteocles, reporting to Oedipus their warring competition for the throne of Thebes. She pointedly grounds their rivalry in a binding pollution, by which she accounts for their fratricidal desire. Oedipus, who is the source of this pollution, mirrors Polyneices's own anger when he describes Polyneices as "my worst enemy."[29] But Oedipus does not challenge the rivalry Ismene describes and bestows no deathbed compassion on Polyneices and Eteocles. Rather than deter Polyneices from embarking on a murderous emulation of his own life, Oedipus curses his sons, describing his words as "weapons" that will bring violence down on their heads. Oedipus's deadly words match Polyneices's and Eteocles's actions, for they take up arms against each other in fatal combat. Antigone's plea to her father that he listen to Polyneices and consider his supplicatory appeal both anticipates and recalls the ethical stance she assumes in *Antigone*. Breaking with the ethic of "helping friends and harming enemies," Antigone calls on her father to show mercy. Antigone reasons that Oedipus's sufferings because of the actions of his own mother and father should have taught him how to identify with the victim: "Come yield to us," she says, for "it would not be right for you to return evil for evil."[30] Although Oedipus professes to be "overcome" by Antigone's words, his words recall those he speaks against the Thebans when he decries their efforts to control his body after his death. "Let no one ever get control over my life!" he shouts.[31]

Throughout, Oedipus remains caught up in a rivalrous competition where his very body is treated as a trophy.[32] Even Theseus, who alone gazes on Oedipus as he departs the earth, does not suggest that he has witnessed a transformation. Theseus's final reflections on Oedipus continue to mirror Oedipus, for Theseus remains caught up in the ethic of helping friends and harming enemies. Promising to act in ways agreeable to the recently departed Oedipus, Theseus asserts that he will grant favor (*charis*) to those who help Athens.[33]

Writing of *Oedipus at Colonus*, Girard confirms that Oedipus experiences no transforming moments as his life draws to a close. He remains always within an economy of scapegoating. Prime evidence, for Girard, comes in looking at the role that Oedipus plays for the Thebans and Athenians. Girard recognizes that Oedipus's life story embodies the stereotypes[34] of scapegoating: he is the polluting monster who must be expunged from the community *and* the king whose body will save the city. Girard explains that the community that attributes peace to the victim remains ignorant of the mechanism of violent unanimity operative among them. He writes:

> At the supreme moment of the crisis, the very instant when reciprocal violence is abruptly transformed into unanimous violence, the two faces of violence seem to be juxtaposed; the extremes meet. The surrogate victim serves as catalyst in this metamorphosis. And in performing this function he seems to combine in his person the most pernicious and most beneficial aspect of violence. He becomes the incarnation, as it were, of a game men feign to ignore, one whose basic rules are indeed unknown to them: the game of their own violence.[35]

Substantive change cannot be tracked from *Oedipus the King* to *Oedipus at Colonus*. Oedipus's story remains subject to a double telling; the face of the polluting monster and blind savior are one. Girard submits that the exile of Oedipus has been "good," but only as "amputation of a gangrenous limb is 'good' for an afflicted body."[36] After all, trauma persists after an infected limb has been severed from the body; the amputation creates a new wound.

Not only do Girard's insights about *Oedipus the King* and *Oedipus at Colonus* prove helpful to my efforts to reflect on trauma in the Theban plays, but also they illuminate Antigone's central place within these tragedies. That Girard is a useful guide is, at first, surprising. After all, in *Violence and the Sacred* and *Oedipus Unbound*, Girard all but ignores *Antigone*, focusing instead on *Oedipus the King* and *Oedipus at Colonus* and arguing that they do not break with sacrificial myth.[37] As I have already noted, an extended discussion of *Antigone* is found only in *Things Hidden since the Foundation of the World*, where Girard valorizes Antigone, likening her to "the most perfect *figura Christi* of the ancient world."[38] Girard never expressly reassesses his position that Sophocles remains caught in a sacrificial universe in light of new evidence from *Antigone*. Nevertheless, observations that Girard makes in *Oedipus Unbound* seemingly allude to Antigone, as if foreshadowing his comments in *Things Hidden since the Foundation of the World*.[39]

Specifically, in the course of explaining how tragedy rectifies (*rectifie*) myth,[40] Girard suggests that, for tragedy not only to break with myth but also to expose it, tragedy must escape the "bad reciprocity" that condemns the house of Labdacus to continued violence. Someone in tragedy must "accept the role of victim."[41] Girard asserts that one who accepts the role of consenting victim is not masochistic; rather, his or her actions follow on a prior recognition that sacrifice ends only when we enter a new space. For Girard, there is only one place where the truth of scapegoating is revealed, and it is not a space occupied by the sacrificer. The revelatory space belongs only to the victim.[42] The shift toward the victim, which Girard claims begins in *Oedipus the King* and continues in *Oedipus at Colonus*, is the "march beneath the unthinkable."[43] But in *Oedipus Unbound*, Girard asserts that Sophocles falls short of a vision that would clearly show the "consent of the scapegoat."[44] Sophocles "arrives obscurely at a domain that is closed to Greek thought." Remaining only "implicit" in Sophocles, identification with the scapegoat awaits "Jewish prophetism" and Christianity.[45] Nevertheless, when Girard writes of conditions necessary for the sacrificial economy to be challenged and contends that such a scandal awaits the arrival of one who will step forth as a victim, he shows tragedy *making space for the victim*. In *Oedipus Unbound*, Girard claims Sophocles locates this space but leaves it empty, for Sophocles's storytelling remains tethered to myth. However, in *Things Hidden since the Foundation of the World*, Girard qualifies his earlier assertion in order to name one occupant of that space—Antigone. From within that domain, Antigone evinces a clear and distinct vision that enables her to embody an antisacrificial stance.[46] Unlike Oedipus, who does not escape the constraints of a sacrificial economy in his ascent to the hero cult, Antigone sees *and* acts differently in the tragedy that bears her name. Antigone speaks out from the wound, breaking through trauma to healing.

The Key to *Antigone*

Before taking up the task of explaining how Antigone moves beyond sacrifice, I want to further secure an interpretive approach to the Theban cycle that accords to Antigone a definitive role. I do so by establishing additional reasons to be skeptical of any traumatic reading of the Theban plays that would focus on *Oedipus at Colonus* but neglect *Antigone*. These reasons emerge when I consider the *order of composition* and the *narrative content* of the plays that constitute the Theban cycle.[47] Sophocles wrote *Antigone* first in the sequence of plays that include *Oedipus the King* and *Oedipus at*

Colonus; yet the narrative chronology of the plays begins with *Oedipus the King*, moves to *Oedipus at Colonus*, and ends with *Antigone*. A traumatic reading of the Theban plays that starts with *Oedipus the King* and concludes with *Oedipus at Colonus* necessarily leaves out *Antigone*. The first composed of the Theban plays, *Antigone* predates a trauma that originates in events recorded in *Oedipus the King*. And, in respect to the narrative chronology of the plays, *Antigone* postdates any resolution of trauma to which *Oedipus at Colonus* might attest. Even though Oedipus clearly is beset by trauma in *Oedipus the King*, if Oedipus plays a *central* role in a traumatic reading of the Theban cycle, Antigone seemingly plays no role at all. But the argument that I introduced in the previous chapter and seek to advance here, building on Girard's affirmation of Antigone as a postsacrificial exemplar, requires that I read the Theban cycle in ways that acknowledge Antigone's role in a movement from trauma to healing, from sacrifice to postsacrificial community. But if *Oedipus the King* and *Oedipus at Colonus* dominate a traumatic reading of the plays, Antigone is the odd woman out.

I propose we not assume that the compositional timeline of the Theban plays matches the timeline for Sophocles's revelatory insights. If *Oedipus at Colonus* is Sophocles's last word on the house of Labdacus, it need not be his definitive word. Assuredly, Sophocles does recast myth when he writes the plays that comprise the Theban cycle. But I detect no compelling grounds for asserting that Sophocles's rectification of myth is least developed in *Antigone* and most developed in *Oedipus at Colonus*. Another scenario is possible: a youthful Sophocles records the most profound insights of his life in *Antigone*, the first play he writes in the Theban cycle. Sophocles uses the dramatic trajectory of *Oedipus the King* and *Oedipus at Colonus* to rehearse the revelatory insights that he already has discovered and to which *Antigone* attests. When we take this perspective on the *compositional timeline* of the plays, the *narrative timeline* of the plays begins in mimetic rivalry with *Oedipus the King* and moves forward with *Oedipus of Colonus*, gradually exposing generative violence and embracing the transformative vision of *Antigone*—again and for the first time.

Significantly, I find strong support in Girard's work for analyzing the Theban cycle from a perspective grounded in a revelatory rehearsal that reserves a central place for *Antigone* and its transformative vision. Girard's *Oedipus Unbound* offers insights about the cyclical configuration of narratives that open up Sophocles's Theban cycle to my interpretation of *Antigone*. These insights emerge when I examine what Girard writes in *Oedipus Unbound* about Sophocles's *Oedipus the King* and *Oedipus at Colonus*. Explicitly juxtaposing Proust's *In Search of Lost Time* with these tragedies, Girard writes that *Oedipus the King* and *Oedipus at Colonus* "allow us to assemble and to articulate all the results of the novelistic analysis."[48] Connections that Girard draws between Proust's novel and these two tragedies support my effort to apply to the Theban cycle a corporeal hermeneutics similar to that which guided my discussion of *In Search of Lost Time*. In doing so, I necessarily move beyond Girard's own observations in *Oedipus Unbound*, which, all but bypassing *Antigone*, focus on *Oedipus the King* and *Oedipus at Colonus*.[49] Nevertheless, when read with an open regard for their potential application to *Antigone*, Girard's comments on these two Theban plays cast light on the singular role *Antigone* plays in the rectification of myth in all three tragedies.

Let's take up Girard's discussion as he compares the journey Proust takes with his novel with the travels of a mythic hero. He asserts that the novelist attains transformative awareness "via the other."[50] True insight in writing emerges when an artist deciphers signs that, previously understood by him to apply to another, are now recognized to be "addressed to the self." Girard notes that, in Proust's early writings, Proust is caught up in dualism: Proust's heroes, set at arm's length, are wholly positive or entirely negative. Not catching sight of himself in the mirror of his doubles, Proust's own desire remains unfounded in his work. As a consequence, his writing lacks perspicacity.[51] Proust's transformation occurs when he recognizes himself in those of whom he writes. Whether he is writing of the snob or the wrongdoer, "signs of the Other have become signs of the Self."[52] At first, Proust's writing attests to his developing awareness in the very process of living through it. However, *Time Regained*, the "definitive version" of Proust's earlier work,[53] shows Proust attaining an insightful perspective on his conversion. Proust no longer only *reflects* illusion and its transformation; he also *represents* transformation. In moving forward on a path from reflection to representation, Proust has experienced "identification with the wicked Other which implies death." Girard locates similar patterns of change in tragedy, comparing Proust with the hero who "is sick, wounded, mutilated, and dying." In tragedy, as in the novel, an ordeal is undergone. Face-to-face with death, one experiences the invasion of the other. Identifying with the other in its wounded and mutilated state, dying with the other, one finds oneself subject to an "invasion by a truth that the previous existence refused."[54]

Examining the novel more closely, Girard wants to know why *Time Regained* holds the key for understanding "dying with the other." Girard writes that a novelistic masterpiece seemingly contradicts authorial intention. A writer confuses "finishing" a work with its publication. Sometimes first attempts at writing result in failure, and the author despairs. Unmindful of the destination toward which he or she is headed, the writer is unaware that, like the writer's hero, the writer will sink in a world of illusion and experience death; resurrection will transpire only at the end.[55] Focusing his attention on what he sees to be the definitive achievement of the novelist, notwithstanding the twists and turns of the writer's journey, Girard observes that the novelist always "rectifies his work" from the conclusion. The "omega immediately precedes the alpha."[56] Indeed, Girard asserts: "Nothing in the order of creation is closer to the conclusion, therefore, than the beginning, understood henceforth as a new beginning. If the inspiration is born at one extremity of the work it is at the other extremity that its effects are felt the most quickly and directly."[57]

Offering a perspective in contrast with that of a novice writer who would map his or her writing along a linear trajectory, Girard observes the writer's work circling around itself. Assuredly, the novel may be permeated at the beginning with the spirit of origin; its end with the sense that what has transpired in its chapters is now surpassed. But Girard asserts that the novel is "transcendence itself transcended." Captured by novelistic genius is an "aesthetic and spiritual movement" that does not follow the "chronology of the story unfolding before the reader." For truly, the novelist has not moved in "a straight line leading from beginning to end." Instead, the novelist's path resembles a spiral: the line curves back, and two extremities move toward each other. Not meeting, not forming a circle, these extremities are superimposed in such a way as to leave a gap. In this space, the author preserves transcendence in the spiraling movement itself.[58]

Seeking to understand this process of transcendence and link it with death, Girard once again reflects simultaneously on the novel and on tragedy. Drawing us into *Oedipus the King*, Girard rehearses its story line. Oedipus sits on the throne of Thebes; he has vanquished the Sphinx. All is well, but for a lingering plague. Believing that the plague is the gods' response to an offending pollution, Oedipus sets out on what he perceives to be a straight path to hunt down the guilty party. He is wholly unaware that the path is about to curve. He cannot imagine that his march toward the truth will eventually lead him to circle around, finally to face himself as the polluting monster he has long hunted.[59] As is the case for the novelist Girard has previously described, so also for the tragic Oedipus: "The conclusion delivers the founding truth."[60] As in the novel, so also in Sophocles's tragedy, signs and oracles reverse while curses become blessings. The novel is thus shown to offer "the intersubjective content and even the form of Sophocles' conclusion."[61]

For Girard, both tragedy and the novel unfold in a spiral pattern. Moreover, in describing this pattern, Girard sees in the novel and tragedy an identical break in the spiral that captures and preserves transcendent movement. For Girard, "the oracle represents the gap between the two extremities of the novel" and "prefigures the catastrophic transcendence of an illusory world."[62] The "oracle" of *In Search of Lost Time* is the madeleine. A bridge to truth, it appears at the beginning of the novel as a "glimmer of novelistic grace" and a "mysterious foretaste" of effects that will be established definitively in *Time Regained*.[63] In *Oedipus the King*, the oracle is "nothing else but the voice of the other."[64] Not the independent Delphic entity of myth, the true oracle of tragedy is subject to repeated incarnations in Laius, Oedipus, Creon, and Tiresias who remain caught up in denying its voice. Only Sophocles, alone in arriving a domain otherwise closed to Greek thought, hints at oracular truth: an identification with the scapegoat necessary to transcendence.[65] For both Proust and Sophocles, the oracle is crucial to the unfolding of the truth: indeed, in functioning as a placeholder, the oracle gap establishes *a protective space for the very act of transcendence*.[66] That is why oracles are ambiguous: they "encode the very act of transcendence," precluding those who encounter them from "stabilizing" them within a controlled interpretive nexus.[67]

Surprisingly, having traced so closely similarities in the novel and Greek tragedy, as Girard concludes his comparative analysis, he dissents from the argument he has taken such care to construct. He suggests that the transformative effects of the spiritual movement he has traced through *In Search of Lost Time* are not observed in *Oedipus at Colonus*, for this tragedy is "a perpetual return backwards." *Oedipus at Colonus* only *symbolizes* a revelatory reversal that Proust commits to *sign*. *Oedipus at Colonus* has an ending but no conclusion: "The content of the revelation remains undecided."[68] Because Girard examines closely only *Oedipus the King* and *Oedipus at Colonus* in his search for the spiral pattern that he associates with artistic transcendence, Girard rightly asserts that Sophocles's art falls short of that transcendence. *Oedipus at Colonus* remains an unfinished work. But were Girard to have included *Antigone* in his discussion, he would have discovered in *Antigone* the spiral pattern and the encoding of spiritual movement in the face of death that he has sought and not found in *Oedipus at Colonus*. Girard would have been able to bring to affirmative closure his definitive comparison of the novel and tragedy.

Taking up Girard's argument where he has dropped it, I offer a traumatic reading of the Theban cycle that centers on *Antigone*. Girard's comparative analysis of the novel and tragedy remains of supreme salience. Because Girard has joined seemingly dissimilar features of the novel and tragedy, *superimposing compositional order on narrative chronology,* Girard has discovered *the* key that opens up the entire Theban cycle to interpretation. Of course, Girard has used this key only to unlock *Oedipus the King* and *Oedipus at Colonus*. Grasping this key where Girard has left it on the pages of *Oedipus Unbound*, I now use it to open *Antigone*, overlaying the *compositional order* of the plays on their *tragic content*: The first of the Theban plays to be written by Sophocles, *Antigone* also is encountered last in the narrative chronology of the house of Labdacus. Thus, *Antigone* is both the end and the beginning—the omega and the alpha—of the Theban cycle. Comprising dual extremities of this tragic sequence, the annunciatory sign that is *Antigone* opens out on transcendence when viewed in light of revelations that, thanks to superimposition, are both later and earlier than *Oedipus the King* and *Oedipus at Colonus*. Most significant, when I lay compositional history over narrative content, the "perpetual return backward" that Girard has ascribed to *Oedipus at Colonus* is interrupted. Breaking with a traumatic repetition of mimetic rivalry that has persisted in *Oedipus at Colonus*, notwithstanding changes in Oedipus, *Antigone* captures transcendence in the act.

My analysis necessarily is linked with a different reading of oracles within the Theban cycle than is offered by Girard. The oracles on which I focus are the Sphinx and Niobe. The Sphinx, as Mitchell has so cogently observed, is "a more primitive version of Antigone."[69] As suggested above, the Sphinx's desire sets the stage for the tragic quandary of Sophocles's Antigone: how are

differences that fade into an annihilating sameness and a sameness that transforms into threatening differences negotiated in a family, in a society? With
the Sphinx, no answers emerge. In this dynamic, the Sphinx is a "failed revelation." Even so, the Sphinx also is an annunciatory sign; her role and meaning will be altered by a more definitive revelation. Sophocles introduces the
Sphinx having already encountered a fulfilled revelation in the composition
of *Antigone*. But with the Sphinx, he makes a new beginning, spiraling forward to produce a cycle of tragedies in which Antigone can be encountered
again by those who have journeyed with her in full aesthetic and spiritual
movement.[70] More crucially, as the two extremities of the novel—*Antigone*
read *first* within the compositional structure of the Theban plays and read *last*
within the narrative chronology of these plays—spiral around each other, the
gap between them is bridged by a second oracle: Niobe. Niobe is the rock to
which Antigone compares herself even as the chorus suggests that Antigone
has stumbled against another stone: the high altar of Dike (justice).[71]

What is the significance of the twin juxtapositions in the text of the stone
edifice of justice and the rock that is Niobe? According to Girard, stones serve
as "symbolic concretions of a mimetic stumbling block" when they appear in
a text. Because mimetic rivalry is a relational structure fundamental to human
society, no one escapes it. Instead we are all imprisoned in it; for that very
reason, our capacity to imagine alternative modes of relationship is "severely
limited." Citing *The Winter's Tale*, *Othello*, and the Christian gospel, Girard
writes that stones appear in a text at a moment of transformation: someone
"stumbles" against a stone, experiencing a form of physical and/or spiritual
death, and a *revelatory exposure of sacrifice* that poses a challenge to the entire
system of mimetic rivalry follows. In the Christian Gospels, the women who
come to the tomb on Easter morning find the stone removed and the tomb
empty. In *The Winter's Tale*, a stone "rebukes" Leontes; in *Othello*, the Moor
feels his heart turn to stone. In each case, the revelatory moment announced
by a stone exposes the "truth of all tragedy, the ultimate truth of sacrificial
culture." As a consequence, instead of turning to a scapegoat to discharge
the violent outcomes of rivalrous histories, these figures turn away. In each
case, a stone stands as oracular witness to transformation as the figures who
encounter "stone" find that the *skandalon* is now their own responsibility.[72]
Niobe—emblematic of sacrificial currents of sameness and difference within
the mimetic economy of the family—is a silent stone.

Mark Griffith's insightful commentary on Niobe in *Antigone* complements Girard's insights. Griffith suggests that the petrification of Niobe is a distinctive form of death. Not strictly speaking a death by violence or disease, petrification falls outside clear categories. It is "an indeterminate transition from a living to an inanimate state."[73] As such, Niobe's death can be said to point toward the distinctiveness of Antigone's own death. Not properly understood in the register of sacrifice, Antigone's death is an "indeterminate transition"; for those steeped in the traditions of sacrifice and scapegoating, her death cannot be understood. But for Antigone, "living neither among the mortals nor as a shade among the shades, neither with the living nor with the dead,"[74] the rock of Niobe bridges the omega and alpha of her life. Oracular in form, the rock marks a moment of recognition: Antigone's "ordeal, death, becomes the invasion of the Other, the invasion of a truth that the previous existence refused."[75]

The chorus, caught in the intensifying currents of mimetic rivalry signaled by Antigone and Creon's ongoing conflict, misses the significance of Niobe and the edifice of justice against which Antigone stumbles. For them, each is a *skandalon*.[76] Niobe is no oracle foreshadowing revelation, and Antigone is only a scapegoat who must take her family's pollution to her tomb in order to save Thebes and its order of justice. But we need not stand with the chorus if we are able to receive the stone of Niobe as an oracle and to join Antigone on a journey away from sacrifice enacted in the shadow of Theban justice and toward a postsacrificial stance.[77]

Having established a foundation for a traumatic reading of *Antigone,* in order to explicate how we might follow Antigone along her path forward to emancipation from trauma, I turn to Caruth in order to recall her careful delineation of problems besetting time that perpetuate trauma. She points out that, when Freud studies dreams of traumatic events, he discovers that the fright one experiences is not so much associated with the violence once has endured as with its aftermath: one is frightened because one has awakened to an event that has happened without one's full knowledge. One is not traumatized by one's brush with death but by one's brush with life: one has gotten away and does not how or why.[78] If we apply Caruth's insights to the Theban cycle, we can understand better how trauma is associated with a wound, and we can locate evidence of that wound as well as testimony to healing in *Antigone.*

Oedipus the King shows a wounded man, but Oedipus is never released from his trauma—not in *Oedipus the King* or in *Oedipus at Colonus*. Instead, trauma moves to Antigone, Oedipus's sister, his daughter. Like Oedipus— her brother, her father—Antigone's life is shaped by trauma as she *circles a future that cannot be claimed*. But only in *Antigone* is *mimetic desire exposed as a false quest to name this future*. Only in *Antigone* does a member of the traumatized family of Labdacus move out of a sacrificial orbit to experience a transformation that promises access to time. *Antigone* shows that mimetic desire in its most lethal expression exacerbates the wound in our being; at its best, desire only bandages the wound.

Most significantly, as Antigone enters a domain closed to sacrifice, *Antigone* demonstrates that only intimacy heals, opening us to time—a time for others lived in accord with an ethics of intimacy. As a consequence, Antigone enables us to understand aspects of the Theban cycle that otherwise we are blocked from understanding. In her suffering, she confronts us with a profound paradox: an immediate encounter with violence may take the form of belated experience. As Caruth observes in her study of trauma, a violent experience may touch us most directly when we are constrained by our inability to know it. Attesting to how violence exceeds what may be seen and known, traumatic repetitions intrude into our lives while remaining unavailable to our immediate understanding.[79] How is it that what we cannot grasp becomes foundational to our very identity? Caruth suggests that the belated immediacy of violence shows that trauma is fundamentally not *epistemological* in nature but *ethical*: We are awakened from the unknowingness of trauma not because we are released from previously repressed memories but because *we hear a call of another*.[80] Trauma's hold on us is not broken when we obtain knowledge of events and persons of which we previously were unaware; rather, we are freed when we awaken to an "urgent responsibility" to the other and become that person's witness.

Caruth's insights illuminate Antigone's experience, attuning us to her voice. Antigone speaks from a wound, initially in a voice that alludes to a contagion of trauma, a repetition of suffering across generations of the house of Labdacus. Eventually, out of her suffering, Antigone responds to her kin when she hears his call. Antigone's mourning permits the reliving and reworking of loss associated with traumatic violence in order to repair a wounded existence. Eventually, her mourning merges with a larger creative process—an ethical imperative for the other.[81] In the next chapter, as I join theories of trauma and mourning sketched here with Girard's depiction of artistic transcendence, I am able at last to show *how* sacrifice in *Antigone* is transformed into positive mimesis. As Antigone mourns her brother and performs burial rituals for him, she reworks a loss that belongs also to Oedipus (although he does not know it). A corporeal hermeneutics oriented toward kinesis guides my reflections, facilitating my efforts to show that affective and bodily features of Antigone's mourning play a critical role in the transformation attested to by *Antigone's* tragic narrative and experienced by its audience. Just as trauma is contagious, so also is healing when sensory experience reverses the effects of trauma and opens up a future to intimacy.[82]

CHAPTER 6

Antigone and the Ethics
of Intimacy

At once she brought in her hands thirsty dust,
and from the well-wrought brazen urn that she was carrying
she poured over the corpse a threefold libation.

—Sophocles, *Antigone*

Traumatic violence has caught Oedipus in an ongoing repetition of mimetic rivalry, rooting him in an eternal present. Compellingly demonstrated not only in *Oedipus the King* but also in *Oedipus at Colonus*, his trauma is visceral. For Oedipus's suffering is written on his body: his unsightly face, expressed pain, and profound exhaustion offer graphic testimony.[1] Others reflect back to Oedipus their horror: Oedipus *is* a polluting presence.[2] Attentive to Oedipus's distress, in this chapter I examine the representation of trauma as well as actions that promise to break open constraints on Oedipus, permitting the transformation of Oedipus's memories.[3] In *Oedipus at Colonus*, these actions occur in ritual. Indeed, as Julia Kristeva observes, the purification rite described in *Oedipus at Colonus* is notable for providing us "with one of the most detailed descriptions of purification in classical literature."[4] Although the ritual in which Oedipus takes part does not result in a magical healing of trauma, he can at last bear his wounds.[5]

To be sure, and notwithstanding the rich descriptions of supplicatory ritual in *Oedipus at Colonus*, Oedipus's experience at the sacred grove remains shrouded in mystery. Even as the rituals enable him to bear his suffering, we receive no assurances that Oedipus is freed of the trauma that has beset him throughout his life. Theseus, who alone observes Oedipus's passing, is uncertain about what he has observed. Moreover, Theseus appears to suggest that Oedipus remains in a sacrificial orbit, for Theseus understands that, if he keeps secret the location of Oedipus's grave, Oedipus's body will protect Athens.[6] But even as *Oedipus at Colonus* does not definitively break with a sacrificial economy, it establishes preconditions for transformation in *Antigone*. A point of kinesic connection for *Antigone*'s audience, ritual constitutes one of the only moments of action in a tragic play that sometimes is cited for its lack of action.[7] Thus, ritual in *Oedipus at Colonus* readies us for a transformation that comes to the fore in *Antigone* when healing powers of ritual evoke "graceful possibilities of imagination."[8]

Turning my attention from *Oedipus at Colonus* to *Antigone* in the second half of this chapter, I explore these graceful possibilities. Throughout *Antigone*, Antigone's imagination risks radical truncation. So also does her speech risk fracture as she struggles to name and offer testimony to generational order that has been implemented only in criminal form in the house of Labdacus. But, when Antigone performs rituals over her brother's body, a barrier of sensation and knowledge that has shielded her from full exposure to trauma is breached, becoming an unexpected instrument of healing that opens onto intimacy. Antigone surpasses mimetic violence and sacrifice when she takes up and transforms the visceral memories that have accrued to Oedipus in the sacred grove at Colonus and whose traumatic form Antigone has inherited. This healing, attested to and witnessed by a revelatory process that has spiraled around and through the three plays that comprise the Theban cycle, elicits a capacity for nonviolent existence that has eluded Antigone and the house of Labdacus previously. No longer mired in traumatic repetition, Antigone, "*figura Christi* of the ancient world," ushers in healing that brings to view a nonsacrificial ethics.[9] Access to an intimate domain that has been blocked in the wake of trauma is opened up, as Antigone's actions enable those who hear of them to imagine and claim forms of human community that are not bound by sacrifice.

My analysis, which focuses on the decisive role of rituals in exposing a sacrificial economy, builds on the multivalent possibilities of ritual. I both confirm Girard's analysis of ritual and challenge it in order to augment it. In *Things Hidden since the Foundation of the World*, Girard writes that rituals "reproduce the mimetic crisis"; moreover, rituals also attest to the resolution of that crisis, moving in microcosmic mimicry from "conflictual disintegration of the community into social collaboration."[10] Thus, in rituals, frenetic actions and discordant sounds transition to a delicate choreography in which individuals, previously at each other's throats, engage in expressive movement framed by mutual recognition. But Girard limits the potential of ritual to play a role in the reconstitution of society in the wake of sacrifice.[11] For Girard, rituals, however peaceful, always harbor a propensity to devolve into renewed violence. Rituals remain vulnerable to expropriation for violent purposes because no harmless mimesis exists.[12]

In his later writings, Girard qualifies his views on mimesis, clarifying that a sacrificial nexus is not wholly definitive of human existence. Girard finds within the biblical traditions "non-rivalrous imitation" or what some scholars of mimetic theory call "positive mimesis."[13] However, when Girard discusses how individuals may choose Christ or a Christlike individual as a model for nonrivalrous desire, *he does not rehabilitate ritual*. Ritual remains solely a feature of a sacrificial economy.[14] As a consequence, missing from Girard's reflections is any analysis of ritual that would highlight the work that ritual can do to establish transformative conditions for nonrivalrous desire. If trauma names the violence done to us by a scapegoating mechanism in society, graceful transformation also catches up bodies; indeed, bodywork is essential to the transformation of traumatic violence.[15]

Mitchell's psychoanalytic theory provides a vocabulary for describing the visceral nature of Oedipus's trauma as well as the healing effects of ritual. For victims of trauma, memory regresses into perception. At the actual moment that a person is traumatized, both perception and memory are in abeyance. Caught up in the experience, all capacity for memory as representation is eradicated. In its place, as described by Juliet Mitchell, are perceptions that appear with "a vividness that is near hallucinatory." And these perceptions may be ongoing, interrupting our days and tormenting our sleep. Even so, these sensory traces of trauma are not memories. They are "iconic": in their distorted repetitiveness, they flood their victim with too much perception.[16]

Mitchell notes that when object relations theorists reflect on trauma, they focus on interactions between one who has been traumatized and that individual's analyst, seeking conditions under which memories can be elicited by the analyst. Memories that release one from the repetition of trauma emerge when the analyst and analysand establish a relationship that can bear that trauma. In the absence of such a relationship, object relations theorists believe, memories "flower over and over again along the same trace marks."[17]

Bolens's theory of embodied cognition aligns with Mitchell and accounts for the process by which traumatic perception, which overwhelms its victims, is countered by healing practices. Bolens has suggested that we have no memories in the absence of kinesis. Although Bolens considers only narrative memory that works positively to connect us with others, grounds exist for claiming that kinesis plays a strong role in traumatic experiences as well. However, kinesis that supports the "I can" of embodied agency is, in the case of trauma, embodied as an "I can't." As Serene Jones observes, trauma fractures speech and action, resulting in existence "marked by fear and constructed for protection."[18] Thus, traumatic kinesis, which Mitchell has described as repetitively tracking a constant set of sensorial markers, subjects Oedipus to repetitive suffering. Oedipus embodies an "I can't." Restorative kinesis, exemplified by rituals in *Oedipus at Colonus* and *Antigone*, opens up possibilities for healing. An "I can" opens onto a future.[19]

Bolens, citing Beilock and Lyons, offers a theory of motor resonance that helps us understand how *Oedipus at Colonus* displays multivalent possibilities of kinesis. Kinesic responsiveness, to which the tragedy attests, establishes conditions for its author and audience (as viewers or readers) to perceive Oedipus's suffering as well as his possibilities for transformation. In what follows, I show that Ruth Padel's insightful analysis of contagion and pollution in Greek tragedy accounts for kinesic elements of trauma in Greek tragedy. I indicate too how narrative kinesis, which Bolens has associated with mirror neural mechanisms, comes to the fore when rituals interrupt trauma and support transformation.[20] Most significantly, gestures take on meaning as somatosensory images are formed in the presence of another. As Bolens has said, quoting Giorgio Agamben, "the gesture is . . . communication of communicability."[21]

For persons beset by mimetic rivalries, healing rituals provide for connection with the being of another. In *Oedipus at Colonus*, these rituals establish the possibility of an ethical connection with others; subsequently, Antigone's rituals on behalf of Polyneices create that connection.

An Unlighted Foundation: Trauma and Supplication at Colonus

Rituals frame the beginning and end of *Oedipus at Colonus*. Concerned with pollution and death, these rites situate Oedipus within a traumatic narrative. Juxtaposed to the heroic narrative or "master thesis" of *Oedipus at Colonus*, these rituals suggest a "counter-thesis."[22] Oriented toward the body and its pain, this counterthesis attests to Oedipus's traversal of a path almost invisible to those whose eyes are riveted on the suffering old man who they would see become a hero. The messenger who reports on Oedipus's departure from the world points to this alternative course when he observes that Oedipus could have been taken away by "some escort come from the gods or the unlighted foundation of the earth that belongs to those below, opening in kindness."[23] This "unlighted foundation that belongs to those below" summons our attention as we seek in the text evidence of an affective and bodily healing of Oedipus's suffering, which has condemned him always to circle a future he is unable to name, to replicate mimetic violence from which he is unable to escape. The rituals of supplication in *Oedipus at Colonus* are directed toward those to whom the earth belongs: the Erinyes, the Semnai Theai, and the Eumenides.[24] Although of ancient origin, these goddesses attest to trauma. Indeed, of the three, the Erinyes fully embody the iconic power Mitchell attributes to the hallucinatory flood of traumatic perceptions. Examining their powers as well as those of the Semnai Theai and the Eumenides, I show how they illumine a traumatic reading of *Oedipus at Colonus*.

The profile of the Erinyes is established in the text of *Antigone*, read first *or* last in the Theban cycle. Their presence in *Oedipus at Colonus* is best understood in that light. In *Antigone* we read:

> From ancient times I see the troubles of the dead of the Labdacus house
> falling hard upon one another, nor does one generation release another,

but some one of the gods shatters them, and they have no means of deliverance. For latterly the light spread out above the last root in the house of Oedipus; it too is mown down by the bloody chopper of the infernal gods, folly in speech and the Erinyes in the mind (*phrenes*).[25]

The chorus sings of an unending, multigenerational contagion that infects speech as well as mind. Padel notes that, in ancient Greece, *phrenes* are associated with multiple internal organs. *Phrenes* are vessel-like, passive receptacles of emotions, practical ideas, and knowledge that are placed in humans by the gods. Not dualistically distinguished from the body, the visceral elements of *phrenes* are well captured by contemporary phrases such as "heartsick" or "torn with grief."[26] Moreover, far from belonging to an individual, as does the contemporary mind, *phrenes* can flow out from one, and *phrenes* also can be penetrated by outside forces. To have *phrenes* is to be in control; to lose *phrenes* is to become mad.[27] When the Erinyes invade, the permeable boundaries of *phrenes* are crossed, with disastrous results.[28]

Erinyes are associated with winds that buffet us and turn *phrenes* toward madness. After Antigone utters her most famous lines, attesting to her singular commitment to her brother, Polyneices, the chorus alerts us to her madness: "The same blasts of the same winds of the spirit still possess her."[29] When they do not permeate our being as wind, the Erinyes swoop among us. Winged creatures, they bombard and seize us, attacking from inside and outside.[30] Linked with darkness, females, and pollution, the Erinyes are a most powerful expression of a *daimōn*. Although the term *daimōn* is inclusive of the Olympian gods, in the tragic context explored here, it most often is linked with chthonic powers. A divinity that "interferes with human lives and minds,"[31] a daemon, like the Erinyes, has superior mobility. Threatening from all sides, daemons abound in tragedy, conveying a sense of a hunted world.[32] When grouped together as concentrated forms of danger, the daemons are almost always female: Erinyes, Gorgons, and Harpies.[33] Daemons show that the divine and the human are not dualistically juxtaposed; rather, in fifth century BCE Greece, all of existence is "naturally charged with the gods." They are in every activity; their power to benefit and harm is everywhere.[34] Emotions and feelings do not stay in place: they may be hurled through the air as Fear or Terror, and they may attack us in creaturely form.

Markers of the daemonic appear on the body as skin ulcers and are expressed in madness, terror, and fear.[35]

The epics establish a context for the Erinyes' ongoing life in tragedy.[36] The Erinyes are especially associated with intrafamilial relationships and strife within the home. Taking a special interest in conflict among blood kin, the Erinyes are present also when *threats are made to a mother-child bond.*[37] They feature in conflict among children, *inhabiting sibling relationships,* especially where these relationships are rent by jealousy and anger.[38] That they activate curses is undoubtedly the case: in the epics, the word *Erinyes* aligns with "curse." Even so, their destructive powers, once loosed, are dangerously free-floating and unpredictable. No clear pattern of justice is detectable in the Erinyes' powerful actions.[39] In tragedy, beginning with the *Oresteia,* the Erinyes maintain their association with familial relationships gone wrong. When curses are hurled on the tragic stage, the Erinyes' power is at work; however, after the *Oresteia,* the Erinyes do not take to the stage. Hidden, they ambush *phrenes.* Working punitively in the mind, they are emblematic of damage that can inhere to a single act or lone word. Emerging microcosmically in this way, they assume mass as multiple external forces whose assaults leave everyone defenseless against them.[40]

Oriented by Padel to the ancient Greek experience of the Erinyes, we can better understand their role in *Oedipus at Colonus.* When Polyneices comes to his father to entreat him to stand with him against Eteocles, Polyneices's initial and concluding speeches reference the Erinyes. In pleading with his father, Polyneices acknowledges long odds, for he knows that what stands between him and his father is the curse of the Erinyes.[41] As Polyneices departs, resigned to the fate that awaits him in Thebes, he attributes his position once again to the Erinyes.[42] For his part, Oedipus references daemonic powers in his angry diatribe against Polyneices. Chastising his son for driving him from Thebes, Oedipus calls Polyneices a murderer and "no son of mine." Summoning his *daemon* to come fight with him and cursing his son, Oedipus proclaims that Polyneices and his brother will fall "polluted by bloodshed."[43] Unable to perceive his sons as kin, but only as polluting monsters (as Oedipus also has been seen to be through his life), in the span of a few strophes, Sophocles vividly portrays a fifth-century world riven with powerful daemonic presences. The Erinyes, experts in sibling rivalry, swoop down on the house of Labdacus, directing curses not only between the brothers Polyneices and Eteocles, but also between these brothers and their father/brother Oedipus.

The Erinyes, pollution, violence, and trauma comprise an experiential and thematic cluster in Greek tragedy. Writing of the Erinyes, Parker notes that the Erinyes are "animate agents of pollution." No difference exists between the effects of the Erinyes and those of pollution, for the operations of each are "co-extensive."[44] Thus, when Oedipus curses his sons, loosing a contagion that will later threaten Thebes, he cannot help but simultaneously invoke the Erinyes. Where there is pollution, we find the Erinyes; and, where we find the Erinyes, contagion also is at hand.

Padel explicitly aligns Erinyes and daemons with trauma when she describes the Erinyes as *daemons of the lasting reality of remembered hurt*.[45] The Erinyes well capture the form of traumatic memory. Unlike narrative memory, which is addressed to others and serves to create and sustain social connections, traumatic memory is inflexible and invariable. The work of traumatic memory is a solitary activity. Flowering over and over again upon itself, when one element of the traumatic memory is evoked, all others follow, including affective and motoric elements.[46] With her sensitivity to the embodied meanings preserved in the tragic text, with which audiences and readers resonate so powerfully, Padel's analysis wonderfully explicates how traumatic kinesis factors in narratives of suffering. The experience of trauma may be a solitary activity; however, when that trauma is brought forth by the Erinyes, the contagion they carry touches all.

In *Oedipus at Colonus*, the Erinyes are emblematic of mimetic violence that destroys relationships, creating monsters of those who would be fathers, sons, and brothers; however, the Erinyes also capture in extraordinarily ways how such violence seeps into the depths of one's being, giving rise to a pollution that is viscerally present in the bodies of the Erinyes' victims. Riven by traumatic memories, the house of Labdacus is plagued by madness. No poet has said it more powerfully than Sophocles: "Erinyes of *phrenes*."[47] With a single phrase, Sophocles captures in one frame winged creatures *and* the traumatized mind, locating "the whole lot, terrifyingly, in the mind as well as out of it." The Erinyes's violence is powerful, not only when it spirals out of control to devastate entire cities, but also when it turns round and burrows into a hapless victim, initiating self-destruction. The Erinyes, summoned by

Oedipus in his final rage against his sons, are shown to be central to *Oedipus at Colonus*. They figure in the trauma that has shaped his whole life, poisoning his relationships with his sons and brothers and contaminating his mind.

Notwithstanding the heroic narrative of *Oedipus at Colonus*, which would see Oedipus freed from his earthly suffering and welcomed by the Olympian gods, no fifth-century Greek audience would have missed the invisible presences that haunt him to the end. The audience would not have needed the Erinyes on stage in order to feel their presence. On edge, awaiting the inevitable flowering of daemonic powers once again, the audience would have been primed for further trauma. They would not have seen closure in Oedipus's departure from this world. Nor should we. We do not need to "believe" in the Erinyes to sense the deadly contagion associated with their names. Kinesis brings powerful metaphors to life as surely today as in ancient Greece. Thus, ever alert to *daemons* that haunt Oedipus and his children and siblings, ancients and moderns still anticipate how Sophocles ends his tragedy. *Oedipus at Colonus* does not conclude with Oedipus's being taken away by "either some escort come from the gods or the unlighted foundation of the earth that belongs to those below, opening in kindness." It ends with Antigone departing for Thebes in the hope that she may prevent another round of violence in an ongoing familial trauma: the slaughter of her brothers.[48]

Is there no revelatory break in *Oedipus at Colonus*? Are Knox, Zeitlin, and Segal wholly misguided when they ascribe heroic glory to Oedipus and celebrate his transfiguration from a polluted and accursed monster into a savior who confers blessings? No; if the Erinyes whom Oedipus summons point to ongoing trauma that does not end at Colonus, the other chthonic entities in *Oedipus at Colonus*—the Semnai Theai—do show that a path away from trauma emerges in the play. Whereas the Erinyes are animate agents of pollution, the Semnai Theai are associated with rituals that cleanse and heal. In his supplication at the sacred grove, Oedipus claims that what he says "will be full of sight."[49] The "all-seeing goddesses (*Semnai*)"[50] will receive him and confer sight on him.

In recognizing the import of the transition that takes place in Oedipus's move from Thebes to Colonus, Keltner and Kristeva highlight the wholly new territory to which Oedipus gains access. In this space of transformation, to which strangeness is central, the Semnai Theai offer shelter.[51] Keltner describes how *Oedipus at Colonus* stages strangeness. As the tragedy begins, the blind, limping Oedipus is a foreigner who declares in his first speech that Antigone and he have "come as strangers" to Colonus. But Oedipus is a foreigner not only to Colonus but also to Antigone, his sister and daughter. The incest that shadows them renders their identities to each other uncertain and alien. Oedipus and Antigone are joined in these first moments of the tragedy by a third individual identified by Oedipus as "stranger." In the conversation that ensues, each calls the other "stranger," creating an uncanny effect that extends outward to include not only to the chorus, who repeatedly call Oedipus a stranger, but also the sacred grove itself. Reminded by the chorus of the inviolable ground that is the home to the Semnai Theai, Oedipus nevertheless describes the grove as "a place of hospitality to strangers."[52]

Instrumental in enabling Oedipus to bear his trauma, if not to overcome it, these goddesses who offer hospitality to a stranger establish a relational context necessary for healing by setting the foundation for that transformation in Oedipus's tactile memories. After all, the hold trauma has on an individual is not severed by reflection. Just as trauma repeats itself through memories of the body, so also does healing take place not only when a story finally is told but also when a body offers up trauma for that reading.[53]

Lawrence Kirmayer helps us understand the role of the body in healing from trauma when he describes trauma in terms of a "landscape of memory." Traumatic memory transitions to narrative memory along a "metaphoric terrain that shapes the distance and effort required to remember affectively charged and socially defined events that initially may be vague, impressionist, or simply absent from memory."[54] These landscapes of memory provide grounds for *encountering the body of trauma*. Bolens suggests that kinesis drives narrative memory. Although she does not specifically address traumatic memory, Kirmayer's account supports the extension of Bolen's theory to include traumatic kinesis. Not only is a reworking of tactile memories critical for the break with traumatic perception that has locked the victim into a timeless present, but also these memories are prerequisite for reestablishing relationships. As Jennifer Griffiths notes, a central feature of trauma is that the traumatized body can be an object of dread and fear to those who encounter it. When others mirror trauma rather than offer healing witness, trauma is secured rather than interrupted.[55] The prurient attention by the chorus to the details of Oedipus's history,[56] articulated in a rapid-fire exchange of details, appear to consolidate rather than free Oedipus from traumatic memories. In order that trauma be interrupted and the truth of the past brought forward, the founding conditions of trauma must be halted. Oedipus, trapped in silence on a landscape of suffering, must be freed to meet and be recognized by others. Rituals, rather than dialogue, provide an intercorporeal and kinesic terrain in *Oedipus at Colonus* on which trauma can at last be born, opening up its victim to the other.[57]

These rituals are performed at the grove of the Semnai Theai, the nameless goddesses.[58] The rituals are performed by women; in *Oedipus at Colonus*, Ismene enters the most sacred area of the grove and prays on behalf of Oedipus. In performing the ritual, Ismene draws fresh water from a spring and pours libations into three bronze bowls. These bowls are crowned with wool from freshly shorn sheep. Ismene adds honey to the third bowl. No wine, which is the liquid used in sacrificial rituals, is used in libations for the Semnai Theai. Instead, the offering is comprised of a mixture of water, milk, and honey.[59] Rites for the Semnai Theai are performed in the spring and are associated with festivals that recall three stories of pollution: These stories, forming an etiology for the cult of the Semnai Theai,[60] also allude to stories that shape Oedipus's traumatic history. Affectively charged events are remembered with these stories—but at a distance from the trauma in which Oedipus and his family have been caught. In the first festival tale, Orestes is a supplicant seeking refuge in Athens. Orestes is hospitably received; however, because he is polluted, he is unable to share wine from a common jug. Everyone drinks from an individual container; so also in the festival of the Semnai Theai is this custom observed.[61] The second story also recalls pollution. Cylon attempts to seize the Acropolis but is attacked. He and his supporters seek sanctuary at the altars of the Semnai Theai; however, only those who appeal to the female devotees of the Semnai Theai are spared. The others are killed.[62] The third story focuses on the pollution of Athens that ensues as a consequence of the Cylonian affair. Epimenides is called from Crete to provide Athens with a cure. Setting a flock of black and white sheep loose to wander the Areopagus, Epimenides has the sheep tracked to where they lie down. When each finally seeks rest, it is sacrificed and a "nameless altar" is erected at the site.[63] Through this means, the Semnai Theai, whose altars had been polluted by the Cylonian violence, are supplicated. This story not only offers an explanation for why, within the historical memory of the

Athenians, altars to the Semnai Theai are found across Athens, but also, and more important for Oedipus, the story establishes the Semnai Theai as buffers between the dead who may fear ill treatment for the living and the living who anticipate attacks from the dead.[64] The tale of black and white sheep offers propitiation that accounts for ambiguity in human affairs and yet resolves the issue of pollution *without taking sides*.

That Ismene's supplications on behalf of Oedipus take place in the early spring is suggested by the reference to young lambs;[65] however, the festival celebration need not be an immediate context for Oedipus and Ismene to have an awareness of the etiology of the cult. In particular, the sheep's wool that features in the supplicatory ritual described in *Oedipus at Colonus* recalls the Cylonian pollution and the role of the Semnai Theai in resolving it. All three stories that establish the parameters for worship of the Semnai Theai mirror Oedipus's own life: he, like Orestes, will come to Athens as a suppliant; he also threatens to pollute this city as he as polluted every city during his long life. What Oedipus needs is what the Semnai Theai promise to provide in the story of the black and white sheep: mediation that replaces revenge with the restoration of community.[66]

But the power these rituals[67] have to end Oedipus's suffering is *affective* rather than *reflective*. Neither Oedipus nor Ismene speaks. Just as speechlessness characterizes the landscape of trauma, so also is silence central to rituals for the Semnai Theai in *Oedipus at Colonus*.[68] Indeed, the Semnai Theai are the unnamed "whom we are afraid to name, and whom we pass without looking, without sound, without speech, moving our lips in respectful silence."[69] Silvia Montiglio notes that, for the Greeks, silence is inclusive of whispers: one is silent if others cannot hear one's low voice.[70] Observing this requirement, Ismene whispers her prayer. With a ninefold gesture, she lays down olive boughs as she prays for a total of "thrice nine."[71] Ritual libations follow, expanding the metaphorical terrain on which the silence of trauma can be met and answered. These rituals are critical to the healing from traumatic suffering, for violence leaves holes and gaps in the narratives of human lives. These spaces are associated with silence because the Greeks understand that contagion can be transmitted through verbal contact. The force of pollution can move between and among persons: one who speaks to a polluted being can contract contagion, and the polluted being can infect others by speaking to them. Pollution therefore creates a break with social existence. Montiglio points out that purifying rituals will work only if they are performed in silence: decontamination of the pathways of communication necessarily precedes speech.[72] As a consequence, gestures rather than words mark initial traversals of this space. Those who have been polluted undertake journeys back to human society through the performance of rituals or other actions: speech that reinstates relationships with others is a final, not an initial step, in this process.[73] Working through trauma, the figures of Greek tragedy begin their journey to healing with embodied, nonvocal forms of communication. Their stories attest to lives caught up in traumatic repetition. Living in utter isolation from others by virtue of silences that attest to the severing of ties with human community, their bodily communication, in movement and gesture, eventually creates a bridge that opens up the future for a life inclusive of others.[74]

Bolens's theory of kinesis and Gallese's theory of intercorporeity contribute to our efforts to understand the role of silent gesture in Greek tragedy, which Montiglio has highlighted. Both scholars understand that corporeal connections—motor resonance and mirror neural mechanisms—undergird our capacity to interact with others. Trauma, I have argued here, destroys that capacity when it mires us in repetitive patterns of suffering that close us off from relationship. Greek tragedy compellingly attests to that trauma with its notion of contagion. So also does Greek tragedy demonstrate a profound awareness of the powerlessness of speech to initiate healing. Because relationships begin with embodied connections, healing must begin there too. Gestures rather than words tap a corporeal potential for healing.[75]

To be sure, even as the rituals Ismene performs on behalf of Oedipus are oriented away from sacrifice, Oedipus does not enter fully into antisacrificial space. The hallucinatory awe that attends experiences of the Erinyes mingles always in *Oedipus at Colonus* with the supplications to the unnamed powers of the Semnai Theai, so that the rituals directed toward the latter are never fully capable of overcoming the lasting hurt of the former. Thus, as Oedipus departs the world, the unlighted foundation remains dark. Falling short of revelatory healing, which would enable the *body's story fully to be told, releasing it from traumatic memory*, the disposition of the hero's body remains shrouded in mystery. If Oedipus's story is to be told, attesting to accomplished healing, that task will fall to someone else. Antigone alone has this power in the Theban cycle. Indeed, the revelatory power of the Theban

cycle, turning on the play that is both first and last in the cycle, rests with
the failure of *Oedipus at Colonus*. There is no apotheosis of tragedy in this
drama, no transfiguration of suffering, and no bestowal of salvation on Athens. Oedipus at Colonus "fails" in order that the task of speaking from the
wound of being fall to Antigone, as it must.

The narrative of *Oedipus at Colonus* offers powerful testimony to this
revelatory failure that also is a new beginning. That the Erinyes are active in
Oedipus's final conflict with Polyneices, late in *Oedipus at Colonus*, precludes
us from imagining that the Semnai Theai somehow overcome the Erinyes, as
the Eumenides domesticate the Erinyes in Aeschylus's *The Eumenides*.[76] That
the Erinyes remain a threat prevents us from deploying a tempting interpretive strategy that would see the Erinyes disappear into Semnai Theai. Were
that to happen, the altars of the Semnai Theai, which grace the landscape of
Athens and attest to the possibility of restorative community, could potentially be approached triumphantly and Oedipus could be celebrated as an
antisacrificial exemplar. But we would only defer violence for another day if
we swept under the altars of the Semnai Theai that strange remainder that
is the Erinyes.[77] Such a tidy ending for *Oedipus at Colonus* would constitute
repression.[78] Indeed, new forms of aggression do emerge in *Antigone*.

Most significantly, the unlighted foundation, referenced at the end
of *Oedipus of Colonus* and harkening to uncanny origins of the earth goddesses, shows that assimilation is never without remainder. An alternative
to repression of the Erinyes is offered by the Theban cycle: bring strangeness
to expression and articulate it, not in order to throttle threat but in order
that we might live with it. Not fleeing mimetic desire but meeting it at its
source, as Kristeva suggests, we can turn toward the other in me that is an
other in the same, *the stranger who is always already myself*.[79] We can learn,
as Girard advises, that "at a certain depth there is no difference between our
own secret and the secret of Others."[80] Only greater intimacy with oneself,
which enables one to see oneself as like others, truly enables us to come to
terms with the uncanny depths of being. We are able to realize our relational
being as "signs of the Other have become the signs of the Self."[81]

Summing up steps taken to arrive at this juncture, with Antigone we
have explored three paths along which she has been presumed to travel:
a sacrificial course, a strategic pathway along which one helps friends and
harms enemies, and a way of devotion along which Antigone's actions are

perceived to align with those of the gods. We have seen Antigone diverge from all of these paths. We also have surveyed these paths with an eye to Oedipus's journey. In Oedipus's quest for healing from long-standing pollution and suffering, Oedipus's actions are most clearly shown not to lie with sacrifice, for the rituals that Ismene performs on his behalf are to chthonic goddesses who have rejected the wine-offerings that attend sacrifice. But I have argued that Oedipus does follow the ethos of his day, replicating rather than transfiguring the ethics of "helping friends and harming enemies"; moreover, when Oedipus is at last welcomed by the Olympian gods, his death confirms rather than transforms divine investment in the mimetic rivalries of humanity. Finally, uncertainty characterizes the conclusion of *Oedipus at Colonus*. The disposition of Oedipus's body remains unclear, and Oedipus's quest for being moves only in a vertical direction. The gods invite Oedipus into their midst; however, human relationships—the lateral axis of a transformative ethics—are not altered.

Nevertheless, in reflecting on the contribution of *Oedipus at Colonus* to the Theban cycle, we can see how the play moves toward and from *Antigone*, contributing to *Antigone*'s visionary achievement. Applying Girard's insights about the power of transformative texts, we have seen that the aesthetic and spiritual movement of the Theban cycle does not move in a straight line from beginning to end; rather, by virtue of the compositional order and narrative chronology, *Antigone* is positioned at the cycle's extremities, so that transcendence is preserved in the spiraling movement of the cycle itself. Caught up in this movement, *Oedipus at Colonus* functions as a bridge to truth, establishing *a protective space for the act of transcendence* that is *Antigone*.[82] It does so in two important ways. *Oedipus at Colonus* instills hope to which the scholars who see in this drama a heroic narrative have so eloquently drawn our attention. That hope is most clearly brought to expression, I have argued, by appeal to a corporeal narratology indebted to Bolens, through ritual invocation of the healing powers of the Semnai Theai who offer hospitality to the stranger Oedipus. Rituals in *Oedipus at Colonus* call our attention to the role of the human body and sensory experience in transformations that challenge generative violence and its traumatic legacy. Thus, as Kristeva observes, "it may be that *Oedipus at Colonus* shows, in addition to other modifications of Greek culture, the path by which Hellenism could meet with the Bible."[83]

Turning our attention once again to *Antigone*, we do not leave *Oedipus at Colonus* behind. Instead, the protective space, to which this tragedy has granted access, enables us to encounter Antigone once more, newly capable of observing how she advances nonsacrificial engagement with others. Indeed, in the absence of the tutelage afforded by *Oedipus at Colonus*, we might be insufficiently attentive to gestures Antigone makes over the body of Polyneices. After all, the guard's report is brief: he heard Antigone cry "with a sound like the piercing note of a bird when she sees her empty nest robbed of her young"; he listened as she called down curses on those responsible; he saw how Antigone "brought in her hands thirsty dust, and from the well-wrought brazen urn that she was carrying she poured over the corpse a threefold libation."[84] We might focus our attention so narrowly on Antigone's conflict with Creon that we might miss how Antigone's actions secure a bond with her brother. Caught up in a desire that is ours as much as hers, we might frame Antigone's actions in terms of rivalry with humans and the gods rather than in terms of relationship with kin. But *Oedipus at Colonus* sensitizes us to that which we would otherwise risk bypassing: the powers of ritual in *Oedipus at Colonus* have accessed a space outside the economy of generative violence. Having glimpsed that space, when Antigone enters it, we will not only notice her but also view her actions in a different light, illuminating a previously unlighted foundation.

A Voice Speaks from a Wound

Girard writes that outside the ancient city, outside every closed city, the only road is the one that *follows the scapegoat*.[85] Joining Antigone along that pathway, toward what end have we traveled? Outside the city, how will Antigone engage in healing that also will enable her to reclaim memories so that her family may be freed from its long history of deadly pollution? We will see that, as Antigone pours libations over the body of her brother, tactile memories critical for a break with traumatic perception that have locked the house of Labdacus in a timeless presence are forged. A prerequisite for reestablishing relationships that are not driven by the mimetic violence that has paralyzed Thebes and its most famous family, Antigone's gestures, creating bodily ties between and among family members, mirror the rituals of Oedipus at the sacred grove, but move in a different register. How so?

As we have seen, a central feature of trauma is that the wounded body becomes an object of dread and fear to those who encounter it. Oedipus has summoned such fear in the final moments of his own life. The Erinyes have lurked in the background, mirroring the distress of those who have expressed great agitation with Oedipus's presence at the sacred grove. Mob action against Oedipus has been threatened, for by such violence his body could become a salvific, restoring harmony and peace to a community that previously had been threatened by Oedipus's pollution.

But rather than sacrifice, a different body of ritual has dominated the text of *Oedipus at Colonus*. Within the sacred grove, rituals have been performed that have broken with sacrifice to make space for the victim to whom is offered the hospitality of the Semnai Theai. Even so, the space established by these rituals has not been wholly occupied. The work of ritual has remained incomplete. Because the power summoned through these rituals to bring an end to Oedipus's suffering has been affective and not also reflective, direct purchase has not yet been taken on the ethical transformation made possible by ritual. In *Oedipus at Colonus*, ritual performance has not become *a praxis of healing witness*. Moreover, what transformation has transpired has moved in a vertical direction. Oedipus may have experienced transformation in his accession to the gods; however, the play ends with others still apparently caught up in a web of violence. It remains for Antigone to complete the work anticipated by the rituals to the Semnai Theai in *Oedipus at Colonus*.

In *Antigone*, harbinger and sequel to the other tragedies within the Theban cycle, Antigone mirrors Ismene's ritual actions at the sacred grove in *Oedipus at Colonus*. There, Ismene offers libations on behalf of Oedipus, both father and brother to Ismene and Antigone. But Antigone's actions take place at the very limits of a mimesis that has so often devolved into monstrous violence within the house of Labdacus. For even as Oedipus has become able to bear his trauma in the wake of libations offered to the Semnai Theai on his behalf by Ismene, he has not been fully released from suffering. Oedipus has remained in thrall to the uncanny: the unlighted foundation has remained dark.

The concept of the uncanny offers insight into Oedipus's situation. As Kristeva observes, the uncanny attests to the work of mimesis, highlighting that which is both doubly familiar and alien. She finds Freud's discussion of the etymology of "uncanny" revealing: *heimlich* refers to what is familiar and secret; *unheimlich* to that which has been hidden, should have remained hidden, but now has come to light.[86] The uncanny thus offers insight into the blurring of boundaries, the confusion of desire, from which Oedipus is never released. Only in Antigone's actions does revelatory healing transpire, as entering into the place of the *unheimlich*, Antigone transforms traumatic into narrative memory, making room for an ethics grounded in love, not sacrifice.

The theme of the uncanny appears in the "Hymn to Man," which is the second *stasimon* following the introductory parodos in *Antigone*.[87] The hymn begins with the proclamation that "many things are formidable [*deina*], and none more formidable than man." *Deina*, suggests Cecilia Sjöholm, has connotations of wonder and marvel but also suggests that which is strange and uncanny. Citing Heidegger's interpretation of the "Hymn to Man," Sjöholm directs our attention to how the text evokes the uncanny.[88] From Heidegger's perspective, "Humankind emerges from uncanniness and remains within it— looms out of it and stirs within it."[89] Heidegger asserts that the "Hymn to Man" suggests that humans are not at home, even before they try to make themselves at home.[90] As a consequence, humans are always "outside being." "Unhomed," humans lack being which would comprise for them at-homeness.[91] Although man has great powers—controlling sea and land, domesticating animals in order that they do his bidding, learning speech—these powers are riven by violence. The chorus attributes this violence to a founding split that establishes the conditions of human existence: an original act of violence of which the human is both maker and object. As a result, the human possesses no original unity. As Sjöholm sums up Heidegger's reading of the hymn, despite all of the skills man has acquired, man may as easily do ill as good: "When he applies the law of the earth and the justice the gods have sworn to uphold he is high in the city; outcast from the city is he with whom the ignoble consorts because of his recklessness." Thus, man is *unheimlich*, estranged from himself. Efforts to expand knowledge and build a world only widen the gap in being that constitutes the human, generating more violence.[92]

Lacan confirms Heidegger's and Kristeva's insights about the uncanny, while emphasizing how the uncanny is linked with humankind's ontological illness. Describing the "Hymn to Man" as a "tall tale," Lacan suggests that the hymn challenges the pretenses of man who "always manages to cause things to come crashing down on his head." Lacan takes a special interest in the concluding lines of the hymn, which note that the ever resourceful human has found no way to conquer death even as man is credited with having "contrived escape from desperate maladies." Lacan understands this phrase to say that man "invents marvelous gimmicks in the form of sicknesses he himself fabricates." Rather than celebrating humankind's resourceful ability to escape *from* sickness, Lacan says the hymn calls humans on their propensity to escape *into* sickness.[93] Although Lacan offers his commentary in a light tone, he is deadly serious: humankind's ploys when confronted with the inevitability of death result in illness. This illness is labeled ontological by Girard.

Only Antigone stands elsewhere to work through trauma at a limit of at-homeness. Antigone comes to grips with the uncanny; indeed, *she is the uncanny*. But why? Why do resolution of trauma and a break with the repetition of violence that has beset the house of Labdacus transpire by way of the uncanny? Does not the notion of the uncanny insert an unwarranted complication into our analysis of how Antigone awakens to her responsibility for another and, in a gesture of love, becomes a model, a *figura Christi*, for us? To the contrary, if we are to understand how Antigone breaks with acquisitive mimesis, which inevitably sees in the other a threat that limits recognition and closes down an ethical imperative for antisacrificial action, we must come to terms with the uncanny. And we can do that only if we follow Antigone so that we might see the uncanny as proper to our being.

Antigone recognizes the curse on her family, stumbling against the scandal it poses.[94] Even so, she prepares her parents' bodies for burial, washes and adorns them, and pours libations on their graves. She confronts the strangeness and contagion that has haunted her family. She goes on to replicate the care she has afforded her parents with like care for the body of her brother Polyneices.[95] She has the courage to confront her origins, not in order to defy or violently assault the problematic legacy that is hers; rather, in order that she may welcome it as her own. The question of this tragic drama—*how are differences that fade into an annihilating sameness and a sameness that transforms into threatening difference negotiated in a family, in a society?*—is answered in Antigone's encounter with the uncanny. After all, as Kristeva says of the uncanny, drawing on Freud: "Freud does not speak of foreigners; he teaches us how to detect foreignness in ourselves. That is perhaps the only way not to hound it outside of us. . . . Freud brings us the courage to call ourselves disintegrated in order not to integrate foreigners and even less so to hunt them down, but rather to welcome them to that uncanny strangeness, which is as much theirs as it is ours."[96] Antigone recognizes that the problems of sameness and difference, which would make even our families threatening to our own being, is not a truth to be identified and bounded outside but a symptom of desire that must be assumed if there is to be healing.

In reflecting on Antigone's achievement and substantiating how Antigone lives an uncanny desire even as she breaks with acquisitive mimesis, I offer two analytic strategies that illuminate Antigone's actions, establishing their significance for us. Under the guise of the "Antigone complex" both *familial* and *social* referents for Antigone's actions are visible. In describing this complex, Mitchell has explained what is entailed in "loving one's brother as oneself." A child emerges from infancy perceiving that siblings are replications of itself. The child's initial enthusiasm about a new brother or sister is that "there will be more of me." But, Mitchell has explained, fear soon replaces joy: How can two share a space of one? Because of the sibling, the young child perceives that its place with the mother will be lost. However, just as the Oedipus complex historically has been understood to teach children to accommodate themselves to lack and difference, so also does the "Antigone complex," oriented around the mother and her body, introduce a child to seriality and sameness. Under tutelage in generational ordering by one's mother, one finds that the presence of a sibling does not mean death or a threatening confusion of boundaries. One is able to form a bond with the other—one's first social group—because one is the same. Division within sameness opens up space for the other who is other in the same, *that stranger who is always already myself.*

In such a context, the "law of the mother" explains how the young child grasps generational ordering, comprehending what a brother or sister is and is not. The young child's awareness differs from that of an older child who negotiates its familial standing under tutelage to the "law of the father." In the Symbolic order, the lack of being that fuels mimetic conflict and confusion is negotiated in words: what is lacking is signified. But Mitchell argues that the seriality associated with a young child's initial encounter with a sibling, while taking place among signs, does not revolve around language. Instead, the Antigone complex establishes "numeracy, not literacy."[97] One who experiences displacement discovers that instead of deathly and deadly exchanges, there is "room for two, three, four or more."[98]

Lacan offers important insights on the familial relationships negotiated by Antigone. Remarkably, in writing about Antigone, Lacan does not employ his signature theme—the law of the father—but locates the meaning of Antigone elsewhere. Setting aside his storied preoccupation with Symbolic order, Lacan articulates a perspective similar to Mitchell's. Lacan notes that Antigone does not invoke an order developed in the field of signification. Seeking to understand the place from which Antigone acts, Lacan attends to the text of *Antigone*. Lacan says that the word "unburied," *adelphus*, eludes to one who is "of the same womb." Antigone will bury the one who is unburied, who is of the same womb as she. Within the strictures of language, as the tragic drama powerfully demonstrates, Antigone's acts are inexplicable—the ties that bind us in language to the state or to the gods apparently do not bind her. But Lacan recognizes that Antigone navigates to a different space. She is not beholden to the words by which she has been expected to judge Polyneices for what he has done or not done. Instead, she claims herself beholden to the very being of Polyneices. Polyneices at the limit, at the boundary, takes Antigone to the edges of language.

Yet, at that limit, Polyneices's sister still speaks. In the brief moment before she becomes victim, she opens up the signifying economy, there to honor the singular existence of her brother. On hearing of her actions, Creon asks, "What kind of man would do this?" Although his words summon the image of one who has defied his edict, they also allude to one who *does not know how to bury someone*. The men who puzzle over Antigone's gesture—Tiresias and Creon—confront the irony of one whose actions challenge the intelligibility of language and law. Antigone's struggle is not with the *how* of burial but with the *who* of burial; after all, as Mader has reminded us, family precedent is "namely that of generating one's own siblings."

When, out of the silence, after a long time, a sound is heard, it comes from Antigone, but no word does she speak. Instead, her voice calls out "the shrill note of a bird as it cries when it sees in its empty nest, the bed bereft of nestlings." The cry of these birds has been heard before. Sophocles borrows from Homer's *Odyssey* the imagery of this scene. Odysseus, returning home to the shores of Ithaca to battle for his family, embraces his father Telemachus. Homer says of them, "They cried shrill in a pulsing voice, even more than the outcry of birds, ospreys or vultures with hooked claws, whose children were stolen away by the men of the fields." Carol Jacobs rightly describes the bird cries as evocations of the uncanny. The cries are not words; nevertheless, they are not bereft of meaning. The cry of a mother bird for her children pierces the conventions of speech, dispossessing us of our standing in the world, evoking primal loss.[99] Recalling a mother who teaches her children how there is a place for more than one, Antigone images loss at the very borders of meaning. As Mitchell says when describing the law of the mother, a law grounded in numeracy rather than literacy, even "birds can 'count' their eggs."[100]

Lacan places Antigone at the very border of meaning by translating *atē* as "limit." For Lacan *atē* marks the annihilation of desire at the point of its inscription. As described by Mohammad Kowsar, the subject who is located "at the limit" by Lacan is endowed with unique "ethical lucidity."[101] Seeking the origins of this capacity in early human childhood, Lacan turns to Freud in order to track a passage from archaic unconsciousness to consciousness, a path that, for Lacan, moves "between skin and flesh."[102] Lacan focuses on the nascent subject's discovery of a sibling: a fellow human being. A division within the subject—at the limit of its being—transpires with this discovery. For the young child perceives that an object like this sibling has been part of the child's life before: a threat, a helping power, a source of satisfaction. The young child has no name or sign for this threat-help-source; however, Lacan calls it "the Thing," and readers recognize in the description features of the maternal body. No matter, the infant's perceptions are rapidly homing in on the new fellow: the sibling's moving hands, soft body, and smell awaken visceral memories in the body of the slightly older child. The anchor of it all—the Thing—is a constant fixture in this scene against which an active subject negotiates its first impressions of an "other." This "other"—also an "outside," is a stranger.

The triangulation visible in Lacan's account of a young child's discovery of its sibling predates in the chronology of childhood the triangle that Freud references by way of the Oedipus complex and Lacan by way of the law of the father. Looking elsewhere to locate the origins of Antigone's ethical lucidity, what Lacan sees through this young child's eyes is of critical importance. The child's recognition of a fellow human being is accompanied by a split, and this split constitutes the subject when the subject discovers "itself to be 'other' to an Other." For Lacan, "the Thing" acts as "the signifying coordinate for the pain of separation." Lacan calls this coordinate "the Thing" because it never has standing as a sign—it is not a "mother." Instead, the Thing exists only by virtue of an affective relationship that is oriented not toward the young child, but toward that child's fellow—the sibling. Disoriented in the presence of a sibling, whose gestures, so like the subject's own, evoke memories and establish the founding conditions of mimesis, the subject is in this moment constituted as a being who lacks. Its desire now revolves around a hoped-for repetition—to be the body that is now its sibling's. But, sums up Kowsar, "alterity and difference are part of the irretrievable nature of the original condition."[103]

With his description of the dynamics of early childhood forming a backdrop to his exploration of Sophocles's tragedy, Lacan traces Antigone's actions on behalf of her brother, so inexplicable to commentators, to the chthonic blood ties that rehearse this early story of desire. Antigone's family has been caught up in the throes of a criminal desire—a desire for a Mother that has been viewed as elicit. That desire has led to a multigenerational confusion of desire. Antigone, the offspring of this "criminal lot," digs down into forgotten family memories. Brought by those memories to the limit—*atē*—at the very edges of being, Antigone identifies with the desire of her mother. Positioned with her on the far side of threat, offering a gesture of love, Antigone moves outside the confusion of a desiring lack to the standpoint of ethical lucidity. She will "be the pure and simple guardian of the criminal as such."[104] Breaking free of traumatic memory, Antigone moves toward an ethics of the uncanny.

The space Antigone enters on the other side of trauma is an intimate domain. Caring for the body of her brother, offering cries of lament, Antigone embraces the healing potential of singularity. With Knox, I already have suggested that Antigone does so because she has moved outside of institutions and relationships that have constrained her words and actions within a framework of generative violence. Out of the confusing history of a family trauma, Antigone will love her brother as herself. She will embrace the *singularity of his being*.

Kelly Oliver's analysis of the concept of singularity helps us to understand Antigone's love and to place that love not only in the familial context of an intimate domain but also within a wider context of our ethical life with others, which we initially glimpsed in *Oedipus at Colonus* when the Semnai Theai offered hospitality to Oedipus, the stranger. Although the social exclusion of which Oliver writes is linked with a different era than that of Oedipus, the wandering stranger, her insights are trenchant. In *The Colonization of Psychic Space*, Oliver names as traumatic the exclusion of colonized peoples from social meanings that shape the culture in which they live. Disowned by those who oversee the society in which they live, often prohibited from speaking their native language, colonized peoples are caught in repetitious patterns, unable to find meaning in anything. In order to be freed from these constraints for a new future, colonized persons must be able to fashion new meanings that open up novel cultural spaces. But how can they do so, when everything around them appears to preclude the creation of new meaning? Drawing on the work of Julia Kristeva, Oliver suggests that a way out of trauma emerges in the affirmation of another's singularity.[105] That affirmation is the product of an "intimate revolt." Distinguishing intimate revolt from common forms of violence, Oliver states that an intimate revolt does not aim at the transgression of law. Displacing generative violence from its place of authority within the psychic economy, intimate revolt installs an ethics founded in singularity in its stead, making it possible for us to live with others. On the basis of such a revolt, we are able to renegotiate the parameters of being.[106] "Intimate revolt" thus names what mimetic theorists call "positive mimesis."

Oliver speaks about "singularity" in ways illuminate Antigone's actions. After all, in some ways Antigone lives in a "colonized" space: she and her kin, strangers to each other and to those around them, are captive to multigenerational violence that is part of a wider sacrificial economy riven by mimetic violence. Moreover, the Erinyes that lurk in the background point to the more radical possibility that Antigone's body has been colonized: indeed, the chorus has expressed fears that Antigone is possessed.[107] Trapped in the generational repetition of violence that has subjected her to bodily contagion, Antigone has few options. She has been caught up in trauma that has left her incapable of assimilating the meaning of that trauma within the social context. But Antigone does revolt; and, when she does so, Oliver's analysis helps us to understand that hers is not fundamentally a political or religious revolt—for such a challenge would ensnare Antigone in mimetic conflict. Instead, the authority of mimetic desire is displaced. When Antigone alludes to the singular standing of her brother, hers becomes an intimate revolt that renegotiates the very parameters of being.

Important for my analysis are Oliver's definitions: "singularity" is distinct from "individuality." For most contemporary Americans, "individualism" references a self-determined person who takes independent action. But Oliver sees in the championing of the individual a defensive position that understands others as a threat. Those who assume that position perceive that their independence requires that they defend against dependence and interdependence on others.[108] Likewise is the singular stance of one who enacts an intimate revolt, not the stance of those Hegel has described. Intimate revolt is not "a battle between two subjects or fledgling subjects for recognition." That kind of struggle inevitably devolves into a "merciless war where self-destruction alternates with destruction of the other."[109]

Interpreted from a perspective informed by Oliver's analysis, Antigone's evocation of the singular rather than the individual coheres well with Girard's discussion of heroic action in Greek tragedy. As Girard so perspicaciously observes in his discussion of Sophocles's ironic approach to heroic difference in tragedy, at the very moment that one would claim "individuality" on behalf of a Greek hero, that hero is "brought into violent opposition with another individual who turns out to be almost identical." Individuality does not survive mimetic rivalry.[110] Thus, if Antigone is to point with her actions beyond generative violence to an alternative, it will not be because of individualism.

In my effort to align Antigone's actions with singularity, Oliver's further discussion of the path to be taken to singularity is instructive. Oliver indicates that an intimate revolt that embraces the singularity of being emerges from a questioning stance. Questioning is necessary for psychic life—it enables one to be open to meaning and creativity. But questioning is not exclusively an act of intellection. Recalling Frantz Fanon's "final prayer" at the conclusion of *Black Skin, White Masks*—"O my body, make of me always a man who questions!"—Oliver suggests that questioning has its source in the body.[111] Because trauma locks one in a bodily prison, in which depression witnesses to isolation from words and representations, the transformative powers of intimacy proceed from the body, enabling the re-creation of meaning.[112] Questioning, a negation of a negation, makes possible a reunion with sensation and affect. The world of the body reunites with language.

Antigone is a story of intimate revolt that opens with Antigone posing questions to her sister: Antigone asks of the obligations of kin and friends and refers to the suffering that is culminating in the desecration of Polynei-ces's body. Her questioning takes her to that body. There Antigone's defiance of Creon is not primarily expressed as a battle of words. Instead, Antigone embodies her defiance: she *is* the questioning body who kneels over the body of her brother. Through her ritual actions on his behalf, she negates the violence that has negated his being and hers. Antigone's questioning breaks out of the destructive cycle of mimesis and sacrifice to become a force that nourishes psychic space. When Antigone is interrogated by Creon and says, "I say that I did it and do not deny it," the brevity of her words and their focus attest also that a questioning body has acted.[113]

Oliver's concept of "intimate revolt," developed from the insights of Kristeva, demonstrates that Antigone does walk a path away from genera-tive violence toward an alternative ethics. That Oliver enables us to frame the actions of Antigone, not as a battle for recognition among those who mirror each other but as a engendering of self-consciousness in the work of a body navigating psychic space, links Oliver closely with Mitchell. Antigone's actions, read from Mitchell's perspective, model a young child's discovery through questioning of the existence of a sibling. The young child queries: Can there be more than one of me? Bodily numeracy, establishing a space for two in relationship with each other *and* the mother, offers an initial les-son in intimate revolt. The child discovers which relationships the child can generate from his or her own being and which the child cannot. The child's questioning is not destructive. Not focused solely on discriminating what separates one from its other; the child's questions open out creatively. As a consequence, this intimate revolt offers what Oliver describes as the "nour-ishing of psychic space" that makes it possible for the child to love rather than hate the other.[114]

Oliver turns to a metaphor for singularity used by Kristeva in order to further elucidate intimate revolt. Contrasting the singular with the univer-sal, Kristeva suggests that a certain tension between the two is reminiscent of music. Music has its "singularities: dissonant keys and counter points go beyond the fundamental tonality of a musical composition."[115] The metaphor of music is not incidental: singularity is accessed initially through affective representations rather than signs. Singularity moves into the order of signs via affect: it is expressed and translated into the social through sublimation. As a consequence, Oliver understands sublimation in a broader way than

Freud. For her, it names processes through which persons negotiate a relationship to meaning, through work of the body and a community's social codes.[116] Singularity, like the counterpoint or dissonant keys in music, does not preclude the "universal." A work of music can have a thematic unity; one can carry "a tune." So also can we speak of laws and shared rights. But so also does singularity not disallow unique differences: that which we thought we were cherishing when we held out for "the individual" we can yet cherish. But singularity points to a process in which tensions that accrue to music or to society in their dissonant moments need not devolve into destructive violence. Singularity, enacted through processes of sublimation, which transpose affect into sign, does so by establishing *a strange uncanniness at the heart of the singular*.[117]

In following Antigone on the path that leads out of the city, we arrive at an ethics of an uncanny singularity. As a consequence, as Cecilia Sjöholm argues in her own study of the Antigone complex, we stand at a distance from Freud's Oedipal complex, for we are brought with Antigone to a place that is not about objects that are subject to contestation among mimetic rivals. The desire toward which Mitchell and Lacan point is not an aim but a cause, for lack comprises our being.[118] *Antigone* is not a drama about acquisitive desire, even though Antigone has been deprived of all possessions, status, and family. Rather, her desire is "a movement of return toward an elusive origin, an unraveling of the structure of the subject."[119] In movement toward the space in which we first encounter an other—that fellow human being our sibling—we "hit upon the shadow of an object." Only a shadow, only the shape of a foreign body and not actually that body, a Thing at the "intersection of nature and transcendence" that is not ours to possess, that strange shadow of an object that *never really was there in the first place*, places us at a limit where desire unravels.[120] Thus, Antigone's ethical lucidity emerges as *atē*—at the limit. When she pours libations on the wounded body of Polyneices, she touches a void inherent in the normative order.[121]

The model of desire embodied by Antigone, in her actions on behalf of her brother, concurs with Girard's. Disavowing the idea that desire has an end, he writes that "the essence of desire is to have no essential goal."[122] From whence comes the good desire that we see in Antigone, *figura Christi*? Girard states that mimetic desire is a condition of our humanity: in its absence we would operate only by instinct; we would express no freedom and therefore not be human. Animal desire does have an end, for instinct guides the animal toward its goals, as cows seek out grass on which to graze. But with freedom comes an elevation of the human outside of need, an elevation that *renders desire aimless.* With no end toward which it intrinsically tends, desire in the human is always borrowed desire: "Truly to desire, we must have recourse to people about us."[123] Thus, desire comes into being only as one imitates a model; in the absence of that model "human desire, lacking its own proper object, cannot come into being."[124] Good desire is an outcome of imitating good beings; bad desire is an outcome of imitating bad beings. Desire itself is neutral.

Lacan and Girard concur about how Antigone's desire is best understood. As Lacan says of Sophocles: "For all his heroes, the race is run."[125] Tragedy is not fundamentally about conflict emerging from our desires; it looks elsewhere, along the path that departs from the city, there to witness an unraveling of mimesis that emerges as "poetic creation or re-creation of a negative space that is to be found at the origins of the community."[126] Thus, there is always an element in tragedy that is irreducible, a limit that cannot be surpassed, an *unheimlich* that cannot be made familiar. As Sjöholm eloquently concludes, when we follow Antigone, we confront the unsurpassable element at the core of tragedy, and we find ourselves at "the void beyond the inscription of desire."[127] The chorus, seeing Antigone approach that void, wonders is she is mad and in the grip of the Erinyes.[128] But as the narrative of the play moves toward its conclusion, Antigone is shown to be lucid. Indeed, Antigone's lucidity, hallmark of her ethics, offers demonstrable evidence of how that void can be negotiated.[129]

Here, the singularity of Antigone's love shows that the ethical register in which she acts is not beholden to a social or normative order that is bound by and, in turn, restrains acquisitive desire. Antigone's desire is "unbound," but not because she is in the grip of runaway mimetic desire. With her gestures over her brother's body, Antigone honors the singularity of his being: *He is what he is.* In so doing, Antigone captures a point in being, a limit, that refuses to give itself to the sacrificial economy. Modeled on the Thing, the impossible object at the origin point of desire, Antigone's gestures on behalf of her brother are anchored to the opaque cause of desire at the zero-point of subjectivity.[130] By bringing us to that limit, Antigone opens up a space for ethics.

Importantly, this ethics revolves around the capacity of the human to be posited by and take a position in relation to others. This ethics requires embodiment. The "ethos" of this ethics attends to our habituation to existence with others, the practices of self-formation that we take up in light of others. *Antigone* shows us both the deformation of self-formation in a normative order riven with generative violence *and* a reformation of that self-formation in gestures of love that are the precondition for ethics.[131] Emerging from a corporeal encounter, this ethics is an alternative to formative processes that position us in the world as victim or persecutor.[132] Embracing the singular existence of another, at the very split in being, we can assume our desire differently. This ethics does not issue in codes of behavior. Rather than focus on the social construction of the good or promote the "good life," it concerns itself with the foundations of the subject. It acquaints us with the failure of all objects of desire to deliver the goods.[133] But it also shows us that the foundations of ethics lie beyond representation, in the shadows of the Thing.[134]

Whereas the Oedipus complex speaks to moments in accession to human society that are characterized by the consolidation and achievement of subject status, the Antigone complex opens out on perpetual unraveling. For the young child whose discovery of a sibling, a fellow human being, creates a rift in the world in which it once had being, the Thing is not a maternal body but a maternal absence, a mark or gap that makes possible human existence, caught between need and desire, bound and unbounded materiality, other and self.[135] The thing is what makes us human, what makes us ethical. It is an alterity that we are, an uncanny that we never assimilate, an other that is other in the same.

Sophocles draws on the extraordinary figure of Eurydice, wife of Creon and mother of Haemon and Megareus, in order to direct us to the space of this ethics. Not only is Eurydice not part of the mythological tradition of the Oedipus, but also she does not approach the stage from a side entrance as have the other characters. Instead, she bursts through the door of the palace at center stage. Eurydice is defined by her epithet, "all-mother of the corpse" (*pammētōr nekrou*)[136] and by her consuming grief.[137] Sophocles draws us toward the ethical limit (*atē*) by creating connections between Eurydice and Antigone. Eurydice is given the fewest lines of any character in Sophocles's tragedies.[138] But in the final moments of the play, at the very edges of signification, where words are replaced by gestures, and sounds by silence,

Eurydice mirrors Antigone.[139] That Eurydice does so is, at first, surprising. After all, Eurydice is portrayed as a model mother, bound to the *oikos*, and Antigone is outside the house from the very first moments of the play. But the juxtaposition of Eurydice and Antigone demonstrates that although they do not share a common space, their bodies offer a common witness. Both women offer material evidence of the consequences of the violence and pollution that has ravaged Thebes and their houses. As Rehm suggestions, the bodies of Antigone and Eurydice, bringing to focus this violence, become also the body of the play "against which the blows of embattled human conflicts are directed and through which they are felt."[140]

In the final moments of the tragedy, Antigone is dead in the cave that is her tomb and Eurydice is about to have her home become a grave. Eurydice enters the stage from the house, distraught over the messenger's description of Haemon's death. She announces that, as she was making her way out of the house to offer prayers, she overheard the messenger.[141] Depicting her grief with language that highlights the visceral impact on her of the messenger's news, Eurydice says that his words have struck her and pierced her ears. She has been "struck dumb" by the horror of what she has heard.[142] Nevertheless, she will listen if the messenger can share his news again. Eurydice does listen: she stands silent on the stage as the messenger describes the last moments in Haemon's life during which Haemon "achieved his marriage rites in the house of Hades."[143] In Eurydice's silent witness to the report of her son's demise, she becomes a double of Antigone, for she is about to turn away from and challenge mimetic rivalries that issue in scapegoating, just as Antigone has done. Antigone's efforts to assume a stance that challenges rather than embodies scapegoating have provided the dramatic focus of the play; Eurydice crystallizes that focus, witnessing to its truth lest anyone, in the absence of Antigone, misunderstand the meaning of Antigone's death.

Juxtaposed silence and speech in these last moments of *Antigone* frame an ethics grounded in a nonsacrificial economy. Eurydice, whether on stage or described in her offstage actions, cycles between silence and sound. Eurydice is silent as she hears of Haemon's death; she speaks to request that the messenger repeat his news; she is silent as she listens; she leaves the stage but subsequently speaks, for her words are heard by the messenger. As she prepares to take her life, Eurydice speaks to link the death of Haemon with that of another son—Megareus. Eurydice draws out of the past the legend that led to the death of Megareus, linking that death and Haemon's in a repetitious cycle of generative violence. The legend decreed that one of the "dragon's seed" must be sacrificed to save the city. Only Creon and his children, the last of this seed, were eligible; Megareus was sacrificed. Eurydice names what Creon has done to Haemon and to Megareus without mythic gloss.[144] She names human sacrifice for what it is: Creon is a "killer of sons." There is nothing redemptive in his actions; the earlier act of violence has resulted not in peace but in a contagion of violence that, defiling the altars of the city, threaten to destroy all. The silence of Eurydice once again fills the stage as her body is pushed out through open doors of the house on the *eccyclema*, becoming visible to all. Is Euridyce's silence a match for the spreading contagion that renders Creon's house and the house of Labdacus indistinguishable as the polluting generativity of the house of Labdacus melds with the violent generativity of the sown men, who emerged from the ground fighting?

We can better understand Eurydice's antisacrificial stance if we reflect once again on silence. As Montiglio explains, when there is silence in a Greek play, persons take notice. Greek drama "favors continuous sound over silence," making silence stand out as something to which attention should be given.[145] In the "continuous circulation of sound" on the Greek stage, actors speak as they enter, stand, or exit. In order that entrances of new characters to the stage not be accompanied by silence, those already present offer comments that mark, by way of description, transitions that are under way. In order that a constant level of sound be maintained on the stage, when the context calls for silence, the characters speak about silence rather than enact it. For example, in *Oedipus at Colonus*, when Polyneices leaves the stage in silence, he uses speech to codify silence as a tactical strategy.[146] So also do the heroes of the Greek stage have noisy deaths. Rather than summon silent awe among those who acknowledge them, hymns by the chorus and long speeches by others attest to the significance of the moment. Thus, in multiple respects, whether the context if life or death, actual silence on the stage is as uncommon as it is significant.[147]

Typically, in those few instances when the Greek stage is silent, silence precedes catastrophe. Silence also can announce forthcoming transformation that will usher in clarity. Silence can precede the unveiling of a truth that will not be silenced. Whether presaging catastrophe or announcing revelatory transformation, when silence is broken by speech, the words so spoken do not always reinstate social bonds. Instead, speech that brushes against silence, liminal speech, may remain so, incomprehensible to those who hear it.[148]

Drawing on conventions for silence in Greek drama, Sophocles magnifies Eurydice's significance in the play. She both portends catastrophe and announces transformation. Eurydice's actions, like Antigone's, brush against *atē*, the limit. Just as Antigone's actions in the moments before she offers libations over the dead body of her brother are preceded by silence, so also is Eurydice's lament for her sons preceded by a long period of silent listening. Neither woman's final moments before her death are saluted or immediately acknowledged by the chorus, as is typical in a heroic narrative. Instead, the death of each woman is reported by the messenger. In the case of Antigone, the chorus does not comment on what the messenger has just reported concerning her demise and that of Haemon; instead, startled by Eurydice's abrupt departure from the stage, they interrupt the messenger to ask, "What do you make of this?" They ruminate with the messenger about what Eurydice's "heavy silence" may mean. When the messenger subsequently announces Eurydice's own death, and her body is wheeled onto the stage, another discussion ensues, as the messenger offers descriptions meant to sort out the awful event that has just transpired. Thus, Eurydice, whether interrupting the speech of the messenger with her own words or interrupting actions on the stage with the silent witness of her dead body, breaks with the conventions of heroic narrative. Moreover, she does so, not on behalf of herself, but on behalf of Antigone. Alternating sounds and silence carve out a liminal space within the play, enabling Eurydice to mirror Antigone when she is unable to do so herself, making visible an ethics that moves in a nonheroic register. This ethics is sketched first by Eurydice through her heavy silence and second through reports of her speech.

Eurydice's *speech* about the death of Megareus, reported by the messenger, sketches a leap into the void. The dragon, from whose teeth the Thebans have been sown, marks the limit-point of human society and renders in story form the alien and uncanny aspects of that society. Human sacrifice has been the favored mode for mastery of that unknown, that frightening void in being. But Creon and his sons, the last of the sown men, are shown by Eurydice to have mastered nothing.[149] Eurydice's dead body is not best understood from the perspective of "suicide." Rather, when her actions are viewed from the perspective that she is Antigone's double, inserted into the final moments of the tragedy in order that Antigone be represented in her absence, we understand that Eurydice dies only because Antigone does. And both do so not as suicides but in gestures of self-giving. They aim to break with generative violence through love, not affirm its potency.

Eurydice's voice, keening in grief as did Antigone's when she poured libations over the body of her brother, is claimed to be a "sorrow in the house" that will not reach beyond its walls. But the mourning cries of these women, like mother birds, have a corporeal effect beyond the boundaries of grief. Contemporary scholars have tried to frame *Antigone* as a debate within Athenian society about appropriate funeral customs. But when *Antigone* is viewed through the lens of Girard's mimetic theory, augmented by the corporeal hermeneutics advanced here, the metaphysical illness that we have tracked to the last pages of *Antigone* points beyond social mores to the very limits of human society. Registered at the limit, at a point where signs break down, is testimony to a foundational ethics, an ethics creative of a human subjectivity capable of reaching out to others in love rather than in hate born of a suspect strangeness.

Eurydice and Antigone accomplish together what alone Antigone could not. Antigone, caught up in generations of trauma, has moved toward transformation by embracing the uncanny. Preparing Polyneices for burial, she has reworked tactile memories of trauma that have locked Antigone and her kin in a timeless present. She has circled the landscape of traumatic memory aiming to bring its strange silence to speech. Eurydice, her double, has similarly encountered and lived the body of trauma. But, in the last moment, Eurydice is the one whose speech releases trauma for narrative memory: *She is the one who sides with the victim to name deadly violence as sacrifice.* As a consequence, she expresses how trauma can at last be borne, how at the limit of human society, one can avert catastrophe with the transformative power of love.

The ethical stance solicited by the narrative of Antigone is not subject to mastery. If Greek drama suggests that silence can lead to transforming clarity, so also does Greek drama demonstrate that the speech of the transformed can be incomprehensible to others. Eurydice listens without speaking to the messenger describe what he has seen in the tomb of Antigone. She hears that Haemon has died and departs without speaking. The chorus is nonplussed: recognizing that her silence is "heavy," they know not what to make of the weight of silence. Minutes later, when the chorus sees Eurydice's body brought forward onto the stage, they may still not understand, for Greece understands suicide as a failure in language, a crisis in the logos.[150] But the heavy silence that characterizes Eurydice's listening indicates that silence is not an absence of words, it is a state. At the margins, at the limit of an economy of sacrifice, Eurydice's silence, mirroring that of the entombed Antigone, means everything. That silence, bathing all who encounter it, promises a break with sacrifice.

Silence, Montiglio tells us, is central in rites of purification. These rites suspend the only real mode of existence in the Greek city: verbal participation. Montiglio also states that, in rituals, silence is observed only as is necessary to maintain the efficacy of the sacred action; a transformative silence culminates in actions and new words. At the end of *Antigone*, the chorus offers closure, intending to tidy things up with reassuring words. But these words, landing in the midst of the heavy silence sustained by Eurydice in the last moments of the tragedy, are platitudes, for silence has brushed up against the Thing, an uncanny we never assimilate, an other that is other in the same.

Notwithstanding his appreciation for Antigone as *figura Christi* of the ancient world, Girard has called *Antigone* a lesser text. But *Antigone* articulates the violence that shapes human existence as well as our abject strangeness in ways that cut to the very heart of human origins. In attesting to the uncanny, *atē*, existence at the limit, Antigone's gestures home in on these origins, offering us a pathway from violence to ethics. If we take tragedy to heart, we may participate in its labor and build an expressive space in which to embrace an otherness that is both our own and that of our cultural heritage. Attentive to tragedy, we may better accept the division in being that is humanity without resorting to scapegoats.

Antigone alerts us to the troubling truth of the human condition: mimesis. Our desires, forged from the maternal body of our origins, tutored in our play with siblings, and perfected in our discourse with culture, are mimetic: we wish to acquire what the other has and desires. We even wish to be that other. Our desire leads to rivalry and violence overcome only through scapegoating. Those who would read in Antigone's own stance the role of a scapegoat know this story well.

But the story *Antigone* tells offers more. With Antigone, we experience how a sacrificial economy can be broken open. Intercorporeal and kinesic connections forged in our encounter with *Antigone* move us toward the standpoint of Antigone so that we may stand with her, if only for a moment. Girard recognizes as much when he writes that, within a sacrificial economy, the truth about violence will not abide in a community. Inevitably driven from the community, the voice of the victim is heard only in the process of being driven out, in the brief moment that precedes its *destruction*.[51] Antigone is a paradigmatic emblem of that voice that is heard only at the boundary and limit (*atē*) of being. What remains for theorists of mimetic violence to more fully appreciate is what Antigone has delineated not only with her voice but with her body, in silent supplication, for love of her brother. Not a deficient instance of a nonsacrificial ethic, *Antigone* offers compelling testimony to a corporeal ethics and its healing truth. We ignore that truth at our own risk.

PART 3

The Old Man and the Wolves

Fathers

Exile is a way of surviving in the face of the *dead father*, of gambling with death, which is the meaning of life, of stubbornly refusing to give in to the law of death.

—Julia Kristeva, "A New Type of Intellectual," *The Kristeva Reader*

The father is dead. On this point, Julia Kristeva and René Girard agree. What then can be said any longer of the paternal function? What legacy of the father persists in ongoing economies of sacrifice? And, if the father is not actually dead but only missing in action within the family romance, site of our earliest mimetic rivalries, what role, if any, could a father play in an intimate domain characterized by positive, nonconflictual mimesis? May a father yet live within intimate spaces? Endeavoring to answer these questions, I turn to literature, for Girard and Kristeva agree that literature is reflective and revelatory of human experience in the world. Literature attests to the vicissitudes of the paternal function in contemporary society; for, in bringing into view mimetic desire, trauma, and conflict, literature offers a setting in which we can analyze the misfortunes of the father. Moreover, literature is especially important because Girard and Kristeva assert that literature can *transform* human experience. If there is any hope for the father, literature may enable us to glimpse that promise.

In what follows, I make Julia Kristeva's *The Old Man and the Wolves* my focus as I assess the paternal function. I take my cue from Maria Margaroni, who states that the Kristeva's novel recasts *Totem and Taboo*. Not a battle between father and sons, the conflict in *The Old Man and the Wolves* turns on scission within the paternal function itself between the dead father of a sacrificial economy and the life-giving father of individual prehistory.[1] In the novel, conflict besets the old men of Santa Varvara when wolves invade the community, setting off a violent contagion to which everyone in Santa Varvara is vulnerable. Nevertheless, woven throughout the narrative is testimony by the old men to affective, embodied experience that promises healing from violence inflicted by wolves. Consisting of memories that the old men retrieve and share, this hopeful narrative is grounded in compassion and intimacy. I focus in the chapters that follow on this narrative. Through our kinesic investments in it, we may find ourselves participating in hope that opens toward positive mimesis. I begin, however, by comparing Girard's and Kristeva's views on the paternal crisis. In the wake of the father's demise, Girard emphasizes spiraling violence while Kristeva highlights suffocating meaninglessness; together, they offer complementary insights on our contemporary situation.

The Demise of the Patriarchs and the Coming Apocalypse

Girard signals in *Violence and the Sacred* that, in the modern world, the father is captured by a generative mechanism that issues in violent mimesis and scapegoating. Thus, the father of the family romance—the term I use to typify fundamental patterns of mimetic desire among family members—is no longer pulling his weight. Girard formulates his case by analyzing two of Freud's most important ideas: the Oedipus complex and the parricide described in *Totem and Taboo*. Girard writes that the competition between father and son, which is the focus for Freud's notion of the Oedipus complex, is of modern origin. In traditional societies, fathers are exemplary instances of external models: wanting to imitate their fathers, children respect the enormous distance between themselves and their fathers. They cannot imagine competing with these towering presences; that they emulate their fathers in small ways is challenging enough. By contrast, in the contemporary world, fathers have become not only models but also obstacles. The weakening of paternal authority, which occurs when external mediation is replaced by internal mediation,[2] makes fathers fair game for children. In a world where a son considers his dad his best friend, the father-son relationship features all the instability that shadows friendship. Thus, as differences between father and son dissolve in the contemporary world, parent and child compete for the same objects. Where paternal law is flouted, its force increasingly blunted, "The son looks everywhere for the law—and finds no lawgiver."[3] For Girard, psychoanalysis emerges at a particular moment in history to "announce and to prepare the way for something it cannot itself describe; an advanced stage of indifferentiation, or 'decoding,' which involves the complete effacement of the paternal function."[4] Although Girard's account moves fluidly between the history of fatherhood and the paternal function on which psychoanalysis focuses, his point is well taken. In a world riven by escalating mimetic rivalries, the dissolution of differences is pervasive and thorough. No aspects of human experience are immune from this spreading contagion, including the family.

When Girard reads Freud's description of the primal murder in *Totem and Taboo*, Girard reaches a similar conclusion. Following Freud's account closely, he finds that it points to the generative mechanism for violence. Although Girard believes that Freud turns from his own insights in order to reconcile the interdictory powers of the Oedipus complex with the radical implications of *Totem and Taboo*, Girard holds to the logic of Freud's argument. Girard emphasizes Freud's discovery of intensified rivalry among brothers after the death of the father. Writes Girard, "The situation described by Freud has supposedly arisen because of the death of the dominant father, but now everything takes place as if the father had never existed."[5] Girard avers that the dynamics of conflict, shifted to brothers who treat each other as enemies, brings Freud to the same outcome as have Freud's writings on the Oedipus complex. We are all enemy brothers who are indistinguishable from each other. As a consequence, we are highly vulnerable to mimetic competition, scapegoating, and violence.

In *Theatre of Envy*, Girard expands on his analysis of the demise of paternal authority. He argues that the patriarchal institution of the family already was in the process of breaking down in Shakespeare's time, as happens to all institutions in a sacrificial crisis. For Girard, Shakespeare provides key evidence of the collapse of paternal omnipotence. When fathers appear in Shakespeare's plays, they are not examples of external mediation: they are not role models for their children. Nor do the rivalries that hold Shakespeare's audiences in thrall feature a father. Although a father in a Shakespearean play may present himself as a candidate for rivalrous attention, dramatic mimesis turns on a fraternal rather than paternal axis.[6] As a consequence, Shakespeare subjects the myth of "fatherly omnipotence" to satiric treatment. For Girard, by the time of Shakespeare, "The paternalistic system, if it ever really existed in the Christian West, had already disintegrated."[7] The father has become an "empty scarecrow" in Shakespearian drama and in real life.[8] Thus, for Girard, external mediation, associated with a strong parental presence, is replaced by conflict-ridden internal mediation. Differences among persons, which could moderate familial rivalries, fade before an "increasingly aggravated state of undifferentiation."[9] In *Things Hidden since the Foundation of the World*, Girard concludes that no one "believes" in the father anymore.[10]

Whether Girard is discussing the family patriarch as viewed by Freud or Shakespeare, Girard associates family stability with fathers who are the focus of external mediation and family instability with the rise of internal mediation among family members. In a January 1989 interview with Richard Golsan, Girard expounds on these terms as he reflects further on Shakespeare. Girard states that he relies on concepts of external and internal mediation to locate in Shakespeare's plays revelatory insights on the loss of paternal authority. According to Girard, "A functional society is one which is dominated by external mediation."[11] In the absence of strong external mediation, societies are beset by unrest. Girard observes, however, that the modern West is an exception to this rule: "Only our society can live in a state of permanent crisis or internal mediation. Modern society can absorb more and more indifferentiation, equality, without disintegrating."[12]

In a subsequent interview with Pierpaolo Antonello in 2007, Girard reaffirms his claim to Western exceptionalism by contrasting modern Western society with traditional Indian society. The latter is dominated by hierarchy and external mediation. Because of principles of dharma, "Everybody does what they are ordained to do."[13] Girard suggests that, during the Middle Ages, a religious and social order existed in the West that was governed by principles of external mediation similar to dharma. But this order declined during the Renaissance and Enlightenment and was replaced by a Christian principle of "an individual who dominates his/her own violent impulses."[14] Thus, according to Girard, Christianity has been instrumental in enabling Western society to exchange external for internal mediation without triggering a contagion of violence. The father who exercises paternal authority over all may be dead; however, lawlessness has not triumphed in the absence of that authority.

Although Girard has claimed that the Christian West is a functional society, notwithstanding the driving force of internal mediation, when Girard takes the measure of our contemporary world in his recent *Battling to the End*, Girard distances himself from his former position. The apocalyptic contours of violence that have emerged in the wake of increasingly rampant undifferentiation among social groups now capture his attention. Confronting the utter "powerlessness of politics against the escalation of extremes," Girard doubts that humans can step back from the brink. Violence no longer can be checked. "From this point of view," asserts Girard, "we can say that the apocalypse has begun."[15]

In *Battling to the End*, Girard no longer espouses a Christian exceptionalism that he previously has credited with undergirding benign forms of internal mediation in modern Western society. Now Girard argues that Christianity itself has "provoked the escalation to extremes" we face.[16] Girard asserts that "Christ will have tried to bring humanity into adulthood, but humanity will have refused." He expressly asks his readers to notice his use of the future perfect tense because he wants them to appreciate the profundity of the "deep failure" he is describing.[17]

What provokes Girard's apocalyptic despair? Apparently, Girard's reading of Carl von Clausewitz's *On War* has had a profound impact on him. Girard typifies the book as a uniquely perceptive account of armed conflict that prophetically forecasts a deadly trajectory for mimetic violence in the modern age. Indeed, according to Girard, *On War* is "the greatest book ever written on war."[18] Published after Clausewitz's death in 1832, *On War* makes the case that Napoleonic conflict lays the groundwork for a new form of warfare, an escalation to extremes, that is the duel writ large in history. Where Hegel sees the age of Napoleon presaging the development of a rational state, Clausewitz sees lying just under the surface of that state massive destructive power that may be unleashed at any time. He foresees that modern warfare, fueled by hatred, will demand the extermination of the enemy.[19] This dark underside of contemporary society now holds Girard's attention.

As Girard's exploration of *On War* is described by Stephen Gardner, Girard attentively follows Clausewitz as he homes in on the phenomenon of "total war." In earlier eras, war was never enacted in its "ideal" structure: a conflict in which opposing forces expend all their violence at once and meet with annihilation. Obstacles—social, natural, political—have always interrupted the trajectory of war, limiting its powers. Determining that currents of democracy coursing across Europe now make possible the "total mobilization" of warring forces, Clausewitz struggles to confine to the pages of his book the forces of modernity that now make "ideal war" possible. Placing obstacles in his own way, Clausewitz veers again and again off the road to cataclysmic violence whose surface his words already have paved. Although Clausewitz sees "ideal war" as a conceptual schema, he resists its pull, holding out for "real wars" that are always constrained by social and political factors. Of course, Clausewitz cannot comprehend technological changes in the twentieth century that make apocalyptic war indisputably possible.[20] But Girard can. Bolder than Clausewitz, who swerves time and again into the ditch in order to escape the consequences of following his own thought to its apocalyptic conclusion, Girard hurtles forward toward that end. Because political and technological limitations to ideal war have been overcome—the former by stateless terrorism and the latter by nuclear arms—Girard believes not only that ideal war is possible, but also that it is inevitable. Moreover, Girard can name the engine of ideal war as Clausewitz has not: human mimeticism.

As explained by Gardner, Girard interprets in apocalyptic fashion Clausewitz's statement that "war is the continuation of politics by other means." For Girard, Clausewitz cannot be saying that war *is* political, and therefore will continue to be checked by politics even as war enacts politics by other means. Nor can Clausewitz be acknowledging in the drift of war a move toward something wholly new that would take flight toward destruction but for being tethered to politics. No, Clausewitz's statement has only one meaning: *Politics has become war.* Peoples and nations will duel and only total destruction will bring that dueling to an end.[21] Girard sees that war, like every other human institution, always operated in the past under a sacred canopy that sacralized human mimeticism and checked it. But with the scapegoating mechanism laid bare, thanks to Christianity, no myths bound war. War beyond politics, beyond the sacred, announces the apocalypse.[22] Humans are caught up in an escalation of violence from which escape is impossible.

Is Girard devoid of hope? Three alternatives to the apocalypse are visible in the Girardian corpus. The first is mentioned in *The Scapegoat*. Initially, Girard renders a grave assessment of the power of violence to destroy human society. With the mechanism of substitutionary sacrifice exposed in the modern world, humans lose their capacity to limit violence as they did in the past because they no longer can exchange unrestrained mutual slaughter for a focused attack on a scapegoat. As a consequence, humanity risks an escalating violent mimesis from which no escape is possible. Nevertheless, *The Scapegoat* ends on a note of qualified optimism. Stepping back from the abyss, Girard offers one alternative to the apocalypse: *If we forgive one another, we still have time to avert cataclysmic violence*.[23] Regrettably, Girard does not describe how we may develop personal and social resources for that undertaking.

In *Things Hidden since the Foundation of the World*, Girard espouses a second alternative to the brutal end game he describes in *Battling to the End*. Girard observes that intensifying mimeticism does not always spiral into conflict; he suggests that waves of meaninglessness can flood society to equally devastating effect.[24] According to Girard, a Puritanism that sought to regulate human sexuality is being replaced by a more dangerous Puritanism: "a Puritanism of meaning that kills all that it touches." Writes Girard of the threat he sees: "This Puritanism desiccates every text and spreads the most deadening boredom even in the newest situations."[25] But Girard gives scant attention elsewhere to this provocative line of thought, nor does he suggest how the threat meaninglessness poses to human society can be countered.

A third alternative to the apocalypse is visible in *Battling to the End*, notwithstanding the grim assessment of the future that pervades this work. Girard proposes that we can exchange undifferentiation from others for identification with others. Girard depicts identification as "Christian love" and states that it "supposes a special aptitude for empathy." Likening "identification" to an "innermost mediation," he links both terms to the imitation of Christ.[26] Girard also uses the phrase "intimate mediation" to name processes that "transform mimeticism and open the door to the other side of violence."[27] But how does one imitate Christ, establishing intimate mediation through identification with him? Girard asserts that *the aspect of Christ that has to be imitated is his withdrawal* to be with his father."[28] Christ's withdrawal is linked too with God's "absence."[29] For Girard, when humans engage in positive imitation of Christ, their actions should take the form of renunciation. In a time of a "corrupted sacred," humans escape the apocalypse only along a route characterized by silence. Indeed, Christ's silence and God's absence are "the new face of the divine."[30]

Hölderlin, the poet who was sequestered from the world for nearly forty years in a tower overlooking the Neckar River, is cited by Girard as an exemplary model for the imitation of Christ. Girard calls on us "to take the measure" of Hölderlin's silence and "to measure up to it."[31] Having suggested that the positive imitation of Christ is enacted through withdrawal, Girard now suggests that Hölderlin points the way.[32] In modeling our own lives on Hölderlin's "mysterious relationship to the absence of God, an imitation of his withdrawal," we may yet escape the apocalypse.

Girard's choice of Hölderlin as a model for our time is troubling.[33] Contemporaries of Hölderlin found their visits to him harrowing: unable to converse, devoid of companionship, Hölderlin exuded acute anxiety rather than contemplative peace.[34] Keeping his distance from Christ and his Father[35] and fleeing all human companionship, Hölderlin was utterly bereft. Has Girard truly pinpointed a viable alternative to the apocalypse? Does the world hold so little potential for positive relationships with others that the poet's tower is our only refuge? With Hölderlin as a model, positive identification is shorn by Girard of all reasonable claims to intercorporeity[36] and intersubjectivity. As a consequence, intimate mediation, a positive mimesis that Girard has offered as the third of his alternatives to an apocalypse, comes up short.

Indeed, all of Girard's alternatives to the apocalypse are problematic. Girard offers forgiveness as an alternative to Hölderlin-like withdrawal; however, we do not learn from Girard how we may forgive or how forgiveness can release us from the grip of runaway violence. Girard suggests also that a contagion of meaningless may pose a threat to humans as dire as physical violence, but he does not elaborate on this claim. Indeed, the body of Girard's work suggests that Girard stands with those who wager that the world will end with a bang, not a whimper.[37]

I attribute inadequacies in Girard's discussion of three alternatives to the apocalypse to the long-term consequences of Girard's abandonment of fundamental concepts that he took from phenomenology as a young scholar. I contend here, as I have throughout this book, that when Girard dismisses sensory experience as a resource for human transformation, believing it to be an inconsequential remnant of his early explorations in phenomenology, he does so at great cost. In the absence of ongoing attention to affective memory and sensory experience, Girard closes humans off from access to a positive mimetic desire that would express itself in mutuality and forgiveness. Like a deeply buried splinter, the deleterious consequences of Girard's change of focus have festered largely unnoticed; in the apocalyptic *Battling to the End*, they are palpably manifest.

With Kristeva, we can chart an alternative course. As we have seen throughout this book, Kristeva makes affective memory and sensory experience central to the work of healing intimacy. She shows how Girard could have proceeded, if phenomenology had continued to inform his work. Supported by Kristeva, we can step back from the brink of apocalypse and envision a future. Kristeva's perspective is needed especially because sensory experience is of decisive import not only when we analyze violence but also when we imagine alternatives. In attending to the role that sensory experience plays in transformational healing, Kristeva not only supplements Girard's views, she also offers hope.

Kristeva is no Pollyanna. She shares with Girard an acute sensitivity to the seriousness of our present situation. She too stands at the edge of the abyss. Like Girard, Kristeva writes of the effacement of the paternal function in the contemporary world and acknowledges a crisis of difference. However, Kristeva finds that a deadening of desire and the atrophy of meaning are the primary threats we confront in the wake of the demise of the paternal function, not the accentuation of desire and increasingly violent rivalries. Where Girard is at his most compelling when speaking of violence that spirals out of control, Kristeva is at her most persuasive when she addresses a spreading sense of meaninglessness that leaves increasing numbers of persons paralyzed.

Of course, only on the most superficial level is the contagion that Kristeva highlights nonviolent. Lacking a raw violence that is more typically associated with the apocalypse, Kristeva reminds us that widespread banality features a hidden violence that "integrates aggression but under the ruinous guise of an erasure of meaning."[38] Although she is comfortable naming this phenomenon "depression," Kristeva does not limit depression to individual pathology; rather, "because of its amplitude, it assumes the seriousness of a society event, a civilization crisis."[39] Apprehensive about our capacity to survive in a "robotizing" society,"[40] Kristeva witnesses to an *implosive violence* that issues in a contagion of suicidal melancholia.[41] Kristeva's perspective balances Girard's, for he has set his sights on *explosive violence* that develops into all-out war.

Even as Kristeva and Girard share in common a concern that spreading violence—implosive and explosive—may prove lethal to human community, Kristeva finds grounds for hope. She explores alternatives to the apocalypse that Girard mentions but leaves undeveloped. Kristeva writes about *forgiveness*, making it an integral aspect of healing from trauma. As Kristeva grounds our capacity for forgiveness in relations that are intercorporeal before they are linguistic, she shows how the foundations of forgiveness are laid for a nascent subject prior to the emergence of desires that are riven by mimetic rivalry. Compassion—lived empathy with another to which we are introduced early in our lives—founds our capacity for forgiveness. As a consequence, as Kelly Oliver reminds us, forgiveness for Kristeva is fundamentally not something that the victim *gives* to perpetrators of violence; rather, forgiveness is something the victim *receives* when the victim's founding capacity for forgiveness is restored to her or him following trauma.[42]

Most significant, Kristeva employs a corporeal hermeneutics to explore *intimacy*. Temporalizing mimetic theory and linking forgiveness with intimacy, she focuses on moments of remembering that, via bodily kinesis, open us for communion with others. In doing so, Kristeva takes up Girard's claim that indifference toward others is not the only way we can respond to undifferentiation under circumstances of acute internal mediation in contemporary society. However, when Kristeva explains how we can exchange undifferentiation from others for nonrivalrous identification with others, her model is not Hölderlin. Instead, her corporeal narratology returns us to the "sensory intimacy" we experience early in our lives, which she associates with the love of a father. Not the father of the law, whose demise Kristeva joins Girard in affirming, this "father of individual prehistory" supports the nascent development of the human subject, establishing its capacity for forgiveness and intimacy.[43] Solicited through affective memory, this father offers protection against deadly ennui. Kristeva's microanalysis of our contemporary crisis, oriented toward intimacy and supported by the father of individual prehistory who is our first teacher of forgiveness, complements Girard's macroanalysis of violence, enhancing our capacity to comprehend our current predicament and to determine how we may hope for the future.[44]

The Loss of the Father and the Rise of Monstrous Insignificance

Kristeva and Girard are in accord about the demise of paternal authority. Moreover, Kristeva has been schooled in her conviction, as has Girard, by her reading of Freud's *Totem and Taboo*. Kristeva reminds us that Freud wrote *Totem and Taboo* on the eve of World War I, a catastrophe of violence that shook Freud's understanding of the nature and limits of human community.[45] For Kristeva, *Totem and Taboo* is a prescient account of paternal loss and unacknowledged trauma. The murder of the father purports to tell a story of how "*Homo sapiens* becomes a social animal," exchanging the "tyranny of the father" for the "function of authority" that the sons assimilate into their own bodies (literally and metaphorically). Kristeva emphasizes that Freud highlights the somatization of the loss of the father in this event, which results in hidden trauma.[46] Reminding the reader that *Totem and Taboo* has been derided by its critics for recording the "delirium" and "personal fantasy" of its author, Kristeva asserts the importance of Freud's theoretical contribution. Freud captures humanity's leap into the Symbolic at the moment of paternal death. The demise of the father creates culture; however, that achievement is never represented in culture. The act that has made possible the emergence of culture is recorded only indirectly—in the sacred.[47]

Acclaiming the significance of *Totem and Taboo*, Kristeva espouses views remarkably similar to Girard's. The alignment of their views comes to the fore when Kristeva explains how psychoanalysis after Freud (e.g., Lacan) bypasses Freud's key insights on the formation of the subject. She cites as evidence interpretations by successors to Freud of a text by Freud that also has World War I as its backdrop. Kristeva asks that we read with particular care Freud's 1914 text on narcissism. Kristeva states that readers of Freud have rightly understood that the text does not refer to an individual who is "full of himself."[48] Rather,

Narcissus does not know who he is. He "invests in his image because he is not sure of his identity." So also do most commentators on the text comprehend Freud's concept of identification (*Einfühling*): identification is a primordial experience of another who supports the emerging identity of the subject, mirroring back to the nascent subject its separate existence. But Kristeva deplores that successors to Freud have not brought to their reflections on the essay on narcissism the lessons of *Totem and Taboo*, which Freud wrote just prior to the essay on narcissism. As a consequence, they have not taken with absolute seriousness the Freudian account of negativity that haunts the emergence of *Homo sapiens*, shadowing the work of identification.[49]

The parricide of *Totem and Taboo* brings into broad relief what otherwise may go missing in the story of Narcissus: an "intersubjective and intrasubjective dynamic" of one who is "cast out as 'I am' by being."[50] Named *signifiance* by Kristeva, the dynamic preserved in the narrative of Narcissus marks a "thetic break" that brings the human subject into existence. A process that can be typified as the birth of desire, the thetic break marks the subject's transition from embodied to symbolic being. An infant who has interacted with the world primarily with its senses now takes its place as a subject of language and signs. The thetic break, initiating in the subject a separation in being, marks a point in which subjects achieve inner coherence and secure a pretense of unity by investing in mirror images at whose sites they establish themselves. The tradition recognizes that this process is fundamentally intersubjective—the subject is founded in being by another. However, that this process also is highly volatile is overlooked by a psychoanalytic tradition that has dismissed *Totem and Taboo*.[51]

Asking that psychoanalysis engage lessons from *Totem and Taboo* that it previously has disregarded, Kristeva calls attention to profound implications for society of the fundamental instability and trauma that attend the process of subject creation. Freud reminds us that *signifiance* opens to "the sacred." Writes Kristeva: "In all known archaic societies, this founding break of the symbolic order is represented by murder—the killing of a man, a slave, a prisoner, and animal. Freud reveals this founding break and generalizes from it when he emphasizes that society is founded on a complicity in the common crime."[52]

The sacred, Kristeva says, "theologizes this event" and reenacts it. That she specifically cites Girard when making this point is not surprising.[53] For Girard is among very few scholars who has given *Totem and Taboo* the attention Kristeva believes it is due. Recognizing, as has Kristeva, the import of humans "positing their own violence as an independent being," Girard writes that "violence is the heart and secret soul of the sacred."[54] Like Kristeva, Girard applauds Freud for laying the foundations in *Totem and Taboo* for this critical insight into the human condition.

Girard and Kristeva thus share a reading of Freud that brings into focus the death of the father and the concomitant birth of the sacred. Similar to Girard, Kristeva explores the demise of the father in two registers: at the origin of human society and within our current society. However, when Kristeva reflects on the backdrop of father loss in our contemporary situation, in contrast to Girard, she observes a spreading contagion of meaninglessness, not a coming apocalypse.

Kristeva is not oblivious to apocalyptic features of our time. She notes that Freud's own attention is drawn to the "*later* products of religions," in which there are new rebellions distinct from "the primary revolt that was the murder of the father." These may take the form of ritual sacrifice or of other forms of "mimesis or representation."[55] However, Kristeva believes that the logic of sacrifice has "reached a saturation point."[56] She is concerned that contemporary society has no communal narrative to sustain belief. No one feels guilt or responsibility, and an amnesiac society of spectacle dulls all human experience.[57] Those who feel that their lives are painful are prescribed medicines to dull the pain, not to work through it.[58] Yes, "monsters" who lash out violently keep the sacrificial economy of old in play; however, equally or more deadly is a "monstrous insignificance" that threatens to consume our contemporary world.[59] Indeed, Kristeva suggests that the alternative we confront today is between "active monsters and monstrous insignificance (*monstre actif ou monstrueux d'insignifiance*)."[60]

Kristeva makes common cause with Girard once again when she associates "monsters" with explosive violence and "monstrous insignificance" with an implosive violence associated with widespread cultural meaninglessness. Girard names as "monsters" our mimetic doubles. Emerging at the height of a sacrificial crisis, when our rivalries are most intense, we do not recognize these monsters as ourselves. Writes Girard,

The subject watches the monstrosity that takes shape within him and outside him simultaneously. In his efforts to explain what is happening to him,
he attributes the origin of the apparition to some exterior cause. Surely,
he thinks, this vision is too bizarre to emanate from the familiar country
within, too foreign in fact to derive from the world of men. The whole
interpretation of the experience is dominated by the sense that the monster
is alien to himself. The subject feels that the most intimate regions of his
being have been invaded by a supernatural creature who also besieges him
without.[61]

Mirroring each other in our rivalries, as differences between us collapse
in the midst of crises, the only difference we can find in the other is that
which we create. We see hideous and ghastly differences in the other even as
this other being draws so close as to invade our very skin. When, in *The Old
Man and the Wolves*, Kristeva describes monsters in Santa Varvara—wolves
from foreign lands that overtake and invade the bodies of Santa Varvara's
residents—Kristeva exactly duplicates in her novel's narrative the monster-
making process Girard has described.

Even though Girard's take on our contemporary crisis brings to the
fore an apocalyptic violence in which monsters proliferate, the theme of
"monstrous insignificance," which Kristeva emphasizes as the primary
feature of our contemporary crisis, is present in Girard's thought. When
Kristeva writes that insignificance can be likened to a loss of difference that
pervades contemporary society, eliminating distinctions between "man and
woman, inside and outside, pure and impure,"[62] Kristeva could be describing
Girard's notion of "undifferentiation"—the state a group enters in the midst
of a crisis when mimetic violence becomes so pervasive that "all differences
(social, familiar, and individual) have disappeared."[63] Similarities in Girard
and Kristeva's perspective are confirmed when, in an interview with John
Lechte, Kristeva laments the cultural proliferation of anxieties at "the limit
of our identities" that point to potential decomposition or explosion in our
contemporary world.[64]

Although Kristeva joins Girard in taking the measure of our global crisis,
she does not succumb to despair. As she makes affective memory and sensory
experience central to addressing this crisis, she demonstrates how Girard too
might have proceeded, had he retained insights from phenomenology that

are featured in his early work. Kristeva holds up revolt as the alternative to monsters and monstrous insignificance, explosive and implosive forms of violence, which threaten human survival in a fatherless age. According to Kristeva, humans take up revolt in two ways: through forgiveness and intimacy. What does Kristeva mean by *revolt*? Further, how do *forgiveness* and *intimacy*—two alternatives to the apocalypse that Girard also mentions but does not address in detail—feature in revolt? As Kristeva answers these questions, she demonstrates how we may step back from the brink and reclaim for mimetic theory the hope that is the most important legacy from Girard's early work.

Revolt is, for Kristeva, a kind of "returning" that she associates with the healing work of memory.[65] In the absence of intimacy, our family romances and social conflicts devolve into mimetic violence, catching us up in ongoing trauma. Trauma, the affective and bodily expression of the lack that haunts human being, closes off the future. Although we look to every new desire as a healing salve, because we are captive to traumatic memory, wounds born of mimetic rivalry only deepen. Only revolt, in the form of forgiveness and intimacy, heals. Only revolt grants access to an intimate domain, an intercorporeal and intersubjective space in which we can be reconstituted within Being, overcoming distortions in human relationships.[66] Revolt is not what mimetic doubles do when they take on each other as rivals. Neither does revolt *transgress* the law that, from Girard's perspective in *Battling to the End*, is the law of war. Revolt *displaces* violent, acquisitive mimesis.[67] As conduits of this displacement, forgiveness and intimacy initiate healing that *structures desire as cause rather than as goal.*[68]

Forgiveness is integral to healing from implosive and explosive violence. Kristeva locates the origin of the human capacity for forgiveness in early childhood, prior to our acquisition of language. For Kristeva, our initiation into language sets off a struggle for recognition, which Girard would typify as acquisitive rivalry. However, before our desire for being in the face of our lack of being is brought to expression in signs and before judgment is rendered within the Symbolic order that we lack being, we are supported by a founding intercorporeity that is experienced as protective of being. As a consequence, when we are caught in the throes of violence or depression, we can tap memories of supportive being. Early on, *before* our desires became acts in the world, we were *for-given*.[69] When we were novices at the task of living, *we found ourselves accepted and protected*. Kristeva writes, "It is possible to forgive ourselves by releasing, thanks to someone who hears us, our lack or our wound to an ideal order to which we are sure we belong."[70] Significantly, a loving father, not the father of the law, is "primitive guarantor of our safeties."[71]

This loving father features also in Kristeva's notion of *intimacy*. Intimacy that makes possible healing from traumatic violence is positive mimesis. Indeed, I have pointed out that Girard also refers to intimacy when he describes as "intimate mediation" processes that "transform mimeticism and open the door to the other side of violence."[72] But, as I have argued throughout, Girard does not offer a fully developed theory of intimate mediation. We do not learn from him how we may develop our capacity for intimacy as a strategic intervention in violent mimesis. Kristeva's notions of forgiveness and intimacy redress a lacuna in Girard's work. With these notions, Kristeva demonstrates how affect—sensation, mood, feeling—facilitates healing from mimesis-induced trauma, opening us to positive mimesis. Further, she shows how affect, linked with our earliest memories, plays a crucial role in the revolt that makes intimacy possible. After all, that we possess an idea of intimate mediation does not, in itself, release us from the grip of violent mimesis. By contrast, the revolt celebrated by Kristeva draws us into positive mimesis. Revolt, a bodily "re-turn," transpires as a sensory experience that restores and protects intimacy.[73]

For Kristeva, like forgiveness, the path humans take to intimacy—Girard's intimate mediation—also is established in early childhood. This is the path to which we return when we revolt. With Kristeva, in previous chapters we have looked at how familial functions associated with the *maternal body* and with *siblings* establish in the human subject initial pathways for mimetic desire as well as for acquisitive rivalries that emerge from that desire and devolve into violence. In examining Proust's *In Search of Lost Time*, we have explored how corporeal memories of early childhood undergird a break with maternally marked trauma. These memories, always tentative, make healing possible, but only as aesthetic promise. In reflecting on Sophocles's *Antigone*, we have seen healing take the form of an ethical praxis. Performing rituals over the body of her brother Polyneices, Antigone has revolted, assuming a stance oriented toward love, not sacrifice. Now we observe how the *paternal function* also establishes conditions for revolt, a return to pathways long neglected, that enable us to exchange apocalyptic violence and deadly meaninglessness for life-giving forgiveness and intimacy. Significantly, forgiveness and intimacy are not only embodied but also inter-subjective: they are *corporeal* and *corporate*. Drawing from *The Old Man and the Wolves* lessons in forgiveness and intimacy, our focus is on the old men of Santa Varvara who create a healing praxis evocative of the father of individual prehistory that can be accessed through narrative kinesis. Encountering paternal figures—fathers past and future—we may glimpse in Kristeva's novel expressions of intimacy and forgiveness that can inspire hope.

How Dead Is Dead? Paternal Memory and the Novel

Kristeva believes that the crisis we face is so close to us that theoretical reflection risks creating a false distance, distorting awareness. She arrives at this realization while grieving her father's death. At first glance, Kristeva's bereavement is unrelated to any larger crisis. However, Kristeva discovers that her loss, framed by the "incompetence and brutality of the medical and political system" in which it occurred, simultaneously mirrors a wider social crisis pervading not only eastern Europe but the global society. Kristeva proposes that a novel will enable her to portray personal and social distress better than would a theoretical work.[74] "A novel," she suggests, is "an immense and very powerful means of guiding us most deeply into our crises and farthest away from them at the same time."[75] Citing Proust, Kristeva points to *memory* and *sensation* as key to the work she takes up in her novel: "Truth shall arise only at the moment when the writer, taking two different objects, will posit their relation . . . in a metaphor." For Kristeva, metaphor enables us to give form "to inscriptions that are located on the border of the unnamable."[76]

As I have argued throughout this book, Kristeva's insights are supported by Guillemette Bolens's theory of narrative, which focuses on kinesis, or motor resonance, that links embodied cognition with narrative. Attested to as strongly in this exploration of *The Old Man and the Wolves* as in Kristeva's commentaries on Proust is Kristeva's belief in the transformative power of metaphor. Bolens's theory, grounded in empirical research, lends weight to Kristeva's claim by showing that, when an author and her readers respond to sensory experiences depicted in a narrative, we summon through kinesis past experiences like those described in that narrative. So also does Vittorio Gallese's notion of intercorporeity support Kristeva's claims that the narrative of *The Old Man and the Wolves* not only documents the loss of human relationship—when humans become mired in wolfish violence or debilitating meaninglessness—but also summons an active relationality among author, reader, and characters that taps into an "I can" of the body, initiating healing that leads to intimacy and positive mimesis.

With *The Old Man and the Wolves*, Kristeva wagers that metaphors shed light on a personal *and* cultural malaise that holds her readers and her in its grip: the imagination is "an antidote for the crisis." Kristeva writes that *The Old Man and the Wolves* is "anchored in a pain to which allegory aims to give significance without fixing it, having it vibrate, in an oneiric way, according to each reader's personal framework of ordeals and choices."[77] In this way the novel can create new spaces in which love still can thrive.[78] Moreover, in enabling us to rewrite the stories of our own lives, the novel facilitates movement away from repetitive engagement with trauma in order that we embrace memories that facilitate new and renewed engagements with others.

Even as Kristeva turns to the old men of Santa Varvara in search of paternal memories that heal, Girard would express skepticism about her quest. Although Kristeva and Girard agree on the demise of the father in modern society, they disagree on the implications of that death. Kristeva wants to work through paternal loss in order to retrieve life-giving paternal memories. But Girard dispenses with the father as a special object of study. Asserting that "the father explains nothing," Girard writes that if we are to get to the heart of the generative mechanism of desire and understand its violent workings, "we must put the father out of our minds and concentrate on the fact that the enormous impression made on the community by the collective murder is not due to the victim's identity per se, but to his role as unifying agent."[79] Of Freud's "murdered father" theory, Girard will keep the murder but not the father.[80] So also does he move the founding murder from a "familial framework" to a "societal framework."[81]

Kristeva is committed to examining our contemporary crisis in light of familial functions that establish initial pathways of mimetic desire in early childhood. She explores the effacement of the paternal function and tries to understand links between that and threats posed to ongoing human community associated with expanding banality. According to Kristeva, the dead father cannot be put out of our minds, as Girard would advise, because the father's legacy persists in the form of a trauma registered in our bodies. This trauma comes to expression not only in the reprise of parricide—sacrificial violence—but also in deadly banality that threatens to overwhelm us. Kristeva's goal is to retrieve a father for our time. This father cannot be the one who functioned as a repressive constraint on sacrificial culture—that father is gone forever. Indeed, Kristeva does not support efforts to "repair the father, soothe the mother, allow them to build a solid, introspective inside, master of its losses and wanderings." Kristeva sees psychoanalysis "rather as the instrument of a departure from that enclosure, not as its warden."[82] Kristeva places her hope in a different father.

This father, the father of individual prehistory or the "imaginary father,"[83] emerges in the process of primary identification or primary narcissism to which Kristeva refers as *Einfühling*. From Freud, Kristeva takes the core of *Einfühling* to be an "objectless and immediate identification."[84] A process initiated prior to the differentiation of subject and object, *Einfühling* is an opening to a nonobjectal other. Thus, a not-yet-a-subject immediately identifies with a not-yet-an-object. Predating triangulation in the Oedipal process, *Einfühling* introduces "thirdness." This process, precursor to the social, features a triad that shapes the dynamics of primary narcissism in each human infant. Held in place by twin magnets of attraction—a father of individual prehistory and an archaic mother—a fragile and unstable subject hangs suspended between them.[85] In its first stage, this ternary structure is "mimetic play" over emptiness.[86] Thus, for Kristeva, the twin parties to narcissism protect emptiness even as they guarantee that their child can bridge emptiness to enter language and society.

Offering a description reminiscent of Girard, Kristeva argues that this mimeticism is nonobjectal. One identifies "not with an object, but with what offers itself to me as a model."[87] Predating the acquisition of language and encountered by the proto-subject in moments that comprise, for it, the very founding of human "society," this model is described by Kristeva as a "pattern" that "reminds us of an archaic reduplication (rather than imitation)."[88] Processes aimed at incorporating the model and assuming its being as one's own do recall processes of oral, maternal assimilation. However, attuned to sounds on the edge of its being, the proto-subject is displaced from its chewing, swallowing, and nourishing existence to become "a subject of enunciation."[89]

Typifying the triadic relationship of which she writes as a "love story," Kristeva states that, at the very splitting that establishes the psyche, a subject emerges in an open system, supported between the One and another. Because love promises that for the One there is an Other, love promises being in difference. This magnet of identification is "neither an object of need or of desire."[90] Experienced only indirectly, as a logical possibility of language, a metaphoricity of being is testified to by sound "on the fringe of my being that transfers me to the place of the Other."[91] Apparent not in the words of the Symbolic, with which One seeks mastery of the Other, but only in the sonorous quality of those words, an infant is rocked gently in a hammock of sound as One says to an Other: "Isn't he beautiful?"[92]

The infant, initially anchored in the maternal matrix or body, finds in the father of individual prehistory a preannouncement of the social. Speaking of this father, Kelly Oliver confirms that he predates the father of the law. Idealization linked to this father turns not on demands but on "the transformation of bodily needs into communication and communion."[93] With the support of the father of individual prehistory, the infant's orientation in the world moves from its mouth to its ears. Just as a present and absent breast within a buccal space demarcates boundaries for a nascent subject *within* the maternal matrix, so also do sounds demarcate sameness and difference for an infant *on the edges* of the social matrix (a voice directed toward the infant now turns away from it toward another).[94] Individuals still attuned to the father of the law, despite his demise, may read this perceived difference as a prohibition and challenge— the mother's desire is directed elsewhere. However, in the Imaginary order of infancy, desire is framed by love rather than by law. Because the vocal chamber that is the nascent subject's world resonates for it as triangulated space, the difference mirrored by this space is not offered to the child as interdiction but as gift. As one's sounds directed toward an Other immeasurably enlarge the infant's world, they promise an alternative to the potentially imploding or exploding space of a mimetic dyad. These words are a sound bridge to communion in difference.

Nevertheless, if a sonorous anchor always founds a subject, securing it in a world of possibility, Kristeva emphasizes that the narcissistic parry reaches out over an abyss. Primary identification is fraught not only with possibility, but also with danger. Precisely because the parental poles are anchored within the Symbolic order, the quest for being is marked necessarily by mimetic desire. As a consequence, Kristeva recognizes that violence always shadows the subject: Trauma may eventually overlay early experience, blocking memories of paternal support that promised access to human community. Even so, the love story of early childhood offers a pathway to positive mimesis that we should revisit. After all, this story has established within us a founding capacity for forgiveness and for intimacy. In our time of crisis, it may provide our only source of hope.

Acting on her belief that artists (writers, musicians, poets, painters) maintain close tabs on the psychic landscape of primary identification (*Einfühling*) and the Imaginary father encountered there, Kristeva writes *The Old Man and the Wolves*. Sensitized to the importance of paternal memory by the loss of her own father, Kristeva seeks a father outside the constraints of a Symbolic order in which the father is always already dead. As novelist, Kristeva exemplifies what she has written elsewhere when she has explained that the artist gives new identifications "a voice, because, I would venture to guess, he clings more than anyone to the 'father in personal prehistory.'"[95] Despite the "widespread myth" that artists express Oedipal longing in their work, Kristeva dissents from this view: "The artist sees himself not as the mother's phallus, but as that ghostly third party to which the master aspires, as a loving version of the Third Party, a preoedipal father 'who first loved you' (according to the Gospels), a conglomeration of both genders (as Freud suggests). 'God is agape.'"[96]

The fathers of *The Old Man and the Wolves* evoke deep memories of fathers of individual prehistory who exemplify the work of artists who bring to voice possibilities for connection to others in difference (*Einfühling*) that is rooted in agape rather than in mimeticized conflict.

In the chapters that follow, I analyze *The Old Man and the Wolves* with a goal of crystallizing similarities and differences in Girard's and Kristeva's theories. I locate instances of mimetic conflict within the narrative and show how the novel supports a journey away from violence and toward reconciliation with others. I juxtapose my reading of *The Old Man and the Wolves* with critical insights about the novel indebted to Kristeva's psychoanalytic theory. As I also examine mimesis within the novel, I argue that an analysis of interrelations between memory, sensation, and violence must be incorporated into Girard's mimetic theory if his theory is to realize its full potential to explain both negative and positive mimesis. Throughout, I emphasize the importance of kinesis to the transformative powers of narrative. When bodily engagement in the world experienced by characters in the novel blends with Kristeva's and her readers' corporeal memories, our kinesic capacities are activated. In this novel, conflict that comes to expression not only in explosive violence directed against others but also in implosive violence directed toward oneself is countered through kinesic engagement with a restorative narrative that opens out on positive mimesis.

In chapter 7, I follow Kristeva as she makes *The Old Man and the Wolves* a vehicle for addressing debilitating emptiness that threatens human survival. Attuned to alternatives to meaninglessness that come into view in the novel, I focus on a specific kind of paternal memory oriented toward forgiveness and sensory intimacy that becomes an occasion for healing from trauma. In chapter 8, I explain how this healing potential may be accessed. Appealing to the Roman poets and to a Christology informed by Girard as well as by Orthodox Christianity, Kristeva shows us how we can step back from the brink of apocalypse and reclaim from Girard's early mimetic theory a hope in the power of positive mimesis.

CHAPTER 7

Not a Country for Old Men: Violence and Mimesis in Santa Varvara

All literature is probably a version of the apocalypse that seems to me rooted, no matter what its sociohistorical conditions might be, on the fragile border where identities do not exit or only barely so—double, fuzzy, heterogeneous, animal, metamorphosed, altered, abject.

—Julia Kristeva, *Powers of Horror*

The *Old Man and the Wolves* begins with a tale called "The Invasion." After crossing a frozen river and a windswept plain, wolves from the north now lurk on the edges of Santa Varvara seeking their prey. These "gray-coated, sharp-nosed carnivores, slinking singly or in packs through houses and gardens," wear people's faces and utter human speech.[1] Yet only the Old Man can see or hear them and smell their musky odor. Only he observes the marks their claws have made on the land and on the throats of "animals, birds, even women,"[2] and only he attributes increasing numbers of missing persons to the violence of the wolves. Are these wolves real? Is the Old Man, once a revered professor, senile? That the Old Man feels as if the wolves have invaded his very body does suggest dementia. He confides in Alba, a devoted student, telling her that the wolves have infected everyone. But she remains skeptical even as she learns that Chrysippus, the Old Man's best student, has disappeared and that Epictetus, her cat, has been found dead from strangulation with fang marks on his neck. Alba attributes Chrysippus's absence to his independent ways and believes hostile neighbors have killed her cat.

But even as the Old Man creates bemusement in his students, readers of the novel are encouraged to take his concerns seriously. The Old Man is Septicius Clarus, a classics scholar.[3] As he draws on Roman history and Ovid's *Metamorphoses* to explain the wolves to his students, we gradually embrace the truth and the horror of his story. After thousands of Santa Varvara guards who are supposed to preserve the city from harm are found dead, buried in a mass grave, we get our first sense that the Old Man can be trusted. Like his Roman namesake, Septicius Clarus, the Praetorian prefect who accompanied Hadrian to Britain to build a wall against the barbarians,[4] the Old Man may be our sole protector in a society that is fast being overtaken by deadly violence.

Although Septicius despises the barbarism of his day, he cautions against misplaced nostalgia for an earlier time. Septicius's missing student, Chrysippus, reminds this classics professor of the Stoics, reasonable men and women who lived "without ties to one another" and "looked unblinkingly at demystified images of self and community."[5] But after Septicius sees Chrysippus devoured by wolves before his very eyes, he now wonders "if anyone of that name ever existed."[6] We, who would join Septicius in following the trail of the wolves, know that his task and ours will be more complex than a Stoic-like Chrysippus could have imagined. Septicius recognizes that his skills in reasoning and his capacity for independent judgment, which he has honed over the years as a professor, may no longer be free of external compulsion.[7] The wolves have not killed him, but he feels them under his skin. If he is to challenge the wolves, it cannot be solely through summoning his powers of reason. Because they have attacked his body, Septicius will need to find a way to free his body, and not only his mind, from their violent grip. Even though Septicius is racked by pain, like the Roman prefect of old, he keeps watch from his window. Suffering, rather than a Stoic reason, will be the source of his salvation even as his "unwavering vigilance . . . prevents the barbarians from approaching his house."[8]

As the violence in Santa Varvara spreads, Septicius moves between two registers: the troubling present of Santa Varvara, in which he is known to most only as the Old Man, and the ancient Roman past, in which Septicius finds solace with the poets Ovid and Tibullus. Emblematic of a scission in the paternal function in Santa Varvara, the Old Man / Septicius draws us into its depths. We find ourselves caught up in a sacrificial economy that is destructive of paternity. Dr. Vespasian, a wolf-like counterpoint to the Old Man, exemplifies one side of the paternal function in a sacrificial Santa Varvara. Warns the narrator of the fate of the Old Man in such an economy: "In Santa Varvara they had killed the 'dead' father. Was the Old Man the last of them? All that remained were such as Vespasian."[9] With Septicius, we hear echoes of voices that attest to a different aspect of paternity. Exemplified by Septicius and by other old men in the novel who are his friends, this paternity is described as Christlike but not sacrificial. As the narrative centers on the figures of the old men, it attests to an affective and embodied experience that can mend division within the paternal function. In this way, the loving paternity which Septicius embodies can counter violence not only in Santa Varvara but in any contemporary locale subject to a similar contagion. Elements of the narrative that focus on Septicius's bodily engagement with the elegies of the Roman poets activate kinesic capacities in Kristeva, as author, and in her readers. As the poets enable Septicius to express compassion for others, the kinesic potential of Kristeva's corporeal narratology establishes a participatory threshold along which we too can experience transformative healing from trauma.

A Scission within the Paternal Function: Vespasian and the Lives of Wolves

The sacrificial side of the division within the paternal function, on which the novel initially focuses, comes to the fore as wolves invade Santa Varvara and Vespasian, emblematic of sacrificial paternity, becomes a dominant force in the narrative. The wolves' incursion, which has inspired the Old Man's watchfulness, lends itself to an analysis grounded in Girard's theory of mimetic rivalry and scapegoating, for the victims of the wolves' violence are scapegoats. According to Girard, individuals who are targets of mob violence are innocent of crimes of which they are accused; nevertheless, they are perceived to be guilty and are slain. Indeed, because Girard understands that scapegoating lies behind acts of human sacrifice, Girard equates the two.[10] In *The Scapegoat*, Girard identifies several characteristics or "stereotypes" of this deadly victimization. Drawing his definition of a stereotype from an early method of printing in which multiple copies of a document are produced from duplicate impressions of an original typographical element,[11] Girard lays out unvarying features of scapegoating that reoccur across time in diverse cultures and locales. An initial indicator that scapegoating may develop in a community is *a breach in the social order*.[12] A community is caught up in a crisis not of its own making: a plague, an epidemic, a cosmic or political disturbance. Santa Varvara is experiencing such a breakdown of order due to the ongoing murderous rampages of wolves, whose violence is reminiscent of the plagues that beset Europe in earlier centuries.[13] A second stereotype emerges as individuals subsequently seek out the origins of disorder and look for its cause (e.g., Jews were blamed for the plague). In the absence of social stability, *conflict among community members develops and spreads*. Individual is set against individual, neighbor against neighbor, as each sees the other as a potentially lethal threat. In time, such a contagion spreads in Santa Varvara. Truly, people are dying and those who are not already dead have begun to look different—even wolf-like.

Girard's theory is especially helpful for understanding how violence in Santa Varvara is both microcosmic *and* macrocosmic, engulfing individuals and the wider society. Girard observes that every human is drawn toward what another human desires because of a more basic desire to be like the other; for each human imagines that another can confer on it a plenitude of being that it lacks.[14] However, because the other also lacks being, both individuals mirror each other in their desires, and both are caught up in an increasingly fraught competition for being. Inclined toward mimetic rivalry, they become even more vulnerable to its excesses in the presence of social disorder. As disruptions in society exacerbate a sense of lack, relationships become more contentious.[15]

The novel's narrative follows a relationship between Alba and her fiancé, Vespasian.[16] When they first meet, Vespasian and Alba discover in each other a way to redress lack, and experience a wholeness of being. Although he is a successful army surgeon, Vespasian is consumed by self-loathing and enraged that he is insufficiently appreciated by others.[17] Vespasian bears disgust on his frame; his eyes are expressionless, as if covered by inoperable cataracts; his nose and mouth are distorted, giving him the appearance of a vulture.[18] That Alba initially is enthralled by Vespasian makes him feel valued. In turn, Alba, an immigrant, desires an enhanced social standing she believes will come to her as the wife of a high-ranking military officer. Each now perceives the other as a salvific being. Alba, the marginalized foreigner, locates in her successful surgeon husband the security and recognition she lacks. Vespasian, who has felt inadequate despite his professional success, sees a successful person reflected back to him in Alba's gaze. However, because their desires for each other emerge out of that fundamental lack of being, each fails the other. Their desire turns to anger when neither can be for the other what she and he have desired. Instead of completing each other's being, they become rivals in an elusive quest for being.

The classic form of mimetic rivalry described by Girard focuses on rivals who quarrel over an object. In Alba and Vespasian's relationship, such an object is missing. Girard recognizes this phenomenon and describes a form of rivalry in which an object has receded from view to be replaced by a competition for prestige. He writes, "Each is concerned with acquiring the prestige that threatens to devolve upon the other." Fighting over prestige is literally fighting over nothing. In the absence of a concrete object, "The 'nothing' of prestige appears to be everything."[19] Alba and Vespasian will be consumed by this fighting.[20]

Alba and Vespasian's relationship transitions into rivalrous and deadly violence. The elevated social status Alba seeks proves unattainable. She loses ground even as Vespasian, mirroring Alba's own sense of inadequacy, lashes out at Alba. He tells her that she is stupid; she makes Vespasian look ridiculous in front of his peers; but for him she would have no status, no excuse for being at all. Alba tries to love and accept Vespasian. At first she attributes his tirades to anxiety about the wolves, but he seems more greedy and angry every day. Alba's physical appearance changes too: her skin becomes dry; her hair loses its luster. Hatred curls up inside her.[21] Alba likes to think of Vespasian's persona as a cancer, a sarcoma of "what, according to the Professor, 'had once been the soul.'" She doesn't realize that, as witness to Vespasian's metamorphosis, she too has become cancerous. Hecuba-like, she plots revenge.[22]

Once each other's cherished model, Vespasian and Alba now regard each other with violent antipathy. Hideous strangers to each other, they also know each other well. As Girard describes this stage of mimetic rivalry, they "cannot say or do or feel anything without finding that their very same words, actions, and feeling are immediately reflected back to them by the 'satanic' mirror of their rival."[23] As their reciprocal hatred of each other intensifies, we recall Girard's assertion that a breaking point will be reached.[24]

That Vespasian and Alba perceive each other as threatening, nonhuman monsters creates a link between them and the wolf-driven, social unrest unfolding around them. Vespasian is attacked by a wolf that injects its venom into him. His eyes change: "They're yellow now, like the eyes of an animal."[25] A witness to her husband's metamorphosis, Alba too "is necessarily contaminated." One day, instead of words, "the barking of a dog" comes from Alba's mouth.[26] Embodying on a small scale the violence spreading through Santa Varvara, Alba and Vespasian's interactions promise to become deadly.

The couple's relationship has an expressly contemporary cast, for Vespasian and Alba exude an overwhelming sense of emptiness. The narrator of the novel observes that a lover typically "selects an idol or at least a fetish to adore. But Vespasian had no inner shrine at which to worship: he had fenced it round with frontiers, and inhabited an area with reversible borders and merely temporary thresholds."[27] Alba speaks candidly of her husband: "He was no one, not really a person at all. We think those who hurt us are devils. But no—all we see is a mask with no one behind it."[28] Alba and Vespasian's mimetic desire is emptied of all affect except the most deadly.

The army surgeon and his wife are like their neighbors in this way. Consumed by "the ordinary," they settle into "banality."[29] Even though they are mimetic rivals, who could summon strong feelings in each other, Alba and Vespasian's conversations are largely characterized by an absence of affect. Discussing Alba and Vespasian in an interview, Kristeva comments that in their speech we see "the integration of aggression but under the ruinous guise of an erasure of meaning."[30] Kristeva describes Alba's actions as neutralized, impossible to describe, even in the extreme murderous facets they might exhibit. Alba does not exhibit an individual pathology; rather, in a world in which Alba doubles have become the norm, her character "assumes the seriousness of a societal event."[31] As for Vespasian, Kristeva describes him as "an individual without inner life, almost psychotic, 'either an active monster or monstrously insignificant'—one can't tell which."[32]

In an earlier era, the residents of Santa Varvara would have been satisfied to seek in each other a fullness of being even when it led to violent rivalry;

now, eye-to-eye relationships are gradually being supplanted. However, as exemplified by Alba and Vespasian, the residents of Santa Varvara are caught between active monsters and monstrous insignificance (*monstre actif ou monstrueux d'insignifiance*).[33] Trapped in an anesthetizing social environment and bombarded by media images, the Albas and Vespasians of Santa Varvara convey no feelings for others or display any depth of expression.[34] Screens—television, computer, mobile phone—already the preferred site for the negotiation of mimetic desire, are also exclusive sites for what passes as human relationships.[35] With mimetic desires displayed on a screen of spectacle as "social media," in Santa Varvara, "the beams of people's eyes never met except in a screen."[36] But spectacle-mediated permutations in mimetic conflict exacerbate the lack of being that initially precipitates this conflict. Alternatively, if these screens prove incapable of bearing the weight of mimetic desire, violence may erupt through the fantasy surface. Kristeva represents this violence with the figure of wolves: Thus, even as Vespasian and Alba are swept into a vortex of violence, Kristeva wants her readers think expansively about violence. Muses Kristeva, "The wolves are contagious; they infect people to the extent that one can no longer make out their human faces. They symbolize everyone's' barbarity, everyone's criminality. They finally signify the invasion of banality, which erases the entire criterion of value amid the racketeering, corruption, wheeling and dealing."[37] While the wolves are blamed for the crisis that now grips the city, in truth, the residents of Santa Varvara are indistinguishable from these wolves.

At this point, a third stereotype that Girard claims is featured in every scapegoating scenario emerges in Santa Varvara. Girard writes that community unrest builds until it eventually polarizes around one apparently random victim who is believed by the others to be the cause of the problem. *The one around whom all the others circle is the scapegoat.*[38] Although the mob latches onto its victim seemingly by chance, Girard identifies *stereotypic victim marks*. Individuals who are attacked typically are outsiders by reason of gender, nationality, or religion; they are likely to stand at either the highest end of a society (as do Oedipus and Marie Antoinette) or at its lowest end (as do lynching victims in the American South). Victims may walk with a limp or have another physical disability; often they are suspected by their persecutors of having a predilection for incest, orgies, or other rule-defying behavior.[39] From the perspective of a neutral outsider, the victim of scapegoating is wholly innocent of all charges; from the perspective of the community that aligns as a mob against the victim, the victim is responsible not only for all that threatens the society but also for the peace that will follow his or her death.[40]

The mob banishes or, more typically, kills its victim. After the sacrifice, a community previously divided and under siege engages in a celebratory feast. In this final moment, another stereotype emerges: *The scapegoat is salvific.* Just as the scapegoat has been the source of absolute threat, so also in death is he or she the locus of restorative power that returns the community to peace. Ever after, the community will see itself as captive of a sacred power that lies beyond them. Thus, for Girard, the sacrificial death of the scapegoat is a founding rite, creative of human society.[41] Over time, when humans are again caught in a cycle of violence, *religion* emerges in the form of *rituals of sacrifice* that re-create in domesticated form the original violence against an innocent victim; *culture* emerges as *myths preserve the logic of scapegoating,* justify the actions of the mob, and confirm the guilt of the victim.[42]

Thus, Girard would not be surprised that Septicius draws on his background as a classics scholar to link Ovid's tale of Lycaon, which hearkens back to Greek myth,[43] with the crisis he observes in Santa Varvara. Indeed so closely does the present mirror the past that the professor becomes disoriented: "Was he in the first century . . . dreaming of the metamorphosis that took place in human beings as they entered upon a new era, a new age just as steeped in brutishness as the old? Or was he in the present, in Santa Varvara . . . ?"[44] Past and present stories join, as if enclosed in a poetic quatrain. Lycaon's tale begins with a sacrificial *feast* and ends with a *man* becoming a wolf; Vespasian's story begins with a *man*—Vespasian—becoming a wolf, "a real Lycaon,"[45] and subsequently ends with a violent *"feast."* That each narrative features an outsider as scapegoat—a Molossian and the immigrant Alba—brings to view the sacrificial mechanism they share.

Ovid attests to this mechanism and its pervasive power when he tells us that humans, born of the remains of giants whose own desires led to their destruction, are beset by problematic desire from the moment of their creation. Envious of the gods' being and unwilling to accept their own lack of being, these humans are violent. Moreover, humans' first efforts at social interaction, memorialized by Lycaon, man-become-wolf, are founded in sacrifice. Significantly, this sacrifice takes the form of scapegoating. Rather than engage in civil discord, this race of humans picks one victim—the Molossian outsider—to dismember, kill, and cook.[46] Scapegoating ending in alimentary sacrifice also is definitive of the contagion of violence that threatens to destroy Santa Varvara.

From a perspective informed by Girard, we should not be surprised that the Old Man forecasts the violent denouement of Alba and Vespasian's relationship.[47] Sitting with the couple in a bar, the Old Man begs Alba and Vespasian not to be afraid of wolves, and he says that he is looking everywhere for signs of his old friends. Vespasian laughs at his delusion as the three of them gaze at the TV behind the bar. Turning away, Septicius thinks, "He was a hard man, this Vespasian, a real Lycaon." As he leaves the bar, Septicius whispers the words of Tibullus, "Soon death will come, its head shrouded in darkness."[48]

A few days after Septicius's warning, a crowd gathers on the street. The authorities have "fished out the body of a woman" from a lake.[49] Clothed in a suit with black dots on a white background that matches one of Alba's suits, its face is blue, bloated, and spattered with mud; the body bears a preternatural resemblance to a gigantic trout. The crowd spies a bite mark on the victim's neck. "The wolves," cries the crowd; "probably stabbed by her lover," someone utters.[50] Back at Vespasian and Alba's apartment, the table is set for a dinner that Alba never serves. One of her specialties—trout marinated in wine and served up with herbs and fresh ginger—has been left "to rot in the oven."[51] The reader understands that, just as the Molossian outsider's death was celebrated with a feast, Vespasian has feasted on a different dish this evening.

Tasked with the responsibility of investigating the mysterious death of the young woman at the lake is Stephanie Delacour, daughter of an ambassador to Santa Varvara, former student of Septicius, childhood friend of Alba, and crime reporter for a French newspaper. Girard's theory sheds light on Stephanie's observations, enabling us to recognize that she is reporting an act of scapegoating and sacrifice. After all, as described by Girard, scapegoating inevitably progresses toward the death of an innocent victim who often is an outsider. In Santa Varvara, suspicion has fallen on marginal foreigners such as Alba. Already her father and mother have been killed. Further, in the hierarchy-bound world of the army, Alba always has been a misfit. Whereas Vespasian has enjoyed top standing among the other army doctors, Alba has been an outsider among their wives. Although Alba has done her best to find her "own proper place" among the other wives, she has never succeeded. Over time, she has become "more and more alienated from those hostile strangers."[52] Although the death at the lake initially does not look like an act of mob violence, as is typically associated with stereotypes of scapegoating, Stephanie discovers the body under such circumstances. As Stephanie walks toward the scene of the crime, she observes something she describes as "odd." Crowds on this street are an uncommon occurrence because there are no stores in the neighborhood to attract groups.[53] Nevertheless, Stephanie has to press through a throng to view the body. As a result, the death Stephanie investigates fully replicates the stereotyped sequence of events that Girard has labeled scapegoating. What initially has appeared to be an isolated instance of domestic violence has galvanized a crowd, implicating all of Santa Varvara.

On the Trail of Mimesis: A Detective Story

Readers inclined to trust the insights of Septicius believe that the dead woman pulled from the lake is Alba and that Vespasian has killed her. Readers attuned to mimetic theory already have anticipated a deadly turn in the spiraling mimetic violence that envelops Alba and Vespasian; they too believe the woman at the lake is Alba. Now, with a dead victim and all but certain knowledge of her identity and that of the person who has killed her, the story should be wrapping up.[54] Nevertheless, in a counterintuitive move, Kristeva titles the next part of the novel, "Detective Story."[55] Puzzled readers wonder if their trust in Septicius has been misplaced.

Anticipating these qualms, Kristeva offers guidance. Speaking directly to her readers, Kristeva explicitly identifies herself as the author of *The Old Man and the Wolves* and the novel's narrator. She issues an invitation: "You're invited into a new and outlandish world inhabited by strange characters . . . unapproachable monsters speaking a dead or even nonexistent language."[56] Kristeva asks that her readers reconsider their confidence in the reliability of the story of "The Invasion," and she decries the presumed neutrality of the narrator's voice. She now ascribes to her tale a degree of arrogance, a "presumptuousness of those who are sure of themselves and of traditions and beliefs that conceal a tendency to jump to conclusions."[57] Kristeva proposes not only to challenge her readers but also to examine her own authority as author. Kristeva will assume the role of detective, engaging in a self-reflective and critical exercise on her mimetic investment in her characters. Writes Kristeva of her new approach, "If I change the way I tell my tale, the meaning of the shadows you identify with changes too, as do the proportions they contain of artifice and plausibility. The Old Man is no longer merely the Old Man; Alba may be you; and as for Vespasian . . . Who is to know who's in charge in Santa Varvara once I start interfering!"[58] Kristeva challenges herself and the novel's readers to explore their own relationships to the story they have been reading. Her call will test readers' confidence in the wisdom of the Old Man and transform their experience of the novel, leading to additional reflections on ways in which mimetic theory can illuminate the novel.[59]

A motif associated with Kristeva's theoretical writings—*intertextuality*—sheds light on the reconfiguration of the novel as a detective story. The transposition of one literary genre into another recalls Kristeva's notion of subjects in process in the analytic encounter. The psychoanalytic concepts of transference and countertransference contribute to our efforts to understand what we may initially perceive to be an abrupt and problematic transition in the novel. Kristeva perceives that, for both the analyst and the author, meaning is forged in a relationship with the other. The reader or analysand who reflects on the story of her life in a novel or analytic encounter transfers those meanings to the author or analyst. Moreover, these transferential relations between author and reader, analyst and analysand, are reciprocated. The "truth in action" that Kristeva associates with analytic and literary settings leads the participants forward, possibly to a future characterized by openness to shared meaning.[60] Thus, in writing *The Old Man and the Wolves*, Kristeva takes full purchase on her theoretical understanding of the relationship between art and analysis. Author and analyst, reader and analysand, are mutually implicated in a quest for narrative meaning and understanding.

In the novel's epigraph, Kristeva likens herself to Ovid when she quotes the first lines of the *Metamorphoses*: "I resolved to tell of creatures being metamorphosed into new forms."[61] Ovid enables Kristeva to highlight uncertainties of speech in storytelling. Advising her reader to anticipate all number of roles for her investigator Stephanie, "Sherlock Holmes, James Bond, and even Mike Hammer,"[62] Kristeva also instructs the reader that the detective in her story "may be metamorphosed into a poet."[63] The speech of the detective may reach "the extreme of its own strength and certainty," which we associate with hardboiled detective fiction, requiring a departure into more flexible speech, speech that is attuned to sensation, speech that is, in a word, poetry.[64] This metamorphosis awaits the final section of the novel; until then, detective Stephanie Delacour will explore all avenues in her effort to find the person responsible for the death of the woman at the lake.

That Kristeva embraces detective fiction midway through *The Old Man and the Wolves* is not surprising. Kristeva recalls that Freud was a reader of detective novels, and that Freud once compared the psychoanalyst to a detective.[65] For Kristeva, the detective novel is the literary genre that most directly exemplifies and invites an intertextual or transferential reading.[66] According to Kristeva, those who perceive the analyst to be "one supposed to know" reductionistically distort complex relations forged in psychoanalysis; so also does Kristeva think that the detective "who is supposed to know" misrepresents the detective's stance. Stephanie Delacour comes to Santa Varvara to solve a crime, "but she can't find out who is guilty because they all turn into wolves."[67] Rather than signal incompetence, Stephanie represents the experience of all of us in a contemporary world in which we are surrounded by crimes and unable to find perpetrators. The detective mirrors the lives of all those who are "supposed to know" but do not.

The impasse at which Stephanie arrives in her efforts to detect the perpetrators of crime in Santa Varvara in order to expose the true identity of the wolves and find the wolf who has killed Alba has a clear relationship to Girard's theory of scapegoating. Girard points out that contemporary society expresses an unprecedented concern for victims.[68] In no other era has there been such a public expression of concern for the sufferings of others. Nevertheless, he recognizes that even though we are equipped, especially in the present day, to recognize victimization, we nevertheless continue to present ourselves as ignorant of scapegoating. We continue to believe in the guilt of our scapegoats; however, we do so in a manner distinctive to our time. Our concern for victims has become a competition of mimetic rivalries. We outbid ourselves in our efforts to "one up" our neighbors: "The victims most interesting to us are always those who allow us to condemn our neighbors. And our neighbors do the same. They always think first about victims for whom they hold us responsible."[69] Thus, from the perspective on "one who is supposed to know," Stephanie wants to find the person or persons responsible for the crimes of the wolves. She wants to "one up" not only her neighbors but all other reporters. She wants to get the scoop on death in Santa Varvara, creating headlines in Paris. Stephanie's gamesmanship shows that she has not yet considered self-reflexively her own involvement in the violence that grips Santa Varvara. She remains caught up in mimesis that Girard ascribes to a mythological universe in which individuals "don't detect mimetic snowballing because we participate in it without realizing it."[70]

As the novel unfolds, Kristeva elects a strategy that resonates with Girard's own thoughts on how one "investigates" scapegoating rituals. Girard specifically mentions detective fiction when he likens an investigation of scapegoating to a criminal investigation. All criminals, Girard states, lay down a trail for their pursuers, notwithstanding their efforts to hide their tracks.[71] Comparing the discerning eyes of the scapegoating investigator with those of a detective, Girard observes that when successive proofs of an engraving (and here he recalls the stereotypic production of prints) are subjected to close investigation, patterns may be discerned. "Once the law of their variations has been apprehended," writes Girard, "the true object is correctly perceived."[72] The detective and the mimetic investigator proceed alike in apprehending this law.

Even so, as Kristeva follows the trail of a criminal, she does not always have Stephanie move in ways similar to Girard; instead, Kristeva takes a distinct approach. Where Girard focuses on obtaining *knowledge* of a crime, exposing bad mimesis,[73] Kristeva is *kinesically engaged* as Stephanie looks for clues about violence in Santa Varvara among the bodies of the living and the dead. She understands that when her corporeal memories and those of her readers are activated by narrative, her readers and she do not only tap trauma, they also access transformative, healing possibilities.

Kristeva's sensitivity to the role of the body in mimetic violence, especially in a time where implosive violence wreaks more havoc than does explosive violence, illuminates mimesis in new ways. In particular, Kristeva's corporeal narratology facilitates our reflection on how negative mimesis can be countered by positive mimesis, thereby augmenting Girard's theory. In this regard, that Stephanie is our guide on this journey is of decisive import. In linking the role of detective with that of analyst, Kristeva is able to share with readers the process by which Stephanie gradually distances herself from involvement with mimeticized violence in Santa Varvara to move toward a nonviolent ethic and practice. This journey also will see Stephanie stand back from her initial efforts to obtain knowledge of a crime ("Detective Story"—Part II). Instead, she will make a poetic, bodily investment in alternatives to conflict ("Capriccio"—Part III).

Stephanie is not cast in the mold of Watson's Sherlock Holmes, a man of whom Watson says, "Thus have you reasoned it all out beautifully in one long chain!"[74] Rather, Stephanie can be likened to the Holmes whose prowess Professor Moriarty tests so profoundly that Holmes wonders if they have exchanged roles.[75] As a consequence, Kristeva brings out in the novel elements of reciprocity that are found also in psychoanalysis when an analyst recognizes that transference is reciprocal and relational. She opens the way not only to transferential relations among characters in the novel, but also to transferential relations between herself, the readers whose skepticism about Septicius Kristeva has just solicited, and the text she now invites us to continue reading.[76] As access to nonsacrificial mimesis becomes a shared goal, these relations prove decisive for Stephanie, Kristeva, and the reader.

Moving forward with the "Detective Story," readers and author are touched by wolfish transformations we have perceived previously to be wholly external to our lives. Mimetic processes in the novel now require that we acknowledge our own wolfishness. Uncomfortable though we may be, when we identify with the wolves, we gain access to the depths of the novel. From that vantage point, the strengths of Girard's theory, as well as the need to augment his theory with Kristeva's insights, become visible.

A new and disturbing image now is associated with Santa Varvara. Whereas Santa Varvara is defined by invading wolves in the Old Man's story, in the detective story, a colorful sculpture is emblematic. This sculpture occupies the center of a fountain that is located at the foot of a modern high-rise that is home to Alba and Vespasian.[77] Said by the city's inhabitants to represent "the future" of Santa Varvara, the sculpture is a mass of disjointed limbs: "a giant eye, an enormous nose, red lips revealing teeth as white and shiny and massive as a kitchen sink, silicone-swollen breasts, and a nymph-like rear . . . not to mention the beautiful ogress's Titanic straw hat and matching sunshade." As the sculpture rotates on its axis, great spurts of water fly up from among the segments of plastic flesh and dowse anyone who comes within range. Rather than attest to a future, the nightmarish body fragments of this monstrous sculpture cause physical discomfort (Septicius shuts his eyes when he passes) and remind us of the violence that has already has decimated Santa Varvara and may do so again.[78]

The fragmented body that is the fountain's focal point recalls the figure of Medusa in Ovid's *Metamorphoses*. In this work, Ovid names the image of a person whose lips are silently contorted or from whose lips spew nonsensical words as "*os*": "a face deprived of the capacity to speak." What is most frightening about Ovid's Medusa is not her head or gaze but her *os*. In a singularly terrifying way, Medusa possesses a "face deprived of a capacity to speak."[79] Just as Ovid calls Medusa a "memorable monster," so also is the sculptural fountain memorable. Here Ovid's use of "monster" recalls "*moneo*": "to point out" or "to warn."[80] The sculpture in the center of Santa Varvara is a portent of a community's *os*: The residents of that city in increasing numbers share an incapacity for human speech.

The sculpture highlights a developing fragmentation of the story in which readers *and* author participate. As a first sign of division, we observe Stephanie's reaction to the body of the woman found dead in the lake. When Stephanie exhibits her press card, the crowd parts and permits her to move toward the body, lift the cloth covering it, and observe it directly. Despite her immediate access to the corpse, Stephanie remains uncertain that the body is Alba's. Familiar with Alba's apparel, Stephanie does note that the suit matches Alba's favorite; further, on hearing that Alba was last seen walking by the lake with a man, Stephanie recognizes that the man's description exactly matches Vespasian. Even so, Stephanie remains unconvinced that the body she has viewed is Alba's or that Vespasian is responsible. Perceiving that a drowning would have been an unlikely conclusion to their psychodrama, Stephanie prefers also to tie the dead body to the wolves. They, rather than a disillusioned lover, are the most prevalent menace in Santa Varvara.[81] Nevertheless, she decides to confront Vespasian with the problem of the missing Alba.

Stephanie hopes that excessive consumption of alcohol will put Vespasian in an expansive mood for conversation. Vespasian does acknowledge that he saw a couple arguing at the lake. He admits that the woman could have been a double for Alba, belligerently proclaims that he could kill Alba though he hasn't yet, and asserts that, when he does so, no one will believe that he did it. But his words are lost on Stephanie. In a fog after sharing too many drinks with Vespasian, she ends up in bed with him. In her head,

Stephanie hears Septicius's voice. He is lamenting the hate that characterizes their time and the wolves that invade and inhabit them. Stephanie hears the professor ask her to remember with him what Ovid's and Tibullus's elegies celebrated: a sense of belonging and bond among persons. By contrast, the citizens of Santa Varvara experience no connection at all or only the kind that functions as "a kind of noose."[82] As they turn into wolves, they are possessed by "a desire for the impossible."[83]

But Stephanie is deaf to Septicius's words: she has slept with a wolf. Soon after, Stephanie receives a letter from Alba in which Alba confesses to Stephanie that she has been poisoning Vespasian by putting sleeping pills and tranquilizers in his coffee and soup. She also has been researching other chemical poisons. Explaining herself to Stephanie, Alba states that there is no difference between what he has been trying to do to her and her actions against him: each has been trying to kill the other.[84] Reflecting on her actions, Alba writes that when she has looked deep within herself, she has found only hatred. Did she catch hatred from Vespasian or he from her? Alba says that she can't tell.[85]

Alba's letter is worrisome. Stephanie has been attempting to find out if Vespasian has killed Alba; now, thinking about his bloodshot eyes and general disarray, Stephanie wonders if she has been seeking the wrong perpetrator.[86] She recalls that her newspaper sent her to Santa Varvara to report on the wolves. Her investigation has focused on the homicide by the lake. Now Stephanie wonders what kind of story she can possibly send home to her editor: Who is the victim? Who is the murderer? Alba and Vespasian appear caught between life and death in a contagion of mimeticized violence. Alba may or may not be dead; and Vespasian, if poisoned, is possibly in the throes of death. If Vespasian succumbs to death from poisoning in the wake of having murdered Alba, each will be a murderer and murdered. Further, Stephanie is complicit. She has spent a night with Vespasian; she has held Alba's letter in trust. Caught in the mirrored violence, she puzzles: "Who is the wolf now? Me?"[87] Mimetic doubling and contagion are proliferating, bringing Stephanie uncomfortably close to Alba. Stephanie appears wholly caught up in a contagion of violent mimesis that characterizes the ongoing metamorphoses of humans into wolves in Santa Varvara.

The Very Picture of a Wolf

After the death of the woman at the lake, a double for Alba,[88] the professor's protective mission reaches a critical juncture. With Stephanie sleeping with wolves, Septicius is all but alone in perceiving that Santa Varvara is being consumed by spreading violence. What lifts Septicius above the mob, enabling him to perceive the threat the wolves pose when others are inured to their violence? How is he able to distinguish the innocent from the guilty and the wolves from their victims when all around him a contagion is obliterating differences? In order to uphold his vigilance, the professor seeks wisdom in figures from the classical past: Suetonius,[89] Tibullus, and Ovid.

Of the three, Suetonius quickly disappoints. His pragmatism—"devoid of irony or reproach, vice or virtue"—is matched by his propensity for telling tales of poisoning, lust, and debauchery. As virtue and vice are treated alike by Suetonius, his history becomes a "porno thriller" of no use to the professor.[90] Septicius finds more to sustain him in the works of Tibullus and Ovid. Tibullus's elegies speak to Septicius of his own suffering. They "sing of infinite death. They drink deep of death, they grow drunk on it, but they don't believe in it." The professor sees Tibullus anticipating Christ even as his melancholy words suggest inconsolability rather than resurrection.[91] Ovid too offers inspiration, for his stories of the metamorphoses of humans into shrubs, rivers, flowers, and animals describe the situation that besets the citizens of Santa Varvara. Yet even as he reads Tibullus and Ovid to his students, Septicius's students find these figures boring and irrelevant in an age of instant communication. Only the professor locates in their writing a way to respond to the current barbarism that infects Santa Varvara. Septicius commits himself to "looking at Santa Varvara through the eyes of Ovid and Tibullus."[92]

Ovid's *Metamorphoses* supports the professor's faculties of discernment. Even as the *Metamorphoses* recounts Greek and Roman myths, which Girard would claim uncritically attest to scapegoating and justify mob violence, Ovid does not preserve the authority of myth when he tells these tales. Unlike metamorphoses in the *Aeneid*, a work that moves toward stable endings and cultural order, Ovid's transformations appear at the end of episodes, inserting instability into his tales.[93] Indeed, as Joseph Solodow reminds us, the narrator of the *Metamorphoses* asserts that his stories may not be reliable.[94]

Because the narrator distances himself from the myths of which he writes, Septicius can find in the *Metamorphoses* maneuvering room he needs to move away from the violence that threatens Santa Varvara. For example, Lycaon's bestial nature is revealed, even as Ovid explains neither why he has changed into a wolf nor if that change is good or bad.[95] Instead, Lycaon's prior native bestiality is appropriately exposed by Jupiter. When Ovid likens Lycaon's transformation to a work of art and suggests that Lycaon has become "the very picture" of a wolf, Ovid highlights elements in his writing on which Septicius can draw to expose scapegoating. Metamorphosis transforms that which is personal or individual, and therefore potentially inaccessible to judgment, into *a perception that can be grasped*.[96] In this way, entry to Ovid's world through kinesis is activated.

Ovid is a rich resource for the professor. For Ovid, violence is associated with the *loss of speech*. As Lynn Enterline observes, Ovid is preoccupied with stories that "testify to the power, failure, and disturbing unpredictability of the human voice."[97] Beings who lose their voices or whose voices fail to effect the change they seek are regularly associated by Ovid with the metamorphoses about which he writes. The speechless face is one most alienated from its previous existence.[98] Lycaon exemplifies Ovid's sensitivity to embodied speech. Lycaon is the first character to lose his human shape, and that change is signaled by a change in the shape of his lips. His foaming mouth, recalling rabies-infected animals, marks Lycaon's transformation from human to animal.[99]

Ovid also is fascinated with the productive possibilities of speech and silence. Song is a focal point, for the narrator claims to be "singing" his stories. Persons typically are more aware of their bodies when singing than when speaking. Recognizing their voices as instruments, they focus not only on words but also on their mouths, diaphragms, and lungs. Singers are sensitive to where they form the words in their mouths: their tongues' proximity to their teeth and the way their lips form around their teeth are critical to the tone and quality of the sounds they emit. Sharing the speech of figures in the *Metamorphoses* with his readers, Ovid expresses a keen awareness not only of the figures' tongues, lips, and breath but also of his own.[100] Thus, when Ovid "resolves to tell of creatures being metamorphosed," he asks that the gods "*breathe* on these my undertakings."[101] The mind is moved to speak by drawing breath from somewhere else. Anima (mind) is linked also with air or breath: breathing marks the possibilities of life, just as death is associated with the exhaling breath into the wind.[102] On the one hand, speech signals death, for one dies when the breath of speech passes for the last time from one's lips; on the other hand, when taken up by others, speech garners one a kind of immortality. Ovid alludes to this aspect of speech when, in the concluding passages of the *Metamorphoses*, he describes how his words and songs will be spoken or sung by others who will revivify them with their lips and breath.[103]

Yet even as Ovid testifies to the enduring power of speech, *how* songs are revivified remains an open question for him. To be sure, the affective power of faces that have been deprived of their capacity to speak (*os*) is a recurrent presence in the *Metamorphoses*. The lips of persons—silent, protesting, uttering monstrous words—do function in the *Metamorphoses* as a critique of fantasies of coherent, meaningful, death-defying speech.[104] Although Ovid displays keen insight, he is unable to break fully with the tales he tells; he does not expose the scapegoat mechanism. So also do the rays of discerning light from Ovid that reach into Santa Varvara not free Septicius from the violence these rays illuminate. Septicius's access to a nonsacrificial alternative to scapegoating must await his encounter with Tibullus.

Nevertheless, Septicius learns from Ovid that the human capacity to attain a critical distance from scapegoating is sustained by our bodies: sensory experiences rather than analytical thought found our capacity to replace sacrifice with nonviolent connection with others. Thus, with Septicius's powers of perception sharpened by his reading of Ovid, he takes the measure of threats to Santa Varvara. Newly sensitive to mouths of its residents, the professor reads faces and looks for the *os* of those whose visages signal that they have fallen victim to the wolves. He spies "furry cheekbones lengthening into muzzles, with lips drawn back to reveal the fangs of wolves"; he observes the face "of someone who might have been a man if his ears hadn't been so hairy and his eyes so phosphorescent."[105] So too does the professor become increasingly attentive to the speech of Santa Varvara's inhabitants, for Ovid has taught him that loss of speech is symptomatic of a loss of humanity. A series of exchanges between Alba and Vespasian to which Septicius has been privy is illustrative: "'Work!' (Vespasian.) 'Power.' (Alba.) 'Exactly!' (Vespasian.) 'So what about boredom?' (Alba.) 'What is it?' (Vespasian.)."[106] In a telling permutation of the metamorphoses of which Ovid wrote, faces on

TV and computer screens represent a new *os*, for screen images radicalize the potential for a "face to be deprived of a capacity to speak" and threaten to shut down the affective power of all human speech. Meaningful connections are wholly missing from the words the citizens of Santa Varvara throw at each other; their inability to converse signals that their humanity has been replaced by wolfishness.

Alerted by Ovid's songs to the deadly tenor of his time, Septicius recognizes the importance of countering life-denying with life-affirming voices. Breathing life into Ovid with his own lungs, the professor seeks to enliven Santa Varvara with the very air of the ancient civilization that was inspirited by the voices of its poets. Asking his students what has become of these men, the Old Man answers his own question: "I think they've undergone a metamorphosis. Into what? Into us. Into you."[107] Others disparage Septicius for clinging to the past; but all he has sought to do "via metamorphoses and elegies set down in a dead language that he rehabilitated was to create a kind of music."[108] Repeatedly, "the bustling crowd of metamorphoses" in his mind divests itself of matter: *'sine materia, exercitium arithmeticae occultum nescientis se numerare animi.'* It was a kind of airy music which carried him away."[109]

With Septicius, Kristeva lays the foundation for a telling criticism of contemporary society, which is beset by scapegoating. Engaged in a protective mission in Santa Varvara, the professor enhances our awareness of threats not only to Santa Varvara but also to every present-day locale.[110] Moreover, with the Roman poets, Septicius discovers that, just as violence is associated with the loss of speech, alternatives to violence and scapegoating emerge with the recasting of speech as transformative "song." But how can the professor's critical perception, in which he has been tutored by Ovid, become a starting point for action against wolves in Santa Varvara or elsewhere? Septicius locates in Tibullus's poetry an alternative to wolfish violence. With Tibullus, Septicius can augment his capacity for song, in which Ovid has tutored him, sustaining his critical acumen and empowering him to act. However, the professor has no opportunity to fully embody the nonsacrificial praxis he has discerned in Tibullus, for he is attacked by the wolves. As a consequence, Septicius's life-affirming praxis is attested to only indirectly, as it is refracted through memories of others.

A Scission within the Paternal Function:
An Innocent Victim

In the absence of paternal authority, wolves have swarmed through Santa Varvara, invading the bodies of some residents and killing others. No one has been exempt. In such a time, intimations of alternatives do not emerge directly. Instead, they appear in the wake of renewed violence. As Girard's theory suggests, calm that follows incidents of scapegoating is temporary; violence eventually returns. When conflict resumes, new scapegoats are sought.[111] Evidence supporting Girard's theory comes to the forefront when the Old Man is hospitalized for illness. The one who has spoken out most strongly against the wolves and has shared healing songs with the community now has become vulnerable. The narrative records the Old Man's delirium as wolves fade in and out of focus in the hospital.

At times, the wolves appear to corner the Old Man, placing him at their mercy. At other moments, it seems that Septicius's eyes have never been more discerning. The wolves are in his crosshairs, confined though he is to a hospital bed. Increasingly detached from his body; Septicius lives in his mind and sees the hatred that surrounds him on a screen.[112] Seeking to preserve as evidence for others the evil that surrounds him, he wants to create an indelible image of Lycaon/Vespasian.[113] Caught between his suffering and the need to bring that suffering to expression, the Old Man dreams of borrowing Goya's palette in order to transmit to others the horror that he confronts:[114] He calls out from his bed to no one: "And still I say 'No!' Until the screen goes blank I shall go on etching on it the grotesque spectacle I see in the world around me. *No!*"[115] Fading in and out of consciousness, Septicius finally sees on the screen before him Lycaon, "the living image of ferocity . . . *eadem ferritatis imago est.*"[116]

Looking toward his window, the professor spies two figures crouched by the window. Sensitized by Ovid to signs of inhuman transformation, he watches the figures' metamorphoses: their furry cheekbones lengthen into muzzles; their lips draw back, revealing fangs. They move away from the window and toward the artificial lung that is keeping him alive. Suddenly, he can't breathe. The only human in a hospital overtaken by wolves, in his last moments, the Old Man hears from afar a voice. Billie Holiday's singing suddenly "overwhelms the Old Man's ears and all his organs . . . Now husky, now shrill; it is full of sighs and strong rhythms." The Old Man, who has "regarded music as the most ineffable and the most sacred of secrets," is ushered from this world by the voice of Billie Holiday singing, "I have a long way to go."[117] In summoning from her readers an association of song and voice with Septicius's last moments, Kristeva draws on the primacy Ovid gives to song in the *Metamorphoses*: From singers' mouths fall words of revelatory beauty.[118]

For those unfamiliar with mimetic theory, the Old Man seems an unlikely scapegoat; in contrast to Alba, a marginal outsider, he is a revered professor from whom others in his city have sought advice. But readers familiar with Girard recall that, according to Girard, scapegoats emerge at both ends of the social spectrum, for social marginality features among those at the pinnacle of a society as well as at its bottom.[119] Indeed, around the time the mass graves are discovered, people are "starting to be frightened" of the Old Man.[120] As he "withdrew into his own aura of wisdom and honor" in the face of a widening contagion of violence, the citizens of Santa Varvara "intensified his isolation with their hints, their furtive looks."[121] The Old Man becomes the object of hostile gossip in Santa Varvara's bars. One day someone whispers, "I think talking about this sort of thing—the wolves, I mean—only makes them more real; you have to believe in them, and you have to do something about them. . . . He's just trying to provoke the wolves, that's all. Our hero must be starting to get bored with his books!"[122] Stephanie seems aware that a contagion of violence in Santa Varvara has placed the Old Man especially at risk: "The weak, the old, and the handicapped don't usually arouse pity . . . they provoke the distorted rages, the masked hatreds, the monstrous acts of vengeance that are revealed to us in our dreams, when the hypocrisy of the day no longer operates."[123] Although the Old Man's death is the work of only a few wolves, Stephanie asserts that "it had been in everyone's interest to get rid of Septicius Clarus." Vespasian and Alba had wanted him dead because he knew too much about their violent relationship. The nurses at the hospital had wanted him dead because they were badly paid and disliked elderly patients. The wolves had wanted him dead "because they were wolves."[124] Further, the Old Man is described as being Christlike, which evokes images of an innocent victim, a scapegoat. He was, Stephanie recognizes, a "single visionary" who could perceive the "extreme limits of being."[125]

At Septicius's funeral, that the professor's powers of perception have transferred to Stephanie becomes evident. Stephanie says that she is the only one to recognize that the marks on the professor's face have not been made by a human hand and that the congealed blood around his mouth is evidence of strangulation.[126] Rather than acknowledge the Old Man's violent death and mourn him, those attending the funeral are transfixed by a poised and perfectly coiffed woman, a plastic surgeon who is Vespasian's colleague. Stephanie previously has dubbed her "the Face-lifter."[127] At the funeral, only Stephanie finds the Face-lifter's visage monstrous. Observing her mouth closely, seeking what the professor would have called her *os*, Stephanie notices that the Face-lifter never speaks; instead, she emits the "laugh of a hyper-efficient madwoman."[128] For Stephanie, the Face-lifter's perpetual smile and laugh are reminiscent of the "red lips as white and shiny and massive as a kitchen sink" of the sculpture at the Santa Varvara fountain.[129]

The Face-lifter and her sculpture-twin are reminiscent of Medusa in Ovid's *Metamorphoses*.[130] As described by Andrew Feldherr, Medusa is noted for her *commutative powers*: "Each person who has gazed at the face of the Gorgon becomes a wondrous image, able to freeze and transform new viewers in turn, sentencing them to death as well."[131] Citing Girard, Feldherr labels these powers a "contagion" and suggests they announce an impending "sacrificial crisis."[132] So also are the Gorgon-like powers of the Face-lifter decidedly transmissible. Just as those who gaze at the Gorgon "absorb the stony nature directly from the image,"[133] so also do those who attend the Old Man's funeral take the Face-lifter's monstrousness into their own being. Stephanie knows that, in their efforts to emulate the Face-lifter, the residents of Santa Varvara will pull "all sorts of faces to arrive at the right look" as they stand "in front of their halogen-lit mirrors" this very evening.[134]

Up to now, as commentator Anna Smith notes, the wolf has served as an image of violence in Santa Varvara: the "impulse in society to savage the outsider who is different."[135] So also has Santa Varvara been depicted as a society flattened by torpor and banality. At the funeral of the Old Man, these features of life in Santa Varvara are joined. An innocent victim has been scapegoated, and no one has acknowledged the crime or cared.

With the death of the Old Man, described in the novel as Christlike, the novel appears ready to resolve into an antisacrificial allegory. However, no one but Stephanie reads in the Old Man's death an indictment of the wolves. In Santa Varvara, mimetic violence against an innocent victim has been exposed but it has not been heeded. If the Old Man is to serve as an antisacrificial exemplar, who will be his witness? Stephanie? The reader? Immediate answers to these questions are not forthcoming. Instead, Stephanie perceives that the residents of Santa Varvara are inured to injustice *and* incapable of mourning, hopelessly infected by monsters *and* monstrous insignificance. At this moment, she makes a decision that signals a turning point in the novel. In the aftermath of the funeral, Stephanie discovers memories of her past coming back to her; "suddenly," she feels like writing about them.[136] Resolving to leave her detective work behind, Stephanie anticipates the jeers of her editor: "So our roving reporter, our great detective, is stumped." But Stephanie is committed to her own "whims and fancies (*J'ai droit à mes caprices*)."[137]

In search of what has been lost, Stephanie changes course and follows a different tack. She moves from her role as detective to that of diarist. As recollections well up in Stephanie, the reader recognizes that metamorphoses that have led to a degeneration of humanity into beastliness have been characterized, above all, by *a loss of memory*. In the absence of memory, connection with others has become impossible.

As a genre, the diary or personal journal suggests a work of memory: it preserves the present and becomes a medium for recollection of the past. Indeed, Kristeva sees the diary as an instrument of revolt, a means for a returning that Kristeva associates with the healing work of memory. Inserted into *The Old Man and the Wolves* as a medium for revolt, Stephanie's diary does not transgress the law, which would only strengthen acquisitive mimesis; rather, it displaces the law. A witness for the past, the diary attests not only that forgiveness is decisive to healing from trauma but also that this healing opens up persons for intimacy. Indeed, as a genre, a diary actively suggests intimacy. In *Intimate Revolt*, Kristeva writes that, in a "robotizing and spectacular society," the alternative is intimacy. For her, the novel is "a privileged terrain for such an exploration." It preserves "a place for meditation." When a diary or personal journal is inserted into a novel, it constitutes the inner chamber of such meditative intimacy.[138] As Stephanie's musings invite a reassessment of the contagion that infects Santa Varvara, they point toward a resolution of mimetic conflict. Although this reassessment echoes Girard's own alternatives to violence, it also augments his theory in ways he has not imagined.

CHAPTER 8

To Glimpse a World without Wolves: From Conflict to Compassion

This compassion for the victim is the deeper meaning of Christianity. We will always be mimetic, but we do not have to engage automatically in mimetic rivalries. We do not have to accuse our neighbor; we can learn to forgive him instead.

—René Girard, Pierpaolo Antonello, and João Cezar de Castro Rocha,
Evolution and Conversion: Dialogues on the Origins of Culture

Kristeva names the concluding section of *The Old Man and the Wolves* "Capriccio." "Capriccio" focuses on multiple metamorphoses. Replicating and augmenting the transferential setting of the detective story, these changes radicalize its questions: What is the ultimate source of the contagion that has transformed Santa Varvara into a city of wolves? Can infected individuals be cured, or will they always be wolves? "Capriccio" investigates the possibility of *reversible metamorphoses*: Can those who have been contaminated by the wolves grasp their humanity again and break free of mimesis-driven scapegoating? Addressing this question are Stephanie, by means of her diary, and Kristeva, by way of autobiographical and theoretical reflections she incorporates into the narrative.

In choosing "Capriccio" for the title of the concluding section of the novel, Kristeva invokes the *Caprichos* of Goya: a series of images that include many in which humans take on animal forms. On his deathbed, the Old Man had tried to "borrow from Goya's palette to translate into a dream what Ovid had once written."[1] The images portrayed in the *Caprichos* are understood by interpreters of Goya to serve as critical commentaries on late eighteenth-century Spanish society. Writing elsewhere about Goya, Kristeva acknowledges that, with his *Caprichos*, Goya aims to respond to violence in Spain and to criticize the moral bankruptcy of its social institutions. However, Kristeva sees that Goya is engaged in a more personal struggle as well: the "loss of identity in the clutches of death."[2] Intertextuality enables Goya's work not only to pose a challenge to society but also to call into question how the subject of a society is constituted as subject.

Goya's images are infiltrated by the abject: that part of us which typically is cast out or excluded as a precondition for our social existence. Although the abject is associated with human infancy, the abject can emerge at any time. When subjects seek objects as an external support in the face of a lack of being, the abject emerges whenever the object fails to deliver the goods. Most succinctly, the abject is refused refuse. As Elisabeth Grosz suggests, the abject is that which exceeds the subject when the subject demands that an object fully fill and define it.[3] Goya's art attests to the abject. The physicality, animality, and hybridism evident in his grotesque images decenter Goya *and* the viewer as subjects, casting doubt on all claims to identity.[4] Moreover, because Goya offers a visual coding of the abject, his images express, perhaps even more powerfully than images evoked by Ovid in the *Metamorphoses*, that *what we seek to exclude is constitutive of us*. This uncomfortable truth in the history of being is what Kristeva's "*Capricho/ Capriccio*" proposes to explore.

For Kristeva, the first chapter in the human history of desire is preceded by a prefatory experience of abjection. A newborn must separate from the maternal body in order to become a subject in the world. This separation in being is a process of abjection; for, differentiation from the mass of being is insufficient to produce an object. Objects that will appear later "caught in the fragile web of desire" are unknown to the abject, which pulls the not-yet-a-subject to a place where meaning collapses.[5] Thus, at the zero degree of being, the lack of being that initiates the history of desire is not a narrative of mimesis: "Mimesis occurs secondarily."[6] In the beginning, abjection "is the avant-garde of the future oedipal revolt."[7] In the throes of abjection, careening between hatred *and* love, the proto-subject approaches bounded being divided *and* overwhelmed. The "borders of the human universe in formation" will be secured only with the achievement of language and entry into the Symbolic order. Under great personal or social strain, when individuals or communities are threatened with a radical loss of place, the subject will return to these borders. Revisiting processes of primordial differentiation that enabled it to secure standing in the world, it will attempt to resecure the borders of being against a rising tide of abjection.

In "Capriccio," Stephanie is pulled back to these borders. Confronted with the deadly contagion of wolves, she comes face-to-face with meaninglessness that Kristeva associates with the abject: "Death had forced me back to square one, and square one was empty. I was a detective in search of the void."[8] Struggling against a debilitating loss of identity, she is fearful of the expanding numbers and power of the wolves. She has thought that she has only "pretended to enter their skins" and has remained in control. Reflecting on that sense of personal agency, Stephanie says, "I experienced Santa Varvara from within, but turned myself inside out like a glove in order to see and hear it [Santa Varvara] from a distance."[9] Now Stephanie wonders about the "reversible space" she has thought was hers. She confronts the possibility that, akin to Alba and Vespasian, she is complicit in the crimes of wolves. She faces the terrifying possibility that what she has most sought to exclude has, in fact, become constitutive of her being. Stephanie realizes that she must refocus her investigation: rather scrutinize the crimes of others, she must explore whether she too is culpable. Her search for the wolf that lies within rather than without presages a change in the novel's narrative.[10]

Renewed attention to the figure of Alba in the final pages of the novel mirrors Stephanie's effort to determine anew the boundaries of being. Having confronted "the void of the wandering shape that is myself," Stephanie suddenly remembers the woman at the lake. She senses that the Face-lifter may have played a role in her death. Alba, with whom Stephanie conversed at the Old Man's funeral, had not seemed at all like herself; her "elliptical way of speaking" had been difficult to comprehend. Stephanie contemplates the possibility of a most disturbing metamorphosis: Perhaps the Face-Lifter has used her skills in plastic surgery to create an Alba-like face for someone in order to hide the actual murder of Alba.[11] But Stephanie immediately second-guesses herself. Of the girls in Santa Varvara she says, "If you dunked any one of them in muddy water long enough she might easily be taken for Alba or anyone else you cared to name."[12] Could that "anyone else" be Stephanie? If so, Stephanie now confronts the prospect that Alba and she are mimetic doubles. Their melding points to an abject menace that poses a threat to Santa Varvara much more profound than the wolves' raw violence.

Kristeva has twice referred to the "muddy water" from which the dead woman's body was pulled.[13] Her language about the scene of death by the lake in *The Old Man and the Wolves* is identical to her description in *Powers of Horror* of Narcissus and the abject. There, describing how the nascent subject becomes part of the social-linguistic order, Kristeva writes that prior to "the mimesis by means of which the subject becomes homologous to another in order to become himself" there is an initial separation in being. Not yet an "I," the subject is abject. Thus, a precondition of narcissism is a primal pulsation of differentiation. Secondary to that is a narcissism more commonly recognized by others, that of a self-sufficient subject.[14] However, Kristeva asks that we recall that the foundational experience of narcissism is never "the wrinkleless image of the Greek youth"[15] in a quiet fountain. The desire for being that initiates speech is a perturbation in being that clouds the waters of Narcissus. As a consequence, that Stephanie recalls the bloated, muddied body of the woman at the lake only to disavow her, denying her the name "Alba" and aligning her with wolves, points to the profound disturbance in being that Stephanie confronts. Mimetic confirmation of identity that would enable Stephanie to distinguish herself from Alba, building boundaries in the exchange of names and conversation within the social order, has been lost. To the scene of a muddied pool that could reflect the face of anyone or no one is now added forfeiture of a capacity for meaningful speech. With sight and speech at risk, we see that Stephanie's very ability *to be* has been profoundly challenged by the wolves. Stephanie's encounter with Alba is the most intimately visceral and disturbing instance of this challenge.

No less disturbing is a complete disinterest among the residents of Santa Varvara in the dead woman by the lake. No one has reported a missing person, even though the authorities in Santa Varvara have a file on every person. "There was no such thing as an unidentified corpse. Or rather, if a corpse was unidentified there was no such thing as a crime."[16] The unsolved murder at the lake captures the key issue of Santa Varvara; if people aren't wolves, they aren't anything. People will die, but there will be no anxiety, no dread, and no criminal charge. A society of spectacle, all surface and no depth, exemplified by utter banality, is a society without crime. With such permutations, the sacrificial system of Santa Varvara exhibits a new threat, for underneath the smooth surface of that society lie the deep perturbations in being represented by the muddy body pulled from the lake. The abject menace in Santa Varvara now doubles: sacrifice and cultural psychosis—the complete collapse of meaning and speech—combine to pose a lethal threat. Significantly, as the stakes rise in Santa Varvara, Stephanie glimpses an alternative to sacrifice *and* psychosis. Intimations of grace appear in the final pages of the novel. When Stephanie shares recollections of her father, which she has cited as the primary occasion for writing in a personal journal, readers should be alert for these revelatory allusions.

As Stephanie takes on the role of diarist, the "duplication (*dédouble-ment*) and dissemination of identities," first visible in the doubling of Alba, the professor's student, with the dead Alba of the lake, extends to the Old Man.[17] Old men proliferate, as Stephanie reveals that the Old Man and Stephanie's father knew each other; indeed they were so inseparable that "people often mixed them up."[18] Each a foreigner—Stephanie's father as ambassador to Santa Varvara, the Old Man as "ambassador" from ancient Rome—each lived with a serene detachment that exasperated the wolves and whetted their hunger.[19] Stephanie muses that it sometimes even seemed as if the wolves might not have become visible, but for these friends, each the double of the other.[20] So also does Stephanie's voice amplify or double when her recollections are joined with Kristeva's memories of Kristeva's own father's life and death.[21] The journal musings becomes Kristeva's as well as Stephanie's.[22] Even Tibullus enters the mix. The wisdom of this Roman poet magnifies the voices of the old men, sustains their daughters' memory-work, and introduces themes that point beyond scapegoating toward human relat-edness not founded on sacrifice.

As Maria Margaroni suggests in her reading of the novel, rather than model lives characterized by mimetic rivalry and sacrifice, the old men exemplify ways of living that point to the renewal of the human subject, notwithstanding its lack of being and the abject threats it confronts.[23] The old men are mimetic copies of each other, yet they are not beset by mimetic conflict.[24] Thus, as Stephanie and Kristeva draw on memories of the old men in their lives to mourn their loss, what Kristeva describes in an interview as an "interior space sculpted out by mourning"[25] comes into view, a space that offers portents of alternatives to sacrifice. In contrast to memories founded in a sacrificial economy that justify scapegoating, Stephanie and Kristeva's diary reflections bring into view a *nonsacrificial memory* that is founded in positive mimesis. Unlike relations based on acquisitive mimesis, which revolve around rivalries, relationships grounded in positive mimesis express love, genuine intimacy, and compassion. In an interview about the novel, Kristeva suggests that these men from whom we can draw insights are attuned to that space by "a Christ-like sensitivity that echoes our own anguish."[26] Significantly, access to this space is proffered to us by men who are endowed with bodies and the "full weight of psychology, affects, fears."[27] Even so, when they attest to compassion and forgiveness, they point to a way out of mimetic conflict that has made sacrifice our cultural inheritance. Glimpsing a way to secure our existence against abjection, the old men suggest that we may break free of Santa Varvara's sacrificial economy via a fully embodied journey.

Not the fathers of the law, the old men who merge with each other in the novel recall the supporting presence of the father of individual prehistory. Described by Kristeva as "an imaginary Surface" (recalling the Imaginary order), this father emerges as a third party to triangulate the turbulent and abject space of nascent being, protecting it.[28] Indeed, so essential is the presence of this paternal function to the capacity of an infant to exist, Kristeva deems it "oblative paternity."[29] Of this father, Kristeva writes:

> This is a fundamental support, without which I would not be able to achieve any norm, accept any frustration, obey any prohibition, take upon myself any law or moral code. The primary identification is the basis of the authority, for, constituted by the loving acknowledgement of a third person, it breaks with the terror and tyranny that threaten the powerless premature being of the newborn—and it initiates culture.[30]

The support of the father of individual prehistory, a bridge over abject waters, makes possible the entry of the subject into history as a desiring being. It can be tapped in times of crisis. In *The Old Man and the Wolves*, Stephanie and Kristeva draw on memories of this father as Kristeva grieves the death of her own father, and Stephanie becomes engulfed in the crisis that besets Santa Varvara. Remembering the fathers, they experience once again the support of being: before they first took their places in the world, they found themselves already for-given by the father of individual prehistory.[31] The early guarantor of their being, the one who accepted and supported them, can be summoned again through the loving gestures and poetic songs of the old men of Santa Varvara.

Breathing with Tibullus

Invocations of Tibullus, which occur throughout the novel, feature especially in Stephanie's reminiscences about the Old Man and her father. Access to the poetry of Tibullus follows the inspiration of Ovid. Ovid has described how his words, with the assistance of the gods, will be revivified with the lips and breath of others. So too does Septicius replace his mother tongue, "breathing new life into Latin tomes":[32]

> He spoke only of Ovid and Tibullus. Song was his way of giving himself to his God. When he listened, his eyes widened and filled with bluish light. His face opened up into something beyond skin and bone, yet despite his rapture what he heard was corporeal, clear, precise.[33]

Stephanie recalls that her father shared with the Old Man a love of song, frequently joining him in singing. When they sang the "sound between them wove one pure language: music flowed into words, word rose up into music."[34] Like the Old Man, Stephanie's father knew that the breath of speech, whether present in songs or poems, wasn't merely a part of everyday life but had "an independent existence that moved in light and air and space, and was free."[35]

Reflecting on memories of her childhood, Stephanie comments that love created an atmosphere in her home that was in marked contrast to her neighbor's, the Aguilars. The seven sons in that family reveled in competition: when swimming in the sea, they boasted about outlasting one another when they submerged under water for long periods *without breathing*. Their father too was consumed by competition in his place of business. Viewing the family from the perspective of the professor, Stephanie now perceives that the Aguilars were wolves. They were "completely immune to poetry."[36] Hoping that she has not become hardened against poetry, Stephanie makes Tibullus's poems a sounding board for her recollections. As the poems reflect and amplify the novel's narrative, the power of the text to resonate is enhanced. Specifically, with Tibullus, Kristeva introduces the reader to themes in the novel that point to an alternative to mimetic violence.

The first of these themes is the *power and form of nonsacrificial memory*. In forging a connection between Tibullus and memory, Septicius has echoed Freud who, in *Civilization and Its Discontents*, likens the history of Rome to the work of memory. Acknowledging that much of the earliest topographies of Rome are lost in rubble, Freud suggests that, if Rome were a psychical entity rather than a habitation in space, all layers of history could be held together at once: "The same piece of ground would support the church of Santa Maria sopra Minerva and the ancient temple over which it was built. And the observer would perhaps only have to change the direction of his glance or his potion in order to call up the one view or the other."[37] Septicius also has pointed to an ancient city's landscape to suggest the power of memory to counter violence that, on the macrocosmic level, is destroying Santa Varvara and, at the microcosmic level, is shattering the psyches of its residents. He has told his students that Tibullus and Ovid still may be found "in the original texts, of course; in the ruins of ancient palaces and churches" but also "in the thoughts of people. There are still traces of their old selves in them, in you."[38]

In appealing to Tibullus, the Old Man mirrors Tibullus's invocation of a golden past as well as his status as an outsider. Living in a time when storytellers are killed as scapegoats and residents of Santa Varvara refuse to remember the past, the *narrative memory* of Septicius is crucial for any vision of an alternative to life in Santa Barbara. Its inhabitants are oblivious to actual experience and are lifted out of their blasé and bored lives only when they become excited by the illusory spectacles created by the media. Nothing lies beneath the fabricated surfaces of their lives: outbreaks of violence that beset Santa Varvara evoke neither memories nor mourning for what has been lost.[39] Recalling her teacher, Stephanie describes him as "fleeing from the present of the wolves to the past of the Romans in the expectations of changes he himself might dream of but would never live to see." With barbarism reigning in Santa Varvara, his migration may be "the only form of civilization," a choice to open up "avenues of memory" that had once made Santa Varvara a "capital of metamorphosis" but now makes it merely a "scene of dreadful transmogrifications (transmutations)."[40] That journey from a past to an open future that could celebrate humankind is lost to monster-making violence in a city that has become oblivious to its ancient topography.

Confronted with a crisis of memory in which a contagion of beastliness threatens to override all traces of humanity, Kristeva suggests that we can turn toward the past in a "reactive, nostalgic fashion," or we can explore "a grafting (à greffer) of what comes from another culture, another mentality," onto our own time.[41] With *The Old Man and the Wolves*, Kristeva chooses the second option in order to move toward "an experience of sorrow and hurt that originates elsewhere and is perhaps liable to awaken other effects."[42] Tibullus's poetry is such a "grafting." From the first pages of the novel, his poems establish a vascular connection between past and present, gradually fusing ancient rootstock with contemporary scion. Late in the novel, Tibullus's poems have the strength of a mature graft, enabling those who grieve in the aftermath of sacrificial violence to awaken other effects.

Early in the novel, Septicius connects with Tibullus's poems through sensory-driven encounters. Rather than read Tibullus in his study, Septicius happens upon Tibullus in natural settings. For example, out for an autumn walk, he finds that Tibullus's words "slip in amongst the leaves." Moreover, "The pleasure he got from the bright-hued season was that of taste and touch. All the shades of brown and yellow and red entered into his skin, warmed his throat, filled his eyes, inducing the overwhelming sense of fulfillment that cannot be adequately expressed except in song." The poem's "resonance reconciles Septicius with lost time."[43] Mirroring Septicius's outdoor locale, the rural setting of the poems further frames the encounter between poet and his readers in terms of mood rather than place.[44] Where Ovid often uses the landscape to signal impending violence in the text, Tibullus's poetry offers nonsacrificial access to a world that is tactile, sensorial, and somatic. Indeed, Tibullus is fascinated by the power of touch: words such as "hands, feet, and hair" are common to his poems.[45] By invoking the past, in memory traces accessed through the body, Tibullus's poetry offers entrée to a psychic space that is all but absent from the environs of Santa Varvara, where a monstrous plastic sculpture graces the public square, abject horror haunts the lake, and surface effects of a media-driven spectacle replace embodied human experience. As others identify with Septicius, sharing his encounter with Tibullus's poetry, the poems' transformative potential is demonstrated. Septicius's bodily engagement with Tibullus's words can be taken up author and reader alike, as their corporeal memories are activated. In this way, kinesic engagement with Tibullus's poetry affords the reader a taste of the restorative powers of word that Septicius celebrates.

Two additional themes in Tibullus's poetry are important in the novel: *outsider status and suffering*. Although these motifs are readily linked with scapegoating—the scapegoat is typically an outsider and is made to suffer by an attacking mob—they take on a different meaning in Tibullus's writings, forming a constellation of alternatives to violence. Associated with Tibullus, these themes recall an earlier time preserved in our capacity for nonsacrificial memory. Tibullus redefines the notion of an outsider when he describes himself as a farmer, not a soldier or urban dweller. He is without a family of his own: he has "no mother here to gather up my incinerated bones in the folds of her mourning veil; I have no sister to bestow in my ashes the perfumes of Assyria and weep with unbound hair beside my grave."[46] Moreover, and in contrast to other elegists, Tibullus also does not speak as an authority or claim as his own an elite audience.[47]

Tibullus's outsider status leads to *suffering*. However, as he describes his pain, suffering born of love is shown to differ from pain experienced sacrificially. Most notably, Tibullus suffers from the remoteness of the woman he loves, Delia. The poems that summon Delia and speak of the rural life they will enjoy depict also the separation they will experience because of death. Even as he asks Delia to come close in order to make her one with him, Tibullus knows that "soon death will come, its head shrouded in darkness."[48] The poet does not fear death itself; he laments only that he may encounter death without Delia. Further, Tibullus contrasts his suffering with that caused by war, which he understands to be caused by greed. Greed, Girard would remind us, is rooted in mimetic rivalry. Tibullus contrasts the world of acquisitive desire that regularly becomes violent with the simplicity and contentment of rural life.[49]

Finally, in Tibullus's poetry, the theme of *connection with others* also stands out. Septicius has celebrated the connection of which Tibullus writes and distinguishes it from Alba and Vespasian's conflict-ridden relationship. Acknowledging that Tibullus's relationship with Delia also founders, the professor nevertheless asserts, "There used to be links between people, and yet they weren't bound." Tibullus's embodiment of freedom achieves balance, drifting neither toward a binding passion nor toward indifference.[50] The classics professor attributes to Tibullus's era the "dawn of connection" when persons forged "a sacred bond both passionate and pious—by which I mean respectful."[51] But also it was "free, questioning, skeptical, intellectual."[52] Thus, after losing Delia to another lover and encountering difficulties along his way, Tibullus revisits earlier themes in a new poem, still moving toward connection. Words can't offset the suffering that he has encountered in his life, but the promise of relationships can.[53] Squabbles of rural life are acknowledged; however, the poet now makes family—husband and wife, son and daughter—the "touchstone" against which all challenges of life are measured. Writes Tibullus, "Peace lifts to the sun the hoe and the plowshare; darkness covers the soldier's broken weapons with rust. Merry with drink, the farmer drives homeward with his wife and children through the sunny dust."[54] In celebrating the ordinary, what Stephanie calls "the happiness of simple folk," Tibullus exemplifies living according to "*quodlibet ens*," which Septicius always translates as "a being that matters, no matter what."[55]

The poems of Tibullus provide direction: love of another *no matter what* has the power to counter the violence that besets Santa Varvara. Tibullus's poems create a kind of music, one that "emerges from a brutish cacophony, refining it into duration, expectation, and promise. The promise of harmony, perfection. Epiphany (*l'avent*)."[56] Pointing to an alternative to scapegoating, Tibullus counsels that the space between sensation and language, to which his poems grant access, is vital to connecting with others in spite of suffering. The narrator suggests that Tibullus anticipates Christ (*pressentant Jésus*).[57] The Old Man, embracing Tibullus's vision, is described by Kristeva as "a man of sorrows, in a certain way, a Christ-like figure."[58] The suffering of Stephanie's father (likewise Kristeva's) is described as "a cross he has to bear."[59]

The prefiguring of Christ by Tibullus and the association of Christ with the other old men should not lead us to ascribe a sacrificial theology of atonement to *The Old Man and the Wolves*. The old men's suffering is not salvific for others: they do not die in order that others may live. Of what the old men's Christ-likeness does consist is signaled by Kristeva's Christological reflections in *Tales of Love*. Echoing Girard, Kristeva establishes a context for understanding the Christology of *The Old Man and the Wolves* when she asserts that sacrifice stems from "the law of the social contract." Just as Girard claims that human society originates in sacrifice, so also does Kristeva assert that sacrifice creates meaning for "a social group that has been offered it and on which that social group is dependent for its being."[60] Elsewhere, Kristeva draws explicitly on Girard[61] to explain that the "socio-symbolic contract" that is fundamental to the formation of any society is based on "the expulsion of an excluded element, a scapegoat."[62] Kristeva follows Girard when she expressly distances Christ from this system of scapegoating. Referencing Girard's *Things Hidden since the Foundation of the World*, Kristeva says that love offered by Christ is "very far removed from the classical concept of sacrifice."[63]

In drawing on Girard for her own understanding of the dynamics of Christlike behavior among the old men, Kristeva rightly understands Girard's claim in *Things Hidden since the Foundation of the World* that the crucifixion of Jesus is *not* a sacrifice. To be sure, elements of scapegoating that Girard has labeled stereotypic in their unvarying regularity are visible in Gospel accounts of Jesus's life and death. The Gospels do describe social disorder, an intensifying conflict, mob action that polarizes around one individual, and escalating violence that culminates in the death of Jesus. On the surface, the Gospels replicate the structure of myth, making Jesus's crucifixion a story of sacrificial scapegoating. But the Gospels differ from myth in a most profound way. In myth, the stereotypical elements of scapegoating, stacked one on top of the other, show the victim of mob violence to be *guilty*; in the Gospels, these stereotypes collapse and shatter, revealing Jesus to be *innocent*. In this way, building on an antisacrificial trajectory already evident in the Hebrew Bible, the Gospels fully expose the scapegoat mechanism and offer an alternative to the mythic justification of sacrifice: a revelation of a loving God who sides with victims. Writes Girard, "To say that Jesus dies, not as a sacrifice, but in order that there may be no more sacrifices, is to recognize in him the Word of God: I wish for mercy and not sacrifices. Rather than become the slave of violence, as our own word necessarily does, the Word of God says no to violence."[64] Girard states that the Gospels understand that God does not work through violence: the "non-sacrificial economy" that Jesus sets forth is "a Kingdom of love."[65]

In transposing her nonsacrificial Christological reflections from her theoretical work to her novel, Kristeva follows Girard in differentiating the Old Man's embodiment of the Christian message from the violent mythos of

Santa Varvara. On the surface, the death of the Old Man is an act of scape-goating that mythic traditions in Santa Varvara will justify. But the narrative of *The Old Man and the Wolves* witnesses to the innocence of the victim. In her theoretical work, Kristeva asserts that love offered by Christ comes as a gift that "assumes total suffering and loss" but manifests itself nonsacrificially in the form of compassion shared among members of a community, a community that stretches to "include neighbors, foreigners, and sinners."[66] So also do Christological themes of compassion and gift feature in *The Old Man and the Wolves*. Embodying nonsacrificial Christlikeness, the old men of Kristeva's novel attest to a Kingdom of love that they offer others as gift.

Girard urges caution in associating a gift with intimate mediation or positive mimesis. He writes that most notions of "gift" actively participate in the victimary mechanism. Moreover, reciprocity associated with gift-giving can exacerbate acquisitive rivalry.[67] But Kristeva's notion of "gift" is aligned with her antisacrificial Christology and is an extension of agape, not acquisitive rivalry. In particular, Kristeva uses the word "*par-don*" (through-gifting) to depict the gift of love as "forgiveness." "Religion that forgives," writes Kristeva, "is greeted as a promise that assures psychical life." *Par-don*, for-gifting, opens up psychical time that has cycled previously between desire and hatred.[68]

In a sacrificial economy such as Santa Varvara, outsiders typically bear the marks of victims and suffer as victims. But in the nonsacrificial economy to which the old men testify, outsider status and suffering are revelatory. As Pamela Sue Anderson notes, exiles (outsiders, aliens, foreigners) have a privileged perspective because they view the center from the margins of speech, community, and consciousness. On the periphery, the old men (Tibullus, Stephanie's father, and Septicius Clarus) can see from a distance what is "eating away at the center of the social-symbolic order."[69] Although those on the margins of society are the most vulnerable when scapegoats are sought—the wolves seek them first—when these individuals persist, they stand as witness to an alternative social *and* psychic order.

Thus, notwithstanding that the Old Man is a scapegoat in the sacrificial economy of Santa Varvara, the novel offers intimations of an alternative economy. In the Christlike suffering of the Old Man may be glimpsed an economy of the gift, a for-gifting, which challenges that of sacrifice. Stephanie notes in her diary that the old men have given her the "gift of tongues."

They have passed on to her their God, as if an "infinity of languages" would "play the part of seraphim for me, flocks of angels helping me soar through secret skies."[70] Stephanie, unable to find a common language with the citizens of Santa Varvara, from whose lips come only wolf sounds, is a first reluctant to accept that words have been her gift from the old men. However, at a later point in her journal-writing, she accepts that they have been "transposed" into her, a "metamorphosis that might have amused that persistent reader of Ovid."[71]

But what has been transposed? Stephanie recalls a time when she was at the Santa Varvara Cathedral with the visiting president of France and saw Septicius singing.[72] When she introduced Septicius to the president, he shared with the president the meaning he found in singing in the choir: on his understanding, "singing transcends prayer." Seeing on the president's face that the president had not followed his train of thought, Septicius brought their conversation to a close with a single enigmatic word: "compassion."[73] Stephanie muses that she recalls nothing further from the conversation except that, for a few moments, Septicius had become "the agent of reconciliation" of which he had dreamed. A reflective Stephanie writes, "I had no part in it, but we were together in that dream, and I'm glad to have dream it with him." For a moment, with the word "compassion" hanging in the air, the Old Man "caught a glimpse of the world without the wolves."[74]

With their lives and words, Kristeva's old men embody Christlikeness because *they offer compassion as an alternative to sacrifice.*[75] If they can be said to save others, it is through this gift, not through the violence they suffer at the hands of others. Compassion points to the possibilities of *connecting with others* nonviolently. The form of connection proffered by the gifts of the fathers is described by Kristeva as *Einfühling*; the bond becomes one of identification (*Einfühling*), and "because of that very fact its name is love. Not sacrifice."[76] So also does Kristeva characterize this bond in terms of empathy and Christian agape.[77] Can Stephanie receive this gift, a *par-don* that for-gifts and for-gives?[78] Can she experience a reverse metamorphosis that frees her of contagion and opens up time for her, enabling her to experience her humanity once again even though she has slept with a wolf?

The Alchemy of the Word

Near the end of *The Old Man and the Wolves*, Stephanie writes in her journal that, although she never anticipated it, her sojourn in Santa Varvara has opened up possibilities. The memories and stories of the past to which the old men—Ovid, Tibullus, Septicius, her father—have testified are enabling her to wrest her way free from the debilitating environment of Santa Varvara. No longer caught between Santa Varvara's Scylla and Charybdis—rapacious wolves and engulfing whirlpools of ennui—Stephanie discovers, much to her surprise, that these men have handed down to her a way of going forward. She hears them calling to her, "From this void new forms will be born. It's up to you now, Stephie."[79] Confronted with the devastating loss of the Old Man to the wolves, Stephanie yet stands in receipt of a possible future: compassion, connection, life with others.

Stephanie's insights are as old as Tibullus's poetry and as contemporary as Kristeva's conversations with clients in her psychoanalytic practice. Writes Kristeva: "I believe we must reinstate a notion of the psyche and the soul that avoid the two major detours the psychoanalytic movement has taken, the first of which seeks to thrust psychic space into biology (which makes it closer to psychiatry) and the second of which considers psychic space to be a product of language alone and disregards the signs emitted by the body."[80]

Kristeva recognizes that human efforts to break open cycles of scapegoating require complex interventions that do not bifurcate along dualistic lines, juxtaposing animalistic violence to a perfected rationalism of the human mind. As a consequence, she emphasizes the healing powers of empathetic identification: *Einfühling*. Further, Kristeva understands that when we seek alternatives to violence, narrative traditions shared by literature and psychoanalysis are critical to our interventions.

Through what process do stories, of which *The Old Man and the Wolves* is an example, become a source of hope for writers and readers, analysts and analysands? How are memories that are attuned to compassion rather than to sacrifice drawn forth from narratives? Kristeva identifies two features of narratives that help us access nonsacrificial memory: *embodied human experience* and *relationships founded in acceptance rather than rivalry*. Although novels purportedly are conveyers of signs, writers and readers of novels are led by narrative back into body practices that trauma previously has prevented them from accessing. Thus, it is not only Ovid's *Metamorphoses* that makes possible the transformation of bodies; rather, this revelatory potential is proper to literature and the arts, including religious art so central to the Orthodox Christianity of Kristeva's homeland.[81] When a reader gets caught up in what Kristeva calls "the alchemy of the word," reading is not exclusively an act of comprehension and cognition; rather, according to Kristeva, through reading one recovers "his own memory, his own body," and this can be "revitalizing." In this way, narratives tap into memories; and, as Ovid has demonstrated so compellingly, memories access perceptions. With ideas joined with embodiment, narratives allow for "a permanent come-and-go that remakes the personality as a whole."[82] Such memory work, Kristeva suggests in an interview, resembles the analytic process,[83] for therapeutic narratives promote forms of relationship that unlock healing powers.

Kristeva's comments echo Guillemette Bolens's observations on narrative, for the process Kristeva describes is akin to Bolens's concept of kinesis. Bolens too writes of corporeal memories that play a key role in the reception of narrative meaning. We respond to sensory experiences depicted in a narrative because we can summon through kinesis memories of a like experience. The perceptions of Septicius, attuned to the sensory experiences of the Roman poet Tibullus, become occasions for him to report on what Bolens would typify as kinesis, for Kristeva to claim as her own the experiences of which she writes, and for readers of Kristeva's novel to experience kinesis. The "I can" of the body, to which Septicius attests when he talks of Tibullus breathing life into his own, becomes an "I can" for Kristeva and for her reader when the sensory images Septicius celebrates in the writing of Tibullus enable both to connect with Tibullus's experience: "affectively, kinesthetically, introceptively, and so forth."[84]

So also in psychoanalysis, when an analyst identifies with an analysand, the connection that the analyst forges draws not only on the analysand's biography and memories but also on "transgenerational memory and imagined sensation" that "mobilize the analyst's entire psychical apparatus." As a consequence, transference and countertransference effect healing through a kind of "transubstantiation."[85] According to Kristeva, Maurice Merleau-Ponty provides language for understanding transubstantiation—a process common to the narrative practices of writers and readers, analysts and analysands—when he attests to the reversible and chiasmic relationship among embodied individuals that connects "the perceiver and the perceived, the feeler and the felt." Reminded by Merleau-Ponty that "touch is always tangible, sight is visible, matter is the body, and the same is other," Kristeva understands that, in relating to each other, we "become flesh."[86] In invoking Merleau-Ponty on behalf of a corporeal narratology, Kristeva's reflections align with those of Vittorio Gallese, who, with Bolens, emphasizes that our interactions with others are grounded in what he calls "intercorporeity."[87] Citing Merleau-Ponty as an influence on his work, Gallese attests to the importance of active relationality to establishing meaningful experiences.[88]

In *The Old Man and the Wolves*, Tibullus's poetry enables Septicius to access an opening to being in the flesh that reconciles him to lost time, a time not carved out by sacrifice. A sacrificial economy, fueled by mimetic rivalries that beset those who lack being, provides only for metamorphoses that deprive us of our humanity. By contrast, a nonsacrificial economy that emerges from positive mimesis—compassion become flesh—opens up possibilities for transubstantiation in being. The compelling message of *The Old Man and the Wolves* is that the memory work we undertake in our narrative practices can establish pathways for such healing transformation through the intercorporeity that connects us with the past. More important, this intercorporeity, connecting us with others by means of somatosensory images that are formed when we put ourselves in another's place, provides for a future. As witness to the "communication of communicability" (Agamben),[89] these images show that on the other side of trauma that divides us from each other are healing experiences oriented toward agape, compassion, and connection with others.

Listening to Tibullus and Ovid, Septicius remembers the past in order to revitalize his humanity in the face of threatening wolves. Reflecting in her journal on the old men—Ovid, Tibullus, Septicius, and her father—Stephanie remembers in hope of creating a bridge to a meaningful future. Writing *The Old Man and the Wolves*, Kristeva remembers in hope that she can experience healing and forgiveness in the aftermath of her father's death in the face of hospital malfeasance. Reading this novel, those who participate in the memories it evokes may yet hope to glimpse alternatives to aspects of their own experience that mirror life in Santa Varvara. In all these ways, Kristeva offers entrée through her novel to key moments of an aesthetic and therapeutic praxis that plumb the healing powers of narrative.

Kristeva has located the origins of this praxis in identification (*Einfüh-ling*) and has linked it with empathy and *agape*.[90] She does not ground this praxis in the Law (the Freudian Oedipal Father; the Lacanian Name of the Father);[91] rather, the anchor of this praxis is the father of individual prehistory, the Imaginary father who supports nascent being. He is not the model the child will know in the world of symbols and signs; rather he is a nonobject, a pattern, with which the child will bind by way of semiotic play—sounds, touch, and laughter. In these ways, he facilitates metaphorical transference to a place of meaning. Taking in these sounds, the child becomes a "subject of enunciation" and love. Writes Kristeva of this moment: "It is on the basis of that harmonious blending of the two facets of fatherhood that the abstract and arbitrary signs of communication may be fortunate enough to be tied to the affective meaning of pre-historical identifications, and the dead language of the potentially depressive person can arrive at a live meaning in the bond with others."[92]

In the absence of nonrepresentational and affective elements in language associated with this paternal function, the world is an alien place. Facilitating a bridging to the social, the Imaginary father enables us to reach across a void. He does not do so by means of representation—mimetic modeling in the Symbolic order is secondary—but by means of embodied patterning. Metaphors link sound, speech, and affect in an original triangle of empathic connection. Through the Imaginary father, our bodies connect with those of others.

Kristeva's reflections on the Imaginary father and his healing powers, linked by way of her corporeal narratology to literary narrative and to psychoanalysis, are powerfully attested to by icons of Orthodox Christianity to which Kristeva alludes in the novel. Indeed, when she titles "Men of Sorrow" ("*Hommes de Douleur*") the chapter in the novel that celebrates the old men's healing powers, she points to the iconic function of the old men within her narrative.[93] The "Man of Sorrows" is a prevalent theme in Orthodox icons of Christ, and Kristeva invokes Orthodox beliefs about icons when she portrays the old men as a source of sacred transformation.

Kristeva's theoretical explorations of icons illuminate their role in *The Old Man and the Wolves*. Just as the "Men of Sorrow" in the novel attest to Imaginary rather than to Symbolic paternity, to the father of individual prehistory rather than to the father of the law, so also do Orthodox icons acquire meaning along an Imaginary rather than Symbolic axis. That Imaginary axis, I suggest, aligns also with positive mimesis. Kristeva links *eikōn* with *oikonomia* in order to highlight that a living economic relation—a "redemptive plan"—exists between the icon and the sacred.[94] Citing Marie-Jose Mondzain's commentary on Nicephorus, patriarch of Constantinople and opponent of the iconoclasts, Kristeva states that the economy of the icon successfully negotiates between that which is deadly and life-giving in the human capacity to see similarity and difference, a capacity that students of Girard understand fuels mimetic desire. Writes Kristeva of the icon: "The icon falls under an economy that is neither similitude nor consubstantiation, neither mimesis nor figure, and it is for this reason alone that it is, rightfully, a visible transition between the visible and invisible worlds."[95]

Kristeva observes that when Nicephorus distinguishes the relation summoned by the icon from the Aristotelian *pros ti*, Nicephorus uses the term *skesis* in order to emphasize that the visible (son) and the invisible (father) have relative similitude.[96] Not caught up in Symbolic representation, not an object, the "icon seems to be an indication of the economy of *passage* between two orders."[97] Not a copy or facsimile of the invisible, the icon attested to by *skesis* allows for the flesh of the incarnation. Nicephorus distinguishes between the representation of the flesh of sacrifice—"demons and vampires"—and Christ. A distinct logic attends appearances of the body of Christ in the icon.[98] Celebrating what John Lechte describes as a "vibrant transition," the icon establishes a real and economic relation between two worlds: the son and the father.[99] Incarnating this relationship, the icon is not an image. While images "inscribe" meaning, icons "manifest" meaning. Drawing on Nicephorus, Kristeva concludes: "The icon is a *graphein*, a sensible trace, not a spectacle."[100] As such, the icon functions as does intimate mediation for Girard: it transforms mimeticism and opens the door to that which lies on the other side of violence.

Kristeva offers an example of the power of the icon in an essay on an icon named the "Holy Face of Laon." This icon is a *mandylion*: an image that bears an imprint of Christ's face. In the case of the *mandylion* of Laon, Christ touched a cloth to his face, transferring his features to the cloth.[101] The "Holy Face" becomes an early instance of icons of Christ in which the painted image features only a face, surrounded by heavy locks of hair and severed from its body. This icon, writes Kristeva, is not a representation of God; rather, "it makes us see God." Standing before it, we are "taken in; it is absorbed, it is experienced: it translates an invisible world into its visible lines."[102] Indeed, that the icon is not a representation is crucial to its positive reception among the iconophiles of Orthodox Christianity.

Kristeva recounts the curious history of the image of Christ as a "severed head." The iconography of the Holy Face of Laon is reminiscent of images of Medusa. Kristeva says that she first arrived at this analogy when she came face-to-face with the icon of Laon; later, her intuition was confirmed by Grabar, who points out that Gorgon heads are common talismans in the Byzantine period. The image of Christ, it appears, resonates particularly in a culture in which images of the severed head of Medusa also dominate the cultural landscape.[103]

But into what experience are we taken by the icon of Christ? Surprisingly, Medusa paves the way. Medusa, as myth records, turns any who touch her (Ovid) or look at her (other traditions) into stone. A monster who terrifies us as she emerges from the abject depths to threaten us, Medusa can be approached but only by way of her reflection.[104] Mimesis offers seeming protection against her powers; indeed, gorgoneia proliferate across the centuries and into the medieval era. When we are face-to-face with a monster, her powers can be thwarted and fear of death surmounted if we confront her with a mirrored image.[105] In this way, writes Kristeva, "the Medusa myth already prefigures an aesthetic of incarnation."[106] After all, artists escape victimization by Medusa when they reflect her "even while being transubstantiations of her blood."[107]

The Man of Sorrows, a *mandylion* of Christ, offers an alternative to the talismanic Medusa. It attests to an incarnation oriented toward life rather than death, toward positive mimesis and intimate mediation rather than acquisitive mimesis and deadly imitation. Nicephorus, expounding a theology of the icon, writes that, within the economy of the icon, the image of Christ is not represented. That would be "to mimic" or "to copy." Especially in the mandylion, the icon is an imprint, an infiltration of the body of Christ into the fabric that contains it.[108] What is formerly Medusan sacrifice is "metabolized before our eyes" in the economy of the icon.[109]

In this way, the icon manifests Gregory of Nyssa's theological interpretation of God's response to Moses: "You cannot see my face, for man shall not see me and live." Kristeva suggests that Gregory cannot think that the face of God can kill—only the face of Medusa kills.[110] Instead, Gregory must be referring to a process that defers full seeing of God; after all, such sight would kill. On Kristeva's reading, Gregory claims for Christians movement along a path toward God. This path, a "training for freedom," prepares Christians to resee God in accord with the Spirit.[111] Understood from a perspective attuned to mimetic theory, this "benevolent plan"[112] of redemption, which is attested to by Gregory and made manifest in the icon, enables persons to escape acquisitive desire and move toward positive mimesis. In the throes of mimetic rivalry, our sight becomes increasingly distorted. Others become monsters before our eyes; our being is secured only in their death. But, we can resee the other as we are tutored in compassion in ways that enable us to participate in positive mimesis. Kristeva suggests that icons testify compellingly to the "training in freedom" she attributes to Gregory. Kristeva understands this training to run through the body and to come to expression in what we might typify as the embodied arts: religion, art, and literature.

Kristeva's comparison of a talisman and an icon, Medusa and the Face of Laon, sheds light on significant motifs in *The Old Man and the Wolves*. Medusa and the Men of Sorrow are counterpoints in Santa Varvara. In the center of the town square, a horrific contemporary sculpture with a grimacing face, which Septicius shuts his eyes to as he passes through the square, attests to the Gorgon and a sacrificial crisis of which she is emblematic. Her powers extend to the Face-Lifter, whose lips resemble those of the plastic Medusa. Performing facial surgeries on the residents of Santa Varvara, the Face-Lifter makes them look like her even as she creates disguises for the wolves that are decimating Santa Varvara. The Face-Lifter provides "training" in death. Seeing the Face-Lifter has brought Stephanie face-to-face with death. Recalling a different iconic history, an *eikos* of love as opposed to sacrifice, are the Men of Sorrow. Encountering them, breathing with them, those who hear their song and respond to them participate in a "training for freedom" that prepares them to retrieve their humanity from the wolves.

When Kristeva forges a connection between the men of sorrow in *The Old Man and the Wolves* and the Man of Sorrows in the icons of Orthodox Christianity, she offers powerful testimony to contrasts between economies of sacrifice and compassion, acquisitive mimesis and intimate mediation or positive mimesis. We see how the *prototypical* powers of the icon[113] counter the *stereotypical* powers of scapegoating. An economy of sacrifice is characterized by replication: just as duplicate impressions of an original typographical element, each the mirror image of another, are produced by a stereotype, facilitating large press runs, so also do stereotypic features of scapegoating drive mimetic rivalry, supporting the spread of violence across time and place. But, in an economy of compassion, the icon always is linked with its *prototype*—God. In this way, the icon functions dynamically as the very transmission of the patristic formula: "God became Man so that man should become god."[114] In this way the icon participates in an ongoing theology of creation. Yes, iconographic protocols for the creation of icons are found in interpretive manuals (*Podlinniks*). Nevertheless, iconography is directed toward protecting the transformative work of the icon from rupture, not enforcing duplicative resemblance.[115] Patterns of form, color, and line promote recognition of holiness; however, the force of this recognition does not result in the melding of the icon with its sacred prototype. Rather, the icon, manifesting the "grace of the Holy Spirit," is harmonized and "united in one general sweeping toward God."[116] As we are addressed by the icon, so too are we brought by the spirit into this upward movement. Citing St. Anthony, Leonid Ouspensky and Vladimir Lossky write that the icon teaches us

> to keep the body in order—all of it, from head to foot: the eyes, to see with purity; the ears, to listen in peace, not to delight in slander, gossip and abuse; the tongue, to say only what is good; . . . the hands, to be above all brought into movement only to be raised in prayer and for works of mercy . . . ; the stomach, to keep the use of food and drink within the necessary limits . . . ; the feet, to walk rightly and follow the will of God. . . . In this way the whole body becomes trained in good and undergoes a change, submitting to the rule of the Holy spirit.[117]

An expression of prayer, the icon enables us to participate in a new creation, and to do so in a fully embodied manner.

The stereotypes of scapegoating drive the replication of sacrificial violence, as acquisitive rivalries devolve into monstrous indifferentiation. By contrast, the prototypes of iconic being evolve in accord with the upward movement of creation. We do not stand as spectators before the icon to observe the sacred as an object distinct from us; rather, we find ourselves already transfigured by the "single Icon, not man-made but painted within us by the Holy Spirit, of which each ecclesiastical icon is but an aspect."[118] The icon assists humanity in achieving likeness with its prototype—God—so that we may "embody in life what was manifested and transmitted by God-Man."[119]

That icons are described as prototypes cautions us against conceiving of an icon as a representation of its model, Christ. An icon is an inscription (*graphe*) of Christ. In this manner, the icon engenders *and* voids meaning. Writes Kristeva of this decisive moment in the Christ event: Kenosis "takes on the radical sense of 'hollowing out' with the genesis of icons."[120] Neither the visible nor the invisible, the icon is, as Lechte so perspicaciously asserts, "the condition of possibility of visibility."[121]

In this way, tenets of Orthodox theology illuminate the transformative potential to which the Old Men witness, for all the Santa Varvara's of our time. The image of God is embedded in humanity "in the beginning," as depicted in Genesis; however, humans fall into a state of disintegration and corruption, in defiance of their potential.[122] Through *kenosis*, in which God dwells in the depths of death and loss with humanity, offering forgiveness that reperfects human nature, humans are able to respond to God and become "re-imaged" in the nature of Christ.[123] Acquisitive mimesis can be re-formed into positive mimesis. Emblematic of this theological re-creation, the men of sorrow in *The Old Man and the Wolves* bear iconic witness to possibilities of healing from trauma. Their witness suggests how the deadly metamorphoses that have proved debilitating to human life in Santa Varvara, which Kristeva understands are metaphors for a dehumanizing loss of meaning that threatens all human life today, may be exchanged for life-giving alterations that draw humanity back from the brink, and forward together as participants in an economy energized by compassion, not violence.

Conclusion

Inspired by Maria Margaroni, we have explored how Kristeva's *The Old Man and the Wolves* recasts *Totem and Taboo*, thereby providing key insights into the status of the paternal function in contemporary society. Not a battle between father and sons, the conflict in *The Old Man and the Wolves* has been shown to turn on a scission within the paternal function between the dead father of a sacrificial economy and the life-giving father of individual prehistory. Thus, we have seen how *The Old Man and the Wolves* tells a story about a threatening invasion from two perspectives: a tale of sacrifice and scapegoating is countered with a story of compassion and intimate mediation rooted in memories of a past. We have explored both narratives with Girard and Kristeva as our guides. Each has sensitized us to the pathology of violence that has beset Santa Varvara, enhancing our capacity to understand sacrifice and scapegoating and their devastating consequences in society. Kristeva also has enhanced our awareness of worrisome permutations in the sacrificial economy: interspersed with moments of raw violence is a spreading paralysis of meaninglessness to which persons increasingly are unable to respond.

We have noted that Girard differs from Kristeva in his inattention to the embodied nature of mimetic processes. Key themes in his accounts of mimetic conflict—*passionate* desire, *feverish* competition, *sacrificial* violence[124]—are suggestive of beings who are affectively and physically engaged in the world. But Girard's analyses of these themes are remarkably and problematically cerebral. In the Girardian universe, mimetic conflict is remarkably lifeless, whether in its traditional explosive form or in the implosive form that Kristeva cites as an especially troubling contemporary feature of violence. If someone tortures another with meticulous attention to the knife point wielded against the skin of his victim's body, if someone's lips curl in disgust at the sight of another, if someone vomits before a corpse, if someone experiences the metallic taste of fear in her mouth or speaks to another with blank eyes and without affect, these moments are not subject to formal analysis by Girard.[125] From a Girardian perspective, visceral aspects of conflictual mimesis are not essential markers of mimetic processes.

In distinction from Girard, Kristeva has demonstrated in this novel as well as in her theoretical writings that a Girardian approach to mimetic violence is incomplete. Accounting for mimetic violence requires more than Sherlock Holmes–like detection by "one who is supposed to know," especially in the time of wolves when we have lost our capacity to make ethical distinctions between humans and wolves. At the brink, at the zero degree of subjectivity, we need resources beyond those provided by Girard. Kristeva facilitates a return to the early Girard and enables us to magnify the significance of insights from phenomenology that have not persisted in his later work. For Kristeva, narratives—whether in a therapeutic session or in literature—can become modes for reconciling human subjects' bodies and memories with a future.[126] In the rhythms, echolalias, and silences of speech, narratives can attest to archaic memories that track the highs and lows of human subjects' efforts to gain standing in the world. In showing how subjects negotiate an abject void in being, supported by a paternal function traceable to individual prehistory, Kristeva assists us in exploring a psychic space etched by mourning. But death does not dominate this space. Instead, such explorations constitute a healing anamorphosis of psychic space. A counterpoint to deadly anamorphoses that have marred our life "portraits" with a skull-like stain, these restorative anamorphoses enable us to re-create our lives. In the aftermath of loss, we can again participate in processes that have made us human.[127] Although these processes are not immune to distortion—threats to our humanity do persist—they yet can play an instrumental role in enabling us to break free from those dangers and move forward. Compassion and forgiveness can open out on intimacy. But interventions in mimetic conflict as well as alternatives to that violence must track the work of the body in mimesis if we hope to access their powers. Thus, Kristeva asserts that human efforts to break open the cycle of scapegoating require not only intervening in mimetic conflict but also practicing positive mimesis grounded in *Einfühling*. As we have seen, *The Old Man and the Wolves* sketches steps in a journey to this praxis.

Memory is key to accessing and claiming our humanity. Crucially, this work is fundamentally embodied. Yes, trauma and suffering are part of human experience in the world; however, suffering need not devolve into sacrifice. Fundamental to our capacity for connection with others is a space between sensation and language, an economy of plenitude that can open us up to connection with others, in spite of suffering. Supported in being by the father of individual history, we span a space between sensation and language. The void in our being, the abject, is not set aside; however, always already forgiven by one we first encountered as we began to find a place in the world, we can creatively meet the tasks of this world. Sharing with others, we can move forward toward positive mimesis.

Ourselves and Others in a Time of Wolves

Precisely because the alternative to mimetic violence and sacrifice that Kristeva traces in *The Old Man and the Wolves* is a practice rather than an idea, the novel ends with the mystery of the wolves unsolved: Stephanie's final entry in her journal reports that "Santa Varvara never did yield me up its secrets."[128] Stephanie tells us, for example, that the Old Man has died from "too much awareness." Although he "caught a glimpse of a world without wolves," he couldn't negotiate the boundaries of human and inhuman life in Santa Varvara.[129] The Old Man couldn't accept that wolves were to be found everywhere, not only among the invaders and "others," but even among his "nearest and dearest, including his own Alba."[130] Stephanie too confronts the wolves directly, in those moments when she feels herself doubling with Alba in an abject loss of meaning. But Stephanie faces the void only to come out the other side; inspirited with the gifts of the Old Man, she takes the measure of the wolves. As a consequence, she has a distinct understanding of logic that must be followed to survive: "A she-wolf. Who understands logic and speaks it (*Une louve. Qui connaît la logique et en parle*)."[131]

As Kristeva began the detective story that forms the second part of *The Old Man and the Wolves* and revealed herself to be the novel's narrator, she referred to this logic: well-constructed stories are "another version of contemplation, an algebraic form of orison. Logic transformed into prayer."[132] Now, as Stephanie concludes the journal that comprises the final part of the novel, she too joins and interfuses the story she has told with its form. Stephanie understands analytically what has happened in Santa Varvara; however, in receiving from the old men the gift of compassion, she prepares to navigate Santa Varvara as the Old Man could not. Distinguishing for the first time the old men in her life, Stephanie chooses against Septicius, who watched Santa Varvara from his window, and for her father, the ambassador. Writes Stephanie of her ambassadorial stance:

> A lot of individuals gathered together generate their own carapace, the kind of biological glue secreted by any tribe of animals. It frightens them. But I learned to penetrate the barrier by pretending to enter into their skins and their ways, pretending to become one of them. I experienced Santa Varvara from within, but turned myself inside out like a glove in order to see and hear it as from a distance. This oscillation might be called a kind of justice; it wasn't respect for good itself, but it was reversible space, the essence of ambassadorship, of mission, a to-ing and fro-ing between compromise and revelation.[133]

Kristeva transports us to the edges of the ethical space of the ambassador that Stephanie hopes to access, wagering that she will be able to reverse the effects of the contagion spread by wolves from within that space. But Kristeva does not deliver Stephanie into this space.

Confounding any reader who has hoped for satisfying closure to the novel is Stephanie's final diary entry. Stephanie has returned from Santa Varvara to her home. Standing at her front door in the darkness of a Paris evening, she turns her key in the lock with the alert assurance she has honed as a hardboiled detective. Summing up all that she has experienced in Santa Varvara as she crosses the threshold of her home, Stephanie asserts: "Expect no quarter. I hate the wolves, and now I've got their measure (*Inflexible est la haine qui vous connaît*)."[134]

Stephanie's admission of hatred is troubling. Hatred was the undoing of Alba; when hatred curled up in her, she became a wolf. Will Stephanie be undone by the wolves? She has sought to know them intimately, but she also has asserted her intent to turn the wolf skin she has worn inside out in order to regain her humanity. Has Stephanie failed? That Kristeva ends the novel on an unsettling note may be attributed to Kristeva's desire to offer a route forward for the reader that the reader may not have expected. If the poetics of the gift, a par-don that for-gifts, is to be claimed, it must be taken up directly by a reader who will disavow the last words of the novel, turning away from an invitation to engage anew in mimetic conflict. Kristeva is calling on her readers to revolt. When proffered an opportunity by Stephanie to model hatred of the wolves, readers may refuse hatred.

Kristeva's concept of revolt supports my interpretive claims and gives insight into how Kristeva believes that the contagion that drives mimetic conflict can be broken. As Kelly Oliver cogently observes, for Kristeva, "the ability to revolt becomes a litmus test for psychic life."[135] The absence of revolt is a symptom of the flattening of psychic space in contemporary media culture where it is easier to take Prozac and surf the Web than it is to create a meaningful life. Revolt is prerequisite to political life and also to creativity, freedom, and happiness.

We have seen that Kristeva associates the capacity for revolt with the Imaginary father. According to Kristeva, intimate revolt presages all other forms of revolt. The child who revolts does not violate the law but displaces its authority, taking up its own authorizing in ways that support creative activity, meaning, and connections with others.[136] What comes from revolt, according to Kristeva, is not only revolt against the old law (familial taboos, superego, ideals, Oedipal or narcissistic limits, etc.) but also a "singular autonomy of each as well as a renewed link with the other."[137] As Kelly Oliver explains, revolt is necessary if individuals are to be healed of trauma. Trauma is that which is inassimilable within the social order. Revolt provides for a for-giving of meaning that makes possible a reconnection with others that has been lost to the traumatic event.[138]

In this way, revolt displaces the past on behalf of a future. The Imaginary father is instrumental to revolt, enabling the young child to undertake a dress rehearsal for all future revolts by supporting it at the zero degree of the social order in its effort to draw away from the maternal matrix and the threats it encounters there.[139] The Imaginary father invites the child into the world and supports its sublimation of drives and affects so that it can become a "builder of spoken spaces."[140] Accessed again through bodily memories of his love, the Imaginary father also supports revolt that heals in the wake of trauma.

In *The Old Man and the Wolves*, Stephanie draws on memories that, like the *mandylion* of the Orthodox icon, inscribe the love of an Imaginary father in her very being, offering support for her to rebuild psychic space. This father's compassionate response to suffering establishes grounds for hope that across the void in being that has been her life in Santa Varvara, Stephanie yet can connect with others. Why then does Stephanie turn from an opportunity to revolt against the wolves? The answer may be found in one of Stephanie's last journal entries. She is remembering the Old Man when he would humor her efforts at gardening: "To please me, he would tirelessly water the element that one day would receive him. I could see that thought didn't occur to him, though: he was just joining in the game I played in the intervals of my expeditions to the four corners of the world. He toyed with the clay in order to tend me: to feed me, wash me, make me beautiful."[141]

The Old Man's creative compassion is reminiscent of the work of the Orthodox icon that draws humanity forward in the unfolding of divine creativity. His actions suggest positive mimesis or intimate mediation. But the Old Man's nurturing, as much psychic as verdant, is not what Stephanie most remembers. Instead, thinking of the Old Man's death, she declares, "I'll never forgive the wolves for refusing him the right of burial." Their cruelty, she says, has "left her speechless . . . a lump of basalt, an incurable anguish."[142] The Old men's gift (par-don) has not healed Stephanie's trauma. Forgiveness has missed its mark.

Forgiveness is a gift of the Imaginary father as well as a central act in the psychoanalytic encounter. In both cases, forgiveness is a form of compassion that facilitates integration of trauma and the reshaping of psychic space. Compassion underlays forgiveness, compassion is forgiveness's prerequisite. Until compassion is inscribed in Stephanie, until she breathes it, she will remain traumatized and unable to forgive.

A recent essay on the implications for psychotherapy of the relationship between compassion and forgiveness helps us better understand how compassion and forgiveness are connected in the narrative of *The Old Man and the Wolves*.[143] Everett Worthington and his coauthors attest to the need communities feel for reconciliation after conflict. In the absence of a renewed commitment to collaborative interactions, communities may devolve into recurring episodes of conflict. Forgiveness emerges as a strategic intervention: vengefulness is set aside because of negative physical, mental, and relational consequences.[144] Significantly, in such cases, compassion does not necessarily precede or follow forgiveness. On such a model, forgiveness still appears constrained to operate within a larger nexus of what Girard would identify as a sacrificial economy. Forgiveness may lead, for the moment, to enhanced living conditions; on a different day and, in a different context, scapegoating may accomplish a like goal. When forgiveness is a strategic decision aimed at producing optimal living conditions, the structure of relationships is not essentially altered.

But the authors of the essay on forgiveness and compassion also advance a different model in which compassion underlays forgiveness. Compassion is defined as a capacity for people to "put themselves in the shoes" of a transgressor. Both receptivity to being forgiven and sensitivity to harm done to a victim intensify through identification with another. The ability to forgive appears rooted in a capacity to empathize with the distress of others.[145]

But what founds our capacity for empathy? Unsatisfied with Girard's answer, which does not explain the process by which we become capable of exercising empathy, we initially sought answers to this question with Proust and Antigone. Tracing our capacity for empathy to work done in the wake of trauma by the maternal function and in our nascent relationships with siblings, we noted that, for the maternal function as well as for sibling relationships, our capacity for compassion is founded prior to our acquisition of language. With Proust, we have grounded compassion in grace, in which our embodied being witnesses to the flesh of Being: we move tentatively but with hope from suffering to connection, in which we experience an intimate regard for another's being. With Antigone, we have linked compassion with singularity: in Antigone's compassion for Polyneices she embodies love for another as other in the same, a love characterized by intimate rather than conflicting mediation. In Antigone's attunement to the singularity of her brother's being, Antigone's stance aligns with Septicius, who cares for the being of others that matter "no matter what."[146]

Now, having explored the paternal function, in particular, the work of the father of individual prehistory, we have again traced our capacity for empathy to early childhood. We have seen that, suspended in time between one and another, when we were novices at the art of living, we found ourselves accepted and protected by the father of individual prehistory. As a consequence, as Kelly Oliver perspicaciously argues in her analysis of forgiveness, although the *vehicle* of forgiveness may be language, the *agent* of forgiveness rests with a transfer of affect.[147] Forgiveness turns on the metaphoricity in being that has undergirded our infant existence when the buccal space has opened up to sounds "on the fringe of my being" that have transferred me "to the place of the Other."[148] The movement between the Imaginary and the Symbolic, affect and linguistic meaning, has been sustained by a third that "produces and presupposes forgiveness." The relationship itself—the bridge of sound—has carried me through to par-don, through-gifting. On this foundation, the par-don of the Old Men escapes the clutches of mimetic reversibility. Forgiveness belongs to no one; however, hearing it, breathing it, we belong to it.

We have seen that critical to Kristeva's understanding of forgiveness is her claim that forgiveness works only if affect is united with language. Forgiveness is not an act of linguistic exchange, a gift of words only. Rather, only as the rhythm, tone, and gestures of love are brought to expression is there a through-gifting that makes possible renewed relations with others.[149] Forgiveness has neither the tone nor the structure of evaluation or censure (a role taken by Fathers of the Law and Oedipal fathers). Instead, for Kristeva, as Maria Margaroni affirms, forgiveness is an act, above all, by which "events are witnessed in order to make them sharable."[150]

As *The Old Man and the Wolves* concludes, we observe that Stephanie, who has described herself as a lump of basalt, has not taken up the pardon.

But Kristeva, who began to write *The Old Man and the Wolves* to work out the grief over her father's death, has experienced for-gifting that has recreated psychic time. In the metaphors of her narrative, which have drawn writer and reader into a transferential relationship to language that has embraced sensation and thought, she has experienced healing. Summoning memories of the Imaginary fathers of her life, Kristeva has forged connections out of suffering: drawn into the community of compassion by the old man, her father, she now is gifted with the "I can" of forgiveness. The transfer of affect that has graced the pages of the novel has offered a pardon to the wolves, a gift, through which Kristeva has found a way to renewed meaning, rebirthing herself in language. The Imaginary father who has toyed with clay in that psychic space, in order to "to feed me, wash me, make me beautiful," has re-created in Kristeva a foundation of support. That support had gone missing in Santa Varvara, lost to the television screens and to the wolves. That support had gone missing in Kristeva's life as well, when her father died.

In these ways, compassion and forgiveness are made integral to healing from trauma. In a time of wolves, they offer protective redress against the wolves' sacrificial violence, enabling us to experience the breath of life, not apocalyptic death or suffocating meaninglessness. As Kristeva has grounded our capacity for forgiveness in relations that are intercorporeal before they are linguistic, she has shown that the foundation of forgiveness is laid for a nascent subject prior to the emergence of desires that are riven by mimetic rivalry. Compassion, lived empathy with another to which we are introduced early in our lives by the father of individual prehistory, founds our capacity for forgiveness. Through kinesis, we can experience compassion; we can meet violence with forgiveness, we can experience healing. As Kristeva's narrative demonstrates, when it attests to her own healing after the death of her father at the hands of incompetent medical staff, forgiveness is not something that she *bestows* on perpetrators of violence; rather, forgiveness is something Kristeva *receives* when her founding capacity for forgiveness is restored to her through loving acts of intimate mediation in the memory work of narrative kinesis.

Storytellers cannot par-don or through-gift those who listen to them or read their words; however, we can become the storyteller's witness. Sharing Kristeva's story with her, each of us can be less the hardboiled detective and more the poet. Taking the measure of the wolves, we yet can exchange mimetic violence for compassion. Having made up our minds to tell stories of revolt and undertake our own metamorphoses, we can make Ovid's speech our own as we ask that the gods "look kindly on our enterprise, guiding the unfolding of our poems from the first beginning of the world down to our own day."[151]

From Kinesis to Kenosis: The Future of the Father

Girard has recognized three alternatives to the apocalypse that threatens in the wake of the dead father: we can become mired in meaninglessness, we can forgive each other, or, following Hölderlin, we can imitate Christ in his withdrawal to be with his Father. I have argued that all three of Girard's alternatives need further elucidation, and I have drawn on Julia Kristeva to redress gaps in Girard's theory. I have sketched a phenomenology of forgiveness that points a way to healing from trauma, opening us to a future that is grounded in an economy of loving compassion, not sacrifice. I have pointed also to a nonsacrificial Christology to which the men of sorrow in Santa Varvara have witnessed. Grounded in compassion and attuned to the sacred kinesis of the icon, the Christlike actions of these men open out on forgiveness.

But Kristeva's theory has even more to offer Girard. Precisely because she views the threat to global survival as acutely as does Girard, she explores how the death of the father impacts the death of the Father-God. Girard exempts the Father of Christ from paternal death, sequestering this Father under circumstances of "withdrawal" or "absence." Kristeva grants the Father no such exemption: for Kristeva, the theological implications of the death of Christ on the cross entail also the death of God. This is the "scandal" of the cross: God is dead.[152] But Kristeva is precise, in a way that Girard is not, about what this death entails. Girard speaks of "absence" and "withdrawal," without clearly stating whether he is referring to a single or dual phenomenon; by contrast, appealing to an Orthodox theology of *kenosis*, Kristeva articulates a theology that disavows God's *withdrawal* from the world while acknowledging God's *absence*.[153] That Kristeva does not conflate absence with loss is confirmed when I employ Dominick LaCapra's categories of loss and absence to analyze dynamics of the paternal function in God.

LaCapra writes that "one cannot lose what one never had."[154] Therefore, absence rather than loss is what we ascribe to absolutes that cannot be treated as objects to be possessed or subsequently lost. LaCapra writes that when absence is converted to loss in the Christian tradition, divinity is treated as "hidden" or "lost" because a fault within the human must be compensated for in order for redemption to occur and for that which has been "lost" to be "regained."[155] Penal, substitutionary theories of atonement are articulated in the shadow of this loss. LaCapra explores what it would mean to affirm "absence as absence" without conflating it with loss. When absence cannot be converted into loss but persists, anxiety arises. In absence, no object can be acquired that redresses or compensates for loss. Absence must be lived through.[156] Even so, when absence creates gaps in existence that threaten to consume one, it also functions as a source of acuity or sublimation: the interplay between presence and absence may be productive.[157]

Importantly, this interplay is not structured by desire, as in the case of loss. Where desire gives impetus to loss, in order that an object of desire be acquired that redresses loss, no object of desire is specified by absence. LaCapra notes that it is especially important when reflecting on trauma to acknowledge an absence that cannot be mediated by the work of desire. When absence and loss are conflated, structural and historical trauma (what Mitchell calls deep and mild trauma) are conflated also. In the wake of that conflation, trauma is understood to be resolved when the losses we have experienced receive compensation; another object of desire fills the space that loss had opened. Absence, by contrast, must be lived with and worked through; it does not lend itself to compensation.[158] When absence is subsumed under loss, trauma is generalized and mimeticized. When trauma is subsumed under loss, victim cultures emerge: everyone is a victim and every historical event is traumatizing.[159] When absence is radically inassimilable to loss, so also are victims radically inassimilable to each other. Mimetic competition for victimization is precluded: In this way, when the binary mechanism along which loss is deployed is broken apart, so also is the scapegoat mechanism broken. Absence establishes permanent distance: there is no option for taking another's place. But this turn of events actually can be life-giving.

LaCapra's comments suggest that Girard should seek a theology for our time that attends to absence rather than to Hölderlin-like withdrawal. Girard states that mimeticism doesn't stay put; we are always too close or too far from the other.[160] Because Girard's commendation of withdrawal is part of a dynamic of loss, a praxis of withdrawal will not give Girard the stability he seeks in relationships among humans. Neither will withdrawal account adequately for humanity's relationship with God. Girard needs a theology of absence. Absence, as conceived by LaCapra, provides for empathy that enables us to work through strong trauma and not conflate it with the weak trauma that is part of a competitive-loss system or victim culture. We need not withdraw from the world in order to stand apart from that system. Working through absence, we need not seek to take the other's place (and thereby fall under thrall of acquisitive rivalry). "Empathic unsettlement" can provide for compassion that actually can be transformative. Trauma need not prematurely brought forward in a recuperation of the past that uplifts and fetishizes loss.[161]

LaCapra states that God who is absent rather than lost "honors the name of God in God's absence."[162] His theology of absence aligns with the Orthodox theology of *kenosis* of which Kristeva writes. For Kristeva, the space of iconic representation "inscribes the void" that is kenosis.[163] *Kenosis*, in Greek means nonbeing, nothingness, empty, cut, wipe out. Indeed, *kenosis* refers to the suspension of the paternal function itself, the canceling out of the capacity to represent or to symbolize that function. This is what is means for God to be dead. In Orthodox theology, *kenosis* is dispassion. The yearning we have for the other, the desire for Being—for the Divine itself—is shown to be empty.[164]

In an essay on Christian mimesis, Jim Fodor links *kenosis* with positive forms of mimesis.[165] Fodor arrives at *kenosis* in his efforts to describe discipleship that is grounded in God rather than in desires of individuals that typically devolve into acquisitive rivalry. That *kenosis* is understood as a "giving over" and "relinquishing" points to a God who is the very movement of self-giving. Fodor uses the metaphor of a Father's love, the movement of God within the Trinity. Key to *kenosis* is the human capacity to mirror God's self-emptying, as it is expressed not only in the doctrine of the Trinity but also in the doctrine of Creation. Citing John Milbank, Fodor notes that creative giving by God is not a loss of being but a self-emptying in order to be. In God's giving up of God's self and in human's imitating God and giving themselves up in Christian mimesis, both receive back being, but in life-giving rather than sacrificial ways.[166]

The utility for Girard of Kristeva's appeal to an Orthodox theology of *kenosis* appears when we note their shared recognition of links that exist between the novel and spiritual experience. In *Battling to the End*, Girard writes that "the hell of desire is contained entirely in our refusal to see imitation." We must descend into the heart of mimeticism and "acknowledge our mimetic nature if we hope to free ourselves of it." Girard reminds us that, in his early work, he associates this descent with "novelistic truth."[167] In writing *The Old Man and the Wolves*, Kristeva explores a like truth. Stephanie has journeyed into the heart of mimeticism in her encounter with the wolves of Santa Varvara. Kristeva has joined Stephanie in exploring whether that which they have sought to exclude—the violent wolfishness of being—has, in fact, been constitutive of their being. In Kristeva's reflections, mimetic awareness that Girard names as a necessary precursor to intimate mediation has been at the heart of Kristeva's own quest to explore the healing possibilities of the novel.

But Kristeva attests in her novel also to a theological vision that can lend precision to Girard's reflections on God's withdrawal and augment his own sparse comments on intimate mediation. Connections that Kristeva forges between novelistic truth and iconic revelation show *how* mimetic awareness that is foundational to intimate mediation is not so much known as lived. In *The Old Man and the Wolves*, Kristeva's theology of absence meets LaCapra's working through: Memories of the fathers, brought forward via the kinesic properties of storytelling, enable trauma to be born as compassion counters deadly violence. In *This Incredible Need to Believe*, Kristeva offers the theological counterpart to the "how" of mimetic awareness, demonstrating that awareness born of suffering can open us for positive mimesis. Kristeva names features of *kénose*—sovereign suffering—that lead from trauma to healing.[168]

Kristeva highlights the innocence of Christ's suffering. She says that Christ does not experience his suffering as punishment; therefore, his suffering does not derive meaning from a place outside of Christ's own life. His suffering must, instead, be something necessary to the reconciliation of humanity with divinity. Compassion therefore first means "com-passion," sharing suffering with others.[169] In this way, writes Kristeva, Christ "confers extraordinary dignity" on suffering at the interface of the human and divine.[170] Kristeva acknowledges that Christ's compassion can be misrecognized: One can invest in suffering mimetically, in masochism. But compassion is open to a different mirroring: when one shares in the vulnerability of humankind, acknowledging this vulnerability also in oneself, one arrives at a copresence with others that galvanizes one to struggle with others who suffer and to embody compassion.[171]

So also does Kristeva note that Jesus's suffering takes us to the limit, where pain and torture can result in death. At these limits, Jesus does not suffer only in his humanity but also in his divinity. In this manner *kenosis* is the radical descent of God into suffering.[172] However, the scandal of God's suffering affords freedom from mimeticism.[173] When God dies, desire for the divine is shown to be empty, vain, useless, and absurd. The nothingness of desire for God exposes the bankruptcy of mimeticism. Apophatic theology becomes a powerful antidote to mimeticism. Kristeva calls our attention to Meister Eckhardt, who prays, "I ask God to leave me free of God."[174]

Finally, compassion means reconciliation. At the juncture of shared suffering and the assumed absence of God, Christianity works through compassion, enabling us to represent that juncture to ourselves and thereby witness to resurrection.[175] Kristeva's insights into Orthodox Christianity's testimony to compassion are well illustrated by St. Isaac the Syrian. Writing of the "charitable heart," he describes it as "a heart which is burning with charity for the whole of creation." One who has such a heart "cannot see or call to mind a feature without his eyes becoming filled with tears by reason of the immense compassion which seizes his heart." On one's way to union with God, which is made possible by Christ, all are gathered into this love.[176]

In the face of a spreading meaninglessness that dulls suffering and paralyzes its victims in a deadly malaise, Kristeva calls us to respond to the crisis in the paternal function by taking up compassion as our heritage.[177] She suggests that religion, psychoanalysis, and art offer the means to do so. The "genius of Christianity" provides a powerful alternative to suffering with its twin emphases on compassion and *kenosis*. In psychoanalysis, Kristeva finds that when the analyst projects herself into another's suffering, in order to interpret it from a position other than her own, her compassion becomes an act of par-don, a for-gifting that elicits in its recipient a rebirth.[178] In this way, the transference relationship embodies the compassionate heritage of Christianity. So also, as we have seen in *The Old Man and the Wolves*, Kristeva understands that stories, painting, and music are ways by which the crisis in the paternal function can also be met, as compassion is transformed into "the art of living."[179] Kristeva concludes that the loving intelligence of God "re-creates" in narratives, art, and music "the fruits of the tree of life."[180]

With *The Old Man and the Wolves*, Kristeva has shown that the imagination is an antidote for a mimetic crisis that attends the death of the father. Anchoring her novel in a corporeal hermeneutics, Kristeva has facilitated movement away from repetitive engagement with trauma and toward compassion, as she has shown how iconic memories of fathers can summon renewal and transformation. Drawing on Kristeva's insights, we can return sensory experience to the center of mimetic theory. We can strengthen mimetic theory's capacity to account for threats we face today, caught as we are in the throes of acquisitive mimesis. So also can we enhance the capacity of mimetic theory to speak with hope of how violence is exchanged for forgiveness and compassion through intimate mediation.

Notes

Acknowledgments

1. "Not a Country for Old Men: Mimesis and Violence in Santa Varvara," in *Kristeva's Fiction*, ed. Benigno Trigo, (Albany: State University of New York Press, 2013), 57–78; "After the Scapegoat: René Girard's Apocalyptic Vision and the Legacy of Mimetic Theory," *Philosophy Today* 56, no. 2 (2012): 141–53.

Preface

1. René Girard, *Violence and the Sacred*, trans. Patrick Gregory (Baltimore, MD: Johns Hopkins University Press, 1979), 180.

2. Ibid., 170.

3. Ibid., 175.

4. Ibid., 171.

5. Ibid., 176, 182.

6. Ibid., 175.

7. Ibid., 174. Traditionally, family relationships exemplify "external mediation." This form of mediation occurs when there is space between a desiring subject and its model large enough that they do not compete for the same object. A parent who serves as a "role model" to whom his or her child looks up and aims to emulate is an external mediator; a parent who is a child's "best friend" may fall under the sway of internal mediation. Under conditions of internal mediation, the model and the subject who would imitate the model share much in common and therefore they become rivals when the subject attempts to acquire an object valued by the model. René

Girard, *Deceit, Desire, and the Novel: Self and Other in Literary Structure*, trans. Yvonne Freccero (Baltimore, MD: Johns Hopkins University Press, 1965), 9.

8. Girard writes that "it has become clear that *Totem and Taboo* is more compatible with the theory of the surrogate victim as the foundation of culture than is any other modern work" (*Violence and the Sacred*, 217). Eugene Webb suggests that Girard is "the only important thinker to take a really serious interest" in this hypothesis. See Eugene Webb, *The Self Between: From Freud to the New Social Psychology of France* (Seattle: University of Washington Press, 1993), 154.

9. One particularly compelling example of this diversity is Randolph Splitter's book on Proust (Randolph Splitter, *Proust's Recherche: A Psychoanalytic Interpretation* (Boston: Routledge & Kegan Paul, 1981). The varying psychoanalytic interpretations he offers of *In Search of Lost Time* are eloquent testimony to psychoanalytic theory as a living system. Splitter includes Girard in his discussion and expresses concern about his narrow treatment of Freud in *Violence and the Sacred* (134–35).

10. René Girard, *"To Double Business Bound": Essays on Literature, Mimesis and Anthropology* (Baltimore, MD: Johns Hopkins University Press, 1988), 67; as cited in "Editor's Introduction: Imitating Oedipus," in René Girard, *Oedipus Unbound: Selected Writings on Rivalry and Desire*, ed. Mark R. Anspach (Palo Alto, CA: Stanford University Press, 2004), xxxvii.

11. Anspach, "Editor's Introduction," xxxvii.

12. Ibid.

13. Girard, *Deceit, Desire, and the Novel*, 92, as cited in Anspach, "Editor's Introduction," xxxix.

14. Fundamental to Freud's approach to the mechanism of desire is his early acquaintance with Charcot, whose demonstrations on hysteria Freud attended in 1885 and 1886 at the Salpêtrière amphitheater. Charcot was researching the perplexing symptoms of hysteria: paralysis, muscle contractions, aphasia, and seizures. When his contemporaries accused the patients of malingering, Charcot took his patients' seriously, struggling to understand the physical *and* psychological aspects of their suffering. Freud's attention was captured by Charcot's search for a nondualistic account of the cause of hysteria. Psychoanalysis, a system for bridging body and mind, is born of Freud's reflections on Charcot's work.

15. René Girard, *Things Hidden since the Foundation of the World*, trans. Stephen Bann and Michael Metteer (Palo Alto, CA: Stanford University Press, 1987), 357. Girard is explicitly glossing his commentary on the Oedipus complex in *Violence and the Sacred* in the paragraph from which I take this citation; however, he expands on that account by directly accounting for prepresentational mimesis with the notion of "animal appetite."

16. In my own *Sacrificed Lives*, I address closely the value for Girard of closer attention to the maternal matrix, as described by Kristeva. In an essay on Winnicott, I also address Girard's dismissal of Melanie Klein's work in *Things Hidden since the Foundation of the World* and indicate how a nuanced treatment of her work offers valuable insights for mimetic theory (Martha J. Reineke, *Sacrificed Lives: Kristeva on Women and Violence* [Bloomington: Indiana University Press, 1997], 65–102; Martha J. Reineke, "Transforming Space: Creativity, Destruction, and Mimesis in Winnicott and Girard," *Contagion* 14 [2007]: 81–82; Girard, *Things Hidden*, 361.

17. René Girard, ed., *Proust: A Collection of Critical Essays* (Upper Saddle River, NJ: Prentice-Hall, 1962), 6–7.

18. René Girard, *I See Satan Fall Like Lightning*, trans. James G. Williams (Maryknoll, NY: Orbis Books, 2001), 189.

19. Girard, *Violence and the Sacred*, 174–75; Girard, *Things Hidden*, 353–54. In the latter text, Girard states that mimetic desire is not "normally" a feature of family life but only appears when the family becomes "pathological." See also René Girard, "Delirium as System," in *To Double Business Bound*, 107. In this essay Girard writes that "parricide and incest do not have their origin in the family life of the child. That idea belongs to adults and to the community in crisis." Thus, for Girard, violence begins in collective public misfortune; when it is "transferred from the collectivity to the individual, the crisis is transfigured and reduced to the proportions of a transgression any individual can commit." Situating violence in an individual helps the community unify around the scapegoat. Thus, for Girard, patricide and incest are myths with the same provenance as all cultural myths: they support the generative mechanism, assisting a community in packaging violence in manageable, single-serving-scapegoat size (108).

20. Kristeva does not privilege the breast. Any marking, scission, or movement in the undifferentiated buccal space of the infant that establishes that space as social can teach lessons in mimesis.

21. Julia Kristeva, *Revolution in Poetic Language*, trans. Margaret Waller (New York: Columbia University Press, 1984), 25–28.

22. Luce Irigaray, "The Gesture in Psychoanalysis," in *Between Feminism and Psychoanalysis*, ed. Teresa Brennan (New York: Routledge & Kegan Paul, 1989), 127–38. See especially 131; Kristeva, *Revolution in Poetic Language*, 170.

23. Girard also argues that the game is an example of sacrifice (Girard, *Things Hidden*, 406–7. On this point Irigaray and Kristeva are in complete agreement with Girard that Ernst "throws away" his mother for having left him. Taking their cues from Lacan, who in writing about the *fort/da* game observes that "the symbol manifests itself first of all as the murder of the thing," they would agree with Girard that the game *is* an expression of the scapegoat mechanism (Jacques Lacan, *Écrits: A Selection*, trans. Alan Sheridan, 6th ed. [New York: Norton, 1977], 104.

24. Girard, *Things Hidden*, 407.

25. Julia Kristeva, *Powers of Horror: An Essay on Abjection*, trans. Leon S. Roudiez (New York: Columbia University Press, 1982), 13.

26. For a fuller account of children's violence and how a psychoanalytic perspective can enhance reflection on that violence within mimetic theory see Reineke, "Transforming Space."

27. Comprehensive access to scholarship in mimetic theory is available on the website of the Colloquium on Violence and Religion (http://www.uibk.ac.at/theol/cover/). This website hosts a large database of publications on Girard and mimetic theory. It also has links to over a dozen international, professional societies and scholars whose websites are compendiums of scholarship in mimetic theory (http://www.uibk.ac.at/theol/cover/link/network.html).

28. An important exception to this neglect are essays published in *Mimesis and Science* by researchers in the area of infant and child development who have initiated a dialogue with mimetic theorists (Scott R. Garrels, ed., *Mimesis and Science: Empirical Research on Imitation and the Mimetic Theory of Culture and Religion* [East Lansing: Michigan State University Press, 2011]). See in particular essays by Andrew N. Meltzhoff and Ann Kruger: Andrew N. Meltzoff, "Out of the Mouths of Babes: Imitation, Gaze, and Intentions in Infant Research: The 'Like Me' Framework," 55–74; Ann Kruger, "Imitation, Communion, and Culture," 111–28. So also does Suzanne Ross address early childhood from a perspective grounded in mimetic theory. See her essay "The Montessori Method: The Development of a Healthy Pattern of Desire in Early Childhood," *Contagion* 19 (2012): 87–122.

29. Exceptions tend to focus on the husband-and-wife relationship, rather than on parents and

children. See for example, Suzanne Ross, *The Wicked Truth about Love: The Tangles of Desire* (Glenview, IL: Doers Publishing, 2009); Jean-Michel Oughourlian, *The Genesis of Desire* (East Lansing: Michigan State University Press, 2010).

30. A recent example of an overly rigid interpretation of Freud that erects barriers between psychoanalysis and mimetic theory where bridges instead could be constructed may be found in Jean-Michel Oughourlian's essay "From Universal Mimesis to the Self Formed by Desire," in Garrels, *Mimesis and Science*, 41–54. Oughourlian characterizes Freudian psychoanalysis as a "subjective psychology" that locates the dynamism of the human subject in energy (libido) that wells up from its "biological mass" (47). According to Oughourlian, a Freudian "instinct" or "drive" governs human interactions: conflict emerges when one subject's energy collides with another's. Labeling the human subject of Freud's inquiry "monadic" (48), Oughourlian depicts interactions between multiple monads in ways that make life in the Freudian universe rather like a game of "bumper cars," a carnival ride of my childhood. But Julia Kristeva describes the Freudian drive very differently. Kristeva builds on Freud and distinguishes her views from Lacan's when she locates the drive within a nexus of human development that is not only interdividual but also mimetic. Specifically, Kristeva draws on Freud to offer a *heteronomous* rather than *dichotomous* model of a subject always in process (*Revolution in Poetic Language*, 167). According to Kristeva, Freud does not hold the drives hostage to a mute biologism; rather his goal, which signals his break with contemporaries in the field of neurology, is to explain how the drives function as "bridge between the biological foundation of signifying functioning and the determination by the family and society" (167). Prior to the onset of language, the drives are nevertheless social because infant experience is already characterized by otherness. In the interactions of a mother and infant (e.g., eye contact, babbling, and other shared sounds), Kristeva sees a division in being—a "riant spaciousness"—that is the Freudian drive. See Julia Kristeva, "Place Names," in *Desire in Language: A Semiotic Approach to Literature and Art*, trans. Leon Roudiez (New York: Columbia University Press, 1980), 283. These sounds and muscular responses of a child, expanding in pleasure or contracting in discomfort, are not the intrusion of a mute physicality into the social world; rather, they constitute the creation and delimitation of meaningful, social space. Thus drives are always already movements of an embodied and communicating being.

31. René Girard, Pierpaolo Antonello, and Joao Cezar de Castro Rocha, *Evolution and Conversion: Dialogues on the Origins of Culture* (New York: Continuum, 2007), 204.

32. René Girard, *Mimesis and Theory: Essays on Literature and Criticism, 1953–2005*, ed. Robert Doran (Stanford University Press, 2008), 191.

33. I define "feminist scholarship" by citing the dual character of feminism's goals: feminism is both "an *analytical* and a *politically prescriptive* project." Although feminist scholars take diverse approaches to this project, their work is broadly characterized by a commitment to a "*diagnosis* of women's status" in a variety of contexts (e.g., social, historical, political, religious) and a "*prescription* for changing the situation of women." That said, feminist scholars' diagnoses and prescriptions vary dramatically. There is no agreement among them on what specific forces marginalize, subordinate, or oppress women, on what positive change would look like, or on how change is to be effected. My definition is from Saba Mahmood, who sets a benchmark for critical reflection on feminist theory in her recent book, *Politics of Piety: The Islamic Revival and the Feminist Subject* (Princeton, NJ: Princeton University Press, 2005). Writing as a feminist scholar, in earlier work (*Sacrificed Lives*) I emphasize *diagnosis*, drawing on mimetic and psychoanalytic theories to assess women's situation. I focus, in particular, on causes of violence against women. In this project, I employ these theories again while placing more emphasis on a *prescriptive* thesis for nonviolent relationships inclusive of all.

34. Luce Irigaray, "Women, the Sacred and Money," *Paragraph* 8 (1986): 6–18; Sarah Kofman,

"The Narcissistic Woman: Freud and Girard," *Diacritics* 10, no. 3 (1980): 36–45; Julia Kristeva, "Women's Time," in *The Kristeva Reader*, ed. Toril Moi (New York: Columbia University Press, 1986), 187–213; Kristeva, *Revolution in Poetic Language*; Kristeva, *Powers of Horror*; Toril Moi, "The Missing Mother: The Oedipal Rivalries of René Girard," *Diacritics* 12 (1982): 21–31.

35. Girard indicates that we would need to undertake extensive empirical research to determine if women are more often victims of scapegoating than men. He expresses skepticism that we would succeed in that effort, arguing that, in many instances, 'it cannot be done." See "An Interview with René Girard," in *René Girard and Myth: An Introduction*, edited by Richard J. Golsan (New York: Routledge, 2002), 141–42.

36. Kofman, "The Narcissistic Woman," 41.

37. Moi, "The Missing Mother," 27.

38. Representative feminist engagements with Girard in the humanities and social sciences include Ann W. Astell, *Joan of Arc and Sacrificial Authorship* (South Bend, IN: University of Notre Dame Press, 2003); Rebecca Adams, "Loving Mimesis and Girard's 'Scapegoat of the Text': A Creative Reassessment of Mimetic Desire," in *Violence Renounced: René Girard, Biblical Studies, and Peacemaking*, ed. Willard Swartley (Telford, PA: Pandora Press, 2000), 277–307; Cheryl A. Kirk-Duggan, *Refiner's Fire: A Religious Engagement with Violence* (Minneapolis: Fortress Press, 2000); Rosemary Erickson Johnsen, *Contemporary Feminist Historical Crime Fiction* (New York: Palgrave Macmillan, 2006); Susan Nowak, "The Girardian Theory and Feminism: Critique and Appropriation," *Contagion* 1, no. 1 (1994): 19–29; Kelley A. Raab, *When Women Become Priests* (New York: Columbia University Press, 2000); Reineke, *Sacrificed Lives*; Jennifer Rike, "The Cycle of Violence and Feminist Construction of Selfhood," *Contagion* 3 (1996): 21–42; Christine Shea, "Victims on Violence: 'Different Voices' and Girard," in *Curing Violence*, ed. Mark I. Wallace (Salem, OR: Polebridge Press, 1994), 252–65.

39. Julia Kristeva, *Intimate Revolt: The Powers and Limits of Psychoanalysis*, trans. Jeanine Herman (New York: Columbia University Press, 2002), 5.

40. "An Interview with René Girard," 145. Girard never states whose pre-Oedipal phase needs to be unloaded. Is he referring only to Moi? Is he referring to Rank's theory or to Klein's? The larger context of Girard's comment seems to be that he hopes feminist theorists will "discover why mimetic desire should interest them," and he seems to think their attention to the pre-Oedipal is an obstacle to that interest. If that is what Girard is claiming, his concerns clearly are misplaced. This book demonstrates that feminist interests in psychoanalytic explorations of infancy and early childhood do not preclude serious engagement with mimetic theory.

41. Kristeva, *Intimate Revolt*, 255; Julia Kristeva, *Hatred and Forgiveness*, trans. Jeanine Herman (New York: Columbia University Press, 2010), 7.

42. John Lechte and Mary Zournazi, eds., *The Kristeva Critical Reader* (Edinburgh: Edinburgh University Press, 2004), 3.

43. Although John Lechte attributes the theme of sacrifice in Kristeva's work to Bataille (John Lechte, *Julia Kristeva* [New York: Routledge, 1990], 74.), Girard figures in her work (*Revolution in Poetic Language*, 249 n. 91, 250 n. 100; *Powers of Horror*, 213 n. 4, 215 n. 17; *Tales of Love*, trans. Leon S. Roudiez [New York: Columbia University Press, 1987], 395 n. 16; "Women's Time," 213). Moreover, as I point out in my discussion of *Old Man in the Wolves* in this project, Kristeva's Christology in this novel is expressly indebted to Girard. Kristeva's detailed knowledge of Girard suggests his direct influence. Michael Payne confirms my assessment in citing Girard's influence on Kristeva (Michael Payne, *Reading Theory: An Introduction to Lacan, Derrida and Kristeva* (Hoboken, NJ: [Wiley-Blackwell, 1993], 182). So also does Stephen Bann suggest that

Kristeva's theory of subjectivity is aided not only by Lacan, but also by "the speculations of René Girard, whose achievement she was one of the first to salute." See foreword to Julia Kristeva, *Proust and the Sense of Time*, trans. Stephen Bann (New York: Columbia University Press, 1993), x. It seems unlikely that Bann's comment would appear in the foreword in the absence of Kristeva's endorsement of his characterization of her perspective on Girard (an insight suggested in personal correspondence with Wiel Eggen). Bann also comments on Girard's influence on Kristeva at a colloquium on Kristeva's work. His lecture is published as Stephen Bann, "Three Images for Kristeva: From Bellini to Proust," *Parallax* 4, no. 3 (1998): 70. In this lecture, Bann cites Girard's influence on comments Kristeva makes on Psalm 118 (the builders reject a stone that will become the cornerstone) and sacrifice in *The Sense and Non-Sense of Revolt*. In Kristeva's response to Bann at the colloquium (also published in the *Parallax* article) she states, "The problems of the corner stone and the lost foundations are very important to me and I am grateful that you have noted this" See Bann, "Three Images for Kristeva," 76. Girard's comments on the cornerstone are made in Girard, *Things Hidden*, 178, 429. Kristeva's discussion (offered without formally citing Girard) references not only the stone rejected by the builders but also sacrifice and mimesis. See Julia Kristeva, *The Sense and Non-Sense of Revolt*, trans. Jeanine Herman (New York: Columbia University Press, 2001), 10–17. That Kristeva's interest in Girard is long-standing is also supported by the essay "Women's Time," originally published in 1979 (French) and 1981 (English) and republished in *New Maladies of the Soul* fourteen years later (1993 in French). Kristeva makes a number of revisions to the original essay, adding and deleting passages; however, references to Girard's theory of sacrifice and scapegoating have not been deleted or altered. See Kristeva, "Women's Time"; Julia Kristeva, *New Maladies of the Soul*, trans. Ross Guberman (New York: Columbia University Press, 1997).

Introduction

1. The diversity of psychoanalytic theory is well represented in multiple definitions of the unconscious. Even Freud struggles to describe the unconscious, offering both a topographical model that makes of the unconscious a kind of storehouse in the mind and a structural model that divides the mind's labor among an ego, id, and superego. (See summary in Jane Milton, Caroline Polmear, and Julia Fabricius, *A Short Introduction to Psychoanalysis*, 2nd ed. [Thousand Oaks, CA: Sage, 2011], 20.) Lacanian theorists such as Julia Kristeva espouse a different notion, displacing the locus of the unconscious from the subject to the other. The unconscious does not so much suggest mysterious forces active in a hidden, interior province of a subject's mind as boundary-making practices that delimit the subject and its other. The unconscious for Lacan is "transindividual," an "outside" to the subject who never "is," but always Other (*Écrits*, 49). Lacan's and Kristeva's notions of the unconscious are most similar to Girard's. Although Girard is wary of the term and prefers not to use it, he acknowledges that, "supposing that there is still any point in keeping such a term," mimetic desire is "the real 'unconscious'" (Girard, *Things Hidden*, 359).

2. The "trail guide" is the psychoanalyst, and support is offered in the clinical practice of psychoanalysis.

3. For a more extended discussion of the italicized themes see Milton, Polmear, and Fabricius, *Short Introduction to Psychoanalysis*, 19–45.

4. *Babes in Toyland* was the first movie I ever saw. As is often the case for young viewers of Disney "children's" movies, the movie gave me nightmares for years. Thanks to YouTube, we can be frightened all over again: "This is the forest of no return. You have stumbled in. You have fumbled in. Now you can't get out" (*Forest of No Return*, 2007), http://www.youtube.com/watch?v=8zQe QunbBmk&feature=youtube_gdata_player.

5. Employing this same metaphor, psychoanalytic therapy creates a safe environment for reassessment of this hard-packed trail. With an analyst, we may revisit regular features of our walk through the woods at a therapeutic distance. Although analysis will not enable us to cut an entirely new path, we may be able to move away from dangerous fallen trees or masses of roots that previously have felled us in "a forest of no return."

6. Girard uses the metaphors of "disease" and "illness" to powerful effect. See Girard, *Deceit, Desire, and the Novel*, disease: 43, 91, 250, illness: 137, 180, 254.

7. Girard, *Violence and the Sacred*, 146.

8. Girard, *Deceit, Desire, and the Novel*, 83.

9. Girard, *Violence and the Sacred*, 146–47.

10. Ibid., 160–61.

11. Ibid., 146; Girard, *Things Hidden*, 29.

12. Girard, *Deceit, Desire, and the Novel*, 16–17.

13. Ibid., 294.

14. Webb, *The Self Between*, 91.

15. Girard, *Deceit, Desire, and the Novel*, 232.

16. Ibid., 221–22.

17. Suzanne Clark and Kathleen Hulley, "Cultural Strangeness and the Subject in Crisis," in *Julia Kristeva Interviews*, ed. Ross Mitchell Guberman (New York: Columbia University Press, 1996), 55.

18. Margaret Waller, "Intertextuality and Literary Interpretation," in Guberman, *Julia Kristeva Interviews*, 194–95.

19. Julia Kristeva, *Hannah Arendt*, trans. Ross Guberman (New York: Columbia University Press, 2003), 73.

20. Adriana Cavarero, *Relating Narratives: Storytelling and Selfhood* (New York: Routledge, 2000), 36.

21. Colin Davis, *After Poststructuralism: Reading, Stories, Theory* (New York: Routledge, 2003), 141.

22. Kristeva, *Powers of Horror*, 140.

23. Guillemette Bolens, *The Style of Gestures: Embodiment and Cognition in Literary Narrative* (Baltimore: Johns Hopkins University Press, 2012), 2.

24. Ibid., 6.

25. Ibid., 3.

26. Ibid., 8. Scenes from *In Search of Lost Time* feature prominently in Bolens's introduction, suggesting that Proust is an artist whose work typifies narrative kinesis. See pp. 6–9, 22–25, and 44–46.

27. Ibid., 183 n. 22.

28. Ibid.

29. See ibid., 12–18, 183, 84.

30. Ibid., 15.

31. Vittorio Gallese, "The Two Sides of Mimesis: Mimetic Theory, Embodied Simulation, and Social Identification," in Garrels, *Mimesis and Science*, 89.

32. Emmanuel Levinas, *Totality and Infinity: An Essay on Exteriority*, trans. Alphonso Lingis (Pittsburgh: Dusquene University Press, 2008), 205–6, as cited in Bolens, *The Style of Gestures*, 24.

33. Bolens, *The Style of Gestures*, 41.

34. Ibid., 23.

35. Gallese, for example, states of his essay on mimetic theory and mirror neurons that "the main ambition of this paper was to show that today we can ground man's openness to others in neurobiological bases" ("Two Sides of Mimesis," 103). Gallese's ambition can be applauded; at the same time, however, we need to explore how, when we fail at being open to each other and our actions devolve into violence, our failure is embodied. Trauma, as explored by psychoanalysis, is a name for failed kinesis or failed intercorporeity. And psychoanalysis offers a powerful theory that seeks to understand the embodied components of that failure.

36. Girard, *Deceit, Desire, and the Novel*, 221–22.

37. Ibid., 34s.

38. Kristeva, *Proust and the Sense of Time*, 56.

39. Ibid., 5. Kristeva's notion has similarities with Jean Ricardou's discussion of the productive metaphor in Proust. Rather than serve a representative function, the metaphor creates a metamorphosis. See Jean Ricardou and Erica Freiberg, "Proust: A Retrospective Reading," *Critical Inquiry* 8 (1982): 532.

40. Kristeva, *Proust and the Sense of Time*, 81–82.

41. Bolens, *The Style of Gestures*, 26.

42. Ibid., 24–25.

43. Peter Brooks, *Psychoanalysis and Storytelling* (Hoboken, NJ: Wiley-Blackwell, 1994), 105.

44. Ibid., 43–44.

45. Marianne Hirsch, *The Mother/Daughter Plot: Narrative, Psychoanalysis, Feminism* (Bloomington: Indiana University Press, 1989), 9.

46. My definitions are analogous to those Dominick LaCapra uses when he contrasts structural trauma with historical trauma, absence with lack. See Dominick LaCapra, *Writing History, Writing Trauma* (Baltimore: Johns Hopkins University Press, 2000).

47. The distinction I draw between strong and weak trauma parallels Dominick LaCapra's effort to distinguish absence and loss. Absence, for LaCapra, is transhistorical and applies to absolute foundations (and their absence). Loss references historical phenomena. LaCapra finds in Girard a missed opportunity to delineate between mimetic desire oriented around absence and loss. By making mourning exclusively the expression of a community becoming reconciled in the wake of its scapegoating of a victim, Girard bypasses mourning as a possible expression of absence associated with a lack of being that is the motor of mimetic desire. My exploration of deep trauma is an effort to take the road LaCapra has recommended in order to augment Girard's theory of mimetic desire. See ibid., 195, 45 n. 2.

48. Juliet Mitchell, "Sibling Trauma: A Theoretical Consideration," in *Sibling Relationships*, ed.

Prophecy Coles (New York: Karnac Books, 2006), 155–74. Although the focus of Mitchell's discussion is sibling relationships, her explorations are more inclusive. She has been prompted in her inquiry by the assumption in psychoanalysis that sibling relationships, unlike children's relationships with their parents, cannot be the occasion for deep trauma. That she believes they can motivates her very careful study of trauma and lays important groundwork for my study of *Antigone* in Part 2.

49. René Girard, *Battling to the End: Conversations with Benoît Chantre*, trans. Mary Baker (East Lansing: Michigan State University Press, 2009), 205.

50. Cecilia Sjöholm, "Fear of Intimacy? Psychoanalysis and the Resistance to Commodification," in *Psychoanalysis, Aesthetics, and Politics in the Work of Julia Kristeva*, ed. Kelly Oliver and S. K. Keltner (Albany: State University of New York Press, 2009), 191.

51. Lechte and Zournazi, *The Kristeva Critical Reader*, 191; Sjöholm, "Fear of Intimacy?" 191.

52. Kristeva, *Sense and Non-Sense of Revolt*, 1.

53. Julia Kristeva, *Revolt, She Said*, trans. Brian O'Keeffe (Los Angeles: Semiotext(e), 2002), 120; Julia Kristeva, "The Revolt of Mallarmé," in *Mallarmé in the Twentieth Century*, ed. Robert Greer Cohn, trans. Louise Burchill (Cranbury, NJ: Associated University Presses, 1998), 31.

54. Kristeva, "The Revolt of Mallarmé," 36.

55. In her commentary on Kristeva's notion of intimate revolt, Kelly Oliver notes the juxtaposition of transgression with displacement. Kelly Oliver, *The Colonization of Psychic Space: A Psychoanalytic Social Theory of Oppression* (Minneapolis: University of Minnesota Press, 2004), 143.

56. Sjöholm, "Fear of Intimacy?" 188, 192–93.

57. Sjöholm argues that Kristeva's way of thinking about intimacy is unique and defines her distinctive contribution to psychoanalysis. See ibid., 180.

58. Juliet Mitchell, *Siblings: Sex and Violence* (Malden, MA: Polity, 2004), 15. Mitchell cites Freud's *Group Psychology and the Analysis of the Ego*. See Sigmund Freud, *The Complete Psychological Works of Sigmund Freud*, vol. 18: *"Beyond the Pleasure Principle," "Group Psychology" and Other Works*, ed. and trans. James Strachey (London: Hogarth and the Institute of Psychoanalysis, 2001), 137. Mitchell's chronology is particularly productive for a study of Girard because of the central role provided for lateral relations in psychic development.

59. In the United States, Nancy Chodorow's work has created confusion about this point. She has developed sociological theories of the family that use the vocabulary of psychoanalysis in service to a feminist-based ideology critique. For a more complete description of how psychoanalytic theory differs from Chodorow's sociological perspective on the family see Reineke, *Sacrificed Lives*, 34–41.

60. Teresa Brennan, *The Interpretation of the Flesh: Freud and Femininity* (New York: Routledge, 1992), 69.

61. Ewa Ziarek, "At the Limits of Discourse: Heterogeneity, Alterity, and the Maternal Body in Kristeva's Thought," *Hypatia* 7, no. 2 (1992): 92–100.

62. Kristeva, *Powers of Horror*, 3–4.

63. Julia Kristeva, *Black Sun*, trans. Leon S. Roudiez (New York: Columbia University Press, 1992), 27–28.

64. Kristeva writes about "The Thing" in her discussion of melancholia. Writes Kristeva of individuals

in the throes of depression: "They have lost the meaning—the value—of their mother tongue for want of losing the mother. The dead language they speak, which foreshadows their suicide, conceals a Thing buried alive. The latter, however, will not be translated in order that it not be betrayed; it shall remain walled up within the crypt of the inexpressible affect" (ibid., 53). Kristeva's account of melancholia differs substantively from Freud's. He sees it as a violent cannibalism: a hidden, hostile attack on the other. By contrast, Kristeva emphasizes that those who are melancholic do not challenge loss by attacking it. As Ewa Ziarek, observes, "Melancholics do not so much refuse loss as they refuse to accept that the Symbolic system compensates adequately for their loss." See Ewa Ziarek, "Kristeva and Levinas: Mourning, Ethics, and the Feminine," in *Ethics, Politics, and Difference in Julia Kristeva's Writing*, ed. Kelly Oliver (New York: Routledge, 1993), 73.

65. Kristeva, *Tales of Love*, 26–28.

66. Mitchell, *Siblings*, 222.

67. Mitchell expresses a preference for a childhood inclusive of actual rather than fantasy siblings because these relationships typically allow children to access hatred and resolve it in productive social engagements. However, she does acknowledge that, when siblings are absent, other relationships oriented around sameness afford children similar opportunities.

68. Kristeva follows Lacan in differentiating between the Imaginary and Symbolic orders. When tracing the history of the human subject, Lacan discovers that infants experience only fragments of being. Only gradually does a sense of "I" emerge out of a chaotic field of sensory experience. Lacan refers to this fragmented nexus of early experience as the Imaginary. It is characterized by an absence of clear differentiation between "I" and "other." As the infant matures, it develops a capacity to take a position in the world. The Symbolic order is the field of exchange, language, and law. Although "I" is part of this order, we do not have a self-possessed unity of being. The human subject achieves identity only in difference and asserts a unity of being only in the context of alienation. The "I" comes to be in the mirror of the other's gaze. The "I" is always grounded in misrecognition of a unity of being. The "I" of the Symbolic order is therefore fundamentally intersubjective. Its identity is fundamentally mimetic, to use Girard's words.

69. Kristeva, *Tales of Love*, 26; Julia Kristeva, "Julia Kristeva in Conversation with Rosalind Coward," in *ICA Documents*, vol. 1 (London: Institute of Contemporary Arts, 1984), 23.

70. Girard, *Proust*; Girard, *Deceit, Desire, and the Novel*; Kristeva, *Proust and the Sense of Time*; Julia Kristeva, *Time and Sense: Proust and the Experience of Literature*, trans. Ross Guberman (New York: Columbia University Press, 1996).

71. Girard, *Deceit, Desire, and the Novel*, 53.

72. Julia Kristeva, "Interview: Sharing Singularity," in *Julia Kristeva: Live Theory*, by John Lechte and Maria Margaroni (New York: Continuum, 2004), 150.

73. Mitchell, *Siblings*, 128–29.

74. Girard, *Violence and the Sacred*, 56–57. Girard accounts for the practice of putting twins to death in many cultures by suggesting that fear of the lack of differences that is always associated with a contagion of violence leads cultures to see twins as a particular threat to be eliminated.

75. Ibid., 61.

76. Mitchell, *Siblings*, 44. This structure underlies later expressions of hatred based on proposed differences of race, class, and ethnicity (for example). Hatred, in this instance, is displaced to an out-group who embodies otherness anew. Although Mitchell does not indicate whether this new

out-group poses a problem of being too different or too similar to those who stand in opposition to it, were she to elaborate on this point, she would find Girard's insights helpful. In *The Scapegoat* he observes that although every culture and person has a perception of those who are "different," attributions of difference are not trustworthy markers of potential victims. Others (e.g., the disabled, foreigners) are reproached "for not being as different as expected, and in the end for not differing at all." Prejudicial hatred "is expressed, not for difference, but for its absence." See René Girard, *The Scapegoat*, trans. Yvonne Freccero (Baltimore: Johns Hopkins University Press, 1986), 21–22.

77. Mitchell, *Siblings*, 10.

78. Ibid.

79. Ibid., 13.

80. Girard, *Oedipus Unbound*, 88.

81. Girard, Antonello, and Rocha, *Evolution and Conversion*, 201.

82. Stacey Keltner, *Kristeva* (Malden, MA: Polity Press, 2011), 108.

83. Kristeva, *Tales of Love*, 38.

84. Keltner, *Kristeva*, 111.

85. Lechte and Margaroni, *Julia Kristeva: Live Theory*, 53.

86. Ibid.

87. Julia Kristeva, *The Old Man and the Wolves: A Novel*, trans. Barbara Bray (New York: Columbia University Press, 1994), 140.

88. Julia Kristeva, *This Incredible Need to Believe*, trans. Beverley Bie Brahic (New York: Columbia University Press, 2009), 10.

89. Keltner, *Kristeva*, 119.

90. The French version of both novels describes their setting as "Santa Barbara." The English translation changes the name, apparently to prevent American readers from confusing the city with the television soap opera or the California city that share the same name. Because barbarism is infecting the city of Santa Barbara, the choice of "Barbara" also may be associated with "barbarian" (Kathleen O'Grady, "The Tower and the Chalice: Julia Kristeva and the Story of Santa Barbara," in *Religion in French Feminist Thought: Critical Perspectives*, ed. Kathleen O'Grady, Judith L. Poxon, and Morny Joy [New York: Routledge, 2003], 90). In *Strangers to Ourselves*, Kristeva discusses the etymology of "barbarian," and suggests that Homer coined the term on the basis of such "onomatopoeia as bla-bla, bara-bara, in articulate or incomprehensible mumblings" of non-Greeks." Later in Greece, "barbarians" are persons who speak Greek clumsily, or with an accent (Julia Kristeva, *Strangers to Ourselves*, trans. Leon S. Roudiez [New York: Columbia University Press, 1994], 51). Comments that Kristeva makes elsewhere undercut the suggestion that Kristeva (rather than someone at the publishing house) wanted "Santa Barbara" changed to "Santa Varvara" in the English translation in order to disassociate the "Santa Barbara" of the novel from the TV soap opera. In her essay "In Times Like These: Who Needs Psychoanalysis?" Kristeva describes a sprawling metropolis that could be New York or "anywhere" and describes our psychic life as degenerating into a "society of spectacle" associated with the psychodrama *Dallas* and other "soap operas" (Kristeva, *New Maladies of the Soul*, 27–29). Because the residents of Santa Varvara/Barbara exemplify such a "society of spectacle," Kristeva may have wanted to evoke connections between the city of Santa Barbara in the novel and the soap opera of the same name.

91. Kristeva, *The Old Man and the Wolves*, 58.

92. Julia Kristeva, *Murder in Byzantium: A Novel*, trans. C. Jon Delogu (New York: Columbia University Press, 2008), 64.

93. Julia Kristeva, "Interview: *The Old Man and the Wolves*," interview by Bernard Sichère, in Guberman, *Julia Kristeva Interviews*, 165.

94. Ibid., 169.

95. Ibid., 170.

96. Kristeva describes herself as an atheist (see Julia Kristeva, "A Father Is Beaten to Death," in *The Dead Father: A Psychoanalytic Inquiry*, ed. Lila J. Kalinich and Stuart W. Taylor [New York: Routledge, 2009], 176). However, Kristeva's demonstrated ability to attest to the functional power of Christian practice and belief, visible across the body of her work, is unparalleled among contemporary psychoanalytic theorists. Born in Bulgaria and raised by an Orthodox father who studied theology before he pursued a career in medicine (Kristeva, *This Incredible Need to Believe*, 84), Kristeva brings to her writings on psychoanalysis and religion a unique knowledge of and affinity for the contributions of Orthodox Christianity to the critical assessment of the role of religious belief in human life.

97. Julia Kristeva, *The Severed Head: Capital Visions*, trans. Jody Gladding (New York: Columbia University Press, 2011), 53.

Prelude. Mothers

1. In the exposition that follows, Girard identifies Proust, the author of *In Search of Lost Time*, with its narrator. Dissenting from literary critics who distinguish Marcel and the narrator from Proust, Girard treats them as one. For him, the novel is a "spiritual autobiography which claims to be rooted in a personal experience." René Girard, "Conversion in Literature and Christianity," in *Mimesis and Theory*, 269. In this work, when I am exposing Girard, I follow his lead, even though recent Proust criticism observes that "Marcel" is "tentatively placed in the manuscripts of Proust's novel." Roy B. Lacoursiere, "Proust and Parricide: Literary, Biographical, and Forensic-Psychiatric Explorations," *American Imago* 60, no. 2 (2003): 207 n. 10, doi:10.1353/aim.2003.0013. Indeed, the name "Marcel" appears twice in 3,000 pages of text. In *The Prisoner*, the narrator indicates that Albertine has referred to him as "my darling" followed by his Christian name. The narrator assigns to the narrator the name "Marcel" with the conditional provision: "if we give the narrator the same name as the author of this book" (64). Also in *The Prisoner*, Albertine once directly addresses the narrator as "Dear darling Marcel." See Marcel Proust, *The Prisoner and The Fugitive*, trans. Carol Clark and Peter Collier, vol. 5 of *In Search of Lost Time* (New York: Penguin Classics, 2003), 140. For a long time, that early versions of the text included "Marcel" (as Marcel was included in the notebooks of *Contre Sainte-Beuve*) was assumed. Scholars imagined that Proust gradually excised the name from his writings; however, late manuscript variants of *The Prisoner* show Proust using the name "Marcel." See Angela Moorjani, *The Aesthetics of Loss and Lessness* (London: Palgrave Macmillan, 1991), 158. Nevertheless, the interpretive waters that link "Marcel" with the narrator are muddy. At first glance, Girard's assumption that the narrator and the author are one also is at odds with recent criticism. Brian Rogers suggests that such a view is antiquated when he asserts that, notwithstanding autobiographical features of the novel, "few readers today, however, are inclined to fall into the trap of identifying the narrator with the author." See Brian Rogers, "Proust's Narrator," in *The Cambridge Companion to Proust*, ed. Richard Bales (Cambridge: Cambridge University Press, 2001), 86. Rogers further asserts, "The Narrator is not Marcel Proust" (98). However, a closer look at the substance of Rogers's

argument suggests that Girard's and Rogers's views are similar. Rogers aims to show how Proust creates characters who act as mirrors of each other. Their identities are not something they possess; rather, the characters negotiate and obtain identity in relationship with each other. Writes Rogers of the narrator, "If we wish to understand him we must look into his mirror, share the images swirling around in his imagination and *unravel the process by which they form patterns* which will turn into a work of artistic creation" (85; emphasis mine). For example, Swann's identity comes into view for the reader because he is a mirror for the narrator (and the narrator for him) (Rogers, 88). Girard shares Rogers's perspective on the text: through his analysis of mimetic/mirror play in the novel, Girard actually takes on the task Rogers commends to us: Girard is unraveling the process by which these mimetic patterns develop and function. So also do Rogers and Girard agree that *Finding Time Again* is "a statement of the author's conception of art and a commentary on his work" (Rogers, 95). Rogers asserts that, in structuring the final volume in this way, Proust "ensures both the reader's contribution to the creation of his hero and his participation in the act of creation which is the climax of the novel" (95). Proust is encouraging the reader to "rewrite the world" (97). For Rogers, when Proust creates a narrator who offers a mirror to the reader (because he is not the author), Proust enables the reader to enter the world reflected in the mirror: "We inhabit the narrator's body, see everything through his eyes, and share his sensibility" (98). Philip Kolb views the conclusion of the novel in a similar light. While distinguishing the narrator from Proust throughout the novel (drawing on Proust's own letters about his novel), Kolb suggests that, in the conclusion of the novel, Proust and the narrator merge, "somewhat as a double image, viewed in a stereoscope, gradually becomes a single image as it comes into focus." Philip Kolb, "Proust's Protagonist as a 'Beacon,'" in *Critical Essays on Marcel Proust*, ed. Barbara J. Bucknall (Boston: G. K. Hall, 1987), 58. Thus, like the artists highlighted in the novel (Vinteuil, La Berma, Elstir, and Bergotte), Proust becomes a beacon who will guide others. Already in the conclusion of *Deceit, Desire, and the Novel*, we see that Girard concurs with Rogers and Kolb about the transformative effect that reading Proust's novel can have on the reader. When Girard talks about the conversion experience, asserting similarities between literary and religious experience, he quotes Aloysha from the *Brothers Karamazov*: "Certainly we shall rise again, certainly we shall see each other and shall tell each other with joy and gladness all that has happened" (*Deceit, Desire, and the Novel*, 314). Despite the similarities of Girard's and Rogers's perspectives, one of Rogers's insights does have constructive implications for my argument. Rogers states that, when the narrator is present in the text, we hear about his reactions to certain stimuli. On these occasions, the narrator is embodied and experiences the world with his body. He falls silent when he is not physically present (Rogers, "Proust's Narrator," 85). Rogers's insight will see further attention as we discuss Kristeva's interpretation of the novel. Kristeva does not refer to the narrator as "Marcel." She does align the author and narrator of the text; however, Kristeva also can be seen to concur with the substance of Rogers's argument. Neither readers nor authors are "one" in relation to a text: we are subjects in process and relationship. Moreover, because Kristeva emphasizes the *bodily* experience of the novel, her commentary on Proust adds further detail to Rogers's observation that the body has significance to the narrator of *In Search of Lost Time* and also to readers, as they respond to that narrator. William C. Carter's depiction of the relation between Proust and the narrator complements Kristeva's. Carter notes that in letters and notes about the novel, Proust usually speaks of the narrator as "I," "making no distinction between himself and his fictional persona." But Carter notes that *In Search of Lost Time* is not an autobiography; instead, as the novel progressed "the 'I' telling the story became both its generator and its subject, like a Siamese twin, intimately linked to Proust's body and soul and yet other." William C. Carter, *Marcel Proust: A Life* (New Haven: Yale University Press, 2002), 474.

2. By "affective memory" Girard references memories that are contrasted with memories we self-consciously recall. Proust calls these memories "involuntary." They are typically associated with "organic" aspects of experience: smell, taste, sound, and kinesthetic sensation. Proust can be

understood to transpose to the locale of the initial experience the work of involuntary memory and also the evocation of emotion. One example is found at the beginning of *Finding Time Again* when Marcel describes waking one night and thinking of Albertine: "One's legs and arms are full of torpid memories. Once, when I had left Gilberte rather early, I woke up in the middle of the night in my room at Tansonville and, still half asleep, called out: 'Albertine!' It was not that I had been thinking about her or dreaming of her, nor that I had mistaken her for Gilberte: but a recollection suddenly burgeoning within my arm had made me reach behind my back for the bell, as if I had been in my bedroom in Paris. And, not finding it, I had called out: 'Albertine!,' thinking my dead lover was lying beside me as she often used to in the evenings." Marcel Proust, *Finding Time Again*, trans. Ian Patterson, vol. 6 of *In Search of Lost Time* (New York: Penguin Classics, 2003), 5.

3. Girard, introduction to *Proust*, 4.

4. Ibid., 6–7.

5. Published four years later (1965) as Girard, *Deceit, Desire, and the Novel*.

6. Ibid., 32–33. Marcel Proust, *In the Shadow of Young Girls in Flower*, trans. James Grieve, vol. 2 of *In Search of Lost Time* (New York: Penguin Classics, 2005), 26–30. Marcel Proust, *Within a Budding Grove*, vol. 2 of *In Search of Lost Time*, trans. C. K. Scott Moncrieff and Terence Kilmartin (Modern Library, 1998), 35–41.

7. Girard, *Deceit, Desire, and the Novel*, 34. In Marcel's childhood, his models are his parents and Bergotte. He imitates them without rivalry (Girard calls this "external mediation"). Later, mediation becomes internal, as Marcel approaches the adult world from a position of acquisitive desire (*Deceit, Desire, and the Novel*, 73–74).

8. Ibid., 77.

9. Ibid., 78.

10. Ibid., 78–79.

11. Ibid., 81.

12. René Girard, "Genesis of Mimetic Theory," Imitatio Conference, April 29, 2008, http://www.youtube.com/watch?v=Ak8VXw-9NBQ&feature=youtube_gdata.

13. Gallese, "Two Sides of Mimesis," 25.

14. Ibid.

15. Ibid.

16. Ibid., 230.

17. Ibid.

18. Girard, Antonello, and Rocha, *Evolution and Conversion*, 25.

19. In "Perilous Balance: A Comic Hypothesis," *MLN* 87, no. 7 (December 1972): 811–26, Girard still is drawing on the language of phenomenology in his discussion of Molière. However, of the original cluster of key terms from Girard's work on Proust—perception, sensory impression, material bridge, affective memory—only "perception" appears to have been retained in Girard's later work and then only in *Things Hidden since the Foundation of the World*. Discussing the victimage mechanism with Girard, interlocutor Jean-Michel Oughourlian mentions a historical stage during which persons exhibit a "limited perception" of that mechanism (Girard, *Things Hidden*, 130). In *Des choses caches*, the phrase is "*reconnaissance limitée*," which suggests cognitive

rather than sensory awareness. René Girard, Jean-Michel Oughourlian, and Guy Lefort, *Des Choses Cachées Depuis la Fondation du Monde* (Paris: Grasset, 1978), 152. In the other places in which the word "perception" is found, the phenomenological meaning is largely absent. For example, in *Things Hidden* (35) the word "perception" is associated with hallucinatory phenomena in ritual trances ("*la perception*," in *Des Choses Cachées*, 43) "Perception" (*la perception*) is used analogically by Girard to compare meanings derived through ethnological interpretations with those associated with the figures that Gestalt psychology produces (*Things Hidden*, 61; *Des Choses Cachées*, 69). Interestingly, in introducing *To Double Business Bound*, xiv–xv, Girard offers insight into his changed focus when he alludes to disjunctions between the argument of *Violence and the Sacred* and the collection of literary essays in *To Double Business Bound*. Explaining that some of these essays predate his discovery of the victimage mechanism, on which he reports in *Violence and the Sacred*, Girard states that he has chosen not to reconcile language and theory in the two works. Rather than update the earlier work with more extensive references to his new discovery, Girard hopes that the imperfections and "lacunae" of *To Double Business Bound* will "spur the reader into active collaboration with the author and improve channels of communication." But Girard anticipates only limited lacunae: the collaborative reader will join Girard in supplementing ideas in the *older* work with his *newer* work but will not need to also supplement the *newer* work with additional appeals to *earlier* work. In responding to Girard's call for collaboration, I take on this neglected task.

20. Girard returns to the theme of spiritual conversion in Girard, *I See Satan Fall*. See also Gallese, "Two Sides of Mimesis," 175, 198, 212. But Girard does not describe a role for affect and sensation in conversion.

21. Girard, "Conversion in Literature and Christianity." "Conversion in Literature and Christianity" is dated "1999" on the title page; a title note indicates that the paper was delivered in December 1998 at the Christianity and Literature session of the Modern Language Association's national convention in San Francisco.

22. Girard, *Proust*, 6; Girard, "Conversion in Literature and Christianity," 269.

23. Girard, "Conversion in Literature and Christianity," 269.

24. Girard, *Proust*, 7.

25. Girard, "Conversion in Literature and Christianity," 270–71.

26. Ibid., 271.

27. Girard, *Deceit, Desire, and the Novel*, 81.

28. Ibid.

29. Stephen J. Duffy, *The Dynamics of Grace: Perspectives in Theological Anthropology* (Eugene, OR: Wipf & Stock, 2007), 390.

30. Paul Ricoeur, *The Symbolism of Evil* (Boston: Beacon Press, 1986), 250. Quoted in Duffy, *The Dynamics of Grace*, 390.

31. Duffy, *The Dynamics of Grace*, 391.

32. René Girard, "Violence, Difference, Sacrifice: A Conversation with René Girard," in "Violence, Difference, Sacrifice: Conversations on Myth and Culture in Theology and Literature," ed. Rebecca Adams, a special issue of *Religion and Literature* 25, no. 2 (Summer 1993): 24–25.

33. Adams, "Loving Mimesis," 284.

34. Ibid., 289.

35. Kristeva, *Proust and the Sense of Time*, 94. Kristeva attributes Proust's interest in mimesis to the philosopher Gabriel Tarde, who wrote about "the herd-like character of social groups, with its basis in *imitation*" (Kristeva, 94). For Tarde, as described by Kristeva, "We are governed, on the one hand, by an implacable heredity, and on the other by the desire to be *like*, to *imitate*, to *believe in common* (94). See pp. 53–76 of *Proust and the Sense of Time* for a summary of her views on Proust's metaphors.

36. "Proust was fascinated with Christian incarnation because before it became the motor for an unprecedented artistic expansion, it wove into the figure of the Passion the indissociable symbiosis between the sensible and the sensed, between the Word and the flesh. This process created a space for the middle term: a state of grace" (Kristeva, *Time and Sense*, 319).

37. Girard, *Deceit, Desire, and the Novel*, 34.

38. Anne-Marie Smith, *Julia Kristeva: Speaking the Unspeakable* (London: Pluto Press, 1998), 67.

39. Kristeva, *Time and Sense*, 168.

40. Proust, *Finding Time Again*, 24–25. Röntgen invented the X-ray in 1895. The invention quickly captured the imagination of the world when X-ray images of the hand of Röntgen's wife were published in numerous countries. X-ray images were passed among friends: An X-ray print of a mother's hand was a popular gift among family members. As Sara Danius suggests, in breaking down barriers between the outer and inner body, the X-ray machine "reorganized epistemological assumptions" not only in the medical field but also in the arts. Revealing previously hidden causes of disease (e.g., a tumor), X-ray machines suggested a model for other efforts to expose previously hidden human "diseases" (e.g., social mores such as snobbism). The X-ray machine as literary image also captured the ambivalence of modern knowledge. On the on hand, in creating an objectified, visual sign of disease, the X-ray machine divested the bearer of disease of full ownership. The cause of disease, such as a tumor, had to be certified by the X-ray operator. On the other hand, an individual's fascination with her or his own X-ray image provided for newfound "ownership." For the first time, "One could claim an exteriorized visual sign of one's own interior." For more on Proust's interest in X-ray technology, see Sara Danius, *The Senses of Modernism: Technology, Perception, and Aesthetics* (Ithaca, NY: Cornell University Press, 2002), 75–78.

41. Kristeva, *Time and Sense*, 168.

42. An example of the former instance would be "the information highway of the Internet": an example of the latter would be "a snowplow works an airport runway with a yellow grimace." This example is from Tucker, "Snowbound," 26.

43. Kristeva, *Proust and the Sense of Time*, 56.

44. Ibid., 5. Kristeva's notion has similarities with Jean Ricardou's discussion of the productive metaphor in Proust. Rather than serve a representative function, the metaphor creates a metamorphosis. See Ricardou and Freiberg, "Proust: A Retrospective Reading," 532.

45. Kristeva, *Proust and the Sense of Time*, 7.

46. Bolens, *The Style of Gestures*; Gallese, "Two Sides of Mimesis," 89.

47. The quote is from Marcel Proust, *Swann's Way*, trans. Lydia Davis, vol. 1 of *In Search of Lost Time* (New York: Penguin Classics, 2004), 45. The pagination for this scene in other translations is: Marcel Proust, *Swann's Way*, trans. C. K. Scott Moncrieff and Terence Kilmartin (New York: Modern Library, 2004), 61; Marcel Proust, *Remembrance of Things Past*, trans. C. K. Scott Moncrieff and Terence Kilmartin, vol. 1 (New York: Random House, 1981), 48. Quotations from Proust in *Deceit, Desire, and the Novel* do not have page citations. When I reference pages in the

novel to which Girard is referring in his commentary, these citations refer to the English language edition(s) of *In Search of Lost Time* that I am using in this work.

48. Kristeva, *Proust and the Sense of Time*, 46–47.

49. In *Tales of Love*, Kristeva explores at length the "catastrophic-fold-of-being" that is the maternal body in its modeling of alterity. Ewa Ziarek typifies this body-work as "the imprint of the other within the same." In a different context, which I will explore in the last part of the book, the founding "triangle" of proto-subject, other, and model in the maternal body is characterized as a division of *sound* within the maternal body. In this context, the model is described by Kristeva as the father of individual prehistory. Because the roles of both parents in this triangle predate language, these points of alteration are not linked to mothers and fathers in the Symbolic/Oedipal order; they could be both parents or even "x and y." See Ziarek, "At the Limits of Discourse," 102. Also Kristeva, *Tales of Love*, 173; Kristeva, "Julia Kristeva in Conversation with Rosalind Coward," 23.

50. Kristeva, *Powers of Horror*, 208.

Chapter 1. The Eyes of a Parricide

1. Girard, *Deceit, Desire, and the Novel*, 301–5; Girard, *Oedipus Unbound*, 8–10.

2. Girard, *Deceit, Desire, and the Novel*, 300.

3. Henri van Blarenberghe was the son of a friend of Proust's parents (H. F. A. van Blarenberghe). Henri's father died in the summer of 1906 and Proust, on behalf of his parents, wrote Henri a letter of condolence. Early in 1907, Proust wrote Henri another letter along with a request for information about an employee in van Blarenberghe's business. Proust received a gracious reply from Henri, in which Henri extended words of sympathy to Proust concerning death of Proust's parents. Approximately a week later, Proust decided to write a letter of response to Henri; however, he sat down to read the January 25 *Le Figaro* before commencing to write Henri. In the newspaper, he learned that Henri van Blarenberghe had killed his mother on the previous day and then shot himself, dying soon after the police arrived. On January 30, the editor of *Le Figaro*, who knew of Proust's acquaintance with the van Blarenberghe family, invited Proust to write a piece for *Le Figaro* about the van Blarenberghe homicide-suicide. Proust wrote quickly and delivered the piece to the newspaper that evening. In a note to Lucien Daudet written at around the same time, Proust observes that he has not written "a word" apart from letters for a year and a half (since his mother's death). We may conclude that the *Le Figaro* essay constituted the first extended piece of writing since her death. See Carter, *Marcel Proust*, 421.

4. Proust, "Filial Sentiments of a Parricide," 96. In my discussion of the essay, I cite Anderson's English translation, referring to the French only when the translation suggests alternatives.

5. Girard, *Deceit, Desire, and the Novel*, 301.

6. Proust, "Filial Sentiments of a Parricide," 98.

7. Girard, *Deceit, Desire, and the Novel*, 301. The English translation contains an error. The French "peut-être celui qui saurait voir cela" is translated in *Deceit* as "perhaps women who could see . . ." René Girard, *Mensonge Romantique et Vérité Romanesque* (Paris: Grasset, 1961), 337. The passage continues, "in that belated moment of lucidity which may occur even in lives completely obsessed by illusions, since it happened even to Don Quixote, perhaps that someone, like Henri Van Blarenberghe after he stabbed his mother to death, would recoil from the horror of his life and snatch up a gun, in order to put an immediate end to his existence." But the opening phrase

"perhaps someone" parallels the subsequent "perhaps that someone," confirming that the text references the son (or sons), not women or mothers (Proust, "Filial Sentiments of a Parricide," 99). See also Marcel Proust, "Sentiments Filiaux d'un Parricide," in *Contre Sainte-Beuve*, trans. P. Clarac and Y. Sandre (Paris: Gallimard, 1971), 159.

8. Girard, *Deceit, Desire, and the Novel*, 301.

9. Ibid., 302.

10. René Girard, "From the Novelistic Experience to the Oedipal Myth," in *Oedipus Unbound*, 1–27.

11. Ibid., 9.

12. Ibid.

13. Ibid.

14. Girard, *Deceit, Desire, and the Novel*, 303.

15. Ibid., 294.

16. Ibid., 298.

17. Ibid., 38.

18. Ibid., 299. Girard contrasts this revelatory sequence from *In Search of Lost Time* with the narrative of Proust's earlier novel, *Jean Santeuil*. Both novels feature a theater scene that utilizes the space of the theater to depict contrasts between the "haves and have nots" of society. In *Jean Santeuil*, Santeuil is an elegant and gifted young man at home with the "haves." Living the dream, Santeuil is a projection of desire attaining its goal. So too does the narrator appear to identify with his hero. Girard notes that the narrator is not unaware of desire and its dangers; however, the narrator sees that the problems of desire apply only to others. Snobbery is always a vice of others; the viciousness of social rivalry belongs only to others. In the end, the hero will triumph, virtue will be rewarded, and snobs will be banished (Girard, *Oedipus Unbound*, 3). By contrast, in writing *In Search of Lost Time*, Proust does not exclude himself or Marcel from the revelations of desire. Proust recognizes himself in the snob. Proust's reflexive awareness—central to *In Search of Lost Time* and absent from *Jean Santeuil*—is the genius of Proust's great novel and that of any great novel (*Oedipus Unbound*, 9).

19. Girard, *Deceit, Desire, and the Novel*, 300.

20. Ibid., 297.

21. Ibid., 301.

22. Ibid., 302.

23. Ibid., 310. On my reading of Girard, he clearly suggests that, when the novelist describes a conversion experience, the reader can be responsive to that account. Girard is committed not only to the notion that writers experience conversion but also to the idea that the reader may be moved in some way toward transformation by his or her experience of the novel. Nevertheless, especially when compared with Kristeva, who regularly writes of the transformative power of art (including literature), religion, and psychoanalysis, Girard only infrequently speaks directly of what the novel does for and to its *reader*. A key exception may be found in "From the Novelistic Experience to the Oedipal Myth" when Girard writes of the oracle (the madeleine in the case of *In Search of Lost Time*). He notes that the experience of the oracle not only "orients the reader" but also is "necessary from the reader's viewpoint" (Girard, "Novelistic Experience," 22–23). Oracles

are "glimmers of novelistic grace," "annunciatory signs," and a "foretaste" of a revelation that is to come (20–21, 23).

24. Girard, *Proust*, 4.

25. Proust, "Filial Sentiments of a Parricide," 92.

26. Ibid., 94.

27. Girard, *Deceit, Desire, and the Novel*, 310.

28. Kristeva, *Proust and the Sense of Time*, 5.

29. Proust, "Filial Sentiments of a Parricide," 95.

30. Ibid., 93.

31. Ibid.

32. Ibid., 96.

33. Ibid.

34. Ibid., 99.

35. That Proust's words can elicit such a powerful response suggests that they attest to Proust's own reaction to the physical presence of an aging maternal body at some time in the past. An obsession with youth in our own time may only have increased our capacity to be physically repulsed by a visibly aging body, to possess uncomfortable memories of that body, and to respond strongly to Proust's words.

36. Proust's mother died in September 1905, and "Filial Sentiments" was published February 1, 1907.

37. Girard, *Deceit, Desire, and the Novel*, 302; Girard, *Mensonge Romantique et Vérité Romanesque*, 301.

38. Girard, *Deceit, Desire, and the Novel*, 301.

39. Girard, "Novelistic Experience," 9–11. Writes Girard, "To turn back against oneself the curse first hurled at the Other, to discover that this wicked Other and the Self are one, means discovering the same in what once passed for absolute Difference, it means unifying reality. But first of all it means *dying*" (9).

40. Ibid., 10.

41. Girard, *Deceit, Desire, and the Novel*, 302.

42. According to letters and correspondence of Proust analyzed by William Carter, Proust began writing the article at 3:00 A.M. and wrote until 8:00 A.M. He decided to sleep before completing the letter; however, he was awakened by workers in the apartment below. He sent the article off without rereading it. That evening, the proofs arrived and he added a concluding paragraph. He returned the proofs with the new conclusion instructing that "they could cut whatever they liked but not a word of the ending must be changed" (Carter, *Marcel Proust*, 420–21). When Proust received the *Le Figaro* and saw that his wishes had not been followed, he sent the editor Calmette a letter of protest: "The only thing I had indicated to M. Cardane as being essential was omitted, though I said that he could cut anything he liked rather than these last few lines. I had indeed in my hurry sent off the article in the morning without an ending. I added one on the proofs, a paragraph in which I gathered my reins, my scattered steeds, at once hurtling and floundering, straying. The article ended thus [Proust copies in full the paragraph I have inserted below]." Marcel Proust, *Selected Letters*, vol. 2: *1904–1909*, ed. Philip Kolb, trans. Terence Kilmartin (New

York: Oxford University Press, 1989), 240, letter #185. Calmette responded by return mail. He asserts that the final paragraph had frightened Cardane (editorial secretary at the newspaper), who also thought that the added text did not show sufficient disapproval of Henri van Blarenberghe's actions. Calmette states that he disagrees with Cardane and that the readers will read his article "with an enchanted heart," notwithstanding the absent text. "From Gaston Calmette" (250, letter #186).

43. Proust, *Selected Letters*, 240, letter #185. For the original French text, see Proust, *Contre Sainte-Beuve*, 786.

44. Oedipus is discussed as an example of a parricide earlier in the newspaper article; however, Orestes, the prototype of matricide, is mentioned only in this last paragraph. The reference to Orestes could be understood as an afterthought by Proust. But the reference may point also to Proust's developing lucidity as he "gathers his reins" and secures his previously floundering steeds (see note above). After all, the reference to Orestes links Henri ever more closely to Proust.

45. Proust, *Contre Sainte-Beuve*, 255–57.

46. In support of his argument that the critical paragraph in "Filial Sentiments of a Parricide" is the one that references Don Quixote, Girard observes that Proust mentions Don Quixote elsewhere in *Contre Sainte-Beuve* along with the writers Stendhal, Flaubert, Tolstoy, George Eliot, and Dostoyevsky (Girard, *Deceit, Desire, and the Novel*, 302). According to Girard, Proust's second reference to Don Quixote, in conjunction with the discussion of other great writers, shows that Proust is consolidating his initial insight in "Filial Sentiments." A review of *Contre Sainte Beuve* for the passage to which Girard refers (page citations are not included in *Deceit, Desire, and the Novel*) shows that Don Quixote is referenced in brief comments on "La Création Poétique." See Marcel Proust, *Contre Sainte Beuve* (Paris: Gallimard, 1954); Proust, *Contre Sainte-Beuve*, trans. Clarac and Sandre, 412–14. On these pages, Proust reflects on the struggles of writers for insight and notes the elusive qualities of creative genius, for whom clarity of insight may be delayed until the moment of death. Goethe and Mallarmé are the other figures named by Proust in this set of comments. Proust's observations lend support to Girard's claims concerning Proust's insights into novelistic genius. Nevertheless, that we seek greater clarity on the last, unpublished paragraph of "Filial Sentiments of a Parricide" remains important. From that exploration we will learn *how* one takes purchase on the lucidity toward which Proust directs our attention with his comments in "La Création Poétique."

47. Kristeva, *Time and Sense*, 171.

Chapter 2. Of Madeleines, Mothers, and Montjouvain

1. Girard, *Oedipus Unbound*, 20; Kristeva, *Proust and the Sense of Time*, 30–48; Kristeva, *Time and Sense*, 3–22.

2. Kristeva, *Proust and the Sense of Time*, 30.

3. Ibid.; Kristeva, *Time and Sense*, 4.

4. Proust, *Swann's Way*, 44.

5. Kristeva, *Proust and the Sense of Time*, 31–32; Kristeva, *Time and Sense*, 5.

6. Kristeva, *Proust and the Sense of Time*, 32–34. Kristeva, *Time and Sense*, 5–7.

7. Proust, *Swann's Way*, 45.

8. Ibid.

9. Kristeva, *Proust and the Sense of Time*, 32. Kristeva cites Notebook 8, 1909 (101 n. 1).

10. Kristeva observes that the Pléiade edition capitalizes "Madeleine." The capitalization is not retained in English translation (Kristeva, *Time and Sense*, 343).

11. Ibid., 6.

12. Kristeva, *Proust and the Sense of Time*, 35.

13. Ibid., 36–37. In the first typewritten text, the mother in the novel is named by Proust as "Madeleine Blanchet." She is named also in the proofs. But in the final published edition, the name "Madeleine Blanchet" has been omitted.

14. Kristeva, *Time and Sense*, 11.

15. Kristeva, *Proust and the Sense of Time*, 35–43. Kristeva, *Time and Sense*, 7–16.

16. Proust, *Swann's Way*, 45.

17. Kristeva, *Time and Sense*, 17.

18. Kristeva, *Proust and the Sense of Time*, 44–45; Kristeva, *Time and Sense*, 17.

19. Proust, *Swann's Way*, 45.

20. Kristeva, *Proust and the Sense of Time*, 46; Kristeva, *Time and Sense*, 18–19.

21. Kristeva, *Proust and the Sense of Time*, 47; Kristeva, *Time and Sense*, 19–20.

22. Kristeva, *Proust and the Sense of Time*, 47.

23. Ibid., 48; Kristeva, *Time and Sense*, 21–22.

24. Kristeva, *Proust and the Sense of Time*, 49.

25. An early example of distancing occurs in the 1905 text, "On Reading." Proust uses the autobiographical "I" and refers to his "mother." In late drafts, he changes the "mother" to a "great aunt" (Carter, *Marcel Proust*, 870 n. 55).

26. Kristeva, *Proust and the Sense of Time*, 41.

27. Proust, *Shadow of Young Girls in Flower*, 153.

28. Kristeva, *Proust and the Sense of Time*, 49.

29. Proust, "Filial Sentiments of a Parricide," 92. See also Proust, "Sentiments Filiaux d'un Parricide," 6.

30. Proust, "Filial Sentiments of a Parricide," 94.

31. Ibid., 94–95.

32. Ibid., 97.

33. Ibid., 99; Proust, "Sentiments Filiaux d'un Parricide," 159. Proust apes the jaded terminology of a society tabloid. His words contrast dramatically with those he uses to describe Greek drama.

34. Proust, "Filial Sentiments of a Parricide," 99.

35. Kristeva, *Proust and the Sense of Time*, 14.

36. Ibid.

37. Ibid.

38. Danius, *The Senses of Modernism*, 95.

39. Proust, *Swann's Way*, 10.

40. Ibid., 28.

41. Moorjani, *Aesthetics of Loss and Lessness*, 165.

42. As described by Freud, Ernst (Freud's grandson) is playing with a reel in his mother's absence. Throwing it away, the child says, "*o-o-o-o* [*fort*]." Retrieving it, the child says "da." Lacan has emphasized the paradigmatic quality of this game: the child is mastering key roles that structure the signifying economy of the Symbolic order (Lacan, *Écrits*, 103–4). Kristeva has emphasized the kinetic, vocal, and gestural components of the game (*Revolution in Poetic Language*, 170). For her, the game is a lesson in visceral acclimation to the Symbolic. Separation from the maternal body and entry into the world of language is not an intellective act; rather the gestural and vocal aspects of the game show that the child demarcates space and meaning with his mouth and teeth.

43. Kristeva suggests that Proust's long-term issues with asthma may be understood in light of his deep-seated ambivalence about differentiation and undifferentiation from his mother: issues of rejection are coupled with issues of a frightening, suffocating proximity (Kristeva, *Time and Sense*, 240). See also Kristeva, *Intimate Revolt*, 58.

44. Proust, *Swann's Way*, 38.

45. Although the narrator of this scene is not an infant or toddler, this scene alludes to the "pre-Oedipal." Like Melanie Klein, in describing the pre-Oedipal, Kristeva emphasizes its sacrificial aspect. The separation of the nascent subject from the maternal matrix of its origin is "a violent, clumsy breaking away, with the constant risk of falling back under the sway of a power as securing as it is stifling" (Kristeva, *Powers of Horror*, 13). Not yet a subject of language, an infant demarcates space with its mouth, biting, chewing, and swallowing sameness and difference. Humans return to this somatic rite, by which they have secured their most basic boundaries of their being, at times of crisis. An infant's "matricide" is limited, but that of older children and adults is immoderate when, torturing substance to make it signify, they somatize signs. They transgress in order to reestablish standing in the world. Sadomasochism, to which the narrator of *In Search of Lost Time* is vulnerable, is one expression of such violence. For more on Kristeva's theory of matricide, see Reineke, *Sacrificed Lives*, 81–93.

46. Marcel Proust, *Sodom and Gomorrah*, trans. John Sturrock, vol. 4 of *In Search of Lost Time* (New York: Penguin Classics, 2005), 153. Proust is setting up a pattern first established in "Filial Sentiments." A scene of violence and debauchery precedes a revelatory scene. As noted above, I see in such regular juxtapositions evidence of trauma and testimony to the long and difficult path one traverses from the depths of metaphysical desire to conversion.

47. Ibid., 154.

48. Ibid., 155.

49. Ibid., 156.

50. Ibid., 157. This scene has autobiographical components: When she was dying, Proust's mother had her photo taken for him (Kristeva, *Proust and the Sense of Time*, 11).

51. Proust, *Sodom and Gomorrah*, 157.

52. Ibid.

53. Ibid., 158.

54. Amber Jacobs, *On Matricide: Myth, Psychoanalysis, and the Law of the Mother* (New York: Columbia University Press, 2007), 79–82. Melanie Klein argues that the ambivalence a young child feels toward its mother's body, which is experienced by the child as source of life and absolute threat, is resolved only through suffering and pain. These experiences must come before the developing child gains a capacity to recognize and understand its own destructive tendencies. On the way to recognition, the child splits the maternal body, resulting in a bad and good mother. The child will direct anger toward the bad mother. The child also will feel guilt about its own violence as well as about its incapacity to protect its good mother from harm. But with guilt comes an eventual recognition by the child that it is not omnipotent. In uniting the split mother into one, the child gains a capacity for relationship with its mother. The child experiences a painful recognition of the damage it has done to its mother and mobilizes care on her behalf. Significantly, Klein does not consider that the processes she describes follow a linear, developmental trajectory. Although these processes emerge early in our life histories, humans can move forward and backward through these processes, as we respond to experiences of threat or feel safe in our relationships with others. Proust exemplifies such a process.

55. Moorjani, *Aesthetics of Loss and Lessness*, 168. The dream is one of several autobiographical dreams that Proust initially recorded in his notebook. It attests to the dislocating role of the "grandmother" in the novel, for the dreams Proust recorded in the notebook were about his mother. Confirming Moorjani's line of thought, Carter suggests that the mother and grandmother are two versions of the same woman at different ages. He notes that the attachments the narrator feels to his mother and grandmother depict Proust's "extraordinary closeness" to his mother (*Marcel Proust*, 471). The conflation of mother and grandmother to which Carter and Moorjani attest is illustrated also by the mirroring of two scenes that I discuss below.

56. Proust, *Sodom and Gomorrah*, 159.

57. Ibid., 161.

58. Ibid., 160.

59. Proust, *Swann's Way*, 527 n. 124.

60. Carter, *Marcel Proust*, 557. In subsequent correspondence with friends, Proust expresses delight that Jammes has praised the skillful composition of *In Search of Lost Time*, for Jammes's assessment countered a common criticism that the novel is a haphazard collection of reminiscences (Carter, 562).

61. Ibid., 701.

62. Proust, *Sodom and Gomorrah*, 527–28 n. 124.

63. The concluding inference is to Proust, *Finding Time Again*, 187. The sounds of cutlery that provoke experiences of involuntary memory pervade *Finding Time Again*. Spoons are mentioned on 176, 179, 181, 186, and 191. Forks are mentioned on 180 and 187. A knife is mentioned on 184.

64. Roger Shattuck likens the scene to one that could be found in a work by Molière. Roger Shattuck, *Proust* (London: Fontana Press, 1974), 73.

65. Kristeva, *Time and Sense*, 179.

66. Ibid., 180.

67. Ibid.

68. Ibid. Kristeva is citing Proust, *Sodom and Gomorrah*, 155.

69. Ibid.

70. In *The Guermantes Way*, the narrator associates such failures in recognition not only with his own response to the photo but also with the inadequacies of photography as a vehicle of communication: "For the first time and for a mere second, since she vanished almost immediately, I saw, sitting there on the sofa beneath the lamp, red-faced, heavy, and vulgar, ill, her mind in a daze, the slightly crazed eyes wandering over a book, a crushed old woman whom I did not know." Marcel Proust, *The Guermantes Way*, trans. Mark Treharne, vol. 3 of *In Search of Lost Time* (New York: Penguin Classics, 2005), 135. The narrator first comments on the human eye. When we first view another, we do so through a prism of memory. Our encounter is refracted by affection and care; as a consequence, the prism of memory hides or distorts the truth of aging and therefore misses the truth of the other. By contrast, as Danius astutely shows, for Proust the camera eye has no burden of assumptions, and is relentless in its "deadly power." The camera offers up only an "uncanny double" of what the narrator previously has beheld (Danius, *The Senses of Modernism*, 15).

71. As cited in Carter, *Marcel Proust*, 452.

72. As cited in Kristeva, *Time and Sense*, 179.

73. Proust, *Sodom and Gomorrah*, 300. Proust suggests that this point would be worth a chapter of its own in the book.

74. J. Theodore Johnson Jr., "Marcel Proust and Architecture: Some Thoughts on the Cathedral-Novel," in Bucknall, *Critical Essays on Marcel Proust*, 137. Kristeva argues that when Proust refers to cornerstones, as he does when discussing Ruskin, he has biblical references expressly in mind, specifically Psalms 118: 22–23 and Matt. 21:42 ("The stone which the builders rejected has become the head of the corner"). He also is thinking of Romans 9:33 ("Behold, I am laying in Zion a stone that will make men stumble, a rock that will make them fall; and he who believes in him will not be put to shame") (Kristeva, *Time and Sense*, 105). The cornerstone, linked with the paving stone over which one stumbles, becomes an image of forthcoming spiritual transformation. Girard understands the meaning of stones in a like manner. Citing *The Winter's Tale*, *Othello*, and the Christian gospel, Girard writes that stones appear in a text at a moment of transformation. They are associated with physical or spiritual death and the revelatory exposure of mimetic rivalry. René Girard, *A Theatre of Envy: William Shakespeare* (New York: Oxford University Press, 1991), 340–41.

75. Proust, *Swann's Way*, 163; emphasis added.

76. Girard, *Deceit, Desire, and the Novel*, 184.

77. Ibid., 176.

78. Ibid., 165.

79. Ibid., 177.

80. Ibid.

81. Ibid., 179.

82. Ibid., 180.

83. Proust, *Sodom and Gomorrah*, 158.

84. Girard, *Deceit, Desire, and the Novel*, 182.

85. Ibid., 184.

86. Ibid.

87. Ibid., 185. As an example, in the Montjouvain scene, when Mlle Vinteuil and her lesbian lover
    participate in the desecration of her father's photo, Mlle Vinteuil embodies sadism. She tormented
    her father during his last years, such that he gave up entirely his goal of transcribing his musical
    compositions before his death (Proust, *Swann's Way*, 163). Now, as Mlle Vinteuil awaits an
    evening visit from her friend, she prepares the room by placing her father's photo close to the
    sofa, the better to prepare for a "ritual profanation" when she spits on the photo while engaged
    in erotic play (166). Girard emphasizes that Mlle Vinteuil's play is a "second-degree imitation."
    She wants to imitate the primary desecration of her father but to do so in ways that double up on
    victimization, rendering Mlle Vinteuil a persecuted innocent rather than the one responsible for
    her father's suffering (Girard, *Deceit, Desire, and the Novel*, 187).

88. Kristeva, *Time and Sense*, 187.

89. Ibid., 188.

90. Ibid., 185.

91. Ibid., 181.

92. Proust examines Jews and anti-Semitism in French society in a similar way. Certainly, elements
    of personal biography are reflected in his comments. But Proust's subjective reference points,
    far from blocking his interpretive insights, enable him to bring a reflective sensitivity to the
    discussion that is notable for his time. Strong confirmation of my assertions can be found in
    comparing aspects of Proust's narrative that focus on homosexuality with those that describe Jews.
    The Dreyfus affair is a point of repeated reference; the characters Swann, Charlus, and Bloch are
    Jews and are described in ways that draw on Jewish stereotypes then current in French society.
    In her extended commentary on Jews and Jewishness in *In Search of Lost Time* (*Time and Sense*,
    141–63), Kristeva argues that Proust's characterization of Jews is motivated by two interests.
    First, especially with the Dreyfus affair, Proust is articulating the dynamics of mimetic rivalry,
    as he has been influenced by the mimetic theory of Gabriel Tarde (*Time and Sense*, 145, 266).
    Second, he is conducting an "experiment" into the dynamics of anti-Semitism in French society
    similar to the one he conducts with reference to the mores of Sodom and Gomorrah. The issue
    of relational identity and its associated threats is key to Proust's treatment of Jews. Characters
    that "double" with the narrator in the text are invariably Jewish, and this doubling enables the
    narrator to explore questions of sameness and difference among clans and groups. He discovers
    that barriers are no longer airtight, and he reflects on the contamination that results (in the case
    of anti-Semitism the linguistic markers of this threat are clear) (Kristeva, *Time and Sense*, 156).
    Sadomasochism figures in the question of boundaries for Jews and homosexuals: Are you one
    of them or not one of them? Writes Kristeva of Proust's instructive pursuit of an answer to this
    question, "Do not think that you can map out a new territory, a separate and innocent clan or
    sect, for you will invariably find yourself caught in the same logical structure: the heady lure of
    being *one of them* or not being *one of them*. Our sadomasochism makes this necessary. I belong
    to him (to them)—he (they) love(s) me; I do not belong to him (to them)—he (they) is (are)
    killing me. Being is a question of *love*, that is, of belonging, of identification–and of regret" (158).
    Proust is showing that Jewishness is not unique; rather, being Jewish in French society is relational.
    Jewishness "reveals that sadomasochism adheres to the dark center of every society." Kristeva
    says that Proust is fascinated by the Jewish/non-Jewish bifurcation of French society because
    he has a hunch that such divisions lie "at the heart of social activity" and are engaged in by all
    humans (*Time and Sense*, 161). As a consequence of Proust's insights, Kristeva heralds his efforts
    as exhibiting "unsurpassed sociological and metaphysical ambition" (163). I emphasize Proust's
    discussion of homosexuality in this chapter rather than his discussion of Jews and anti-Semitism

because I think the intimate bodily contours of that discussion advance our understanding of the novel more directly. Intimate markers are referenced in Proust's discussion of Jews, and there is a cross-contamination between Jews and homosexuals in French social views of Proust's day; however, pivotal scenes in my discussion align most strongly with the dynamics of sadomasochism within a setting of physical and erotic intimacy.

93. Proust, *Finding Time Again*, 126.

94. Kristeva, *Time and Sense*, 93.

95. Proust read Kraft-Ebbing's *Psychopathia Sexualis*, and commented to Paul Morand that it would seem that even homosexuality is now among the "exact sciences" (George D. Painter, *Marcel Proust: A Biography*, vol. 2 [New York: Vintage, 1978], 270).

96. Proust, *Swann's Way*, 38.

97. For careful documentation and textual support of Proust's theory see Elisabeth Ladenson, *Proust's Lesbianism* (Ithaca, NY: Cornell University Press, 2007), 36–42.

98. Two theories from which I dissent attempt to account for Albertine's significance in the novel. Both foreground the theme of homosexuality and make Albertine the central figure in Proust's development of that theme. As described by Ladenson, the "transposition theory" asserts that Albertine is Alfred Agostinelli, Proust's occasional chauffeur and companion (Ladenson, *Proust's Lesbianism*, 13). A version of this theory also claims that, even when Albertine is not present in the text, whenever females are an object of desire in the text, the reader should replace "she" with "he" in order to arrive at Proust's otherwise hidden characterizations. The transposition theory holds that Proust wanted to write a novel about homosexual love; however, under the constraints of his era, he could not convey directly what he knew of desire among men. Therefore, he changed his male into female characters. But whenever one attempts to consistently apply the logic of transposition, large sections of the text cease to make sense. The narrator's desires, his jealousies, his joys and sufferings simply do not align with a mechanical transposition of male into female characters. Ladenson observes that in his analysis of homosexuality in the novel Harry Levin shows how transposition creates problems for the Albertine/Andrèe relationship, rendering discussion of bisexuality in the novel an impossible proposition (Ladenson, *Proust's Lesbianism*, 14). For Ladenson, Eve Kosofsky Sedgwick offers the definitive criticism of this theory, by showing how the theme of transgression becomes hopelessly tangled by a transposition of characters, rendering both transgressive and nontransgressive readings of the novel inconsistent and ultimately incoherent (Ladenson, *Proust's Lesbianism*, 15). By point of contrast, the "symmetry theory" (Ladenson, *Proust's Lesbianism*, 11) understands Gomorrah to be the female counterpart of Sodom, and Sodom is a world populated by sexual inverts. As previously noted, Proust rejects a theory of male homosexuality that would suggest that men who are attracted to other men want contact with "the same." He prefers to typify homoerotic behavior as inversion because he understands that male subjects who see other men as attractive sexual objects are actually woman-like in their interest in these male sexual objects. The symmetry theory argues that Gomorrah is Proust's imagined representation of the lives of female inverts. But the symmetry theory founders when, along with Ladenson, we look closely at Gomorrah, for the women whom the narrator suspects harbor a Sapphic interest are not inverts in the manner Proust has described: they are not mannish. Nor is their "boyishness" (*garçonne*) just another term for masculinity. Albertine and her friends call to mind the flappers of the 1920s who challenged social mores with their dress, dancing, drinking, and smoking; however, their boyish demeanor did not typically attest to a specific sexual preference (Ladenson, *Proust's Lesbianism*, 47–48). And that indeterminacy of being is, precisely, the attraction Albertine poses for the narrator. Albertine, who flaunts social conventions, is elusive, mysterious, possibly a lesbian, perhaps a bisexual. Always

alluring, she is not a "mannish" invert. In rehearsing here major features of Elizabeth Ladenson's argument, I set aside significant supporting argumentation. Interested readers can access full documentation in *Proust's Lesbianism*. For example, Ladenson demonstrates that Proust's theory of lesbian sexuality at one time expressly parallels his theory of male inversion; however, by the time he writes *In Search of Lost Time*, he is advancing a distinct theory of lesbian sexuality.

99. Ladenson, *Proust's Lesbianism*, 7.

100. Ibid., 50. The mystery is exacerbated for the narrator by the exhibitionism of lesbian sexuality. Mlle Vinteuil and her friend leave the blinds open; performing before others is part of their erotic play. But the narrator cannot see what they are doing. So also is the scene in the hotel between Bloch's sister and another woman carried on in full view of the hotel guests. But whenever Proust tries to spy on an intimate scene in order to comprehend female eroticism, notwithstanding the purported exhibitionism of lesbians, he is unable to detect anything. The scene of the laundresses, in which the narrator pays to watch two women and yet is unable to decipher what is going on (whereas when the narrator only hears Charlus and Jupien engaging in a sexual act he knows what they are doing) humorously depicts the narrator's dilemma (Ladenson, *Proust's Lesbianism*, 67, 73–75).

101. Kristeva highlights similarities in the narrator's depictions of paintings and descriptions of Albertine (*Time and Sense*, 73).

102. Proust, *The Prisoner and The Fugitive*, 39.

103. Proust, *Sodom and Gomorrah*, 193.

104. Proust, *The Guermantes Way*, 361.

105. Victor E. Graham, *The Imagery of Proust* (New York: Barnes & Noble, 1966), 66.

106. Without appealing to fantasies of the womb, that the maternal body of infancy be experienced as a sea of plenitude for a small infant can well be imagined.

107. Nicholas Kostis, "Albertine: Characterization through Image and Symbol," in Bucknall, *Critical Essays on Marcel Proust*, 70–92. The citation is from the Gallimard French edition, *Nouvelle Revue Francaise*, 3:393. The sea imagery is from Proust, *The Prisoner and The Fugitive*, 60–61.

108. Carter, *Marcel Proust*, 606; emphasis mine. In Aristotle's *Poetics*, XI, the peripeteia references a character whose impact is the opposite of what has been anticipated. The anagnorisis is the part of the plot in which ignorance is transformed into knowledge (recognition). Ideally, the peripeteia leads directly to the anagnorisis. Aristotle, *Poetics* (New York: Cosimo, 2008), 20.

109. Proust, *Finding Time Again*, 166–225.

110. Proust, *Sodom and Gomorrah*, 499.

111. Ibid.

112. Ibid., 500.

113. Ibid.

114. Ibid., 501, 506, 512.

115. Ibid., 513.

116. Ibid., 514.

117. Proust, *The Prisoner and The Fugitive*, 418. Kristeva's analysis of the figure of Albertine also arrives at this conclusion (Kristeva, *Time and Sense*, 82–83).

118. Proust, *Sodom and Gomorrah*, 513.

119. Ladenson's major contribution to the critical literature on Proust rests on this point. Proust's obsession with lesbian desire, as displayed throughout *In Search of Lost Time*, has no counterpart in his own life. His letters and notebooks do not attest to a fascination with lesbianism. In creating Albertine and a world of Sapphic desire, we see Proust as architect of a fictional world that will prove to be his salvation. Albertine is the figure of grace in the novel. Emerging as a self-projection, Albertine offers Proust a mirror image oriented toward positive rather than acquisitive mimesis.

120. This insight is from Moorjani, *Aesthetics of Loss and Lessness*, 170.

121. Proust, *The Prisoner and The Fugitive*, 463.

122. Ladenson points out that this splitting is unprecedented in Proust's writings. There is no "division of labor" between a grandmother and mother prior to *In Search of Lost Time* (Ladenson, *Proust's Lesbianism*, 110).

123. Proust, *Sodom and Gomorrah*, 167–68, 512.

124. The term is coined by Ladenson (*Proust's Lesbianism*, 112).

125. Ibid., 113. Kristeva chooses different supporting evidence to show how Proust traverses a maternal terrain that he has perceived previously to alternate unstably between absolute threat and salvific ground. Drawing on Proust's biography, she suggests that Proust's relationship with his housekeeper, Céleste Albaret, which developed during the time he was writing the novel, enabled him to come to terms with the maternal figures in his life. Céleste offered a nonthreatening counterbalance to Proust's mother. Kristeva, *Time and Sense*, 181–84.

126. Proust, *Sodom and Gomorrah*, 168.

127. Ladenson argues that Proust identifies strongly with the wayward son whom Mme de Sévigné characterizes in one of her letters as "a certain 'he' who adores me, and another 'he' who is the torment of my life" (November 2, 1679, in *Letters from the Marchioness de Sévigné*, 6 [London: Spurr & Swift, 1927], 156–57, as quoted in Ladenson, *Proust's Lesbianism*, 126). Ladenson thinks that Proust demonstrates in his novel his familiarity with this particular letter by Mme de Sévigné when he describes the contents of a letter the narrator receives from his mother (*Proust's Lesbianism*, 125–26). Here the narrator's mother criticizes the narrator's handling of finances, suggesting that he is like Charles de Sévigné because "you do not know what you want and are 'two or three people at once'" (125). Ladenson also notes that Charles de Sévigné shares similarities with Henri van Blarenberghe (127). Charles, Henri, and Proust have in common a propensity to both adore and harm their mothers. Thus, references in the novel to the Sévigné family—mother and son—thematically mirror "Filial Sentiments of a Parricide" and are part of a common nexus of suffering and (eventual) transformative "lucidity."

128. Proust, *Sodom and Gomorrah*, 513–14.

129. Quoting Agamben (Bolens, *The Style of Gestures*, 23).

130. Proust, *Sodom and Gomorrah*, 514.

131. Carter, *Marcel Proust*, 802. At the time of his death, Proust was working on revisions for *The Prisoner*. In one proposed scenario, Albertine dies from a horseback riding accident in Montjouvain rather than in Tourain.

132. Indeed, the final paragraph of *Sodom and Gomorrah* represents such a false start when the narrator announces to his mother that he will marry Albertine. So also will the discussion of the visit to Venice in my next chapter show the narrator initially taking two steps forward and one step

backward as he tentatively explores the transformation of desire that he has glimpsed at the end of *Sodom and Gomorrah.*

133. Maurice Merleau-Ponty, *Phenomenology of Perception*, trans. Colin Smith, 2nd ed. (London: Routledge, 1962), 151. My attention was called to this wonderful discussion of the unity of the body and a work of art by Bolens. See Bolens, *The Style of Gestures*, 27–28.

134. Proust, *The Prisoner and The Fugitive*, 61.

135. Merleau-Ponty, *Phenomenology of Perception*, 151.

136. Ibid.

Chapter 3. The Journey Home Is through the World

The title of this chapter is inspired by Richard Kearney, who links the healing potential of memory with an "odyssey of alterity." Speaking of what Irish migrant monks called *circumnavigatio*, Kearney states that "the path home through the detour of the world" is the shortest route to encounter a self, who is a self "always through the other." See Richard Kearney, *Strangers, Gods and Monsters: Interpreting Otherness* (New York: Routledge, 2002), 189. The citation is Proust, *Finding Time Again*, 174.

1. Proust, *Finding Time Again*, 354.

2. Proust, *Swann's Way*, 39; Proust, *Sodom and Gomorrah*, 157.

3. Proust, *Sodom and Gomorrah*, 158.

4. Cathy Caruth, *Unclaimed Experience: Trauma, Narrative and History* (Baltimore: Johns Hopkins University Press, 1996), 2.

5. Ibid., 6.

6. Ibid., 61.

7. Ibid., 62.

8. Ibid., 64–65.

9. Ibid., 70–71.

10. That would not have surprised Klein, who understood that mourning can be productively engaged in the cultural domain of art and religion. Harriet Lutzky, "Mourning and Immortality: Ritual and Psychoanalysis Compared," in *Mourning Religion*, Wiliam B. Parsons, Diane Jonte-Pace, and Susan E. Henking, eds. (Charlottesville: University of Virginia Press), 149.

11. Serene Jones, *Trauma and Grace: Theology in a Ruptured World* (Louisville: Westminster John Knox Press, 2009), 86, 92–93.

12. Ibid., 96–97.

13. Girard, *Deceit, Desire, and the Novel*, 79–81.

14. I am not suggesting that the young Marcel was a victim of incest. But the narrative of the novel does attest to trauma. In young children, an emotionally fraught relationship with their mothers can be exacerbated by scenes such as the one described in the novel, in which the mother's acquiescence to the child's wishes, combined with the subject matter of *François le champi*, enables the child to experience his heightened power as well as his mother's to a degree that may be deeply disturbing and from which the child will seek to protect himself by erecting a barrier to

full awareness of all of its features, perhaps especially his powerful ambivalence before a maternal presence that alternately summons in him the emotions of adoration and violent aggression.

15. Proust, *The Prisoner and The Fugitive*, 115.

16. Ibid., 116.

17. The narrator describes the joy he has found in contemplating writing a book. He states that he will prepare it scrupulously, "constructing it like a church," even as he anticipates that due to the "very extent of the architect's plan" he may not complete the book just as "many great cathedrals have been left unfinished" (Proust, *Finding Time Again*, 342–43).

18. Stephen Gilbert Brown, "Desire on Ice," *College Literature* 32 (2005): 45.

19. Proust, *The Prisoner and The Fugitive*, 418.

20. Ibid., 594.

21. Proust, *Finding Time Again*, 175.

22. Kristeva, *Time and Sense*, 109–10.

23. Proust, *Finding Time Again*, 178.

24. Draft XV, sec. 2, of *In Search of Lost Time*, as cited in Kristeva, *Time and Sense*, 113.

25. Ibid.

26. This important insight is Collier's (Peter Collier, *Proust and Venice* [New York: Cambridge University Press, 2005], 126–27).

27. Kristeva, *Time and Sense*, 112–13.

28. Proust, *The Prisoner and The Fugitive*, 590.

29. As cited by Collier, *Proust and Venice*, 138. Collier suggests that Ruskin's description of the tomb of the Doge Dandolo, who designed the interior of the baptistery and is buried in it, may have inspired Proust's discussion of the stones of St. Mark's, in which his mother's memory will be preserved (as discussed below). But Collier does not note that the scene in St. Mark's is foreshadowed in the descriptions of Proust's mother at the hotel, which parallels Ruskin's description of the tomb in St. Mark's. Collier's argument could be strengthened by this comparison. Kristeva makes a similar argument, linking the scene at the Venetian window with the subsequent scene at St. Mark's and noting that Ruskin's commentary is the bridge between the two scenes (Kristeva, *Time and Sense*, 113).

30. Proust, *The Prisoner and The Fugitive*, 610.

31. Ibid., 611.

32. Ibid., 612.

33. Ibid., 609.

34. The author does record his ambivalence about what happened in Venice. Proust wrote multiple drafts of the Venice narrative, some with disquieting scenes of erotic conquest that Proust acknowledged would shock his readers. In these drafts, scenes of transporting beauty depicting St. Mark's are juxtaposed with vulgar sexual dramas. Revisions that Proust was completing at the time of his death omit most of these observations. Remaining in the narrative is the narrator's late-aborted plan to remain in Venice after his mother has left in order to rendezvous with the maid of Mme Putbus. But the draft that became the published *The Fugitive* does retain of the visit to

Venice the narrative sequences focused on the mother. Kristeva suggests that we not consider this draft the "last word," but see in undercurrents in the drafts further testimony to a developmental trajectory that ends with *Finding Time Again* (Kristeva, *Time and Sense*, 115–17).

35. Stephen Gilbert Brown, *The Gardens of Desire: Marcel Proust and the Fugitive Sublime* (Albany: State University of New York Press, 2004), 200.

36. Moorjani, *Aesthetics of Loss and Lessness*, 173.

37. The salvific powers of sensation were identified by Proust in 1907, the same year that began with Proust writing "Filial Sentiments of a Parricide." In November 1907, Proust writes an essay for *Le Figaro*, "Journées en automobile." Whereas the year began with Proust musing, in the wake of his mother's death, about an ancient tragedy—the *Oresteia*—at year's end, Proust's gaze is transformed. As he writes for *Le Figaro* about motoring that fall in a car around France and finding himself spiritually transported by the experience, he is positioned on the forward edge of the modern age. Only one in 1,000 persons in France had access to a car in 1907. There were 37,295 cars in France in 1907 out of a population of 38,343,000 (A. L. Clough, ed., *The Horseless Age* [New York: Horseless Age, 1903], 681). In this essay, Proust records animate nature: the sea pulls back behind the car as they pass it, houses rush toward them, fir trees leap out of their way (see Danius, *The Senses of Modernism*, 140). Proust will reprise this narrative, exchanging a car for a carriage, in his discussion of the steeples of Martinville in the novel (Proust, *Swann's Way*, 185). An animated nature also features (as discussed above) in Proust's depiction of Venice. Proust's insights about sensation and perception and their role in what we have typified as the transformation of metaphysical desire are developed in the aesthetic theory of *Finding Time Again*.

38. Proust, *Finding Time Again*, 354.

39. Ibid., 355.

40. Ibid., 356.

41. Kristeva, *Time and Sense*, 189.

42. Proust, *Finding Time Again*, 355–56.

43. Proust would have learned of Tarde's work from his philosophy instructor and personal tutor, Alphonse Darlu (Kristeva, *Time and Sense*, 259). Interestingly, Girard discusses Tarde in *Evolution and Conversion*. He indicates that Tarde had "tremendous phenomenological insight" but identified imitation across a broad cultural spectrum; even so, Girard judges Tarde's insights as "superficial" because he did not discover mimetic rivalry or its consequences (Gallese, "Two Sides of Mimesis," 139). Given Girard's understanding that Proust did understand mimetic rivalry and articulated that understanding in the course of writing *In Search of Lost Time*, Girard might be open to the notion that Tarde's insights reached fuller development in their application and extension in Proust's novel.

44. Quoted in Kristeva, *Time and Sense*, 266.

45. Ibid.

46. Moorjani, *Aesthetics of Loss and Lessness*, 174. Moorjani amplifies Kristeva's comments on Schopenhauer with an example of his influence on Proust. For Schopenhauer, music is a direct expression of psychic forces. She suggests that Proust "undeniably followed Schopenhauer" when writing of "the translation music effects of an ineffable text inscribed within a hidden place." She also links the work of metaphor with the narrator's negotiation of maternal loss. For Proust, writes Moorjani, music "reiterates the infant's first motions, voicings, and play with shapes and colour

on the border of social codings." Repetition of a drama of love and loss, music establishes and maintains a relation to the maternal body, the Lacanian imaginary mother.

47. Kristeva, *Time and Sense*, 268.

48. Ibid., 267.

49. Proust, *Finding Time Again*, 356.

50. Ibid., 356–57.

51. Ibid., 198.

52. Ibid., 205.

53. Ibid., 207.

54. Ibid., 217. Although the narrator uses cinematography as a counterexample to the revelations he associates with writing, he turns to optical instruments to describe the work of the writer. The writer offers readers various lens, knowing that some will result only in blurred vision but that others will set the imagination in motion. The written work functions as an optical instrument so that the reader may see what could not be seen without it (220).

55. Kristeva, *Time and Sense*, 214.

56. See Moorjani, *Aesthetics of Loss and Lessness*, 174.

57. Kristeva, *Proust and the Sense of Time*, 5. Kristeva's notion has similarities with Jean Ricardou's discussion of the productive metaphor in Proust. Rather than serve a representative function, the metaphor creates a metamorphosis. See Ricardou and Freiberg, "Proust: A Retrospective Reading," 532.

58. Kristeva, *Time and Sense*, 213.

59. Ibid., 193.

60. Ibid.

61. Ibid., 195.

62. Proust, *Finding Time Again*, 75, 179.

63. Ibid., 180.

64. Ibid., 181.

65. Ibid., 183.

66. Ibid., 186–87.

67. Ibid., 189.

68. Ibid., 192.

69. Ibid., 193.

70. Ibid., 194.

71. Ibid., 196.

72. T. M. Lennon, "Proust and the Phenomenology of Memory," *Philosophy and Literature* 31, no. 1 (2007): 63–65, 55.

73. Kristeva, *Proust and the Sense of Time*, 57.

74. Ibid., 53.

75. Ibid., 70–72.

76. Ibid., 77.

77. Ibid., 79.

78. Ibid., 81–82.

79. Kristeva, *Time and Sense*, 239–40. Kristeva sees special significance in Proust's lifelong struggle with asthma. With asthma he lived with his body the unresolved struggle between differentiation from the maternal body and suffocating subsumption by it. This "impossible individuation process" in which mother and son "lay coiled up beside one another" makes his efforts to write sensation and to bring experience to expression all the more an aesthetic and therapeutic victory.

80. Ibid., 269. Kristeva's comments echo Girard's, who has singled out Merleau-Ponty as an influence on his early work (Gallese, "Two Sides of Mimesis," 25), and help us link Girard's interest in Merleau-Ponty to his fascination with Proust. Merleau-Ponty, like Proust, is a student of metaphysical desire. In his essay "The Child's Relations with Others," he draws on the research of child psychologist Henri Wallon, who studied infants' reactions to their images in a mirror. For Merleau-Ponty, image-reflection is primarily a living relation with others that the child discovers by drawing on multiple senses (Maurice Merleau-Ponty, "The Child's Relations with Others," in *The Primacy of Perception*, trans. William Cobb [Evanston, IL: Northwestern University Press, 1964], 140). Merleau-Ponty's awareness of mimeticism is clearest in his discussion of jealousy and sympathy. A jealous child defines himself "entirely in relation to others and by the lack of what others have" (144). In adulthood, Merleau-Ponty observes, a jealous man (perhaps rivalrous with a competitor for the attention of a woman) does not know how to act because in jealousy he has become a spectator possessed by the action of the rival. For Merleau-Ponty, sympathy is primarily postural rather than specular (as is jealousy). Although sympathy appears in the child on the foundation of mimesis, in assuming a sympathetic stance one takes up the gestures, conduct, and ways of doing things of those with whom one is in contact (146). In adulthood, just as jealousy is a primary manifestation of mimetic desire, sympathy is expressed as love. Merleau-Ponty realizes that sympathetic connection with others is a fragile achievement. Rivalry is a more likely scenario. However, he still attests to a dialogical experience of embodied communion. The world, he believes, arises as a response to the touch and gesture of another. This syncretic sociability is not exhausted in adult life; rather, the passage from implicit to exploit sociability is also the journey of Being (155). Mimetic theorists would typify this passage as "positive mimesis."

81. Maurice Merleau-Ponty, *The Visible and the Invisible*, trans. Alphonso Lingis (Evanston, IL: Northwestern University Press, 1969), 149; Kristeva, *Time and Sense*, 272.

82. Merleau-Ponty, *The Visible and the Invisible*, 12.

83. Merleau-Ponty, *Phenomenology of Perception*, 218.

84. Merleau-Ponty, *The Visible and the Invisible*, 155; Kristeva, *Time and Sense*, 273.

85. Merleau-Ponty, *The Visible and the Invisible*, 133.

86. Ibid., 136.

87. Ibid., 137–38.

88. Ibid., 153.

89. Ibid., 142.

90. Kristeva, *Time and Sense*, 226.

91. Ibid., 308.

92. Merleau-Ponty, *The Visible and the Invisible*, 150.

93. Ibid., 151.

94. Ibid., 151–52.

95. Girard, *I See Satan Fall*, 189.

96. Jones's concerns about grace suggests that, for one who has been traumatized, physical intimacy and not only loquacious verbal acceptance poses risks: one fears being hugged to death. Victims of torture and abuse need indirect grace, characterized by proximity rather than by contact.

97. Jones, *Trauma and Grace*, 156.

98. That familial violence may be done in the name of "love" exacerbates the confusion a victim of trauma may feel between incoming "grace" and incoming "violence."

99. Jones, *Trauma and Grace*, 156.

100. Ibid., 157.

101. Kristeva, *Time and Sense*, 308.

102. Ibid., 319.

103. Ibid., 325.

Prelude. Siblings

1. Mitchell, *Siblings*, 32.

2. Ibid., 32. Oedipus also refers to Antigone and Ismene as his sisters in *Oedipus at Colonus*, l. 535. As the chorus identifies the two women as his daughters and begins to ask him whether they are also his siblings, Oedipus interrupts the chorus and confirms, "yes, sisters to their father."

3. Estelle Roith suggests that Freud represses painful issues associated with his own siblings and, as a consequence, neglects to give sufficient attention to siblings in his work. Freud was the eldest son and experienced strong ambivalence when his brother Julius was born. When Julius died a few months after birth, Freud experienced lasting guilt. Freud also found the birth of his sister, Anna, problematic. Freud did, however briefly, acknowledge the deep feelings associated with siblings when he wrote, "A child who has been put into second place by the birth of a brother or sister, and who is now for the first time almost isolated from his mother, does not easily forgive her this loss of place; feelings . . . arise in him and are often the basis of a permanent estrangement." Freud, *Introductory Lectures in Psychoanalysis*, as quoted in Estelle Roith, "Ishmael and Isaac: An Enduring Conflict," in *Sibling Relationships*, ed. Prophecy Coles (London: Karnac Books, 2006), 57.

4. Mitchell, *Siblings*, 35. Mitchell notes that Freud asserts that he has never met a woman patient who has never dreamed of murdering a sibling; however, Mitchell observes that Freud does not incorporate this insight into his psychoanalytic theory (134).

5. Ibid., 35.

6. Ibid., 15.

7. Ibid., 36. Jacques Lacan makes a similar point. In *Seminar XI*, he writes that Augustine "sums up his entire fate, namely, that of the little child seeing his brother at his mother's breast, looking at him *amare conspectus*, with a bitter look, which seems to tear him to pieces and has on himself the effect of a poison" (Jacques Lacan, *The Four Fundamental Concepts of Psychoanalysis*, ed. Jacques-Alain Miller, trans. Alan Sheridan [New York: Norton, 1998], 116). Lacan returns to the theme in *Seminar XX*, and writes of the hatred that "'sprimages forth' (*s'imageaillisse*) from the gaze of the little guy observed by Saint Augustine." Describing Augustine as "a third party," Lacan says that when he observes his brother at the breast of their mother he experiences a "desire evoked on the basis of a metonymy" (Jacques Lacan, *On Feminine Sexuality: The Limits of Love and Knowledge*, trans. Bruce Fink, book 20 of *The Seminar of Jacques Lacan*, ed. Jacques-Alain Miller [New York: Norton, 1999], 100). Lacan asserts that this scene does not depict jealousy: The child does not want the object his brother possesses. Rather, "The subject pales before an image of a completeness closed upon itself," for the child experiences, without having "the least idea" of what he is seeing, that the mother (*das ding*) from whom he is separated is, for his brother, the source of satisfaction (*befriedigung*). Lacan understands this scene in terms of metonymy, which he aligns with the path of desire oriented toward the mother (*das ding*) and distinguishes from the metaphorical expression of the Law of the Father. Mitchell's Law of the Mother, which aligns metonymy with seriality and sameness, is an intriguing counterpoint to Lacan. On the one hand, the seriality to which she points has similarities with Lacan's notion of the signifying chain along which desire is deployed. So also does she share with Lacan an understanding that the child is not beset by object-driven envy. On the other hand, in focusing on this sibling drama, Mitchell broadens the field on which human subjectivity develops. By contrast, Lacan tends to treat metonymy only as a deferral of desire for the mother. For Mitchell, even when a child has no idea what he is seeing when he observes his mother and the infant on her lap, the mother is not mute "completeness closed upon itself"; rather, according to Mitchell, the mother introduces her children to a world oriented toward love rather than hatred of the other. One loves because one is the same. Significantly, Lacan moves toward a similar insight late in *Seminar VII*, in his discussion of Antigone (Jacques Lacan, *The Ethics of Psychoanalysis*, trans. Dennis Porter, book 7 of *The Seminar of Jacques Lacan*, ed. Jacques Alain-Miller [New York: Norton, 1997], 243–87.

8. Mitchell, *Siblings*, 65.

9. Ibid., 41.

10. Ibid., 29.

11. Ibid., 43.

12. Ibid., 27–28, 128. Cecilia Sjöholm, whose work will be cited later, also talks about the "Antigone complex" in her book by that same name (Cecilia Sjöholm, *The Antigone Complex: Ethics and the Invention of Feminine Desire* [Stanford, CA: Stanford University Press, 2004]). Mitchell and Sjöholm appear unaware of each other's books; however, their insights complement each other well.

13. Mitchell, *Siblings*, 44.

14. Ibid., 54.

15. Girard, *Violence and the Sacred*, 252.

16. By contrast, in "Oedipus Analyzed," based on a 1965 lecture and published in *Oedipus Unbound*, Girard identifies the Sphinx as male and paternal rather than female and fraternal. He cites the Egyptian origins of the Sphinx and its image as a "deceased king." Oedipus's competition with the Sphinx is therefore a competition between a son and its paternal obstacle. However, if the Sphinx is a sibling to Oedipus, as Mitchell suggests, Girard has a more direct route to his larger

claim: Mimetic doubling is about competitors. Siblings are paradigmatic competitors, in this case. Can this sibling be a sister? Although Girard acknowledges that "one can easily see what tends to feminize" the Sphinx, he does not elaborate (Girard, *Oedipus Unbound*, 29–30).

17. Mitchell, *Siblings*, 57.

18. Mary Beth Mader, "Antigone's Line," in *Feminist Readings of Antigone*, ed. Fanny Söderbäck (Albany: State University of New York Press, 2010), 163.

19. Ibid., 164–65.

20. Mitchell's suggestion that the sibling relationship founds mutuality characteristic of the ethical life may bring to mind Hegel's comments on sibling relationships. In *The Phenomenology of Spirit* he credits sisters with possessing the "feminine element" that "premonizes and foreshadows most completely the nature of ethical life (*sittliches Wessen*)." Georg W. F. Hegel, *The Phenomenology of Spirit (the Phenomenology of Mind)*, trans. J. B. Baillie (Lawrence, KS: Digireads.com Publishing, 2009), 205. Mitchell cites Hegel only once, founding her theory in psychoanalysis rather than Hegelian philosophy. I follow Mitchell's lead here; psychoanalysis offers a productive alternative to Hegel, who so often is the primary mode of entry for reflection on *Antigone*. In particular, Mitchell joins Girard in having a more expansive vision of mimetic desire than does Hegel. As Oughourlian states eloquently in *Things Hidden since the Foundation of the World*, Hegel looks only at one variant of desire: "desire *for* the other's desire; desire for recognition." By contrast, Girard looks at "interdividual desire . . . desire *according* to the other's desire" (Girard, *Things Hidden*, 320).

21. Girard, *Oedipus Unbound*, 78.

22. Girard, *Violence and the Sacred*, 61.

23. Girard, *Oedipus Unbound*, 91.

24. Mark R. Anspach, "Imitation and Violence: Empirical Evidence and the Mimetic Model," in Garrels, *Mimesis and Science*, 140.

25. Ibid., 130.

26. Anspach suggests that the empirical literature testing Girardian hypotheses is limited. But if we consider that the laboratory is not the only setting for empirical research, the literature of child analysis, represented by psychoanalysts such as Mitchell and Klein, is replete with founded observations of early childhood in a clinical setting that offer evidence of mimetic hypotheses, as Mitchell recognizes in citing Girard in her work.

27. Girard, *Things Hidden*, 39, 159. Girard also cites the Roman story of Romulus and Remus, in which Romulus's violence against Remus is a justified action that founds society (*Oedipus Unbound*, 112). See also Mitchell, *Siblings*, 35, already cited above.

28. Girard, *Oedipus Unbound*, 112.

29. Girard observes that, at the height of the sacrificial crisis, there is no way out: One must kill or be killed. Either Oedipus or Creon will be the sacrificer; either Oedipus or Creon will be the victim. There is no other role, no other stance. Only the accepting scapegoat, who puts his or her life on the line, can break through the symmetry of sacrifice, which cycles permanently between sacrificer and victim. For Girard, Sophocles is constrained in some ways to "respect the legend" of Oedipus, from which he draws his tragic narrative. But within this framework, Sophocles brings to the fore the symmetries that comprise mimetic desire and its violent outcomes. Shining an extraordinary light on them, Sophocles "rectifies" myth and focuses our attention on the scapegoat himself rather than on his expulsion. As a consequence, the tragic shift that myth undergoes in Sophocles

is "nothing other than the 'march beneath the unthinkable' of which Hölderlin speaks." By inviting us to follow the scapegoat, Sophocles the poet moves very close to biblical prophetism (ibid., 84–86).

30. Girard, *Things Hidden*, 144.

31. Girard, *Oedipus Unbound*, 112–13.

32. Girard, *Things Hidden*, 238.

33. Ibid., 241.

34. Ibid., 244.

35. Ibid.

36. Ibid.

37. Ibid., 245.

38. One might argue that Girard's inattention to sensory experience after his early work on novels is an artifact of Girard's change of focus with *Violence and the Sacred* and *Things Hidden since the Foundation of the World* from literature to anthropology and psychology. Perhaps sensory experience falls out of view when he begins to explore new topics and engage new conversational partners in these fields. However, Girard's work on Oedipus in *Violence and the Sacred* and in essays spanning three decades (late 1960s to the mid-1980s) shows that, without regard for content (sometimes literature, sometimes anthropology and psychology, sometimes literature *and* anthropology *and* psychology), the phenomenological themes of affective memory and sensory experience do not persist in his work midcareer. Girard's inability to explain how one experiences transformation from acquisitive to positive mimesis after he sets aside the explanatory schema grounded in phenomenology on which he draws in his early work is a systemic rather than incidental issue in his mid- and late-career work.

Chapter 4. The House of Labdacus: On Kinship and Sacrifice

1. Sophocles, *Sophocles' "Oedipus at Colonus,"* trans. Mary Whitlock Blundell (Newburyport, MA: Focus, 1990), 1. 3, 16.

2. Aeschylus, *The Seven against Thebes*, ed. Julie Nord, trans. Edmund Doidge Anderson Morshead (Toronto, Ontario: Courier Dover, 2000), 15 n. 7.

3. Froma I. Zeitlin, "Thebes: Theater of Self and Society in Athenian Drama," in *Nothing to Do with Dionysos? Athenian Drama in Its Social Context*, ed. John J. Winkler and Froma I. Zeitlin (Princeton, NJ: Princeton University Press, 1992), 131–32.

4. Ibid., 144.

5. Ibid., 145; emphasis mine.

6. Indeed, Sophocles introduces Thebes as a city defined by its secure boundaries (Sophocles, *Antigone*, in *Antigone, The Women of Trachis, Philoctetes, Oedipus at Colonus*, Loeb Classical Library (Cambridge, MA: Harvard University Press, 1994), l. 101, 119, 141). Unless otherwise indicated, citations are to this edition of *Antigone*. See also Vincent Rosivach, "The Two Worlds of the *Antigone*," *Illinois Classical Studies* 4 (1979): 16. Early in *Antigone*, the chorus references the city's gates three times, as if to summon in the minds of those who hear their words images of Thebans atop the gates defending their city and rendering it inaccessible to outsiders. Thebes's autochthonic origins and the prevalence of incest within its borders attest also to boundedness:

pollution within the city will harm only itself. Further, that Thebes is the home of tyrants who confuse the appropriate relationship between a ruler and the city mirrors the errors within the familial domain in Thebes. There, acts of patricide and incest distort appropriate relationships among kin. The desires of Thebes devolve finally into the extremes of misdirected desire; crossing the last boundary "in demanding equivalence for the self with the gods and taking their power for its own" (Zeitlin, "Thebes," 149).

7. Zeitlin, "Thebes," 132.

8. Girard, *The Scapegoat*, 25.

9. Zeitlin, "Thebes," 133; Sophocles, *Oedipus at Colonus*, in *Antigone, The Women of Trachis, Philoctetes, Oedipus at Colonus*, ll. 299–400, 784–86, 1342–43. Unless otherwise indicated, citations are to this edition of *Oedipus at Colonus*.

10. That Oedipus actually confronts Athens with itself and does not remain bounded off from Athens as a Theban other is attested to by Bernard M. Knox, who argues that Athens is itself "the inspiration for the figure of Oedipus tyrannos" (*The Heroic Temper: Studies in Sophoclean Tragedy* [Berkeley: University of California Press, 1983], 60).

11. Christian Meier, *The Political Art of Greek Tragedy* (Baltimore: Johns Hopkins University Press, 1993), 3–7, 215. In *Antigone*, Meier sees Sophocles's efforts to share his political wisdom with the citizens of Athens. Perceiving the fragility of Athenian democracy, Sophocles demonstrates with the figure of Creon the risks of tyranny. Creon initially acts appropriately as a leader. He acts on behalf of the city, assuming personal risk, and he is open to the advice of others. However, he is soon exposed as a tyrant, a leader who refuses to acknowledge that he has made a wrong decision. He closes his ears to the advice of others. Meier suggests that Sophocles may have had Pericles in mind as he wrote, for concerns about Pericles's leadership are similar to those associated with Creon. Pericles was not a tyrant; however, Sophocles may have seen in him the potential to become one (196). Pericles was criticized by some of his contemporaries for exercising a heavy hand in the conduct of policy with little regard for the views of others (199). On Meier's understanding, Antigone represents the citizen who speaks out against the abuse of power. Precisely because she is a woman and fundamentally powerless, she can model civic responsibility and still challenge a tyrant. For Meier, the civics lesson that Sophocles creates in *Antigone* put enough distance between the play and Athens that the audience was able to remain open to tutelage and could "explore political matters which would otherwise be too daring and unyielding" (203).

12. Charles Segal, "Spectator and Listener," in *The Greeks*, ed. Jean-Pierre Vernant (Chicago: University of Chicago Press, 1995), 211–12.

13. Wm. Blake Tyrrell and Larry J. Bennett, *Recapturing Sophocles' "Antigone"* (Lanham, MD: Rowman & Littlefield, 1998). Burial practices and concern about them are a common motif in several tragedies. Foley, writing in *Female Acts in Greek Tragedy*, examines not only Antigone but also Euripides's *Helen* and *The Suppliants*, Aeschylus's *Choephoroi* and *Seven against Thebes* (Helene P. Foley, *Female Acts in Greek Tragedy* [Princeton, NJ: Princeton University Press, 2002]).

14. Foley, *Female Acts*, 27.

15. Ibid., 25. In particular, public funerals had emerged as a custom in Athens in the years preceding the writing of the play. Paid for at public expense, the remains of soldiers killed in war were returned to Athens and buried following a public funeral (Tyrrell and Bennett, *Recapturing Sophocles' Antigone*, 7). Public funerals became ever more elaborate, perhaps to counter this stress. When this happened, tensions associated with women's traditional roles in rituals of burial were exacerbated (Foley, *Female Acts*, 22). Within the household, women had traditionally prepared

bodies for burial and led rites of lamentation for the dead. When burial rituals moved into public spaces, anxieties about proper treatment of the dead by the living increased. These anxieties intensified whenever a body could not be retrieved from a distant site of battle and the funeral proceeded in the absence of a body. In the wake of these transformations in burial practices, women still participated in public mourning, and their cries of lamentation continued; however, their actions became subject to formal restrictions. Lamentation could be offered only on the occasion of the death of one's immediate kin and then only by one's closest relatives (no more distant than first cousins). Women were required to stay behind men during funeral processions; they could not mark their faces or tear their clothes (Foley, 23). With increasing frequency, women were precluded from exercising their traditional roles during any of the public rites (Tyrrell and Bennett, *Recapturing Sophocles' Antigone*, 12–14).

16. See Tyrrell and Bennett, *Recapturing Sophocles' Antigone*, 1–28. Creon's and Antigone's actions in the play attest to opportunities the play afforded Athenians for such reflections. On the one hand, Creon, exemplifying Thebes, is an impious tyrant—a mirror opposite to leaders of a democratic Athens. But on the other hand, Creon acts in ways reminiscent of the Athenian demos: Antigone is denied the right to bury members of her family just as Athenian women in the decades preceding the writing of *Antigone* have been denied the right by the demos to perform customary burial rituals. So also do Antigone's actions invite a mixed response from the audience. On one level, Antigone's devotion to her brother—to the point of placing her own life at risk—would appear incomprehensible to those watching the play. But on another level, Antigone's strong emotions mirror Athenian concerns that have led to restrictions on women's participation in funerals in the decades preceding the writing of *Antigone*. Antigone embodies the dangers and incendiary powers of uncontrolled women, although she is Thebes's problem, not Athens's (Foley, *Female Acts*, 199–200). Moreover, in contesting Creon's edicts, she violates Athenian social norms concerning authority (as might be expected of a woman from Thebes). The response of the chorus to Antigone suggests that she errs not in her defense of the familial rituals but in choosing the wrong context (public rather than private) for expressing devotion to her kin at the time of Polyneices's death (Tyrrell and Bennett, *Recapturing Sophocles' Antigone*, 27–28; Foley, *Female Acts*, 180).

17. Tyrrell and Bennett, *Recapturing Sophocles' Antigone*, 18. Tyrrell and Bennett claim too that their interpretation of the play is faithful to its era. They do not impose on *Antigone* an interpretation out of keeping with ancient traditions and customs. Rather, by grounding their analysis in cultural and political issues of Sophocles's day, they show the play to be an artifact of its time. Because their interpretation of *Antigone* brings to expression social issues known to historians of the era, Tyrrell and Bennett assert that they avoid speculations that would impose modern categories of analysis of an ancient text (21). In this chapter, I regularly cite Tyrrell and Bennett even though I dissent from their overarching thesis. That thesis, attesting to a functional perspective on the text, unduly constrains their rich and highly suggestive close reading of the text. I am indebted to that reading in my own analysis, and I hope to show that a metaphysical thesis, grounded in mimetic theory, is more compatible with Tyrrell and Bennett's reading of the text than is their functional framework.

18. Foley, *Female Acts*, 55.

19. In Nicole Loraux, *The Mourning Voice: An Essay on Greek Tragedy*, trans. Elizabeth Trapnell Rawlings (Ithaca, NY: Cornell University Press, 2002). Loraux notes that the political interpretations exemplified in this discussion have "dominated studies in tragedy" for several decades. She includes not only political interpretations, such as I describe here, but also anthropological studies oriented toward civic institutions (she places Zeitlin in this group) and sociohistorical approaches exemplified by scholars such as Goldhill (Loraux, 14, 97 n. 2).

20. Rush Rehm, *Marriage to Death: The Conflation of Wedding and Funeral Rituals in Greek Tragedy* (Princeton, NJ: Princeton University Press, 1996), 9.

21. Ibid., 140.

22. Jean-Pierre Vernant and Pierre Vidal-Naquet, *Myth and Tragedy in Ancient Greece*, trans. Janet Lloyd (Cambridge, MA: Zone Books, 1990) as cited in Keltner, *Kristeva*, 112–13.

23. Girard, *Oedipus Unbound*, 26.

24. Girard, *Things Hidden*, 297. In referencing a "metaphysical threshold," Girard indicates that he is not in any way summoning traditional metaphysics. Rather, he suggests that "types of rivalry regulated by society" including, we might imagine, rivalry about public/private, male/female control of funerary rituals, have "no tangible reality" in themselves. When we dig beneath the surface of these rivalries, we arrive at the metaphysical threshold that confronts us with the reality behind all rivalries: metaphysical desire.

25. Mitchell, *Siblings*, 170. As discussed above in my introduction, weak trauma is what usually comes to mind when we think of trauma. In the wake of personal suffering that we perceive to be traumatic, we work through our pain; we cope; we recover. Strong trauma, by contrast, does not resolve over time. It ruptures the very structures of psychic life, immersing us in suffering that cannot be grasped or understood. Instead, it is subject to ongoing repetition.

26. Charles Shepherdson, "Antigone: The Work of Literature and the History of Subjectivity," in *Bound by the City: Greek Tragedy, Sexual Difference, and the Formation of the Polis*, ed. Denise Eileen McCoskey and Emily Zakin (Albany: State University of New York Press, 2009), 61.

27. Ibid., 62.

28. Sophocles, *Antigone*, l. 175.

29. Ibid., l. 90.

30. Ibid., ll. 65–66.

31. Ibid., l. 68.

32. Ibid., ll. 1320–25.

33. Girard, *Violence and the Sacred*, 150.

34. Ibid., 158.

35. Ibid.

36. Sophocles, *Antigone*, ll. 1–3.

37. Tyrrell and Bennett, *Recapturing Sophocles' Antigone*, 31–32.

38. The threat of pollution associated with the womb is augmented by the theme of shared sowing. The wombs of women are like the earth: both are dark places; both are the origin of life and violence; both are fertile and fearful. Adding incest to that darkness multiples pollution (Ruth Padel, *In and Out of the Mind* [Princeton, NJ: Princeton University Press, 1994], 101). Even were the audience to react to Antigone and Ismene's conversation on the level of public rather than mythic discourse, Antigone will not do right by Polyneices because her challenge to authority (however misguided that authority may be in the person of Creon) takes place in a public forum. Therefore, even apart from problems associated with Ismene's need to participate in the rites, the rites Antigone would perform for her brother (however laudatory they may be in a woman) are tainted (Tyrrell and Bennett, *Recapturing Sophocles' Antigone*, 73).

39. Moreover, Ismene mirrors Antigone in posing her own challenge to Creon, although, unlike Antigone, she does not challenge his role as public leader. Ismene challenges him as a father, asking if he will fulfill his obligations to his son, Haemon, who is to marry Antigone. Antigone fails in her efforts to defend the funeral bed, Ismene in her effort to defend the marriage bed (Tyrrell and Bennett, *Recapturing Sophocles' Antigone*, 79).

40. Ibid., 35.

41. Sophocles, *Antigone*, ll. 37–38.

42. Wm. Blake Tyrrell and Larry J. Bennett, "Sophocles' Enemy Sisters: Antigone and Ismene," *Contagion* 15–16 (2008–9): 1–18.

43. Sophocles, *Antigone*, l. 569.

44. Ibid., l. 571.

45. Ibid., l. 572.

46. Tyrrell and Bennett, "Sophocles' Enemy Sisters," 9.

47. Ibid., 10.

48. Ibid., 12.

49. Ibid., 10; translated by Tyrrell and Bennett, 13.

50. Tyrrell and Bennett, "Sophocles' Enemy Sisters," 13.

51. Sophocles, *Antigone*, ll. 184–86.

52. Ibid., l. 738.

53. Mary Whitlock Blundell, *Helping Friends and Harming Enemies: A Study in Sophocles and Greek Ethics* (New York: Cambridge University Press, 1991), 127.

54. Sophocles, *Antigone*, ll. 737–39.

55. Girard, *Violence and the Sacred*, 44–49. Citing Girard in support of their thesis, Tyrrell and Bennett join him in attesting to the brothers' symmetry within the play (*Recapturing Sophocles' Antigone*, 43–44 n. 1).

56. Ruth Padel, *Whom Gods Destroy: Elements of Greek and Tragic Madness* (Princeton, NJ: Princeton University Press, 1995), 253.

57. Sophocles, *Antigone*, ll. 582–626.

58. Ibid., l. 620.

59. Padel, *Whom Gods Destroy*, 255.

60. Blackness and darkness are associated with madness in Greek tragedy. Black bile in the human body offers evidence of internal pollution. But brought by the gods, the blackness of sand and sea points to a destructiveness that crosses inner and outer boundaries, overwhelming barriers just as the sea too would surge across the sand. For discussion of blackness and darkness and their relation to madness in Greek tragedy see ibid., chapters 5 and 6.

61. Sophocles, *Antigone*, ll. 585–606.

62. Ibid., ll. 600–620.

63. *Iliad* 19.86–88, as cited in Tyrrell and Bennett, *Recapturing Sophocles' Antigone*, 83.

64. Sophocles, *Antigone*, l. 755.

65. Padel, *Whom Gods Destroy*, 167.

66. Ibid., 168. Padel argues that we cannot locate an original or primary meaning of *atē* that would predate Homer. Padel recommends that we watch "how a word behaves in use," exploring it in its native habitat. For Padel, when we look at Greek tragedy, Homer is helpful to our efforts to offer a contextual interpretation of *atē* because Homer is a living tradition for a poet such as Sophocles and for his audience.

67. Ibid., 188.

68. Ibid., 205.

69. Ibid., 191. Padel cites Girard's *Violence and the Sacred* as the source for her discussion of generative violence in Greek tragedy (Girard, *Violence and the Sacred*, 9–32, 81–86, 93–96).

70. Padel, *Whom Gods Destroy*, 192.

71. Ibid., 210.

72. Ibid., 196.

73. Ibid., 242–43. Madness can visit the tragic hero. Heroes are violent, and their violence is sometimes likened to madness, or their violence can be treated as a sign of impending madness.

74. Ibid., 243. They may be characters on the stage, but they often are invoked in the absence of explicit characterization. Vase paintings depicting scenes from Greek tragedies will include images of the Erinyes as if they had been present during the staging of the scenes.

75. Ibid., 214.

76. Although Padel cites Girard in developing her concepts of reciprocal and generative violence, when she discusses the double bind, she does not cite Girard's own discussion (Girard, *Violence and the Sacred*, 146–47). Instead, she cites multiple texts by Bateson, suggesting his direct influence on her use of the term and her analysis.

77. Sophocles, *Oedipus at Colonus*, l. 755. This line plays on line 754 with its reference to mindlessness See James C. Hogan, *A Commentary on the Plays of Sophocles* (Carbondale: Southern Illinois University Press, 1991), 157.

78. Sophocles, *Antigone*, ll. 640–55.

79. Ibid., ll. 685–700. Haemon likens himself to the Athenian youth who serve on the frontiers, having sworn an oath of citizenship. As scouts, they are on the lookout for danger and regularly report back to their superiors. See Tyrrell and Bennett, *Recapturing Sophocles' Antigone*, 89.

80. Tyrrell and Bennett, *Recapturing Sophocles' Antigone*, 90.

81. Sophocles, *Antigone*, l. 746.

82. Ibid., l. 750.

83. Ibid., l. 751.

84. Ibid., l. 761.

85. Ibid., l. 775. "*Mainomai*" (I am mad) is linked in the Greek imagination with "*miainomai*" (I am polluted). Thus madness and pollution, human error and divine hostility, come together as Creon leaves Haemon and prepares to make offerings that will cancel the pollution associated with killing kin (Padel, *Whom Gods Destroy*, 200).

86. Padel, *Whom Gods Destroy*, 149.

87. Sophocles, *Antigone*, l. 776; Tyrrell and Bennett, *Recapturing Sophocles' Antigone*, 95.

88. Sophocles, *Antigone*, ll. 1284, 1274.

89. Rush Rehm notes that marriages and funerals are frequently juxtaposed in literature (Shakespeare, Racine, Ibsen) and opera (Donizetti, Verdi, Wagner) and are given a "powerful instantiation" in Greek tragedy. He attributes this juxtaposition of events that seem disparate to their shared liminality. Both have the three-part structure identified by Victor Turner (separation from a prior state; transition in liminal period, reincorporation in changed form). The liminal period is decisive in the work of tragedy because it represents a dangerous vulnerability that can issue in loss or in enhanced freedom or creativity (Rehm, *Marriage to Death*, 3–5).

90. Sophocles, *Antigone*, l. 852. *Metoikos*, "resident alien," wonderfully captures the liminal standing of Antigone, betwixt and between worlds. See Knox, *The Heroic Temper*, 114. Of course, the links Sophocles forges between death and marriage are not unique to *Antigone*, for Greek culture marks these connections and knows them well (Nicole Loraux, *Tragic Ways of Killing a Woman*, trans. Anthony Forster [Cambridge: Harvard University Press, 1991], 37–38. Marriage always is colored by intimations of death because child-bearing that follows marriage is, in ancient societies, fraught with risk. Maternal and infant deaths are all too common outcomes of childbirth. Thus, both weddings and burials track transitions from life to death (potential in the case of marriage; actual in the case of death). Moreover, marriage and death rituals share in common the capacity to effect irreversible transitions: the dead enter the house of Hades and never leave it; when a bride leaves her father's home and enters her husband's, she will "perish" as a virgin. The liminal state into which brides and the dead enter require similar attention to preparation of bodies for transition, call forth similar hymns and sacrifices, and proceed in similar ways. In both ceremonies, a procession by mule cart accomplishes a physical transition from the space of life to the space of death (Tyrrell and Bennett, *Recapturing Sophocles' Antigone*, 98).

91. Sophocles, *Antigone*, ll. 820–25.

92. Ibid., ll. 853–56.

93. Ibid., l. 1003. Hogan suggests that the allusion is to the gadfly who hounds an animal or human (e.g., Io) into madness (*Commentary on the Plays*, 167).

94. Charles Segal, *Tragedy and Civilization: An Interpretation of Sophocles* (Cambridge: Harvard University Press, 1981), 164.

95. Sophocles, *Antigone*, ll. 1006–22. Tiresias describes in repulsive detail the failure of the sacrifice. The fire that should burn as a hot flame merely smolders; the oozing flesh reminds the audience of Polyneices' corpse; the fat that should create a rich smoke for the gods fails to burn. The appalling scene powerfully evokes the complete break in communication between gods and humans. See Griffith's commentary in Sophocles, *Sophocles' "Antigone"*, ed. Mark Griffith (New York: Cambridge University Press, 1999), 299–300.

96. Sophocles, *Antigone*, l. 1035.

97. Girard, *Violence and the Sacred*, 151; see also Tyrrell and Bennett, *Recapturing Sophocles' Antigone*, 134.

98. Sophocles, *Antigone*, l. 1040.

99. Ibid., l. 1075. See Blundell, *Helping Friends*, 129.

100. Sophocles, *Antigone*, l. 1095.

101. Ibid., l. 1100. Hogan suggests that *blabē*, which means "swift-footed," is a synonym for *atē* that personifies *atē* (*Commentary on the Plays*, 170).

102. Sophocles, *Antigone*, l. 1232. The Lloyd-Jones translation says "spat." In his commentary on *Antigone*, Griffith notes that the ferocity and "almost sub-tragic" aspect of Sophocles's description of Haemon's attack has startled translators and commentators. Rather than translate the Greek literally, some have suggested only that Haemon "looked with contempt at his father" (*Sophocles' "Antigone"*, 338).

103. What is savage (*agrion*) is outside the polis. Centaurs, mountain-dwelling beasts, are regularly referred to as *agrion*. They are a distorted form of the male body and represent a confusion of boundaries. One with savage eyes is also a madman. See Segal, *Tragedy and Civilization*, 30–33, 159.

104. Sophocles, *Antigone*, l. 1235.

105. Ibid., l. 1281.

106. *Sophocles' "Antigone"*, ed. Griffith, 328.

107. Sophocles, *Antigone*, ll. 1304–5; see also Griffith's commentary in *Sophocles' "Antigone"*, 351.

108. Sophocles, *Antigone*, l. 1320.

109. Ibid., ll. 705–10. The reference is to a writing tablet, which is decorated on the outside but can be "opened up" to read the truth inscribed inside. Euripides uses similar language in *The Trojan Women* (l. 662) and *Medea* (ll. 659–61). A drinking song from the time wishes "if only it were possible to open up a man's breast, to find out what he is like; then, after looking at his thoughts to close him up again and regard him for sure as your friend." See Griffith's commentary (*Sophocles' "Antigone"*, 244).

110. The chorus well mirrors uncertainties the audience may have about how to understand Antigone's entombment and death. After Antigone is led away, the chorus compares Antigone to Danaë, Lycurgus, and Cleopatra Ibid. (ll. 945–60). Each figure suggests a different interpretation of how Antigone's impending death may be best understood; however, the chorus does not advocate for one. Danaë's story suggests that divine fate is at work. The case of Lycurgus suggests that Antigone, like Lycurgus, is mad and deserves punishment by the gods. The third case suggests that Antigone is a victim of Creon's brutality. See C. M. Bowra, *Sophoclean Tragedy* (New York: Oxford University Press, 1970), 105.

111. Loraux, *Tragic Ways*, 33–34, 46.

112. Sophocles, *Antigone*, ll. 817–22. See also Loraux, *Tragic Ways*, 48. As Hogan points out, this compound adjective "self-law," denoting what is voluntary and self-chosen, occurs fifteen times in *Antigone* and nineteen times in the remaining extant plays of Sophocles (*Commentary on the Plays*, 160).

113. Sophocles, *Antigone*, l. 875.

114. Blundell, *Helping Friends*, 26.

115. Ibid., 28.

116. Ibid., 39.

117. Ibid., 32.

118. Ibid., 41–44. The "help friends and harm enemies" code is most unambiguously visible in military

conduct. "Citizen" and "enemy" are opposites and clearly dictate how warriors will perceive those they engage in battle. In other contexts, the lines separating *philos* from *echthros* (enemy) are less clear. Conflicts of interest may create tensions between and among *philoi*. Moreover, because friends are designated as such by principles of loyalty and reciprocal benefit, friends may have problematic qualities and still be counted as friends. So also can individuals with positive personal characteristics be subjected to ill-treatment because they are enemies. The blurring of categories has an impact on the implementation of the talion: the court of law and the gods may be referenced as the source of justice when lines separating friends from enemies blur (Blundell, *Helping Friends*, 51–53).

119. Sophocles, *Antigone*, ll. 523, 512.

120. Ibid., ll. 927, 93; see also Blundell, *Helping Friends*, 113.

121. Sophocles, *Antigone*, ll. 29–30, 461–68; Robert F. Goheen, *The Imagery of Sophocles' "Antigone": A Study of Poetic Language and Structure* (Princeton, NJ: Princeton University Press, 1970), 14–16.

122. Sophocles, *Antigone*, ll. 1040–45; see also Goheen, *Imagery of Sophocles' Antigone*, 16–17.

123. Sophocles, *Antigone*, l. 1063.

124. Ibid., ll. 188–90.

125. Girard, *Things Hidden*, 198–99. Significantly, Girard finds "primitive" and traditional societies more acutely aware of the mimetic features of social violence than contemporary societies. Today we tend to view violence as an isolated crime enacted by a single perpetrator. However, the formulaic "help friends and harm enemies" attests to the propagation of imitation along symmetrical lines. Girard attributes the loss of such ancient symmetries of violence to the development of a "judicial institution that transcends all antagonists" (*Things Hidden*, 11–12). In ancient Greece, the code of "help friends and harm enemies" demonstrates that transcendence had not yet been secured.

126. In *Oedipus Unbound*, Girard references the reciprocity of Creon and Antigone's rivalry. He writes that the "two attitudes are intertwined; each reveals the hubris of the other." He also asserts that Sophocles "does not get to the bottom of things" until *Oedipus the King* (*Oedipus Unbound*, 53). However, by the time he writes *Things Hidden since the Foundation of the World*, Girard acknowledges that Antigone breaks through the cycle of doubles. My discussion points to a direction in which Girard could have moved were he to have developed these insights further.

127. Sophocles, *Antigone*, ll. 45–64.

128. Goheen, *Imagery of Sophocles' Antigone*, 17.

129. Even Blundell acknowledges Antigone's move away from the code of "help friends and harm enemies." True, Blundell consistently treats Antigone and Creon as mirrors of each other and shows them to be one-sided in their commitments. However, Blundell states that Antigone does abide heroically in the end to a *philia* of kin and can make some claim to a *philia* of citizen-community; however, Creon is a failure at both. In the final analysis, Blundell acknowledges that Antigone "rises above conventional self-interest to embrace personal loyalty even at great personal cost" (*Helping Friends*, 145–48). That move, I suggest, takes Antigone outside of the help/harm nexus that Blundell has analyzed.

130. Segal, *Tragedy and Civilization*, 166.

131. Sophocles, *Antigone*, ll. 450–51.

132. Ibid., ll. 810–16.

133. Ibid., ll. 898–904, 913–15.

134. Some commentators typify the conflict between Creon and Antigone in terms of law, bypassing religion altogether: Creon cleaves to the laws of the polis, Antigone to the unwritten laws of nature. But the religious context of their conflict is missed when it is described in this way. Antigone does support the *nomina*, which specifically refer to "customs" associated with burial of the dead. However, in doing so, she does not juxtapose the customs to which she appeals with the laws of the polis or with some kind of natural law (as Aristotle suggests in writing about *Antigone* in his *Rhetoric*). Rather, the customs Antigone follows evince her proximity to a sacred domain. When she states her intent to bury her kin in accord with *nomina*, she is not referencing law but *devotion*. Her devotion to the gods is a lived practice. See Knox, *The Heroic Temper*, 96–99.

135. Sophocles, *Antigone*, ll. 163, 185.

136. Ibid., l. 282; see also Knox, *The Heroic Temper*, 101.

137. Knox, *The Heroic Temper*, 102.

138. Sophocles, *Antigone*, ll. 1068–73.

139. Girard, *Violence and the Sacred*, 135.

140. Shepherdson, "Antigone," 54.

141. Sophocles, *Antigone*, ll. 416–20.

142. Segal, *Tragedy and Civilization*, 171.

143. Tyrrell and Bennett point to problems with other explanations. The dusting is definitely not a burial by either human or divine action since actions associated with a burial require multiple rituals (whether the agents of these rituals are humans or gods). Nor is it "symbolic" of burial, for dusting a corpse is an actual ritual to prevent pollution in ancient Greece (Tyrrell and Bennett, *Recapturing Sophocles' Antigone*, 57). Segal affirms as plausible that the gods are responsible for the dusting of Polyneices's corpse (*Tragedy and Civilization*, 160).

144. Tyrrell and Bennett, *Recapturing Sophocles' Antigone*, 58.

145. Sophocles, *Antigone*, ll. 422–35.

146. Tyrrell and Bennett, *Recapturing Sophocles' Antigone*, 66.

147. Segal, *Tragedy and Civilization*, 179.

148. Sophocles, *Antigone*, l. 443.

149. See Girard, *Violence and the Sacred*, 135. I suggest too that the audience for Sophocles's play, steeped in the religious traditions of the fifth century BCE, would have been caught up in uncertainties and confusions, wondering if Antigone acted or if she was a bystander to the actions of the gods. Today's audience, living in a world from which divine whirlwinds are generally absent, may too readily dismiss the multivalent aspects of the text. More likely to take Antigone at her word and Creon at his, a contemporary audience may be less likely to hear in the witness of the watchman evidence of the work of the gods.

150. Foley indicates that Antigone's last speech is directed toward the chorus. I join Knox in asserting that Antigone's speech is expressed from within the liminal context of tomb / bridal chamber (Foley, *Female Acts*, 177; Knox, *The Heroic Temper*, 103). That the chorus is witness to her speech but is not the addressee of her words is an important distinction to draw because the chorus does not recognize that Antigone is moving away from the sacrificial economy in which they live. Knox points out that interpreters such as Jebb have questioned the authenticity of Antigone's words

because they seem at odds with her last words, which are addressed to "the rulers of Thebes," whom she asks to look upon her house and on her suffering as she summons the gods of Hades ("reverent observance of reverence") (*Antigone*, l. 940). But I concur with Knox that Antigone is not being inconsistent in her words; rather, she is distinguishing her audience in each speech (Knox, *The Heroic Temper*, 105). Antigone utters one speech from within the liminal frame, as she stands on the threshold of death; she addresses the other to Thebes and expresses herself in the language of defense within the communicative context of mimesis.

151. Sophocles, *Antigone*, ll. 890–910. A body of literature (some of which will be referenced in the next chapter) has debated the authenticity of Antigone's surprising words. I align my own interpretation with Knox, who points out that Aristotle refers to this speech and does not imagine it to be an interpolation (*The Heroic Temper*, 104).

152. Foley does suggest that the fifth-century audience could have been surprised but not shocked by Antigone's speech. That Antigone does not frame her final words in terms of her devotion to the gods (a focus that has been central throughout much of the play) is surprising. But Foley points out that in aligning herself with her natal family, as the last living family member of that family, Antigone recognizes responsibilities she has to her brother. Ancient Greece did provide for daughters to perform rites for their families in such exceptional circumstances. Thus, her comments cannot be viewed as shocking. Moreover, obligations she would have to the family into which she was about to marry have become moot due to Creon's actions. See Foley, *Female Acts*, 177–80.

153. Sophocles, *Antigone*, ll. 484–85, 1167. See Butler, *Antigone's Claim*, for an insightful discussion of how Creon describes his conflict with Antigone in terms of manhood and its (monstrous) reversal by Antigone. Judith Butler, *Antigone's Claim* (New York: Columbia University Press, 2002), 9–10. See Knox for comments on the mirrored imagery of death (*The Heroic Temper*, 116).

154. Blundell suggests that the code of "help friends and harm enemies" extends beyond the grave (*Helping Friends*, 114). Heroes are expected to continue to help friends and harm enemies. Antigone's distance from this model (as argued above) is confirmed by her distance from it at the moment of death.

155. Although the gods affirm Antigone's right to bury Polyneices and even "do the deed" as argued above, they do not praise Antigone. When she makes her final speech on behalf of Polyneices, she remains *metoikos*, a resident alien with the gods above and below. When Tiresias, speaking for the gods, condemns Creon for his actions, Tiresias does not lift Antigone up. The gods will punish Creon and speak against what he has done to Antigone (l. 1070) but they will not save Antigone. See Knox, *The Heroic Temper*, 115.

156. Knox, *The Heroic Temper*, 107.

157. Julia Kristeva, "Antigone: Limit and Horizon," trans. Ella Brians, in Söderbäck, *Feminist Readings of Antigone*, 216.

158. Genesis 42–45; Girard, *Oedipus Unbound*, 112–13.

159. Girard, *Oedipus Unbound*, 112–13.

160. Sophocles, *Antigone*, ll. 420–35.

Chapter 5. Trauma and the Theban Cycle

1. The human is the most *deinon* of all creatures. *Deinon* means "fearful" or "wonderful." It can also mean "uncanny" (Sjöholm, *The Antigone Complex*, 68–69). Charles Segal notes that the

conjoining of terror with wonder encapsulates the human as a tragic figure. The wonderful powers of the human free the human from the constraints of nature; however, these powers make the human more terrible (*deinoteron*) than natural phenomena because these powers undergird a human capacity for extremes of violence. See Segal, *Tragedy and Civilization*, 153.

2. These insights are helpfully offered by Cecilia Sjöholm ("Fear of Intimacy?" 180).

3. Sjöholm argues that Kristeva's way of thinking about intimacy is unique and defines her distinctive contribution to psychoanalysis (ibid.).

4. Caruth, *Unclaimed Experience*, 2.

5. Ibid., 61.

6. Ibid., 62.

7. Ibid., 4–10.

8. Charles Segal, *Interpreting Greek Tragedy: Myth, Poetry, Text* (Ithaca, NY: Cornell University Press, 1986), 69.

9. Ibid., 70.

10. Girard, *Violence and the Sacred*, 74.

11. Ibid., 79.

12. Girard, *Oedipus Unbound*, 31.

13. Ibid., 32.

14. Girard, *Violence and the Sacred*, 81.

15. Ibid., 82.

16. Caruth, *Unclaimed Experience*, 4.

17. Ibid., 7–8.

18. In ancient Greece, the hero's traits do not include wisdom and justice. Rather, the hero is a man of forceful personality, achievement, great suffering, and anger. He is a larger-than-life figure who is distinguished from others by passions that compel fear and admiration, even after his death. His fearlessness is attested to by battles with humans and with gods. Hero cults arise in order to propitiate these men whose powers issue from raw strength, untutored by justice and wisdom (Knox, *The Heroic Temper*, 55–56). As the account that follows indicates, according to Knox, Oedipus is distinctive among the Greek heroes; having been given superhuman vision by the gods, he acts from "knowledge, certainty, and justice" (148).

19. Ibid., 160–61.

20. Ibid., 148; Sophocles, *Oedipus at Colonus*, 1627.

21. Otfried Becker, *Das Bild des Weges und Verwandte Vorstellung im Frühgriechischen Denken*, vol. 4 (Wiesbaden: Hermes Einzelschrift, 1937), 212, as cited in Segal, *Tragedy and Civilization*, 406.

22. Segal, *Tragedy and Civilization*, 407–8.

23. Zeitlin, "Thebes," 155, 163–64. Zeitlin actually assigns to Antigone the legacy of violence from which Oedipus has been freed. My argument opposes Zeitlin's on that count also.

24. Sarah Iles Johnston, *Restless Dead: Encounters between the Living and the Dead in Ancient Greece* (Berkeley: University of California Press, 1999), 153.

25. Ibid., 155–59. Hogan observes that, in acknowledging the ongoing power of the heroized dead, the Greeks sought to limit or direct that power through their offerings. In *Oedipus at Colonus* (l. 407), Ismene and Oedipus discuss his grave—near Thebes or Athens—in ways that demonstrate the complex powers associated with dead. The Thebans want Oedipus close but not so close as to incur pollution. Ismene states the concern bluntly when she says that the Thebans need Oedipus's grave close "where they can control you" (l. 400) rather than at a distance where "[you] would be your own master" (l. 406). See Hogan, *Commentary on the Plays*, 118.

26. Sophocles, *Oedipus at Colonus*, ll. 1720–60.

27. Ibid., l. 788. The wording belongs to Robert Parker, *Miasma: Pollution and Purification in Early Greek Religion* (New York: Oxford University Press, 1996), 320. See also Rosalyn Diprose, *The Bodies of Women: Ethics, Embodiment and Sexual Differences* (New York: Routledge, 1994), 32: "not me but my daemon will bring vengeance."

28. Knox, *The Heroic Temper*, 149.

29. Sophocles, *Oedipus at Colonus*, l. 1172.

30. Ibid., ll. 1190–95.

31. Ibid., ll. 405, 1200–1202.

32. The gift of Oedipus's body (*charis*) is described in terms of grace from the deities (ll. 1751–52). But commentators place the multiple references to *charis* in the text within the context of favors and benefits that Oedipus will provide. See lines 586, 636, 1109, and 1489. For commentary see G. M. Kirkwood, *A Study of Sophoclean Drama* (Ithaca, NY: Cornell University Press, 1994), 244–45; Hogan, *Commentary on the Plays*, 120, 124.

33. Sophocles, *Oedipus at Colonus*, l. 1775. See also lines 1488, 248, 767, and 779b. Blundell translates *charis* as "favor" and places *charis* squarely within the ethics of helping friends and harming enemies (*Helping Friends*, 33, 45).

34. "Stereotypes" refer to the replication, without regard to differences in time, place, or context, of set features of the scapegoat. See Girard, *The Scapegoat*, 12–23.

35. Girard, *Violence and the Sacred*, 85–86.

36. Ibid., 85.

37. In *Violence and the Sacred*, Girard describes "two Oedipus plays," excluding *Antigone* from the Theban cycle (91). So also in *Oedipus Unbound*, Girard does not note that the narrative trajectory of *Oedipus at Colonus* moves forward and includes *Antigone*. However, with the exception of one essay that does not discuss Oedipus, the essays in *Oedipus Unbound* were written between 1968 and 1973. These essays predate Girard's insights about *Antigone* discussed in *Things Hidden since the Foundation of the World* (1978). As a result, insights in the former essays are never synthesized with Girard's comments in the latter. My reflections in this chapter may be viewed as a contribution to such a synthesis.

38. Girard, *Things Hidden*, 244.

39. In *Oedipus Unbound*, when Girard associates the limping gait of Oedipus with "scandal," he may be anticipating his assertion in *Things Hidden since the Foundation of the World* that Antigone breaks out of an economy of sacrifice. Girard introduces the theme of "scandal" when he argues that the Oedipus stories, to the extent that they depart from myth, move forward against a false sacred. These stories constitute an obstacle to a mythic reading of Oedipus's life (Girard, *Oedipus Unbound*, 68–69). Girard traces how this transition from myth to tragedy is matched by

a transition in focus from a paternal to fraternal relationship, underscoring how son and father are scandalized by that transition. When Girard observes that limping is passed on to "Labdacus' entire male line," Antigone is excluded as a point of reference (79). Perhaps Girard has no inkling of the insights he will offer ten years later about Antigone. But in speaking exclusively of the *male* line in the house of Labdacus, Girard seemingly forecasts the definitive move away from sacrifice with which he will credit Antigone in *Things Hidden since the Foundation of the World*.

40. Girard, *Oedipus Unbound*, 87. That Girard has chosen his words well is demonstrated by the cluster of terms that define "rectify." Webster's dictionary states that to "rectify" an object (a globe) is "to adjust it in order to prepare for the solution of a proposed problem." So also does "rectify" mean to correct by calculation or adjustment (mathematics) and to refine and purify (chemistry). In functioning to correct and refine myth, tragedy moves humans forward toward a solution to generative violence. For Girard, tragedy does not arrive at the solution, which he associates only with Jewish and Christian scriptures.

41. Ibid., 86. Girard presumes that the reader will be familiar with his work and will understand the larger context in which he places the notion of the consenting scapegoat or victim. Girard does *not* valorize "self-sacrifice." The critical context for establishing what he means when he writes about the consenting victim is his analysis of Jesus as such a victim. Girard points out that the revelatory meaning of Jesus is not appreciated by those who are caught up in a "logic of sacrifice." For them, Jesus is a threat, a corrupter of order, and therefore a perfect victim. He is one who can justifiably be attacked. From inside the sacrificial economy, Jesus is not unique; he fits the typical victim profile. Moreover, within a sacrificial economy, "consent" of the victim is gamesmanship. The consenting victim actually is being coerced by others or is caught up in mimetic desire, in which one engages in self-sacrifice to "sacralize *oneself* and make *oneself* godlike" (Girard, *Things Hidden*, 236). By contrast, and from the perspective of revelatory insight, Jesus is not a scapegoat. Jesus is "the victim par excellence" (209). However, his actions and words fall outside the context of mimetic gamesmanship. In saying this, Girard intends that we acknowledge the arbitrariness of victimization (an arbitrariness to which Jesus is subjected) but also note that Jesus is the least violent of victims. As a consequence, Jesus transcends the sacrificial economy. There is no action or word from Jesus that participates in violence; all is love for neighbor (211). Jesus does not "consent" within the strictures of a sacrificial economy. He neither acts at the behest of a violence-loving God to harm himself nor to sacralize his life. Rather, breaking with the reciprocity of violence (kill or be killed) and its multiple distorted forms (including self-sacrifice that benefits the one who dies) Jesus lays down his life out of love, thereby "breaking the circle" of death (214).

42. Girard, *Oedipus Unbound*, 86.

43. Ibid., 87. The reference is to Hölderlin.

44. Ibid., 88.

45. Ibid., 56, 88–89.

46. Girard, *Things Hidden*, 245. As noted in my introductory comments above, Girard does qualify Antigone's achievement, stating that Antigone assumes a nonsacrificial stance in relation to *dead* kin, whereas the exemplar in the Judgment of Solomon assumes a like stance on behalf of a *living* child. But Girard offers no evidence that a selfless regard for kin is different for the person who embodies that love if the kin is dead rather than alive. Certainly, the fluid boundaries between living and dead in ancient Greece obligate Girard to offer detailed support for the hard distinctions he wants to draw between Antigone and the mother in the Judgment of Solomon.

47. *Oedipus the King* was written around 430–429 BCE; *Oedipus at Colonus* was performed after

Sophocles's death and believed by most scholars to have been written shortly before his death, between 406 and 401 BCE; and *Antigone* was written around 442–441 BCE.

48. Girard, *Oedipus Unbound*, 13.

49. Girard speaks of Antigone in only one paragraph of *Oedipus Unbound*, in a chapter dating from 1965 (ibid., 53). He describes her conflict with Creon in terms of perpetual mimetic doubling, and states that Sophocles "does not get to the bottom of things" until *Oedipus the King*. Not only does this cursory account of *Antigone* overlook this tragedy's complexity, but also Girard's dismissal of Antigone is at odds with his comments on Antigone a decade later in *Things Hidden since the Foundation of the World*.

50. Ibid., 3.

51. Ibid., 4.

52. Ibid., 9.

53. Ibid., 8. In *Oedipus Unbound*, Girard builds his cyclical theory by juxtaposing Proust's writings prior to *In Search of Lost Time* with *Time Regained*, the final volume of the novel, not mentioning the other volumes. But his theory applies equally well to the volumes of the novel. The 1911 typescripts that comprise the first version of *In Search of Lost Time* consist of *Swann's Way*, parts of *In the Shadow of Young Girls in Flower* (with no Albertine), portions of *The Guermantes Way*, drafts of the material on homosexuality, and "numerous drafts of *Time Regained*." *Time Regained* is present at the beginning of *In Search of Lost Time* as well as at the end when, in the spring of 1922, Proust works on it prior to his death in November. See Marion Schmid, "The Birth and Development of *A la Recherche du Temps Perdu*," in Bales, *Cambridge Companion to Proust*, 64–65, 70.

54. Girard, *Oedipus Unbound*, 9–10.

55. Ibid., 11.

56. Ibid., 21.

57. Ibid.

58. Ibid., 21–22. Girard states that "*The Past Recaptured* [*Finding Time Again*] was entirely conceived, if not entirely written, before any other portion of the novel. This conclusion is, therefore, both an end and a beginning" (Girard, *Proust*, 10). The core of the final volume of the novel, *Finding Time Again*, had been drafted by 1910. See the introduction by Ian Patterson in *Finding Time Again*, ix. Segments of *Swann's Way* were published in *Le Figaro* in January 1912 and by Grassett in November 1913. Lydia Davis's statement on the compositional history of the novel is more subtle but equally clear: As she says of the first volume in her introduction to the 2002 Penguin edition of *Swann's Way*, "Even as he wrote the opening, however, he *foresaw* the conclusion, and in fact the end of the book was completed before the middle began to grow." See Proust, *Swann's Way*, xiii; emphasis mine. *Finding Time Again* would not be published until after Proust's death. When he died, it was not yet in typescript. The margins were filled with changes and additions, and additional pieces of paper were glued to early versions of the manuscript. See Proust, *Finding Time Again*, ix–x.

59. Girard, *Oedipus Unbound*, 13.

60. Ibid., 14.

61. Ibid., 15.

62. Ibid., 22.

63. Ibid., 19–20.

64. Ibid., 49.

65. Ibid., 56.

66. Ibid., 23.

67. Girard notes that the chorus in *Oedipus the King* says that oracles are now disdained and that has caused Thebes's problems. Acknowledging that the chorus risks granting too much power to an oracle, Girard still affirms Sophocles's recognition of the oracle. In reviving with his art the forgotten oracle, Sophocles encodes revelation and transcendence (ibid., 26).

68. Ibid., 16.

69. Mitchell, *Siblings*, 54. Girard observes only Oedipus's sphinx whom he identifies as the paternal obstacle in *Oedipus the King*. As a consequence, the sphinx is not oracular but symptomatic of how Oedipus lives subject to the constraints of mimetic desire and a sacrificial economy (Girard, *Oedipus Unbound*, 29.)

70. See Girard, *Oedipus Unbound*, 21, for details of this journey in Girard's discussion of the oracle. The express application of this argument to *Antigone* is mine.

71. Sophocles, *Antigone*, ll. 853–56.

72. Girard, *A Theatre of Envy*, 340–41. Texts cited by Girard are Mark 16 1–4; *A Winter's Tale* V.ii.37–38; and *Othello*, V.ii.63–65). Interestingly, Lacan invokes the notion of scandal when he discusses how Antigone's claim to act as she did only for a brother has been a scandal (*de scandale*) to interpreters (*commentateurs s'en soient scandalisés*). Lacan, *The Ethics of Psychoanalysis*, 255–56, 280; Jacques Lacan, *Le Séminaire de Jacques Lacan Livre VII*, ed. Jacques-Alain Miller (Paris: Seuil, 1986), 297–98, 326.

73. Griffith in *Sophocles' "Antigone"*, 268.

74. Ibid., 850.

75. Girard, *Oedipus Unbound*, 10.

76. For a clear account by Girard of the notion of the *skandalon* see René Girard and Willard Swartley, "Response by René Girard," in *Violence Renounced*, 310. Imitation of Christ is necessary to avoid scandals. Antigone, *figura Christi* of the ancient world, effects that *figura* with the result that the power of scandal vanishes.

77. Debates over the translation of *Antigone* ll. 853–56 well illustrate this point. According to Dora Pozzi, "stumble" has become the preferred translation among interpreters who understand that the chorus is faulting Antigone for having challenged Creon's authority. Dike (Justice) sides with that authority. Others have suggested that Antigone "kicks" the altar of Justice. But if she does so, the meaning of her actions does not change. Rather, Antigone's "kick" merely extends her inappropriate actions to include another institution of authority. Further, Pozzi argues that "kick" can only awkwardly be reconciled with the grammatical requirements of the Greek. For her part, Pozzi suggests that Antigone does not stumble but "falls on her knees," depicting her willingness to be sacrificed. Pozzi says that Antigone's action brings her to the "limit of daring." Moreover, in offering herself up, Antigone is able to counter Creon's perverted ritual of sacrifice (Antigone's entombment) with her own "true sacrifice" that will cancel the pollution of her family. Whether Antigone "stumbles" or "falls" against the altar, Pozzi suggests that Antigone reaches "the limit" with her action. See Dora Pozzi, "The Metaphor of Sacrifice in Sophocles' 'Antigone' 853–856," *Hermes* 117, no. 4 (1989): 500–505. Pozzi, exemplifying an agonistic history of translation, does

not appreciate the radicalism of Antigone's gesture. As Griffith and Girard suggest, not only Antigone but also translators stumble over her words and actions. At the limit, Antigone's actions do not neatly fit into any *known* scheme because she is moving toward *transformative* action beyond the limits of a sacrificial economy.

78. Caruth, *Unclaimed Experience*, 70–71.

79. Ibid., 91–92.

80. Ibid., 100.

81. Contemporary psychotherapy concurs. In *Trauma and Recovery*, psychiatrist Judith Lewis Herman identifies as key features of recovery from trauma reconnection with others in which the victim of trauma acts on behalf of others to make their lives safer. Some persons take on explicit commitments to social actions that embrace educational, political, or legal initiatives to prevent victimization by others in the future. In each of these instances, healing is interwoven with an ethical commitment to the other. See Judith Herman, *Trauma and Recovery: The Aftermath of Violence—from Domestic Abuse to Political Terror* (New York: Basic Books, 1997), 207–9.

82. The contagion of trauma and healing is attested to by psychoanalyst A. Modell. He writes that affect is at the core of healing in therapeutic relationships that aim to address trauma: "Affects are communicative and contagious, so that the other person is involved in the affective repetition and will collude, either consciously or unconsciously, in confirming or disconfirming the subject's category of perception." As quoted in Bessie Van der Kolk and Onno Van der Hart, "The Intrusive Past: The Flexibility of Memory and the Engraving of Trauma," in *Trauma: Explorations in Memory*, ed. Cathy Caruth (Baltimore: Johns Hopkins University Press, 1995), 168.

Chapter 6. Antigone and the Ethics of Intimacy

1. Sophocles, *Oedipus at Colonus*, ll. 283, 513, 576.

2. Ibid., ll. 1132–37. Trauma can be exacerbated by others' responses. Others experience dread and fear when they encounter a traumatized being, and their powerful emotions are mirrored in their faces. See Jennifer L. Griffiths, *Traumatic Possessions: The Body and Memory in African American Women's Writing and Performance* (Charlottesville: University of Virginia Press, 2010), 175.

3. For a discussion of this process in a general context of trauma recovery, see Jones, *Trauma and Grace*, 158ff.

4. Kristeva, *Powers of Horror*, 87. The ritual is described at Sophocles, *Oedipus at Colonus*, ll. 466–91.

5. Jones, *Trauma and Grace*, 160. Trauma theory indicates that trauma is not so much overcome as it is borne: those who have been wounded, are able, at last, to bear up. Bearing our pain typically is made possible with the support of others, whether in formally therapeutic or informal settings.

6. Sophocles, *Oedipus at Colonus*, l. 1760.

7. A. E. Haigh, *The Tragic Drama of the Greeks* (Oxford: Clarendon Press, 1896), 198–200.

8. This apt phrase attesting to the power of ritual is from Jones, *Trauma and Grace*, 165.

9. Girard, *Things Hidden*, 244.

10. Ibid., 19–20.

11. Ibid., 23.

12. The strongest language confining ritual to a sacrificial economy belongs to Girard's interlocutor,

Jean-Michel Oughourlian. Summing up Girard's discussion, Oughourlian states, "Your point, then, is that all prohibitions and rituals can be related to mimetic conflict. The common denominator is the same, but there is a paradox in that what is prohibited in one case is required in another. If the mimetic crisis is indeed as threatening as our reading of prohibitions leads us to believe, it would seem incomprehensible that the ritual should be an attempt to reproduce, often in a frighteningly realistic manner, precisely what societies fear the most in normal times, with an apparently well-justified fear. There is no innocent, harmless mimesis, and one cannot ritually imitate the crisis of doubles without running the risk of inciting real violence." In this passage, Girard does not challenge Oughourlian's summative comments. Ibid., 21.

13. In *Battling to the End*, Girard acknowledges positive mimesis. He typifies it in terms of "positive identification" (131). Girard further describes positive mimesis as an "innermost mediation" experienced through the imitation of Christ (133). So also does he suggest that an "intimate mediation transforms mimeticism, opening the door to the other side of violence (205).

14. Girard does acknowledge the existence of rituals "that include no sacrifice whatsoever[,] not even of a symbolic kind," but he suggests that discussion of this point would be a digression and he does not elaborate (Girard, *Things Hidden*, 23). The Eucharist is an obvious candidate for the discussion that Girard defers. Girard begins a discussion that could develop that point when he affirms the origins of the Eucharist in "archaic cannibalism" (Mitchell, *Siblings*, 217). But even as Girard tries to show how recognition of scapegoating in the Gospels, as it comes from Christ, transforms a history of sacrifice, he does not explain how the Eucharist is similarly transformed from a cannibalistic rite into a ritual of Christlike imitation. In *Covenant of Peace*, Willard Swartley offers the kind of analysis of the Eucharist not yet fully developed by Girard. See Willard M. Swartley, *Covenant of Peace: The Missing Peace in New Testament Theology and Ethics* (Grand Rapids, MI: Eerdmans, 2006), 177–88.

15. The literature on trauma makes this point. In addition, scholars of Christianity and Islam who explore an ethical pedagogy drawing on an Aristotelian model note how ritual acts create corresponding internal dispositions. The notion of *habitus* (Bourdieu) expresses this ethical pedagogy; scholars of medieval Christianity and contemporary Islam establish this Aristotelian understanding of piety as a bodily learning that produces virtue not as knowledge one possesses but as something that one is. See Mahmood, *Politics of Piety*.

16. Juliet Mitchell, *Mad Men and Medusas: Reclaiming Hysteria* (New York: Basic Books, 2001), 281–83.

17. They concur on this point with Lacanian analysts who assert that memories are not held in a hidden reservoir of our minds. To the contrary, taking up Freud's notion of deferral (*nachtragichkeit*), Lacanian analysts locate trauma in traces without content or origin. These traces can be rearranged and retranscribed but they are never "found." Ibid., 285.

18. Jones, *Trauma and Grace*, 86, 92–93.

19. Bolens, *The Style of Gestures*, 3.

20. Ibid., 11–16; See also Gallese, "Two Sides of Mimesis," 89.

21. Bolens, *The Style of Gestures*, 23.

22. I take this term from Diane Jonte-Pace, "At Home in the Uncanny: Freudian Representations of Death, Mothers, and the Afterlife," *Journal of the American Academy of Religion* 64, no. 1 (1996): 61–88. Jonte-Pace argues that much of Freud's work was oriented toward a "master thesis" about death that featured a death drive oriented toward the father and the Oedipal paradigm. But especially when Freud was talking about religion, a "counter thesis" oriented toward an uncanny

maternal body "haunted" Freud. Jonte-Pace's argument is highly suggestive of the position I argue here.

23. Sophocles, *Oedipus at Colonus*, ll. 1660–65.

24. Scholars have struggled to understand relations among the goddesses depicted in *Oedipus at Colonus*, often conflating their identities. One interpretive strand has assigned especially ancient origins to the Erinyes: they are a curse-force rather than fully developed deities (Lewis Richard Farnell, *The Cults of the Greek States* [New Rochelle, NY: Caratzas Brothers, 1977], 437–38). This line of thought has the merit of accounting for the deeply personal association between the Erinyes and persons who have been wronged (an association to which Padel is especially sensitive). Moreover, the curse-force theory explains why more powerful persons have more potent Erinyes (Farnell, 439). Other scholars, citing evidence from ritual sites in Greece, believe that the curse-force is an attenuated form of an earlier earth-goddess. Her powers would be summoned by the curser; in later times, this power would be detached from its association with a deity (Farnell, 440). Johnston argues that "Erinu" is an early form of "Erinyes" and appears on a tablet specifying cultic worship (*Restless Dead*, 250). Moreover, in arguing that "Erinyes" was the name for the negative aspect of a dual-nature goddess (Eumenides being the positive) she argues that it would be unlikely for cultic practices to directly invoke that side; instead, suppliants would summon the positive form (270). Robertson addresses the association of the Erinyes and the Eumenides. According to Robertson, some scholars (Jameson, Jordan, Kotansky, Dubois) have frequently suggested that they are two names for two side of the same powers, kind and cruel (Noel Robertson, *Religion and Reconciliation in Greek Cities: The Sacred Laws of Selinus and Cyrene* [New York: Oxford University Press, 2009], 89). Hogan concurs with that analysis when he writes of lines 40–43 in *Oedipus at Colonus* that the "daughters of darkness and earth" are the Erinyes in their violent aspect and the Eumenides in their benign aspect (*Commentary on the Plays*, 80). In distinction from Johnston, Robertson states that he joins Clinton in suggesting that there is no historical or archeological evidence for cult worship of the Erinyes, whereas strong evidence exists for worship of the Eumenides (Robertson, *Religion and Reconciliation*, 89 n. 7). Johnston suggests that, from the fifth century, "Erinyes" is used to describe the negative aspects of the Semnai Theai and the Eumenides (which she understands to be similar, though important in different areas of Greece). She states that the three entities do not have an "original identity"; however, they share similarities that enable the tragedians to link the three (Johnston, *Restless Dead*, 268). Farnell and Robertson agree that Aeschylus's effort to link the Erinyes with the Eumenides succeeds with the popular imagination and is taken up by Sophocles (*Oedipus at Colonus*, l. 44) even though the links he forges *are without historical grounding in cultic practice*. By contrast, *distinct sites for worship of the Eumenides are found at Colonus and for the Semnai Theai at the Areopagus*. The Semnai are earth goddesses who serve as guardians of society and oversee laws against bloodshed. They receive cereal and nonalcoholic libations. Farnell argues that the Eumenides and the Semnai Theai *are* "of the same nature and origin: they are both earth goddesses and both receive the same wineless libations" (*Cults of the Greek States*, 442). Robertson's research, drawing on publication in 1993 of the contents of a mid-fifth century BCE tablet describing ritual calendars, which was found in an archeological dig in Sicily, builds on Farnell's, offering clarifying insights. Rituals associated with the Eumenides and the Semnai Theai are described on the tablet (Robertson, *Religion and Reconciliation*, 4). Robertson says that the Eumenides are associated with rituals of spring. Both the Semnai Theai and the Eumenides are agrarian deities: the former are associated with an Athenian cult and the latter with a cult in Peloponnesus. Their worship is matched in time (early spring—the end of February) and in "all essentials" (105). Women are the worshippers in both cults, and they carry torches to plunge into the earth to bring warmth. Cultic sites for the Eumenides and the Semnai Theai are distinct; however, in *Oedipus at Colonus* they are conflated as Oedipus alternately uses the name Eumenides (ll. 42, 486) and Semnai Theai (ll. 89–90,

458) as well as *semno* (ll. 41, 100), even as he states the names are a mystery (ll. 43, 129) and joins the tradition in referring to the Semnai Theai as the "nameless goddesses" (l. 123). Further, the goddesses appear as the Erinyes at lines 1299 and 1434. Like Farnell, Robertson attributes Sophocles's use of all three names to the influence of Aeschylus. Interestingly, he also sees some historical evidence for the conflation of the Eumenides with the Semnai Theai. An inscription of "Semnai Theai" on a roof tile that was reused for a second-century grave is located approximately 850 meters from the hill at Colonus. This artifact places the Semnai Theai closer to Colonus than to the Areopagus, suggesting that Sophocles's attribution is perhaps not solely an act of creative conflation (Robertson, *Religion and Reconciliation*, 107). In sum, the association of the Erinyes with the Eumenides is solely the work of Aeschylus. However, that conflation resonates powerfully with the tragic poets who follow him and with the popular imagination. That Johnston argues for a more balanced profile of the Erinyes, suggesting that no Greek divinity is entirely negative, could explain the appeal of Aeschylus's conflation (Johnston, *Restless Dead*, 250). The Eumenides and Semnai Theai are distinct traditions of agrarian goddess worship; however, they are highly similar and their conflation by Sophocles is not at odds with the historical and archeological record (Robertson, *Religion and Reconciliation*, 106–7). In what follows, I take into account the historical joining of the Eumenides and the Semnai Theai as well as the creative conflation of the Erinyes (for which there is no evidence of cultic worship) with both the Eumenides and the Semnai Theai. I especially make note of the powerful resonance that the three-way alignment and conflation of these goddesses has for the tragic poets and their audiences and draw on that creative alignment in my own analysis. While acknowledging the conflation or fusion of positive and negative features in these three entities, I do not argue for their utter confusion, which would justify using a single English word to describe them, as does the Lloyd-Jones when he refers to the Semnai Theai as "goddesses" (89) and the Erinyes (Oedipus's daemon) as "goddesses" (1390) in his translation of *Oedipus at Colonus*. I carefully distinguish when supplication of the Semnai Theai in ritual is directed to their positive attributes and powers, whether the Erinyes are understood to be the "dark side" of the Semnai Theai or independent entities.

25. Sophocles, *Antigone*, ll. 586–603.

26. Padel, *In and Out of the Mind*, 34.

27. Ibid., 35.

28. Ibid., 88.

29. Sophocles, *Antigone*, l. 929.

30. The daemonic is associated not only with the Erinyes but also with other winged creatures. Eagles and vultures are the most common of these aerial assailants. Just as birds tear at the flesh, so also are daemons such as the Erinyes likened to these carnivorous invaders of the body. The emotional impact of these figures is traceable to their invasive nature: their assault begins in the air, mingles with it, but becomes an attack on the innermost elements of human being. See Padel, *In and Out of the Mind*, 129–31. Science fiction film visually conveys some of the sense of assault by alien flying creatures that featured so prominently in the tragic landscape. So also do these films enable us to sense a world teaming with powers that, whether beneficial or harmful, observe no boundaries of the human body. We may think, for example, of the rapacious velociraptor of *Jurassic Park* or the invasive, life-destroying creatures of the *Alien* movie series featuring Sigourney Weaver. To the extent that our dreams feature voracious dinosaurs or monstrous creatures invading our bodies or exploding out of them, the psychological field of trauma and the imaginative possibilities of traumatic anxiety merge.

31. Ibid., 141, ix.

32. Ibid., 138.

33. Ibid., 161.

34. Ibid., 139. Kirkwood conveys a similar understanding of the daemonic when he writes, "It is the driver, the guide, the fulfiller; and nearly always it brings to pass suffering and disaster. The 'daemonic' seems to be Sophocles' customary way of expressing the dark and enigmatic agency by which disaster is flung suddenly upon unsuspecting man. Neither wholly separate from deity nor identical with it, neither wholly external to man nor entirely a part of his own nature, neither an impersonal force nor a wholly definable spirit, the 'daemonic' is as close to an answer as Sophocles gives to the question whence suffering comes to man" (Kirkwood, *Study of Sophoclean Drama*, 285).

35. Padel suggests that we err if we claim the Greeks were only "personifying" emotions: "Personification as the fifth century inherited and used it was not an isolatable trick of language, but part of explaining what happened to and inside people." They are summoned and dealt with in the cultic, ritual lives of the people. See Padel, *In and Out of the Mind*, 158–59.

36. Ibid., 164.

37. Johnston, *Restless Dead*, 252–57.

38. Padel, *In and Out of the Mind*, 165. In "Erinyes" we see also the Greek word "eris," which means "strife" or "rivalry." See Helen H. Bacon, "Woman's Two Faces: Sophocles' View of the Tragedy of Oedipus and His Family," in *Sexuality of Women: Scientific Proceedings of the Tenth Annual Spring Meeting of the American Academy of Psychoanalysis* (New York: Grune and Stratton, 1966): 17.

39. Padel, *In and Out of the Mind*, 167.

40. Ibid., 172. Padel observes that some scholars think that the Erinyes live in tragedy only as fictional creations of the poets. But Padel finds it unreasonable to believe that the Erinyes are the only daemons not to have survived into the fifth century, especially when other daemons enjoy a healthy, vibrant existence, as detailed in chapters 2, 5, and 7 of Padel's *In and Out of the Mind*.

41. Sophocles, *Oedipus at Colonus*, l. 1299.

42. Ibid., l. 1434.

43. Ibid., ll. 1370–75, 1390.

44. Parker, *Miasma*, 107.

45. Padel, *In and Out of the Mind*, 171. Padel cautions against "psychologizing" the trauma undergone by figures in Greek tragedy. Gods, not the psyche, control life in the fifth century BCE. Padel does not challenge all interpretations of tragedy grounded in psychology; rather, she is critical of dualistic interpretations that align the psyche with an interior space whose contents, often repressed, belong to an individual. I would suggest that Padel is opposing the kind of psychological understanding of traumatic memory that Mitchell assigns to ego psychology, which locates trauma in "repressed memories" and treats the unconscious as a kind of private container of the individual that is accessible only through therapeutic probing. But, as I have described above, Lacanian accounts of trauma, at odds with ego psychology, are compatible with Padel's notions: Not belonging to a subject, memory is subject to persistent deferral, and trauma flowers over and over again along trace marks that are given to bodily expression. Fifth-century Greece gives powerful testimony to these trace marks with the Erinyes, who embody the hallucinatory perceptions typical of trauma. Indeed, when Padel says that these daemonic presences control one's life, she captures the power of trauma, which can be broken only through a reorientation

of one's whole existence. That reorientation of one's whole being, whether in ancient Greece or today, alone brings change and healing.

46. Van der Kolk and Van der Hart, "The Intrusive Past," 163. Language that Padel uses to describe daemonic powers directly matches Mitchell's depiction of trauma. Drawing on Lacan, Mitchell observes that traumatic memories *flower over and over along the same trace marks* (Mitchell, *Mad Men and Medusas*, 285–88). These marks can be rearranged and repeated, but they will not offer themselves up to healing transformation. Padel notes that the daemon in tragic poetry is depicted as a *flowering* growth. But its growth outward (*exanthein, thremma hudras*) is not a celebratory profusion of spring blooms; rather, growth is poisonous, or, if initially is associated with health, the growth withers (Padel, *In and Out of the Mind*, 134). The flowering of daemonic powers of the Erinyes thus brings to mind the spreading cells of a cancer or a deadly contagion, not a healthy profusion of vegetation.

47. Sophocles, *Antigone*, l. 603. See Padel for a discussion of and justification for this reading of line 603 (Padel, *In and Out of the Mind*, 186, and see especially n. 61).

48. Sophocles, *Antigone*, ll. 1660, 1770.

49. Sophocles, *Oedipus at Colonus*, l. 74.

50. Ibid., l. 40.

51. Kristeva, *Powers of Horror*, 86–88.

52. Sophocles, *Oedipus at Colonus*, l. 90. The translation is Grene's (*Sophocles*, trans. David Grene [Chicago: University of Chicago Press, 1991] as quoted in Keltner, *Kristeva*, 115). In Lloyd-Jones's translation, Oedipus refers to "a seat of the dread goddesses and a shelter."

53. Griffiths, *Traumatic Possessions*, 2.

54. Lawrence J. Kirmayer, "Landscapes of Memory: Trauma, Narrative, and Dissociation," in *Tense Past: Cultural Essays in Trauma and Memory*, ed. Paul Antze and Michael Lambek (New York: Routledge, 1996), 175.

55. Griffiths, *Traumatic Possessions*, 6.

56. Sophocles, *Oedipus at Colonus*, ll. 510–50.

57. In writing about healing from trauma, Jones mentions that acupuncture, yoga, as well as prayer are healing 'rituals." In each of her examples, a tactile bridge from traumatic to narrative memory enables one to emerge from the timeless present of trauma into a present oriented toward acting and loving others. See Jones, *Trauma and Grace*, 160–61.

58. As established in a note above, the Semnai Theai and the Eumenides are conflated in *Oedipus at Colonus*. Sophocles refers to their names as a "mystery" and joins the tradition in calling them the "nameless goddesses." Given that Robertson has documented an inscription referencing the Semnai Theai on a tile found near Colonus (as discussed above), I choose this representative appellation in what follows.

59. Sophocles, *Oedipus at Colonus*, ll. 101, 466–507. See also Matthew Dillon, *Girls and Women in Classical Greek Religion* (New York: Routledge, 2003), 71; Robertson, *Religion and Reconciliation*, 108.

60. Robertson, *Religion and Reconciliation*, 110.

61. Ibid., 110–11.

62. Ibid., 111–12.

63. Ibid., 110–12. Johnston underscores the significance of this ritual by comparing it with a psychagogic ritual. In this ritual the location of a dead boy whose ghost is causing trouble cannot be known. A black sheep is led around, forced to walk on its hind legs. When it finally collapses, a sacrifice is performed. Johnston suggests that, with the violation of the Semnai Theai's altar at the Areopagus, a similar technique may have been employed to locate the divinities. Once traced to their new sacred locales, altars could be built and the goddess supplicated (Johnston, *Restless Dead*, 279).

64. Johnston, *Restless Dead*, 281.

65. Sophocles, *Oedipus at Colonus*, l. 475.

66. Johnston, *Restless Dead*, 281. Johnston suggests that the story of Epimenides's cure probably dates from the late seventh or very early sixth century BCE and thus is older than the plot of the *Oresteia*, which it very much resembles, albeit with heightened references to revenge-seeking divinities (284). In arguing that the ritual referenced in *Oedipus at Colonus* moves away from revenge sacrifice toward collaborative, community building, I follow Girard's analysis of ritual. As discussed above, he allows for ritual to diffuse mimetic conflict, as the black and white sheep surely do. I also agree that ritual evocation of the black and white sheep is a fragile, first step away from sacrifice (just as the Crucifixion of Jesus is a fragile step). Because sheep are killed, even though the outcome of the ritual lifts it out of a sacrificial nexus, the ritual could yet be returned to a sacrificial nexus. However, because I focus on the ritual history within the context of Oedipus's life, the trajectory I follow with this ritual does not move back into ancient Greece but forward as it spirals toward transcendence.

67. Although another ritual associated with the Semnai Theai—burying torches in the ground—is absent from *Oedipus at Colonus*, the association of the Semnai Theai with the earth is maintained in *Oedipus at Colonus* even in the absence of this particular ritual. Euphorion confirms this association in his genealogy for the Semnai Theai of Colonus, for which he finds support in a passage from *Oedipus at Colonus*, The chorus, singing of the sacred grove in which Oedipus finds himself, depict it as "fed by the dew from heaven, the narcissus with its lovely clusters, the ancient crown of the two great goddesses." Euphorion describes these goddesses as the "frightful granddaughters of Phorcys." Drawing on an orphic genealogy, Euphorion links the Semnai wholly to chthonic rather than Olympian gods (Robertson, *Religion and Reconciliation*, 125–27). Phorcys is an "Old Man of the Sea," a parent of monsters. In Orphic genealogy he mates with Hecate, and Persephone is their daughter. This genealogy locates the Semnai Theai among the deities of the earth, in contrast to the Olympian gods of civic religion. Thus, the Semnai Theai are goddesses who dwell in the earth, forces whose "unlighted foundation" contrasts with the gods on high. That sacrifice is alien to this terrain is attested to by links between the rituals to the Semnai Theai and Orphic genealogy. Lucien Scubla links the Orphic tradition with an antisacrificial stance not unlike that which Girard sees in the Gospels. Six centuries before Jesus, that tradition "condemned with vigor all forms of blood sacrifice and already reproached men with having founded their polis on murder, not only in the myth of the dismemberment of Dionysus by the Titans but also in the story of the death of Orpheus, savagely lynched for having denounced the pernicious character of sacrificial rites." Girard confirms that the Orphic tradition "comes close to the Christian conception in some respects" but states that its vision is fragmentary and lacks the power of the gospel. See Lucien Scubla, "The Christianity of René Girard and the Nature of Religion," trans. Mark R. Anspach, in *Violence and Truth: On the Work of René Girard*, ed. Paul Dumouchel (Stanford, CA: Stanford University Press, 1988), 161; Mitchell, *Siblings*, 212. The narrative memory underscored by Euphorion's orphic genealogy of the Semnai Theai establishes important features of a nexus for healing featuring earth and its divinities in which Oedipus can at last find himself able to bear his trauma.

68. Sophocles, *Oedipus at Colonus*, ll. 131–33, 156–57, 488–89.

69. Ibid., ll. 120–35. See also Robertson, *Religion and Reconciliation*, 115; Silvia Montiglio, *Silence in the Land of Logos* (Princeton, NJ: Princeton University Press, 2010), 39.

70. Montiglio, *Silence in the Land of Logos*, 13. To pray in one's heart is to be absolutely silent.

71. Sophocles, *Antigone*, ll. 483–84. Robertson associates the worship of the Semnai Theai with Nine Gates, a formal entrance to their closed precinct. In turn, the Nine Gates are associated with silence. The allusion to Ismene's gesture thus links her silence with supplication of the Semnai Theai. See Robertson, *Religion and Reconciliation*, 115–16.

72. Montiglio, *Silence in the Land of Logos*, 18–19.

73. Ibid., 21–22. Montiglio's example in this context is Orestes, who travels in exile, undertaking a long, silent journey, in order to work out his pollution. When he arrives in the end at Athens, Apollo permits him finally to speak.

74. Jones affirms that healing from trauma in therapeutic contexts with which she is familiar proceeds from embodied work to speech. See Jones, *Trauma and Grace*, 94–95.

75. Robertson, *Religion and Reconciliation*, 117.

76. My assertion applies whether the Erinyes are "the other side" of the Semnai Theai or distinct entities.

77. In analyzing Aeschylus's *Eumenides*, Girard conveys a similar suspicion about the tidy amalgamation of the Erinyes with the Eumenides. He points out that the Erinyes, in celebrating a new world in which love and joy will play a greater role, do not disavow hatred; they retain a place for unanimity in violence in order to "hate with a single soul." They would have the city accommodate itself to violence "under the pretext that 'much wrong in the world thereby is healed.'" But violence cannot be domesticated or "shepherded" in this way, writes Girard. It lurks beneath the surface to rise again. See René Girard, *Job: The Victim of His People*, trans. Yvonne Freccero (Stanford, CA: Stanford University Press, 1987), 147–51. As I argue throughout, where Girard asserts in this discussion that only the Bible speaks of the victim as victim, I include Sophocles's *Antigone* among texts that critically expose the generative mechanism.

78. My analysis is indebted to Emily Zakin, "Marrying the City: Intimate Strangers and the Fury of Democracy," in McCoskey and Zakin, *Bound by the City*, 179. Zakin analyzes Aeschylus's *The Eumenides*, tracing the transformation of the Erinyes into the Eumenides.

79. Kristeva, *Strangers to Ourselves*, 191.

80. Girard, *Deceit, Desire, and the Novel*, 298.

81. Girard, *Oedipus Unbound*, 9.

82. Ibid., 23. This space, recognized by Girard, is presumed empty by him in *Oedipus Unbound*.

83. Kristeva, *Powers of Horror*, 89.

84. Sophocles, *Antigone*, ll. 420–35.

85. Girard, *Oedipus Unbound*, 87.

86. Kristeva, *Strangers to Ourselves*, 183.

87. Sophocles, *Antigone*, ll. 332–70.

88. Martin Heidegger, *Hölderlin's Hymn "The Ister"*, trans. William McNeill and Julia Davis (Bloomington: Indiana University Press, 1996), 61. See Sjöholm, *The Antigone Complex*, 67.

89. Heidegger, *Hölderlin's Hymn "The Ister,"* 72.

90. Ibid., 75.

91. Ibid., 76.

92. Sjöholm, *The Antigone Complex*, 68–69.

93. Lacan, *The Ethics of Psychoanalysis*, 275–76.

94. Sophocles, *Antigone*, ll. 840–65.

95. Ibid., ll. 895–900.

96. Kristeva, *Strangers to Ourselves*, 191–92.

97. Mitchell, *Siblings*, 44.

98. Mitchell writes that children's games such as "musical chairs" and "duck, duck, goose" are all about seriality. Children in play to manage the question of space and how it can be shared (or not) (ibid., 54).

99. Carol Jacobs, "Dusting Antigone," *MLN* 111, no. 5 (1996): 904.

100. Mitchell, *Siblings*, 44.

101. Mohammad Kowsar, "Lacan's 'Antigone': A Case Study in Psychoanalytical Ethics," *Theatre Journal* 42, no. 1 (1990): 97, doi:10.2307/3207560.

102. P. 46 of seminar VII by Lacan as cited in Kowsar, "Lacan's 'Antigone,'" 99.

103. Kowsar, "Lacan's 'Antigone,'" 101.

104. Ibid., 105.

105. Oliver, *Colonization of Psychic Space*, 144.

106. Ibid., 143.

107. Sophocles, *Antigone*, l. 929.

108. Oliver, *Colonization of Psychic Space*, 175.

109. Kristeva, *Sense and Non-Sense of Revolt*, 54; Oliver, *Colonization of Psychic Space*, 148. Because Hegel, Sartre, Freud, and Lacan share similar vocabularies and concerns about humankind, that we demarcate Kristeva's views is important. Oliver very well articulates Kristeva's difference from Hegel: "While for Hegel only reason can resolve the conflict that engenders self-conscious subjectivity, for Kristeva only the imagination operating at the level of the unconscious can engender self-conscious, but always only provisional, subjectivity" (148). Kristeva's position on Hegel echoes my position on mimetic theory: Sensory experience plays a critical role in opening humans to healing alternatives to ontological illness. Routes of access to sensory experience identified by psychoanalytic theory, especially Kristeva's, helpfully augment mimetic theory.

110. Girard, *Violence and the Sacred*, 204.

111. Oliver, *Colonization of Psychic Space*, 147.

112. Ibid., 149.

113. Sophocles, *Antigone*, l. 443.

114. Oliver, *Colonization of Psychic Space*, 146.

115. Julia Kristeva, *The Portable Kristeva*, ed. Kelly Oliver (New York: Columbia University Press, 2002), 408; Oliver, *Colonization of Psychic Space*, 173.

116. Oliver, *Colonization of Psychic Space*, 174.

117. Ibid., 176–77.

118. Sjöholm, *The Antigone Complex*, 100.

119. Ibid.

120. Ibid., 101.

121. Ibid., 107.

122. Girard, *I See Satan Fall*, 15.

123. Ibid.

124. Ibid., 40.

125. Lacan, *The Ethics of Psychoanalysis*, 272. Writes Lacan of Sophocles's heroes (with the exception of Oedipus in *Oedipus the King*): "They are characters who find themselves right away in a limit zone, find themselves between life and death." Later he says of Antigone's claim on behalf of Polyneices that "the stance of the-race-is-run is nowhere better illustrated than here" (279).

126. Sjöholm, *The Antigone Complex*, 102.

127. Ibid., 107.

128. Sophocles, *Antigone*, l. 929.

129. Sjöholm, *The Antigone Complex*, 126.

130. Ibid., 108–9.

131. Diprose, *The Bodies of Women*, 18–21.

132. Sjöholm, *The Antigone Complex*, 127–28.

133. Ibid., 130.

134. Ibid., 135.

135. Ibid., 140.

136. *Sophocles' "Antigone"*, ed. Griffith, 1282.

137. Sophocles, *Oedipus at Colonus*, l. 1282; see Charles Segal, *Sophocles' Tragic World: Divinity, Nature, Society* (Cambridge: Harvard University Press, 1998), 134.

138. Rehm, *Marriage to Death*, 68.

139. Ibid., 67.

140. Ibid., 67–69.

141. Sophocles, *Oedipus at Colonus*, ll. 1183–89.

142. Ibid., ll. 1188–89.

143. Ibid., ll. 1240–42.

144. Hogan states baldly that "a member of Creon's family must be sacrificed to appease the God." Line 1302 states that the one who dies is called Megareus. Steiner points to some ambiguity in whether Megareus's death was self-sacrificial or sacrificial. See Hogan, *Commentary on the Plays*, 168; George Steiner, *Antigones* (New Haven: Yale University Press, 1996), 245. In *Phoenician Women* Euripides calls him Menoeceus and presents him choosing to "go and save the city and give my life to die for this country" (Euripides, *Electra, Phoenician Women, Bacchae, Iphigenia at Aulis*, trans. Cecelia Eaton Luschnig and Paul Woodruff (Indianapolis: Hackett, 2011), ll. 995–1000. Denial of sacrifice is endemic in sacrificial economies, according to Girard.

145. Montiglio, *Silence in the Land of Logos*, 160.

146. Ibid., 243; Sophocles, *Oedipus at Colonus*, l. 1445.

147. In his groundbreaking study of masks in the Greek theater, Gregory McCart sheds light on Eurydice's silence when he describes how the performance of tragedy by masked actors changed the experience of drama for actors and audience. He comments specifically on how a masked, silent actor exerted a compelling presence on the Greek stage. Agreeing with Montiglio that silence is uncommon on the stage, McCart points out that when the audience is confronted with the masked actor, the theatrical effect of silence is all the more profound. See Gregory McCart, "Masks in Greek and Roman Theatre," in *The Cambridge Companion to Greek and Roman Theatre*, ed. Marianne McDonald and Michael Walton (New York: Cambridge University Press, 2007), 253–54. The masked actor cannot rely on changes in his facial expressions to elicit from the audience specific emotions and thoughts. Rather than create an illusion of emotion, the masked actor must demonstrate emotion through his entire presence: gestures, bodily demeanor, and silence drive the actor's performance (252). McCart helps us to understand how masked actors make trauma manifest on the Greek stage. Trauma, an amplified, endless presence, is well depicted by an unchanging mask. The mask covering the faces of the actors prevent the audience from seeing in facial expressions an actor's musings about past experiences or his anticipation or dread of the future. As a consequence, the unchanging features of the mask offer a visual representation of traumatic memory, what Karmen MacKendrick calls that "strange forgetfulness in which the body itself cannot forget, cannot let go, but must recreate the past." See Karmen MacKendrick, *Fragmentation and Memory: Meditations on Christian Doctrine* (New York: Fordham University Press, 2008), 74. If a tragedy is to move from traumatic repetition toward transformation, how might a masked actor attest to change? As we previously have noted with Jones and Caruth, sensory experience and witnesses are critical to change. Are these precursors to change visible on the Greek stage, or is tragedy synonymous with unending trauma? McCart's analysis of masks helps us to see how both conditions are met in *Antigone*. Because masks remove from the stage the actor's face as a primary conduit of emotion, an actor's broad, embodied performance, especially his gestures, become of critical import. In order to interact with another actor, an actor must turn his entire body; in order to make a point, an actor must draw his whole body into a gesture. McCart writes that when his students and he first began to work with masks in performance of Greek tragedy, the actors' bodies appeared to be too small: The students looked "like walking tadpoles." The students had to offer much more strongly physical performances; when they did so, the tadpole effect was eliminated. See McCart, "Masks in Greek and Roman Theatre," 252. When Eurydice takes the stage, effecting a strong presence, a presence that is made all the more powerful by her silence, she creates preconditions for movement away from trauma. But her masked presence seems to be an especially ideal medium for the work of witnessing: Just as Eurydice partners with Antigone to facilitate a transition from repetition to narrative, so also does Eurydice partner with the audience, who are called to witness to her heavy silence. Prevented by her mask from reading in her face clues to her story, the audience must be her witness. In witnessing for her, the messenger offers vital assistance to the audience. Telling Eurydice's story, the messenger provides an opening for the re-creation of humanity, for healing.

148. Montiglio, *Silence in the Land of Logos*, 160.

149. Segal, *Tragedy and Civilization*, 196, 204.

150. Montiglio, *Silence in the Land of Logos*, 238–39.

151. Girard, *Things Hidden*, 218; as cited in James G. Williams, *The Bible, Violence, and the Sacred: Liberation from the Myth of Sanctioned Violence* (New York: HarperCollins, 1991), 239–40.

Prelude. Fathers

1. Lechte and Margaroni, *Julia Kristeva: Live Theory*, 53.

2. Relationships between parents and children traditionally have been primary examples of "external mediation." This form of mediation occurs when there is space between a desiring subject and its model large enough that they do not compete for the same object. Other role models, persons we admire and seek to emulate, also are examples of external mediation. By contrast, in internal mediation, the model and the subject who would imitate the model are perceived by the subject to share a world or situation. As a consequence, they become rivals when the subject attempts to acquire an object valued by the model. Girard, *Deceit, Desire, and the Novel*, 9.

3. Girard, *Violence and the Sacred*, 189.

4. Ibid., 190. Beginning with *Violence and the Sacred*, Girard uses the words "indifferentiation" and "undifferentiation" to describe the loss of all differences among those caught up in the mimetic excesses of sacrificial crises. The loss of difference is destabilizing and results in violence. In *Battling to the End*, Girard settles on the term "undifferentiation," and this word becomes a key explanatory term, appearing twenty-nine times in the text.

5. Ibid., 212.

6. Girard claims the same in describing the father Karamazov. Girard writes, "Despite his title of father and his role as progenitor, father Karamazov is nothing but a bad brother, a sort of double. We are in a universe where there are no more fathers in the sense meant by Freud." See Girard, *To Double Business Bound*, 56.

7. Girard, *A Theatre of Envy*, 94.

8. Ibid., 295.

9. Girard, *Things Hidden*, 359.

10. Ibid.

11. "An Interview with René Girard," interview by Golsan, 136.

12. Ibid. As noted above, having used the terms "indifferentiation" and "undifferentiation" interchangeably in his early work, in *Battling to the End* Girard makes "undifferentiation" his term of choice. The term captures the loss of all differences in sacrificial crises. Those who have become caught up in "undifferentiation "are now "indifferent" to each other. Girard, *Battling to the End*, 89.

13. Girard, Antonello, and Rocha, *Evolution and Conversion*, 240.

14. Ibid., 241.

15. Girard, *Battling to the End*, 210.

16. Ibid., 118.

17. Ibid.

18. Ibid., xi.

19. Ibid., 18–19.

20. Stephen L. Gardner, "The Deepening Impasse of Modernity," *Society: Journal of the Social Sciences* 47, no. 5 (2010): 454.

21. Ibid., 456.

22. Ibid.

23. Girard, *The Scapegoat*, 212.

24. Girard, *Things Hidden*, 442.

25. Ibid.

26. Girard, *Battling to the End*, 133.

27. Ibid., 205.

28. Ibid., 50, 120.

29. Ibid., 125.

30. Ibid., 122.

31. Ibid., 44–45.

32. Ibid., 51, 112.

33. James Williams notes that Girard's positive assessment of Hölderlin represents a change in Girard's thinking. Williams observes that, in *Violence and the Sacred*, Girard acknowledges that Hölderlin suffered from mental illness, and Girard casts this illness in terms of Hölderlin's own experience of mimetic desire. Williams writes that, in *Battling to the End*, Girard now sees Hölderlin's withdrawal from the world and turn toward Christ as a healing from mental illness, not a manifestation of it. See Girard, *Violence and the Sacred*, 155–58. Also see René Girard, *Resurrection from the Underground: Feodor Dostoevsky*, trans. and ed. James G. Williams (East Lansing: Michigan State University Press, 2012), x.

34. Girard states that Hölderlin never showed signs of "excessive madness" and displayed instead a "nobility of silence" (*Battling to the End*, 121). An interdisciplinary inquiry arrives at a different conclusion. See Roman Jakobson and Grete Lübbe-Grothues, "The Language of Schizophrenia: Hölderlin's Speech and Poetry," trans. Susan Kitron, *Poetics Today* 2, no. 1a (1980): 137–44. Separated by an "unbridgeable abyss" from others, Hölderlin's infrequent attempts at conversation featured nonsensical words. Works of poetry from his tower years are sensible "monologues"; however, in stark contrast to his early work, deictic referents (i.e., who, when, where) are absent from these poems, reflecting Hölderlin's profound isolation.

35. Girard, *Battling to the End*, 123.

36. As I have noted in earlier chapters, I take the term "intercorporeity" from Victorio Gallese ("Two Sides of Mimesis," 89).

37. The reference is to T. S. Eliot, "The Hollow Men," in *Collected Poems 1909–1925* (Orlando, FL: Harcourt Brace Jovanovich, 1991), 77.

38. Kristeva, "Interview: *The Old Man and the Wolves*," 167.

39. Ibid.

40. Kristeva, *Intimate Revolt*, 5.

41. Kristeva's focus is undoubtedly influenced by her psychoanalytic practice as well as by her attention to women's experiences in the contemporary world. In *Black Sun*, a study of depression and melancholia, Kristeva draws examples from her psychoanalytic practice as well as from literature and art. She suggests that implosive mimetic violence is more common among women and explosive violence is more common among men. See Reineke, *Sacrificed Lives*, 91–93.

42. Oliver, *Colonization of Psychic Space*, 191.

43. Because the "father" of individual prehistory references experiences prior to the child's acquisition of language, I emphasize again that, for Kristeva, paternity refers to a *function*, not to empirical fatherhood. She writes (quoting Freud), "This identification anterior to any objective relation of desire is not destined for the Oedipal father but for a . . . loving father, who would have . . . the "attributes of both parents." Kristeva, *This Incredible Need to Believe*, 10.

44. Terrorism illustrates the importance of addressing violence on micro and macro scales inclusive of political, economic, and historical perspectives. Moreover, given problematic relationships that many young, male terrorists have with their fathers, a psychoanalytic perspective also is important, lest key indicators for violence be missed. Girard acknowledges as much when he inquires of the young men who give their lives to terrorist acts. He writes, "We do not know whether such phenomena belong to a special psychology or not." See Girard, *Battling to the End*, 212, 214. Psychoanalyst Ruth Stein documents the breakdown of the paternal function in the lives of young terrorists, using as an example Mohammed Atta, who headed the 9/11 group that flew into the World Trade Center. See Ruth Stein, *For Love of the Father: A Psychoanalytic Study of Religious Terrorism* (Palo Alto, CA: Stanford University Press, 2009).

45. Kristeva, *Sense and Non-Sense of Revolt*, 44.

46. Ibid.

47. Ibid., 44–45.

48. Ibid., 46. Kristeva points to what would be a difference between her views and Girard's, if she had in mind only one form of narcissism. When Girard talks about narcissism, he is clearly talking about what Kristeva calls "secondary narcissism," a deployment of mimetic desire that constitutes a failing in relationships of adult life. But Kristeva is writing here about "primary narcissism," the mirror-work that a nascent subject must make in order to attain any standing at all in the world.

49. Ibid., 57.

50. Ibid., 58.

51. Ibid., 59–60.

52. Kristeva, *Revolution in Poetic Language*, 70.

53. Ibid., 75, 249 n. 91.

54. Girard, *Violence and the Sacred*, 31.

55. Although Kristeva has asked that psychoanalysis keep ever in mind World War I as a backdrop for Freud's reflections on *Totem and Taboo* and his writings on narcissism, as she makes a transition in her discussion from reflecting on a culture of sacrifice to a culture of meaninglessness, she does not follow her own advice. She says that, for Freud, religious experience is the "fruit" of parricide and that rebellion will need to be repeated whenever bonds between brothers start to weaken.

It will be necessary "to repeat the rebellion, particularly in the form of ritual sacrifice." Could Freud be assessing whether World War I is, itself, such a repetition? Kristeva reports Freud's list of precipitating factors for violence: "unemployment, exclusion, lack of money, failure in work, dissatisfactions of every kind." However, that these precipitating factors weakened the bonds of human community in Europe, leading to World War I, is never stated. See Kristeva, *Sense and Non-Sense of Revolt*, 13–14.

56. Ibid., 14–15.

57. Ibid., 5.

58. Kristeva, "Interview: *The Old Man and the Wolves*," 167.

59. Ibid., 171.

60. Kristeva, *The Old Man and the Wolves*, 51; Bernard Sichère, "Roman Noir et Temps Présent," *L'Infini* 37 (Spring 1992): 82.

61. Girard, *Violence and the Sacred*, 165.

62. Kristeva, "Interview: Sharing Singularity," 155.

63. Girard, *Battling to the End*, 220 n. 20.

64. Kristeva, "Interview: Sharing Singularity," 155.

65. Kristeva, *Revolt, She Said*, 120; Kristeva, "The Revolt of Mallarmé," 31.

66. Kristeva, "The Revolt of Mallarmé," 36.

67. In her commentary on Kristeva's notion of intimate revolt, Kelly Oliver notes the juxtaposition of transgression with displacement. Oliver, *Colonization of Psychic Space*, 143.

68. Sjöholm, "Fear of Intimacy?" 188, 192–93.

69. Kristeva, *Black Sun*, 200.

70. Ibid., 216.

71. See Oliver, *Colonization of Psychic Space*, 139.

72. Girard, *Battling to the End*, 205.

73. Sjöholm argues that Kristeva's way of thinking about intimacy is unique and defines her distinctive contribution to psychoanalysis. See Sjöholm, "Fear of Intimacy?" 180.

74. Kristeva, "Interview: *The Old Man and the Wolves*," 163–64. In another essay, Kristeva writes that her father "died in my native Bulgaria, two months before the fall of the Berlin Wall, murdered in a supposedly socialist hospital where experiments were performed on elderly patients; family members were forbidden to visit for fear of germs. Since bodies of practicing Christians who died were cremated to prevent religious gatherings, while mourning I could only talk about this through writing a novel." See Kristeva, "A Father Is Beaten to Death," 175.

75. Waller, "Intertextuality and Literary Interpretation," 194.

76. Kristeva, "Interview: *The Old Man and the Wolves*," 164.

77. Ibid., 165.

78. Kristeva, *Tales of Love*, 383. Kristeva mentions also music and film.

79. Girard, *Violence and the Sacred*, 214.

80. Ibid., 216.

81. Ibid., 218.

82. Kristeva, *Tales of Love*, 379.

83. Although Kristeva takes the terminology from Lacan, she develops a unique understanding of the concept. As Kelly Oliver explains, when Kristeva exchanges "maternal" for the "father or parents of pre-history," thereby inserting division within the prespecular, Kristeva expresses her view that the earliest prerepresentational experiences of difference and alterity feature "pleasurable excess rather than painful gap." See Kelly Oliver, *Reading Kristeva: Unraveling the Double-Bind* (Bloomington: Indiana University Press, 1993), 80. The "Imaginary" father or parents of prehistory reference a fragmentation of infant being. The infant's world is a chaotic field of sensory experience without the clear differentiation between and I and Other that is proper to the "Symbolic," a field of exchange, language, and law (Jacques Lacan, *Feminine Sexuality: Jacques Lacan and the École Freudienne*, ed. Juliet Mitchell and Jacqueline Rose, trans. Jacqueline Rose [New York: Norton, 1985], 163). Yet, as Noëlle McAfee observes, the Imaginary division within infant being creates a basis for future idealization. The Imaginary father is "a phantasm of the logic of identifying one thing with another. See Noëlle McAfee, *Julia Kristeva* (New York: Routledge, 2003), 67.

84. Kristeva, *This Incredible Need to Believe*, xi. Girard too observes that Freud discusses a kind of identification that takes place "anterior to any choice of object." See Girard, *Violence and the Sacred*, 171. Like Kristeva, Girard recognizes that Freud is on the trail of a distinctive idea; indeed, he credits Freud with seeing the path of mimetic desire stretching out before him, for Girard believes that Freud is referencing the phenomenon of mimesis (201). However, when Freud's attention turns to the Oedipus complex, Girard reads Freud to have evaded his preliminary insight and criticizes Freud for going on to develop the Oedipus complex while setting aside fundamental insights about the mimetic structure of desire to which his original concept of identification attests. Not only does Freud turn his back on mimesis, but also, because he has done so, he does not recognize that secondary narcissism (which Girard regularly exemplifies with the figure of the coquette) is a species of mimetic desire. See Girard, *Things Hidden*, 368–70. Kristeva takes a different tack than Girard that both complements his own approach and revises it in order to establish positive mimesis at the foundation of human experience. Distinctions between primary and secondary narcissism that Freud makes are not based on a misunderstanding of mimetic desire; rather, what is distinct about *Einfühling*, or primary identification, is that in its preobjectal dynamic what connection there is to the other is immediate because it is embodied (e.g., tactile, sonorous). Language and symbol do not mediate the relation, as happens later in secondary narcissism (e.g., the Oedipal process). As I have argued throughout, Kristeva's subject is mimetic: it comes to be in a place where it is not, its lack of being countered by a mirroring desire that, by way of misrecognition, promises being. What Kristeva adds to Girard with her attention to and expansion of Freud's concept of *Einfühling* is a recognition that subject-creation is fundamentally transitive or metaphorical (to use Kristeva's language). Primary narcissism, home to this transitivity, is distinct from secondary narcissism. That the infant experiences nonthreatening "thirdness" prior to differentiation of subject/object lays a foundation in later life for positive mimeticism, which becomes acquisitive in the wake of the subject/object division within language.

85. Kristeva, *Tales of Love*, 374.

86. Ibid., 23–24.

87. Ibid., 25.

88. Ibid.

89. Ibid., 26.

90. Ibid., 36.

91. Ibid., 37.

92. Ibid., 34.

93. Oliver, *Colonization of Psychic Space*, 157.

94. Of course, the Symbolic order or Father's law, with which we are familiar from Freud's description of the Oedipus complex, will read this perceived difference as an interdiction: the mother's desire is directed elsewhere and I am not the phallus she seeks. But the Father of individual prehistory suggests a metaphorical reading of the social space that balances the interdictory Law of desire with the gift of love. See Kristeva, "Julia Kristeva in Conversation with Rosalind Coward," 22. Because the vocal chamber that is the world resonates for the child as triangulated space, the difference harbored by this space is offered to the child not only as interdiction but also as gift.

95. Kristeva, *New Maladies of the Soul*, 180.

96. Ibid.

Chapter 7. Not a Country for Old Men: Violence and Mimesis in Santa Varvara

1. Kristeva, *The Old Man and the Wolves*, 7.

2. Ibid., 4.

3. Kristeva uses both names throughout the book. She calls the professor "the Old Man" when she is describing his interactions with the residents of Santa Varvara. When he is engaged in communicating with the past, breathing new life into the figures of the Roman Empire, she calls him "Septicius Clarus."

4. The office of prefect was created by Augustus in order to oversee his personal guards. The prefect also had juridical duties to prosecute persons who were charged with lèse-majesté and high treason. In his role as prefect, Septicius Clarus accompanied the emperor Hadrian on his journey to Britain in 122 BCE that resulted in the building of an eighty-mile wall to separate the barbarians from the Romans. In Britain, Septicius Clarus and Suetonius were banished by Hadrian, due to an unspecified breach of etiquette. See Anthony R. Birley, *The Roman Government of Britain* (New York: Oxford University Press, 2005), 121, 223.

5. Chrysippus of Soli oversaw the Stoic school in Athens, specializing in logic. The quotes are from Kristeva's own characterization of the Stoics from *In the Beginning Was Love: Psychoanalysis and Faith*, trans. Arthur Goldhammer (New York: Columbia University Press, 1988), 51, 57. In *Strangers to Ourselves*, Kristeva writes about Chrysippus and the Stoics. She applauds their "tolerant cosmopolitanism" but descries their "elitism," which, as it developed, undercut their claims to an inclusivity that saw "distinctions fade between Greeks and barbarians, free men and slaves" (Kristeva, *Strangers to Ourselves*, 58). The "wise man" became separated from the rest of humankind. Thus Stoicism became "less a thought of the other that would integrate the foreigner's difference than an autarchy that assimilates the other and erases him under the common denominator of reason" (59). Kristeva's Old Man, in valuing connection to others, does not embrace the Stoic ethic (*The Old Man and the Wolves*, 97).

6. Kristeva, *The Old Man and the Wolves*, 6.

7. The reader may recognize these attributes also as characteristic of Stoic philosophy.

8. Kristeva, *The Old Man and the Wolves*, 12.

9. Ibid., 140.

10. Girard offers a particularly clear commentary on this point in his recent book *Sacrifice*. René Girard, *Sacrifice*, trans. Matthew Pattillo and David Dawson (East Lansing: Michigan State University Press, 2011).

11. In addition to representing a formulaic or oversimplified concept, a "stereotype" also is a type of printing plate developed in the eighteenth century and widely used in newspaper printing. Stereotypes are created with molds that are mirror images of each other. Stereotypes facilitate large press runs that would stress less durable type. By referencing this meaning of a "stereotype," Girard suggests that victims of scapegoating fit a certain type or "mold" that has durability and staying power across long periods of history or "press runs." That the victims are "mirror images" of others facilitates links between this metaphor, associated with Girard's scapegoat theory, and his larger theory of mimetic conflict.

12. Girard, *The Scapegoat*, 14.

13. Ibid.

14. Girard, *Violence and the Sacred*, 146–47.

15. Ibid., 160–61.

16. Dr. Vespasian is a medical doctor, whose position would suggest trust. The doctor's namesake, Emperor Vespasian, was installed by his troops as ruler, challenging constitutional precedent and establishing an autocracy. Although Vespasian demonstrated acumen in financial management, his single-minded efforts to stabilize the empire gave him a reputation for ruthlessness and greed. Possible name-associations with the Roman Empire for the character "Alba" are less clear. Alba Longa is the name for an ancient city near Rome that was destroyed by Rome in 600 BCE. Some families from Alba are said to have migrated to Rome at that time. Alba Graeca was the name for Belgrade, Yugoslavia, under Byzantine rule. In all instances, the name "Alba" seems to be associated with a location rather than a person. In Ovid's *Metamorphoses*, landscapes and geographical locations are often antipastoral. They become the locus for myths that entail sexual violence and failed courtships. In this mode, landscape descriptions are treated by Ovid as "narratological cues" for such impending action (Stephen Hinds, "Landscape with Figures: Aesthetics of Place in the *Metamorphoses* and Its Tradition," in *The Cambridge Companion to Ovid*, ed. Philip Hardie [Cambridge: Cambridge University Press, 2002], 130–31). In naming a female character after a city called Alba, Kristeva may be employing the Ovidian narratological strategy of signaling impending violence that proves destructive of Alba and Vespasian's relationship.

17. Kristeva, *The Old Man and the Wolves*, 38–39.

18. Ibid.

19. Girard, *Things Hidden*, 304–5.

20. Kristeva, *The Old Man and the Wolves*, 56.

21. Ibid., 40–42, 48–50.

22. Ibid., 51–52.

23. Unpublished translation in English of the introduction to the Grasset one-volume republication of Girard's major works. René Girard, "Introduction," trans. Andrew McKenna, n.d.

24. Girard, *Things Hidden*, 413.

25. Kristeva, *The Old Man and the Wolves*, 8, 5.

26. Ibid., 51.

27. Ibid., 50.

28. Ibid., 100.

29. Ibid., 46. See also Szu-chin Hestia Chen, *French Feminist Theory Exemplified through the Novels of Julia Kristeva: The Bridge from Psychoanalytic Theory to Literary Production* (Lewiston, NY: Edwin Mellen Press, 2008), 97–98.

30. Kristeva, "Interview: *The Old Man and the Wolves*," 166.

31. Ibid., 166–67.

32. Ibid., 171.

33. Kristeva, *The Old Man and the Wolves*, 51; Sichère, "Roman Noir et Temps Présent," 82.

34. See McAfee, *Julia Kristeva*, 106.

35. Part of this chapter was written in various airports where screens abound. Few persons converse with each other (even families or persons traveling together). Instead, they watch TVs in the airport bars and those that hang from the ceilings in every waiting area. Many travelers are absorbed in the screens of their laptops, tablets, and smart phones. My own navigation of airports now focuses on finding Wi-Fi hotspots and outlets for my laptop, which one airport identifies with glowing blue lights on stations placed every hundred feet or so. Persons who are oblivious to each other gather around these blue orbs of light in order to gain sustenance from the images transmitted to them on their laptop screens.

36. Kristeva, *The Old Man and the Wolves*, 60. As the discussion of Proust has demonstrated, neither Kristeva nor Girard believes that the society of spectacle is entirely new. The Internet salons of today (Facebook, YouTube, etc.) and the Paris salon may appear to be very different social settings; however, Kristeva and Girard identify similarities in mimetic conflicts visible in both settings. However, Kristeva and Girard also agree that our contemporary spectacle poses a more lethal threat than did the salons of the early twentieth century.

37. Kristeva, "Interview: *The Old Man and the Wolves*," 165.

38. Girard, *The Scapegoat*, 20.

39. Ibid., 20–22.

40. Girard, *Violence and the Sacred*, 85–88.

41. Ibid., 306–7.

42. Ibid., 235, 257–58; Girard, *Things Hidden*, 105ff.

43. Girard would find of particular interest that one of the oldest renderings of this myth has Lycaon serve Zeus a dish created from the sacrifice of Lycaon's son. According to Girard, child sacrifice is one of the most ancient expressions of the "victim mechanism." Abraham's near sacrifice of his son Isaac is cited by Girard as an example. See Girard, *I See Satan Fall*, xv.

44. Kristeva, *The Old Man and the Wolves*, 120.

45. Ibid., 60.

46. Ovid, *Metamorphoses: A New Translation* by Charles Martin (New York: Norton, 2005), ll. 220–335. Ovid writes that Jupiter destroyed with a flood the race of humans that had originated from the bodies of the giants. If so, one could posit that the second creation of humans was less violent. For his part, Girard understands that humans are uncomfortable with acknowledging that human society begins with sacrifice. The truth of origins is glossed over and obfuscated by myth. See Girard, *Things Hidden*, 103–4. For his part, Feldherr argues that Ovid's mythic stories also obscure any clear separation between the two "races" of humans. They share the human form in common; further, as the story of the second creation progresses, clearly rivalry with the gods persists. The "second" race of humans "reduplicates" all the questions raised about the first race. The flood resolves nothing about the nature of humanity. See Andrew Feldherr, *Playing Gods: Ovid's Metamorphoses and the Politics of Fiction* (New York: Columbia University Press, 2010), 126–28.

47. Kristeva, *The Old Man and the Wolves*, 50–52.

48. Ibid., 60.

49. Ibid., 92.

50. Ibid., 85.

51. Ibid., 87.

52. Ibid., 101.

53. Ibid., 84.

54. With Alba's death, we are only at the halfway point in *The Old Man and the Wolves*. Girard's insights are helpful here. In contrasting Greek tragedy with Shakespearean tragedy, Girard notes that death in the Shakespearean tragedy comes at the midpoint of the play, not at its end. Shakespeare's goal, after all, is to expose the structure of mimetic violence. See Girard, *A Theatre of Envy*, 223–24. So too does Kristeva's primary interest lie with the systemic violence that holds Santa Varvara in its grip.

55. The French title of Part II of the novel is "Série noire," after the French series of crime fiction. Anglo-American hardboiled detective stories are featured in the collection (e.g., Chandler, Hammett, Burnett).

56. Kristeva, *The Old Man and the Wolves*, 63. Although Kristeva appears to be describing the world of Santa Varvara, her words readily apply to Ovid's *Metamorphoses*. Having previously linked her novel with Ovid's in her epigraph, Kristeva now models her novel on his, for Ovid regularly cast into question the reliability of tales he had just told (as noted by Solodow; see above).

57. Ibid., 64.

58. Ibid., 66.

59. Already in the previous section, titled "Anamorphoses," Kristeva has offered clues that the reader is going to experience uncertainty. The most famous image of anamorphosis, one cited by Lacan, is Hans Holbein's painting *The Ambassadors*. In a group portrait of several men, a large stain appears to mar the lower part of the painting. However, when the viewer moves toward the side of the painting, so that she or he views it from an angle, the stain changes shape, becoming a skull. The remainder of the painting becomes distorted. The men in the painting represent the arts and sciences and the collective knowledge they embody. But the viewer does not possess that knowledge; rather, when she or he becomes aware of her or his relation to the painting (a

recognition forged when viewers move into a position in relation to the painting that enables them to see an undistorted skull), the viewer confronts the ultimate human failure to know. Knowledge that would counter mortality with immortality escapes the human gaze—the human is left only with a skull. See Jacques Lacan, "Anamorphosis," in *Four Fundamental Concepts of Psychoanalysis*, 79–90. In Kristeva's chapter, "Anamorphoses," Alba and Vespasian's marriage is a similar "stain" or "skull" on the margins of the text. As their relationship comes into focus, everything else in Santa Varvara becomes distorted. The reader wonders if there is any place from which she can accurately assess what threatens Santa Varvara.

60. In an interview, Kristeva says, "You cannot analyze someone without yourself being part of the listening situation. We have transference and counter transference. The patient transfers something to the analyst, but the analyst transfers something in return. Through this exchange new truths emerge, new accords, not the purely scientific truths and accords, but a kind of truth in action" (Birgitte Midttun, "Crossing the Borders: An Interview with Julia Kristeva," *Hypatia* 21, no. 4 [Fall 2006]: 167).

61. Kristeva, *The Old Man and the Wolves*; epigraph is Kristeva's translation.

62. Ibid., 64.

63. Ibid., 65.

64. Ibid.

65. Kristeva, "Crossing the Borders," 173. See also Sergius Pankejeff, *The Wolf-Man: With the Case of the Wolf-Man* (New York: Basic Books, 1971), 146. Here, Pankejeff (the Wolf Man) notes, "Once we happened to speak of Conan Doyle and his creation, Sherlock Holmes. I had thought that Freud would have no use for this type of light reading matter, and was surprised to find that this was not at all the case and that Freud had read this author attentively."

66. Kristeva, "Crossing the Borders," 172–73.

67. Ibid., 172.

68. Girard, *I See Satan Fall*, 163.

69. Ibid., 163–64.

70. Ibid., 183.

71. Girard, *Violence and the Sacred*, 200.

72. Ibid.

73. Girard, Antonello, and Rocha, *Evolution and Conversion*, 225.

74. Brooks, *Psychoanalysis and Storytelling*, 53.

75. I take this insight from Peter Brooks. Contrasting Watson's Holmes with the Holmes revealed in Holmes's own musings about Professor Moriarty, Brooks creates an analogy between the detective and the psychoanalyst. The young Freud was like Watson's Holmes. The mature Freud, Brooks asserts, would have understood that the detective who best represents the analyst is not the Holmes who is the object of Watson's fawning comments but the Holmes who is the adversary of Professor Moriarty, the "Napoleon of Crime." Holmes parries and thrusts for three months with Moriarty, only to confess that Moriarty is his intellectual equal and has skills that Holmes admires. Brooks sees in the Holmes and Moriarty relationship a transference necessary to the eventual detection of a crime: Moriarty and Holmes exchange moves and countermoves. Each is a detective *and* the one detected. Because Moriarty and Holmes are caught in the unstable

dynamics of reciprocal relations, Holmes is unable to offer a perspicacious assessment of Moriarty as villain that would summon Watson's accolades. Mentally and emotionally taxed, he works at a loss. Nevertheless, the dialogue and struggle in which Holmes is caught up with Moriarty, far from functioning as obstacles to knowledge, are decisive for Holmes's understanding of Moriarty. Freud came to appreciate that, when analyst and analysand enter into a complex relationship, they exchange roles, work at a loss, and often struggle. No one stands in the position of one who is supposed to know. See ibid., 61–64.

76. For readers familiar with Freud's case of the Wolf Man, Kristeva has alluded to the stance she will assume (and invite her readers to assume) from the first pages of the novel. The first time Vespasian speaks in the novel, "affecting the assurance of the self-proclaimed expert," he derisively dismisses the professor as an "old dodderer." He asks Alba if she isn't familiar with Freud's case of "The Wolf Man," and jeeringly alludes to the dream of the Wolf Man reported by Freud. He asks how many wolves the Old Man has seen, "Not five, by any chance? On a tree outside his window?" (Kristeva, *The Old Man and the Wolves*, 8). The case of the Wolf Man does play a decisive role in the narrative of *The Old Man and the Wolves*, but not because the Old Man emulates the Wolf Man; rather, Kristeva the novelist emulates Freud. After writing the case history of the Wolf Man between 1914 and 1915, Freud returns to it in 1918, adding an analysis in which he reassesses his initial interpretation of the Wolf Man's dreams. In question is whether the wolves in the Wolf Man's dream refer to an actual event (parental coitus) or to a primal fantasy. Rather than erase his earlier analysis, Freud includes both interpretations in his 1918 discussion, juxtaposing one with the other. Kristeva's novel duplicates this structure: the certainty to which she brings the reader at the conclusion of Part I (that Vespasian is a murderous "wolf") is juxtaposed with new reflections of Part II, which undercut her initial "case" against Vespasian. So also do transference and countertransference, which are illuminating themes in *The Old Man and the Wolves*, feature in the case of the Wolf Man. There, the priority of Freud's narrative analysis is repeatedly challenged by the analysand. The dialogue that ensues between Freud and the Wolf Man, attested to in Freud's case and in the writings of the Wolf Man, has been preserved in Pankejeff, *The Wolf-Man*, which includes Freud's case, the autobiography of the Wolf Man, and other analyses of the case. See also "Fictions of the Wolf Man," in Peter Brooks, *Reading for the Plot: Design and Intention in Narrative* (New York: Knopf, 1984).

77. Kristeva likens this sculpture to those at the Centre Georges Pompidou designed by Niki de Saint Phalle. Kristeva, "Interview: *The Old Man and the Wolves*," 164.

78. Kristeva, *The Old Man and the Wolves*, 69–70.

79. Lynn Enterline, *The Rhetoric of the Body from Ovid to Shakespeare* (Cambridge: Cambridge University Press, 2006), 16.

80. Ibid., 118.

81. Kristeva, *The Old Man and the Wolves*, 87–88.

82. Ibid., 97.

83. Ibid., 98. "Ils sont possédés par une soif d'impossible" (Julia Kristeva, *Le Vieil Homme et Les Loups: Roman* [Paris: Fayard, 1991], 139).

84. Kristeva, *The Old Man and the Wolves*, 99.

85. Ibid., 103.

86. Ibid., 104.

87. Ibid., 106.

88. Kristeva never states that the young woman at the lake is Alba, the student of Septicius; instead, she is "Alba's double" (ibid., 108). Late in the novel, when Alba is observed by Stephanie "hand in hand with Vespasian" (126), Stephanie continues to honor the memory of Alba of the lake. In Kristeva's interview with Sichère, she explains that "the duplication and dissemination of identities refer to the obvious fact that we are experiencing contemporary culture in a process of metamorphosis." "Interview: *The Old Man and the Wolves*," 165; Sichère, "Roman Noir et Temps Présent," 76.

89. Suetonius wrote *De vita Caesarum*, a scandal-filled record of the lives of the first eleven emperors. His patron was Septicius Clarus, the Praetorian prefect. Both Suetonius and Septicius Clarus were banished by Hadrian over an issue of disrespect to Hadrian's wife.

90. Kristeva, *The Old Man and the Wolves*, 18–21.

91. Ibid., 15.

92. Ibid., 16–17.

93. Andrew Feldherr, "Metamorphosis in the Metamorphoses," in Hardie, *Cambridge Companion to Ovid*, 169.

94. Joseph B. Solodow, *The World of Ovid's Metamorphoses* (Chapel Hill: University of North Carolina Press, 2002), 64–68.

95. Ibid., 175–76.

96. Ibid., 213–14.

97. Enterline, *Rhetoric of the Body*, 11.

98. Ibid., 15–16.

99. Ibid., 43.

100. Ibid., 41.

101. Ibid., 206.

102. Ibid., 50.

103. Ibid., 54; Ovid, *Metamorphoses*, 554.

104. Enterline, *Rhetoric of the Body*, 16.

105. Kristeva, *The Old Man and the Wolves*, 35, 120.

106. Ibid., 56.

107. Ibid., 58–59.

108. Ibid., 16.

109. Ibid., 22.

110. Ibid., 51.

111. Girard, *Things Hidden*, 103.

112. Kristeva, *The Old Man and the Wolves*, 113.

113. Ibid., 114.

114. Ibid.

115. Ibid., 116–17.

116. Ibid., 119.

117. Ibid., 121–23. Kristeva, *Le Vieil Homme et les Loups*, 176. The quotation (in English in the French) is from "Billie's Blues," also known as "I Love my Man." The actual phrasing of the lyric is, "I had a long, long way to go."

118. Enterline, *Rhetoric of the Body*, 40–41. Among all singers for whom we have recordings, Holiday's voice is perhaps most recognizable; indeed, her voice rather than the words she sings are what those who hear her sing most remember about that experience.

119. Girard, *The Scapegoat*, 18.

120. Kristeva, *The Old Man and the Wolves*, 10.

121. Ibid., 11.

122. Ibid., 24.

123. Ibid., 11–12.

124. Ibid., 123.

125. Ibid., 126.

126. Ibid., 178.

127. Ibid., 78.

128. Ibid., 129.

129. Ibid., 69.

130. Ovid, *Metamorphoses*, 154–56.

131. Feldherr, *Playing Gods*, 325.

132. Ibid., 327–29.

133. Ibid., 327.

134. Kristeva, *The Old Man and the Wolves*, 129.

135. Anna Smith, *Julia Kristeva: Readings of Exile and Estrangement* (New York: Palgrave Macmillan, 1996), 191.

136. Kristeva, *The Old Man and the Wolves*, 130.

137. Ibid.; Kristeva, *Le Vieil Homme et les Loups*, 186.

138. Kristeva, *Intimate Revolt*, 5.

Chapter 8. To Glimpse a World without Wolves: From Conflict to Compassion

1. Kristeva, *The Old Man and the Wolves*, 115.

2. Kristeva, *Intimate Revolt*, 66.

3. Elizabeth Grosz, *Sexual Subversions: Three French Feminists* (Crow's Nest, Australia: Allen & Unwin, 1989), 73.

4. Antonio Lázaro-Reboll, "Counter-Rational Reason: Goya's Instrumental Negotiations of Flesh and World," *History of European Ideas* 30 (2004): 109–19.

5. Kristeva, *Hatred and Forgiveness*, 184.

6. Ibid., 187.

7. Ibid., 186.

8. Kristeva, *The Old Man and the Wolves*, 134.

9. Ibid., 141.

10. Sylvie Gambaudo, *Kristeva, Psychoanalysis and Culture* (London: Ashgate, 2007), 77.

11. Kristeva, *The Old Man and the Wolves*, 179.

12. Ibid.

13. Ibid., 85, 179.

14. Girard appears to recognize in Freud both primary and secondary narcissism when he says that "there are two pools of desire; the maternal object and the unique type of object that I am for myself" (*Things Hidden*, 368). However, he almost immediately loses sight of primary narcissism (what Kristeva associates with the abject, prespeaking being) and focuses only on what Kristeva identifies as secondary narcissism and associates with mimesis. When Girard does recognize two forms of narcissism, he assigns one to the classic mimetic pattern and the other to the desire of the feminine, defining it as "coquetry." Coquetry is a misfiring of object-centered desire. Girard analyzes coquetry in order to show that it too is a species of mimetic desire. Lost in his discussion is any referent to the primary narcissism associated with the initial differentiation of the human subject who is not yet an "I." See *Things Hidden*, 371–73.

15. In the scenes in the book that take place at the edge of the lake, Stephanie names only one witness to the events that led to the death of the woman at the lake: the "Clean Youth" ("*Le Clean*") (*The Old Man and the Wolves*, 85; Kristeva, *Le Vieil Homme et les Loups*, 124). Both at the time of the initial discovery of the body of the woman at the lake and at the end of the novel, Stephanie disavows the reliability of the Clean Youth's testimony. Early on, she finds him an implausible witness but decides to "play along" (85). At the end of the novel, she recalls his testimony and states that she would like to find him, because he has the "gift of gab" (180). The "Clean Youth" who would stand as witness to the identity of Alba appears to be the "Greek youth" in *Powers of Horror* (14), which is a reference to Narcissus. In *Powers of Horror* Kristeva associates the fountain into which Greek youth looks with the Symbolic, the world of signs (home to the gift of gab?). Kristeva's claim in *Powers of Horror* is that the fountain is always muddy, precluding the Greek youth/Clean Youth from finding a clear image in it. Stirrings of the pool that muddy the waters are associated with challenges to the identity of speaking being. Mimesis gives way to violence and to a loss of being, which exposes an archaic economy that lies, as it were, at the bottom of a pool. This archaic economy is linked with abjection. Before subjects become objects for each other in the Symbolic order, they are "abject." Primary narcissism develops on the way to subject status, after which subjects attain their "*corps proper*" and participate in sign-driven secondary narcissism. In French, *propre* means "clean" as well as "proper." Indeed, in the English translation of *Powers of Horror*, the translator uses the phrase "clean and proper body" whenever Kristeva is describing the *corps propre* of the subject within the Symbolic Order (viii). In *The Old Man and the Wolves*, presumably in order to doubly emphasize the alienation of subjects in the Symbolic order, Kristeva names the "proper youth" the "Clean Youth." Those who are abject in Santa Varvara are therefore twice removed from the Symbolic order: they do not possess the *corps propre* (clean and proper body) that they should and they don't speak the language of "the Clean." This double alienation

is particularly apparent in the French version of the novel because Kristeva uses the English word "Clean" to describe the youth.

16. Kristeva, *The Old Man and the Wolves*, 180.

17. Kristeva, "Interview: *The Old Man and the Wolves*," 165; Sichère, "Roman Noir et Temps Présent," 76.

18. Kristeva, *The Old Man and the Wolves*, 153.

19. Ibid., 139.

20. Ibid., 163.

21. Kristeva suggests that she is replacing a "hidden, anonymous observer, the author in disguise, with a "master of ceremonies" who will "reveal himself and include himself in the story" (ibid., 63). In Kristeva's interview with Sichère, she comments that she wrote the novel in the aftermath of her father's death, which occurred "in a Sofia hospital through the incompetence and brutality of the medical and political system" ("Interview: *The Old Man and the Wolves*," 163). Especially when scenes are not explicitly placed in Santa Varvara and refer to incidents from Kristeva's own life (as in a visit Kristeva made to the cathedral in Sofia with the president of France), it is evident that Stephanie and Kristeva's father are one.

22. Unless necessary for adjudicating the full meaning of the text, having made the connection between Kristeva and Stephanie in the last pages of the novel, I will revert back to describing Stephanie as the author of the journal.

23. Lechte and Margaroni, *Julia Kristeva: Live Theory*, 55.

24. Kristeva, *The Old Man and the Wolves*, 163.

25. Kristeva, "Interview: *The Old Man and the Wolves*," 169.

26. Ibid.

27. Ibid., 170.

28. The founding triangle of proto-subject, other, and model in the maternal body, which was my focus in reflecting on Proust, is oriented toward orality and touch. Here a like triangulation features a division of sound within an original triangle, and the model is described by Kristeva as the father of individual prehistory. Because the roles of both parents in this triangle predate language, these points of alteration are not linked to mothers and fathers in the Symbolic/Oedipal order; they could be both parents or even "x and y." See Ziarek, "At the Limits of Discourse," 102. Also Kristeva, *Tales of Love*, 173; Kristeva, "Julia Kristeva in Conversation with Rosalind Coward," 23.

29. Kristeva, *This Incredible Need to Believe*, 10.

30. Ibid.

31. Kristeva, *Black Sun*, 200.

32. Kristeva, *The Old Man and the Wolves*, 151.

33. Ibid.

34. Ibid., 152.

35. Ibid., 165.

36. Ibid., 157–58.

37. Sigmund Freud, *Civilization and Its Discontents*, trans. James Strachey (New York: Norton, 2005), 34.

38. Kristeva, *The Old Man and the Wolves*, 59.

39. Gambaudo, *Kristeva, Psychoanalysis and Culture*, 77–78.

40. Kristeva, *The Old Man and the Wolves*, 149–50; Kristeva, *Le Vieil Homme et les Loups*, 213.

41. Kristeva, "Interview: *The Old Man and the Wolves*," 169; Sichère, "Roman Noir et Temps Présent," 81.

42. Kristeva, "Interview: *The Old Man and the Wolves*," 169.

43. Kristeva, *The Old Man and the Wolves*, 13–14.

44. Michael in Albius Tibullus, *The Poems of Tibullus*, ed. E. M. Michael (Bloomington: Indiana University Press, 1968), 16–17.

45. Michael C. J. Putnam, *Tibullus: A Commentary* (Norman: University of Oklahoma Press, 1979), 11.

46. Kristeva, *The Old Man and the Wolves*, 15.

47. Francis Cairns, *Tibullus: A Hellenistic Poet at Rome* (Cambridge: Cambridge University Press, 1980), 28.

48. Kristeva, *The Old Man and the Wolves*, 60; Tibullus, *Poems*, 351.1.69.

49. E. M. Michael, introduction to *The Poems of Tibullus*, 13.

50. Kristeva, *The Old Man and the Wolves*, 58.

51. Ibid., 15.

52. Ibid., 97.

53. Putnam, *Tibullus*, 99.

54. Tibullus, *Poems*, 62, Book I, Poem 10.

55. Kristeva, *The Old Man and the Wolves*, 145–46.

56. Ibid., 16; Kristeva, *Le Vieil Homme et Les Loups*, 31.

57. Kristeva, *Le Vieil Homme et Les Loups*, 29; Kristeva, *The Old Man and the Wolves*, 15, 17.

58. Kristeva, "Interview: *The Old Man and the Wolves*," 170.

59. Kristeva, *The Old Man and the Wolves*, 153.

60. Kristeva, *Tales of Love*, 142–43.

61. Kristeva, "Women's Time," 213 n. 21.

62. Ibid., 202.

63. Kristeva, *Tales of Love*, 142, 395 n. 16.

64. Girard, *Things Hidden*, 210.

65. Ibid., 197. Girard discusses at length that the historical religion of Christianity has frequently ignored the message of the Gospels and regularly has been a primary instigator of cultural scapegoating. See, for example, *Things Hidden*, 224–62. Christianity also has developed theologies

of atonement in total forgetfulness of the Gospels' message. These theologies reinstate a God who wants human sacrifice. In order to satisfy this God, even his son must die. But God is not the problem that theologies must resolve; rather, mimetic contagion among humans that mutates into scapegoating is the problem. With Jesus, theologians are given a new task by God: to disseminate the gospel message that has exposed the truth of sacrifice and revealed a God who defends victims and offers love. See Girard, *I See Satan Fall*, 150. That Christianity has not absorbed or acted on the nonsacrificial message of Christ is a focus of critical exploration for many students of Girard. See for example, Swartley, *Violence Renounced*.

66. Kristeva, *Tales of Love*, 146–47. Kristeva is sympathetic toward much of the Christian story. However, even as she recognizes its antisacrificial message, enabling her to draw close to Girard, she is not a Christian apologist. For Kristeva, the message of Christian love comes at a price: the disavowal of the human body. Christian love becomes implicated by its theologians in a worship of a Father who welcomes us "as pure spirit, as name, and not as body" (*Tales of Love*, 144). *Powers of Horror* is Kristeva's extended commentary on problems that have accrued to Christianity over the centuries because of its choice against corporeality. In seeking to join Hebraic flesh (a body bounded by the law) with the pneumatic body (that flesh subdued), Christianity has created the "lining and the cloth of one and the same economy" (*Powers of Horror*, 124–25). But that economy, fundamentally sacrificial, moves Christianity away from its antisacrificial origins, creating a history with onerous consequences for those within Christian history who most obviously represent the body. For further discussion of this sacrificial history, see my *Sacrificed Lives*, 93–102 (for nonsacrificial alternatives that Kristeva observes Christianity has retained, see pp. 189–90). Kristeva's discussion of icons in *The Severed Head*, as summarized here, qualifies arguments that she has made in earlier writings about disembodied Christianity.

67. Girard, *Battling to the End*, 60.

68. See Girard, Antonello, and Rocha, *Evolution and Conversion*, 252; Kristeva, *This Incredible Need to Believe*, 25; Kristeva, *Hatred and Forgiveness*, 192–93.

69. Pamela Sue Anderson, "Writing on Exiles and Excess: Toward a New Form of Subjectivity," in *Self, Same, Other: Re-visioning the Subject in Literature and Theology* (Sheffield, UK: Sheffield Academic Press, 2000), 114–15.

70. Kristeva, *The Old Man and the Wolves*, 166.

71. Ibid., 170. The reference is ostensibly to the Old Man; however, in this context, the Old Man and Kristeva's father have become one. Kristeva laments the "fire that ravaged and destroyed the Old Man," which is an oblique reference to the cremation of Kristeva's father after his death, an act mandated by the government of Bulgaria. In the novel, Vespasian defends the cremation: "We don't have graves any more in Santa Varvara." Labeling burial an "anachronistic ritual," he says that "only atheists will be allowed to have mausoleums in the future" (169). In Bulgaria, only Communists can be buried because they presumably have no religious reasons for their choice of burial. The cremation of her father was a cause of great anguish by Kristeva because it violated her father's wishes for the burial of his body (see Kristeva, "Crossing the Borders," 172). Kristeva's father, a devout Orthodox Christian, was opposed to cremation because he was an adherent of the Orthodox belief in the bodily resurrection. Death is a time of "sleep" for the body; following Christ, the dead will rise at the end of time and their souls will once again be united with their bodies. That Kristeva's father's body was assaulted in death compounds his mistreatment by medical authorities, amplifying Kristeva's grief.

72. Kristeva, *The Old Man and the Wolves*, 172. Again, this reference includes Kristeva's father. In an interview with Clark and Hulley, Kristeva describes the same scene. She notes that she

accompanied President Mitterand to Bulgaria and went with him to a church, where her father was singing (Clark and Hulley, "Cultural Strangeness," 50–51).

73. Kristeva, *The Old Man and the Wolves*, 173.

74. Ibid., 173–74.

75. Ibid., 173.

76. Kristeva, *Tales of Love*, 143.

77. Kristeva, *New Maladies of the Soul*, 178–79.

78. Kristeva, *Hatred and Forgiveness*, 192–93.

79. Kristeva, *The Old Man and the Wolves*, 176.

80. Catherine Francblin, "On *New Maladies of the Soul*," in Guberman, *Julia Kristeva Interviews*, 86.

81. Vassiliki Kolocotroni, "Avant-Garde Practice," in Guberman, *Julia Kristeva Interviews*, 220. Kristeva cites in this interview the example of Joyce—who speaks of "transubstantiation"—while describing writing as "the passage of words into the body and vice versa."

82. Ibid.

83. Ibid., 221.

84. Bolens, *The Style of Gestures*, 41.

85. Kristeva, *Intimate Revolt*, 61.

86. Ibid.

87. Gallese, "Two Sides of Mimesis," 89.

88. Ibid., 97, 102.

89. Bolens, *The Style of Gestures*, 23.

90. Kristeva, *New Maladies of the Soul*, 178–79.

91. In the novel, the only fathers recognized in Santa Varvara are dead fathers, except for the wolf-like Vespasian. Alluding to the Father of the Law, Kristeva writes, "When there's no father, the wolves prowl" (*The Old Man and the Wolves*, 140). In her interview with Sichère, Kristeva asserts that the professor and ambassador are "far from being a master, even less so a hero, but who remains an enigma at the very bottom of a sea of insignificance or brutality." The fathers summoned in *The Old Man and the Wolves* are "orphaned, suffering, uprooted fathers." Their task is not to represent a stern or abstract law but to "prepare a place for possible law" ("Interview: *The Old Man and the Wolves*," 170). The most powerful attestation to the kind of father who graces the pages of *The Old Man and the Wolves* is visible in Stephanie's recording of a dream in her journal. It is a classic Freudian dream: Stephanie dreams of a train that runs over her father's throat and cuts his head off. The next day, Stephanie recalls that her father did acquire a sore throat in the days that followed her dream. In fact, "He was always coughing afterward. I don't think he ever stopped" (*The Old Man and the Wolves*, 139). Writing of this scene, Margaroni suggests that Kristeva is saying that Stephanie's father cannot speak in the Lacanian Name of the Father, without coughing or breaking up sounds (Lechte and Margaroni, *Julia Kristeva: Live Theory*, 56). Perhaps in choosing a train to represent the Symbolic order/order of language that has decapitated her father, Kristeva has Lacan's train in mind. In *Écrits*, Lacan likens the Symbolic order of language to a train (152).

92. Kristeva, *Black Sun*, 23–24.

93. The origin of "man of sorrows" is Isaiah (52:13–53:12). This figure, assumed by Christians to be an anticipatory reference to Christ, is also the focus of an antisacrificial message within the Hebrew Bible. The man of sorrows is an outsider to the community; he becomes despised by them and appears to have a disfigured face from whom others hide; he bears the pains of that community, is crushed by that community even though he has not been the source of that community's suffering and has done no violence; and he becomes the source of healing for the community. But the text of Isaiah is not myth: myths justify mob action; but, in the text of Isaiah, the persecutors recognize that the suffering servant is innocent of the charges for which he has been held culpable (53:9). In myth, gods do not challenge scapegoating; in Isaiah, Yahweh sides with the victim. Although human violence is not wholly supplanted by Yahweh, Yahweh does not have his servant repay violence in kind. In this way, the power of violent mimesis is broken in the Hebrew Bible, whereas it is not broken in myth. See Raymund Schwager, *Must There Be Scapegoats?* (New York: Herder & Herder, 2000), 126–33; Julia Kristeva, *Crisis of the European Subject*, trans. Susan Fairfield (New York: Other Press, 2000), 153.

94. Kristeva, *The Severed Head*, 49. Extended discussion of Kristeva's commentary on *oikos* takes us beyond the focus of this chapter. This commentary is located in Kristeva's book *Hannah Arendt*. Kristeva criticizes Arendt's treatment of *oikos*, which Kristeva sees as unduly bifurcating the private and the public, the household (society) and the state, while relegating the work of the household economy to *animal laborans*. Calling for "a more thoughtful political anthropology," Kristeva reminds Arendt of the meaning of "economy" in the Gospels and Byzantine Christianity. Here, "economy" suggests both "negotiation" and "transition" between an invisible and immortal universe and a visible and mortal world. As such, "economy" does not cede the mortal to "an unhappy life of labor" but makes possible the emergence of divine presence within the visible world. Historical links between "icon" and "oikos" are forged from this connection. See Julia Kristeva, *Hannah Arendt*, 160–62.

95. Kristeva, *The Severed Head*, 51.

96. Ibid., 52.

97. Ibid., 53.

98. Ibid., 54.

99. John Lechte, "Love, Life, Complexity and the 'Flesh' in Kristeva's Writing Experience," in Lechte and Zournazi, *The Kristeva Critical Reader*, 196.

100. Kristeva, *Crisis of the European Subject*, 153.

101. Legend has it that the leprous King Abgar of Edessa in Mesopotamia received a letter from Christ (his contemporary) along with a "portrait": a cloth Christ had used to wipe his face had become imprinted with Christ's features. See Kristeva, *The Severed Head*, 38.

102. Ibid., 41.

103. Ibid.

104. Ibid., 29.

105. Ibid., 31.

106. Ibid., 36.

107. Ibid.

108. Ibid., 49.

109. Ibid., 55.

110. Ibid., 50.

111. Ibid.

112. For Kristeva's discussion of the meaning of "economy" as "redemptive plan," see ibid., 139 n. 13. Kristeva quotes Ephesians 1:9: "He made known to us the mystery of his will, this *benevolent design*." She also links economy with dispensation. "God has *dispensed* his grace" (Ephesians 3:2) according to God's "eternal design" (Ephesians 3:11). Emphases Kristeva's.

113. The language of "prototype" is Lossky and Ouspensky's in their study of icons. See Vladimir Lossky and Leonid Ouspensky, *The Meaning of Icons* (Crestwood, NY: St. Vladimir's Seminary Press, 1982), 37.

114. Ibid., 36.

115. Ibid., 37.

116. Ibid., 38.

117. Ibid., 39.

118. Lev Gillet, *Orthodox Spirituality: An Outline of the Orthodox Ascetical and Mystical Tradition* (Crestwood, NY: St. Vladimir's Seminary Press, 1978), 108.

119. Lossky and Ouspensky, *The Meaning of Icons*, 44.

120. Kristeva, *The Severed Head*, 55. Kristeva is quoting Philippians 2:7.

121. Lechte, "Love, Life, Complexity," 196.

122. Dumitru Staniloae, *Orthodox Spirituality: A Practical Guide for the Faithful and a Definitive Manual for the Scholar*, trans. Archimandrite Jerome and Otilia Kloos (South Canaan, PA: St. Tikhon's Seminary Press, 2003), 15.

123. Ibid., 17.

124. Girard, *Things Hidden*, 306, 307, 32; emphasis mine.

125. We can see the challenges that Girard faces in addressing the lived experience of mimetic desire in his conversation with Jean-Michel Oughourlian and Guy Lefort about manic depressive disorders (bipolar disorders) and psychosis (ibid., 306ff.). Girard struggles to explicate how the expression of these disorders, which have strong physical components (examples would be slow or fast speech, euphoria, or crying spells) can be integrated into a mimetic analysis. Oughourlian suggests an "organic" component that can be temporarily "neutralized with chemical products." Girard responds that "the mimetic context" must play a central role in such events. Moving to the subject of madness, Girard observes that Freud was aware of this "dynamic force" but that he erred in inventing a "death instinct" because "mimetic desire can account for it all more directly and efficiently." "Being rational—functioning properly—is a matter of having objects and being busy with them; being mad is a matter of letting oneself be taken over completely by mimetic models, and so fulfilling the calling of desire. It is a matter of pushing to final conclusions that distinguishes desire—only very relatively of course—from animal life and of abandoning oneself to a fascination with the model, to the extent that it resists and does violence to the subject" (311). Confronted with the lived expression of mimetic desire where it simply cannot be avoided (the extreme affect of a bipolar disorder). Oughourlian and Girard are caught in a dualism. For them, affect is animal or organic (subject to chemical alteration); mimesis is a rational process

that is human to the extent that one is not completely taken over by desire that would lead one to abandon oneself to violence. But psychoanalysis began as an effort to end dualistic analyses of human suffering: Freud sought to address through *conversation* the symptoms of hysteria, which included *paralysis* of limbs, *constrictions* of the throat, *grimaces* of the face. That psychoanalysis was and still is an effort to offer a nondualistic account of mimetic desire is dismissed by Girard as a suspect mythology. In exploring options for augmenting Girard's theory, I not only am showing that Girard's dismissal of psychoanalysis needs to be revisited, but also that the actual circumstances of mimetic conflict mandate analyses that acknowledge the embodied nature of mimesis, moving beyond an animal/human, mad/rational dualism. Kristeva, I suggest, addresses both issues.

126. Gambaudo, *Kristeva, Psychoanalysis and Culture*, 74.

127. In a fascinating discussion of Klein's theory of the unconscious, Kristeva applauds Klein for recognizing that the work of the unconscious is a work of anamorphosis: "body into the mind, of sensations and affects into signs, and vice versa." Kristeva links anamorphosis with Christian theology, suggesting that the process Klein identifies is named "incarnation" within that theology. Julia Kristeva, *Melanie Klein*, trans. Ross Guberman (New York: Columbia University Press, 2004), 148.

128. Kristeva, *The Old Man and the Wolves*, 182.

129. Ibid., 174.

130. Ibid., 177.

131. Ibid., 183; Kristeva, *Le Vieil Homme et les Loups*, 269. I agree with Anna-Marie Smith that the English translation "A female wolf who knows what's behind it all and is prepared to talk about it" may not wholly convey Kristeva's intent. Therefore, I am following Smith in using the more literal translation of the French.

132. Kristeva, *The Old Man and the Wolves*, 65.

133. Ibid., 140–41.

134. Ibid., 183; Kristeva, *Le Vieil Homme et les Loups*, 269.

135. Kelly Oliver, "Revolt and Forgiveness," in *Revolt, Affect, Collectivity: The Unstable Boundaries of Kristeva's Polis* (Albany: State University of New York Press, 2005), 77.

136. For a discussion of Kristeva's point, see Oliver, *Colonization of Psychic Space*, 143.

137. Kristeva, *Intimate Revolt*, 8.

138. Oliver, *Colonization of Psychic Space*, 144.

139. Kristeva, *New Maladies of the Soul*, 122. See also Oliver, *Colonization of Psychic Space*, 137.

140. Kristeva, *Tales of Love*, 382.

141. Kristeva, *The Old Man and the Wolves*, 168.

142. Ibid., 169.

143. Everett L. Worthington et al., "Compassion and Forgiveness: Implications for Psychotherapy," in *Compassion: Conceptualisations, Research, and Use in Psychotherapy*, ed. Paul Gilbert (New York: Routledge, 2005), 168–92.

144. Ibid., 168–70.

145. Ibid., 172–74.

146. Kristeva, *The Old Man and the Wolves*, 145–46. In a fascinating discussion of the meaning of singularity across Greek, Jewish, and Christian traditions, Kristeva links the singular with the Greek *daimōn* and points to the association of the daimon with a god "who watches over each man, thing, place, state." Tracing the history of this "communion," Kristeva states that the copresence of the human and the divine becomes in Christianity (and here she asks to be "allowed a giant step!") the good news of the Parousia, a "gift of love." That which is singular participates in this history when from the "singular experience of the love of God" one embodies a desire to surpass oneself (here she cites a connection with "genius"). The singular, in Christianity, thus becomes "a fulfillment of Jewish messianism." Kristeva is profoundly concerned that, in contemporary society, the singular has been lost to "the mirror and its narcissistic consolations," which replace "reverence for the peerless singular in others and oneself." The singular, on this reading, aligns with positive mimesis. Kristeva, *This Incredible Need to Believe*, 30–31, 37.

147. Oliver, *Colonization of Psychic Space*, 185–86.

148. Kristeva, *Tales of Love*, 37.

149. Oliver well describes the work of the third, the imaginary father: "An identification with this mingling of maternal and paternal positions (needs and demands) loads language with preverbal and nonrepresentable drives and affects. It is not a matter of articulating affect, which is impossible, since, strictly speaking, they are nonrepresentable; rather, it is a matter of supporting them, giving them form, for-giving them, allowing them access to the symbolic." Oliver, *Colonization of Psychic Space*, 138, 187.

150. Lechte and Margaroni, *Julia Kristeva: Live Theory*, 55.

151. Kristeva, *The Old Man and the Wolves*, 181.

152. Kristeva, "A Father Is Beaten to Death," 180–81; Kristeva, *This Incredible Need to Believe*, 61.

153. Kristeva, "A Father Is Beaten to Death," 182.

154. LaCapra, *Writing History, Writing Trauma*, 50.

155. Ibid., 51.

156. Ibid., 57.

157. Ibid., 58.

158. Ibid., 64–65, 77.

159. Ibid., 66, 77.

160. Girard, *Battling to the End*, 134.

161. LaCapra, *Writing History, Writing Trauma*, 78.

162. Ibid., 67 n. 34. For LaCapra, this acknowledgment brings integrity to atheism. In the comments that follow, I suggest that atheism is not the sole response we can make. Kristeva, herself an atheist, articulately sketches contours for a theology of absence grounded in Orthodox Christianity.

163. Kristeva, *The Severed Head*, 55.

164. Kristeva, "A Father Is Beaten to Death," 182.

165. Jim Fodor, "Christian Discipleship as Participatory Imitation: Theological Reflection on Girardian Themes," in Swartley, *Violence Renounced*, 256.

166. Ibid., 259, 272.

167. Girard, *Battling to the End*, 205.

168. Kristeva, *This Incredible Need to Believe*, 89.

169. Ibid., 91.

170. Ibid.

171. Ibid.

172. Ibid., 94.

173. Ibid., 95.

174. Ibid.

175. Ibid., 96.

176. Vladimir Lossky, *The Mystical Theology of the Eastern Church* (St. Vladimir's Seminary Press, 1997), 111.

177. Kristeva, *This Incredible Need to Believe*, 97.

178. Ibid., 85.

179. Ibid., 96.

180. Kristeva, "A Father Is Beaten to Death," 184. Although Kristeva does not cite Gregory of Nyssa by name, Gregory seemingly facilitates Kristeva's efforts to link faith and art with a healing praxis. As Gregory's thought is exposited by Dumitru Staniloae, Gregory characterizes the fall of humanity as a fall into an aridity of mind that understands humans only as objects and never as "partners in a dialogue of love." The tree of the knowledge of good and evil described in Genesis depicts this problematic human condition. But Gregory draws attention to another tree that is found in paradise: the tree of life. Distinct from the tree of knowledge only in its relationship to God, the "tree of life" is any person I encounter through love, just as the "Tree of Life" is the Person of God, the source of all love. Dumitru Staniloae, *Orthodox Dogmatic Theology* (New York: Continuum International Publishing Group, 2002), 175.

Bibliography

Adams, Rebecca. "Loving Mimesis and Girard's 'Scapegoat of the Text': A Creative Reassessment of Mimetic Desire." In *Violence Renounced*, edited by Willard Swartley, 277–307. Telford, PA: Pandora Press, 2000.

Aeschylus, *The Seven against Thebes*. Edited by Julie Nord. Translated by Edmund Doidge Anderson Morshead. Toronto, Ontario: Courier Dover, 2000.

Anderson, Pamela Sue. "Writing on Exiles and Excess: Toward a New Form of Subjectivity." In *Self, Same, Other: Re-visioning the Subject in Literature and Theology*. Sheffield, UK: Sheffield Academic Press, 2000.

Anspach, Mark R. "Imitation and Violence: Empirical Evidence and the Mimetic Model." In *Mimesis and Science: Empirical Research on Imitation and the Mimetic Theory of Culture and Religion*, edited by Scott R. Garrels, 129–54. East Lansing: Michigan State University Press, 2011

Aristotle. *Poetics*. Translated by S. H. Butcher. New York: Cosimo, 2008.

Astell, Ann W. *Joan of Arc and Sacrificial Authorship*. South Bend, IN: University of Notre Dame Press, 2003.

Bacon, Helen H. "Woman's Two Faces: Sophocles' View of the Tragedy of Oedipus and His Family." In *Sexuality of Women: Scientific Proceedings of the Tenth Annual Spring Meeting of the American Academy of Psychoanalysis*, 10–24. (New York: Grune and Stratton, 1966).

Bann, Stephen. "Three Images for Kristeva: From Bellini to Proust." *Parallax* 4, no. 3 (1998): 65–79.

Birley, Anthony R. *The Roman Government of Britain*. New York: Oxford University Press, 2005.

Bolens, Guillemette. *The Style of Gestures: Embodiment and Cognition in Literary Narrative*. Baltimore: Johns Hopkins University Press, 2012.

Bowra, C. M. *Sophoclean Tragedy*. New York: Oxford University Press, 1970.

Brennan, Teresa. *The Interpretation of the Flesh: Freud and Femininity*. New York: Routledge, 1992.

Brooks, Peter. *Psychoanalysis and Storytelling*. Hoboken, NJ: Wiley-Blackwell, 1994.

——. *Reading for the Plot: Design and Intention in Narrative*. New York: Knopf, 1984.

Brown, Stephen Gilbert. "Desire on Ice." *College Literature* 32 (2005): 43–61.

Brown, Stephen Gilbert. *The Gardens of Desire: Marcel Proust and the Fugitive Sublime*. Albany: State University of New York Press, 2004.

Blundell, Mary Whitlock. *Helping Friends and Harming Enemies: A Study in Sophocles and Greek Ethics*. New York: Cambridge University Press, 1991.

Bucknall, Barbara J., ed. *Critical Essays on Marcel Proust*. Boston: G. K. Hall, 1987.

Butler, Judith. *Antigone's Claim*. New York: Columbia University Press, 2002.

Cairns, Francis. *Tibullus: A Hellenistic Poet at Rome*. Cambridge: Cambridge University Press, 1980.

Carter, William C. *Marcel Proust: A Life*. New Haven: Yale University Press, 2002.

Caruth, Cathy. *Unclaimed Experience: Trauma, Narrative and History*. Baltimore: Johns Hopkins University Press, 1996.

Cavarero, Adriana. *Relating Narratives: Storytelling and Selfhood*. New York: Routledge, 2000.

Chen, Szu-chin Hestia. *French Feminist Theory Exemplified through the Novels of Julia Kristeva: The Bridge from Psychoanalytic Theory to Literary Production*. Lewiston, NY: Edwin Mellen Press, 2008.

Clark, Suzanne, and Kathleen Hulley. "Cultural Strangeness and the Subject in Crisis." In *Julia Kristeva Interviews*, edited by Ross Mitchell Guberman, 35–58. New York: Columbia University Press, 1996.

Clough, A. L., ed. *The Horseless Age*. New York: Horseless Age, 1903.

Collier, Peter. *Proust and Venice*. New York: Cambridge University Press, 2005.

Danius, Sara. *The Senses of Modernism: Technology, Perception, and Aesthetics*. Ithaca, NY: Cornell University Press, 2002.

Davis, Colin. *After Poststructuralism: Reading, Stories, Theory*. New York: Routledge, 2003.

Dillon, Matthew. *Girls and Women in Classical Greek Religion*. New York: Routledge, 2003.

Diprose, Rosalyn. *The Bodies of Women: Ethics, Embodiment and Sexual Differences*. New York: Routledge, 1994.

Duffy, Stephen J. *The Dynamics of Grace: Perspectives in Theological Anthropology*. Eugene, OR: Wipf & Stock, 2007.

Eliot, T. S. *Collected Poems 1909–1925*. Orlando, FL: Harcourt Brace Jovanovich, 1991.

Enterline, Lynn. *The Rhetoric of the Body from Ovid to Shakespeare*. Cambridge: Cambridge University Press, 2006.

Euripides. *Electra, Phoenician Women, Bacchae, Iphigenia at Aulis*. Translated by Cecelia Eaton Luschnig and Paul Woodruff. Indianapolis: Hackett, 2011.

Farnell, Lewis Richard. *The Cults of the Greek States*. New Rochelle, NY: Caratzas Brothers, 1977.

Feldherr, Andrew. *Playing Gods: Ovid's Metamorphoses and the Politics of Fiction*. New York: Columbia University Press, 2010.

Fodor, Jim. "Christian Discipleship as Participatory Imitation: Theological Reflection on Girardian Themes." In *Violence Renounced*, edited by Willard Swartley. 246–76. Telford, PA: Pandora Press, 2000

Foley, Helene P. *Female Acts in Greek Tragedy*. Princeton, NJ: Princeton University Press, 2002.

Freud, Sigmund. *Civilization and Its Discontents*. Translated by James Strachey. New York: Norton, 2005.

———. *The Complete Psychological Works of Sigmund Freud*. Vol. 18: *"Beyond the Pleasure Principle," "Group Psychology" and Other Works*. Edited and translated by James Strachey. London: Hogarth and the Institute of Psychoanalysis, 2001.

Gallese, Vittorio. "The Two Sides of Mimesis: Mimetic Theory, Embodied Simulation, and Social Identification." In *Mimesis and Science: Empirical Research on Imitation and the Mimetic Theory of Culture and Religion*, edited by Scott R. Garrels, 87–108. East Lansing: Michigan State University Press, 2011.

Gambaudo, Sylvie. *Kristeva, Psychoanalysis and Culture*. London: Ashgate, 2007.

Gardner, Stephen L. "The Deepening Impasse of Modernity." *Society: Journal of the Social Sciences* 47, no. 5 (2010): 452–60.

Gillet, Lev. *Orthodox Spirituality: An Outline of the Orthodox Ascetical and Mystical Tradition*. Crestwood, NY: St. Vladimir's Seminary Press, 1978.

Girard, René. *Battling to the End: Conversations with Benoît Chantre*. Translated by Mary Baker. East Lansing: Michigan State University Press, 2009.

———. "Conversion in Literature and Christianity." In *Mimesis and Theory: Essays on Literature and Criticism, 1953–2005*, edited by Robert Doran, 263–73. Palo Alto, CA: Stanford University Press, 2008.

———. *Deceit, Desire, and the Novel: Self and Other in Literary Structure*. Translated by Translated by Yvonne Freccero. Baltimore: The Johns Hopkins University Press, 1965.

———. "From the Novelistic Experience to the Oedipal Myth." In *Oedipus Unbound: Selected Writings on Rivalry and Desire*, translated by Mark R. Anspach, 1–27. Stanford, CA: Stanford University Press, 2004.

———. "Genesis of Mimetic Theory." Imitatio Conference, April 29, 2008. http://www.youtube.com/watch?v=Ak8VXw-9NBQ&feature=youtube_gdata.

———. *I See Satan Fall Like Lightning*. Translated by James G. Williams. Maryknoll, NY: Orbis Books, 2001.

———. "An Interview with René Girard." Interview by Richard J. Golsan. In *René Girard and Myth: An Introduction*, edited by Richard J. Golsan, 129–49. New York: Routledge, 2002.

———. *Job: The Victim of His People*. Translated by Yvonne Freccero. Stanford, CA: Stanford University Press, 1987.

———. *Mensonge Romantique et Vérité Romanesque*. Paris: Grasset, 1961.

———. *Oedipus Unbound: Selected Writings on Rivalry and Desire*. Edited by Mark R. Anspach. Palo Alto, CA: Stanford University Press, 2004.

———. "Perilous Balance: A Comic Hypothesis." *MLN* 87, no. 7 (December 1972): 811–26.

———, ed. *Proust: A Collection of Critical Essays*. Upper Saddle River, NJ: Prentice-Hall, 1962.

———. "Response by René Girard. In *Violence Renounced: René Girard, Biblical Studies, and Peacemaking*, edited by Willard Swartley, 308–20. Telford, PA: Pandora Press, 2000

———. *Resurrection from the Underground: Feodor Dostoevsky*. Translated and edited by James G. Williams. East Lansing: Michigan State University Press, 2012.

———. *Sacrifice*. Translated by Matthew Pattillo and David Dawson. East Lansing: Michigan State University Press, 2011.

———. *The Scapegoat*. Translated by Yvonne Freccero. Baltimore: Johns Hopkins University Press, 1986.

———. *A Theatre of Envy: William Shakespeare*. New York: Oxford University Press, 1991.

———. *Things Hidden since the Foundation of the World*. Translated by Stephen Bann and Michael Metteer. Palo Alto, CA: Stanford University Press, 1987.

———. *To Double Business Bound: Essays on Literature, Mimesis and Anthropology*. Baltimore: Johns Hopkins University Press, 1988.

———. "Violence, Difference, Sacrifice: A Conversation with René Girard." "Violence, Difference, Sacrifice: Conversations on Myth and Culture in Theology and Literature." Edited by Rebecca Adams. Special issue of *Religion and Literature* 25, no. 2 (Summer 1993): 11–33.

———. *Violence and the Sacred*. Translated by Patrick Gregory. Baltimore: Johns Hopkins University Press, 1979.

Girard, René, Pierpaolo Antonello, and Joao Cezar de Castro Rocha. *Evolution and Conversion: Dialogues on the Origins of Culture*. New York: Continuum, 2007.

Girard, René, Jean-Michel Oughourlian, and Guy Lefort. *Des Choses Cachées Depuis la Fondation du Monde*. Paris: Grasset, 1978.

Goheen, Robert F. *The Imagery of Sophocles' "Antigone": A Study of Poetic Language and Structure*. Princeton, NJ: Princeton University Press, 1970.

Graham, Victor E. *The Imagery of Proust*. Oxford: Blackwell, 1966.

Griffiths, Jennifer L. *Traumatic Possessions: The Body and Memory in African American Women's Writing and Performance*. Charlottesville: University of Virginia Press, 2010.

Grosz, Elizabeth. *Sexual Subversions: Three French Feminists*. Crow's Nest, Australia: Allen & Unwin, 1989.

Haigh, A . E. *The Tragic Drama of the Greeks*. Oxford: Clarendon Press, 1896.

Hegel, Georg W. F. *The Phenomenology of Spirit (the Phenomenology of Mind)*. Translated by J. B. Baillie. Lawrence, KS: Digireads.com Publishing, 2009.

Heidegger, Martin. *Hölderlin's Hymn "The Ister"*. Translated by William McNeill and Julia Davis. Bloomington: Indiana University Press, 1996.

Herman, Judith. *Trauma and Recovery: The Aftermath of Violence—from Domestic Abuse to Political Terror*. New York: Basic Books, 1997.

Hinds, Stephen. "Landscape with Figures: Aesthetics of Place in the *Metamorphoses* and Its Tradition."

In *The Cambridge Companion to Ovid*, edited by Philip Hardie, 122–49. Cambridge: Cambridge University Press, 2002.

Hirsch, Marianne. *The Mother/Daughter Plot: Narrative, Psychoanalysis, Feminism*. Bloomington: Indiana University Press, 1989.

Hogan, James C. *A Commentary on the Plays of Sophocles*. Carbondale: Southern Illinois University Press, 1991.

Irigaray, Luce. "Women, the Sacred and Money." *Paragraph* 8 (1986): 6–18.

Jacobs, Amber. *On Matricide: Myth, Psychoanalysis, and the Law of the Mother*. New York: Columbia University Press, 2007.

Jacobs, Carol. "Dusting Antigone." *MLN* 111, no. 5 (1996): 890–917.

Jakobson, Roman, and Grete Lübbe-Grothues. "The Language of Schizophrenia: Hölderlin's Speech and Poetry." Translated by Susan Kitron. *Poetics Today* 2, no. 1a (1980): 137–44.

Johnsen, Rosemary Erickson. *Contemporary Feminist Historical Crime Fiction*. New York: Palgrave Macmillan, 2006.

Johnson, J. Theodore, Jr.. "Marcel Proust and Architecture: Some Thoughts on the Cathedral-Novel." In *Critical Essays on Marcel Proust*, edited by Barbara J. Bucknall, 133–61. Boston: G. K. Hall, 1987.

Johnston, Sarah Iles. *Restless Dead: Encounters between the Living and the Dead in Ancient Greece*. Berkeley: University of California Press, 1999.

Jones, Serene. *Trauma and Grace: Theology in a Ruptured World*. Louisville: Westminster John Knox Press, 2009.

Jonte-Pace, Diane. "At Home in the Uncanny: Freudian Representations of Death, Mothers, and the Afterlife." *Journal of the American Academy of Religion* 64, no. 1 (1996): 61–88.

Kearney, Richard. *Strangers, Gods and Monsters: Interpreting Otherness*. New York: Routledge, 2002.

Keltner, Stacey. *Kristeva*. Malden, MA: Polity Press, 2011.

Kirk-Duggan, Cheryl A. *Refiner's Fire: A Religious Engagement with Violence*. Minneapolis: Fortress Press, 2000.

Kirkwood, G. M. *A Study of Sophoclean Drama*. Ithaca, NY: Cornell University Press, 1994.

Kirmayer, Lawrence J. "Landscapes of Memory: Trauma, Narrative, and Dissociation." In *Tense Past: Cultural Essays in Trauma and Memory*, edited by Paul Antze and Michael Lambek, 173–98. New York: Routledge, 1996.

Knox, Bernard M. *The Heroic Temper: Studies in Sophoclean Tragedy*. Berkeley: University of California Press, 1983.

Kofman, Sarah. "The Narcissistic Woman: Freud and Girard." *Diacritics* 10, no. 3 (1980): 36–45.

Kolb, Philip. "Proust's Protagonist as a 'Beacon.'" In *Critical Essays on Marcel Proust*, edited by Barbara J. Bucknall, 50–58. Boston: G. K. Hall, 1987.

Kostis, Nicholas. "Albertine: Characterization Through Image and Symbol." In *Critical Essays on Marcel Proust*, edited by Barbara J. Bucknall, 70–92. Boston: G. K. Hall, 1987.

Kowsar, Mohammad. "Lacan's 'Antigone': A Case Study in Psychoanalytical Ethics." *Theatre Journal* 42, no. 1 (1990). doi:10.2307/3207560.

Kristeva, Julia. "Antigone: Limit and Horizon." Translated by Ella Brians. In *Feminist Readings of Antigone*, edited by Fanny Söderbäck, 215–29. Albany: State University of New York Press, 2010.

———. "Avant-Garde Practice." Interview by Vassiliki Kolocotroni. In *Julia Kristeva Interviews*, edited by Ross Mitchell Guberman, 211–25. New York: Columbia University Press, 1996

———. *Black Sun*. Translated by Leon S. Roudiez. New York: Columbia University Press, 1992.

———. *Crisis of the European Subject*. Translated Susan Fairfield. New York: Other Press, 2000.

———. "Crossing the Borders: An Interview with Julia Kristeva." Interview by Birgitte Midttun. *Hypatia* 21, no. 4 (Fall 2006): 164–77.

———. *Desire in Language: A Semiotic Approach to Literature and Art*. Translated by Leon S. Roudiez. New York: Columbia University Press, 1980.

———. "A Father Is Beaten to Death." In *The Dead Father: A Psychoanalytic Inquiry*, edited by Lila J. Kalinich and Stuart W. Taylor, 175–87. New York: Routledge, 2009.

———. *Hannah Arendt*. Translated by Ross Guberman. New York: Columbia University Press, 2003.

———. *Hatred and Forgiveness*. Translated by Jeanine Herman. New York: Columbia University Press, 2010.

———. *In the Beginning Was Love: Psychoanalysis and Faith*. Translated by Arthur Goldhammer. New York: Columbia University Press, 1988.

———. "Interview: Sharing Singularity." In *Julia Kristeva: Live Theory*, by John Lechte and Maria Margaroni, 143–63. New York: Continuum, 2004.

———. "Interview: *The Old Man and the Wolves*." Interview by Bernard Sichère. In *Julia Kristeva Interviews*, edited by Ross Mitchell Guberman, 162–75. New York: Columbia University Press, 1996.

———. *Intimate Revolt: The Powers and Limits of Psychoanalysis*. Translated by Jeanine Herman. New York: Columbia University Press, 2002.

———. "Julia Kristeva in Conversation with Rosalind Coward." In *ICA Documents*, 1:22–27. London: Institute of Contemporary Arts, 1984.

———. *Melanie Klein*. Translated by Ross Guberman. New York: Columbia University Press, 2004.

———. *Murder in Byzantium: A Novel*. Translated by C. Jon Delogu. New York: Columbia University Press, 2008.

———. *New Maladies of the Soul*. Translated by Ross Guberman. New York: Columbia University Press, 1997.

———. *The Old Man and the Wolves: A Novel*. Translated by Barbara Bray. New York: Columbia University Press, 1994.

———. "On *New Maladies of the Soul*." Interview by Catherine Francblin. In *Julia Kristeva Interviews*, edited by Ross Mitchell Guberman, 85–91. New York: Columbia University Press, 1996

———. *The Portable Kristeva*. Edited by Kelly Oliver. New York: Columbia University Press, 2002.

———. *Powers of Horror: An Essay on Abjection*. Translated by Leon S. Roudiez. New York: Columbia University Press, 1982.

———. *Proust and the Sense of Time*. Translated by Stephen Bann. New York: Columbia University Press, 1993.

———. *Revolt, She Said*. Translated by Brian O'Keeffe. Los Angeles: Semiotext(e), 2002.

———. "The Revolt of Mallarmé." Translated by Louise Burchill. In *Mallarmé in the Twentieth Century*, edited by Robert Greer Cohn, 31–52. Cranbury, NJ: Associated University Presses, 1998.

———. *Revolution in Poetic Language*. Translated by Margaret Waller. New York: Columbia University Press, 1984.

———. *The Sense and Non-Sense of Revolt*. Translated by Jeanine Herman. New York: Columbia University Press, 2001.

———. *The Severed Head: Capital Visions*. Translated by Jody Gladding. New York: Columbia University Press, 2011.

——— "Interview: Sharing Singularity." Interview. In *Julia Kristeva: Live Theory*, edited by John Lechte, 143–63. New York: Continuum, 2004.

———. *Strangers to Ourselves*. Translated by Leon S. Roudiez. New York: Columbia University Press, 1994.

———. *Tales of Love*. Translated by Leon S. Roudiez. New York: Columbia University Press, 1987.

———. *This Incredible Need to Believe*. Translated by Beverley Bie Brahic. New York: Columbia University Press, 2009.

———. *Time and Sense: Proust and the Experience of Literature*. Translated by Ross Guberman. New York: Columbia University Press, 1996.

———. *Le Vieil Homme et Les Loups: Roman*. Paris: Fayard, 1991.

———. "Women's Time." In *The Kristeva Reader*, edited by Toril Moi, 187–213. New York: Columbia University Press, 1986.

Lacan, Jacques. *Écrits: A Selection*. Translated by Alan Sheridan. 6th ed. New York: Norton, 1977.

———. *The Ethics of Psychoanalysis*. Translated by Dennis Porter. Book 7 of *The Seminar of Jacques Lacan*, edited by Jacques Alain-Miller New York: Norton, 1997.

———. *Feminine Sexuality: Jacques Lacan and the École Freudienne*. Edited by Juliet Mitchell and Jacqueline Rose. Translated by Jacqueline Rose. New York: Norton, 1985.

———. *The Four Fundamental Concepts of Psychoanalysis*. Edited by Jacques-Alain Miller. Translated by Alan Sheridan. New York: Norton, 1998.

———. *On Feminine Sexuality: The Limits of Love and Knowledge*. Translated by Bruce Fink. Book 20 of *The Seminar of Jacques Lacan*, edited by Jacques-Alain Miller. New York: Norton, 1999.

———. *Le Séminaire de Jacques Lacan Livre VII*. Edited by Jacques-Alain Miller. Paris: Seuil, 1986.

LaCapra, Dominick. *Writing History, Writing Trauma*. Baltimore: Johns Hopkins University Press, 2000.

Lacoursiere, Roy B. "Proust and Parricide: Literary, Biographical, and Forensic-Psychiatric Explorations." *American Imago* 60, no. 2 (2003): 179–210. doi:10.1353/aim.2003.0013.

Ladenson, Elisabeth. *Proust's Lesbianism*. Ithaca, NY: Cornell University Press, 2007.

Lázaro-Reboll, Antonio. "Counter-Rational Reason: Goya's Instrumental Negotiations of Flesh and World." *History of European Ideas* 30 (2004): 109–19.

Lechte, John. *Julia Kristeva*. New York: Routledge, 1990.

———. "Love, Life, Complexity and the 'Flesh' in Kristeva's Writing Experience." In *The Kristeva Critical Reader*, edited by John Lechte and Mary Zournazi, 185–201. Edinburgh: Edinburgh University Press, 2004.

Lechte, John, and Maria Margaroni. *Julia Kristeva: Live Theory*. New York: Continuum, 2005.

Lechte, John, and Mary Zournazi, eds. *The Kristeva Critical Reader*. Edinburgh: Edinburgh University Press, 2004.

Lennon, T. M. "Proust and the Phenomenology of Memory." *Philosophy and Literature* 31, no. 1 (2007): 52–66.

Loraux, Nicole. *The Mourning Voice: An Essay on Greek Tragedy*. Translated by Elizabeth Trapnell Rawlings. Ithaca, NY: Cornell University Press, 2002.

———. *Tragic Ways of Killing a Woman*. Translated by Anthony Forster. Cambridge: Harvard University Press, 1991.

Lossky, Vladimir. *The Mystical Theology of the Eastern Church*. St. Vladimir's Seminary Press, 1997.

Lossky, Vladimir, and Leonid Ouspensky. *The Meaning of Icons*. Crestwood, NY: St. Vladimir's Seminary Press, 1982.

Lutzky, Harriet. "Mourning and Immortality: Ritual and Psychoanalysis Compared." In *Mourning Religion*, edited by Wiliam B. Parsons, Diane Jonte-Pace, and Susan E. Henking, 141–157. Charlottesville, VA: University of Virginia Press, 2008.

MacKendrick, Karmen. *Fragmentation and Memory: Meditations on Christian Doctrine*. New York: Fordham University Press, 2008.

Mader, Mary Beth. "Antigone's Line." In *Feminist Readings of Antigone*, edited by Fanny Söderbäck, 155–72. Albany: State University of New York Press, 2010.

Mahmood, Saba. *Politics of Piety: The Islamic Revival and the Feminist Subject*. Princeton, NJ: Princeton University Press, 2005.

McAfee, Noëlle. *Julia Kristeva*. New York: Routledge, 2003.

McCart, Gregory. "Masks in Greek and Roman Theatre." In *The Cambridge Companion to Greek and Roman Theatre*, edited by Marianne McDonald and Michael Walton, 247–67. New York: Cambridge University Press, 2007.

Merleau-Ponty, Maurice. "The Child's Relations with Others." In *The Primacy of Perception*, translated by William Cobb, 96–155. Evanston, IL: Northwestern University Press, 1964.

———. *Phenomenology of Perception*. Translated by Colin Smith. 2nd ed. London: Routledge, 1962.

———. *The Visible and the Invisible*. Translated by Alphonso Lingis. Evanston, IL: Northwestern University Press, 1968.

Meier, Christian. *The Political Art of Greek Tragedy*. Baltimore: Johns Hopkins University Press, 1993.

Milton, Jane, Caroline Polmear, and Julia Fabricius. *A Short Introduction to Psychoanalysis*. 2nd ed. Thousand Oaks, CA: Sage, 2011.

Mitchell, Juliet. *Mad Men and Medusas: Reclaiming Hysteria*. New York: Basic Books, 2001.

———. "Sibling Trauma: A Theoretical Consideration." In *Sibling Relationships*, edited by Prophecy Coles, 155–174. New York: Karnac Books, 2006.

———. *Siblings: Sex and Violence*. Malden, MA: Polity, 2004.

Moi, Toril. "The Missing Mother: The Oedipal Rivalries of René Girard." *Diacritics* 12 (1982): 21–31.

Montiglio, Silvia. *Silence in the Land of Logos*. Princeton, NJ: Princeton University Press, 2010.

Moorjani, Angela. *The Aesthetics of Loss and Lessness*. London: Palgrave Macmillan, 1991.

Nowak, Susan. "The Girardian Theory and Feminism: Critique and Appropriation." *Contagion* 1, no. 1 (1994): 19–29.

O'Grady, Kathleen. "The Tower and the Chalice: Julia Kristeva and the Story of Santa Barbara." In *Religion in French Feminist Thought: Critical Perspectives*, edited by Kathleen O'Grady, Judith L. Poxon, and Morny Joy, 85–100. New York: Routledge, 2003.

Oliver, Kelly. *The Colonization of Psychic Space: A Psychoanalytic Social Theory of Oppression*. Minneapolis: University of Minnesota Press, 2004.

———. *Reading Kristeva: Unraveling the Double-Bind*. Bloomington: Indiana University Press, 1993.

———. "Revolt and Forgiveness." In *Revolt, Affect, Collectivity: The Unstable Boundaries of Kristeva's Polis*. Albany: State University of New York Press, 2005.

Oughourlian, Jean-Michel. *The Genesis of Desire*. East Lansing: Michigan State University Press, 2010.

Ovid. *Metamorphoses: A New Translation by Charles Martin*. New York: Norton, 2005.

Padel, Ruth. *In and Out of the Mind*. Princeton, NJ: Princeton University Press, 1994.

———. *Whom Gods Destroy: Elements of Greek and Tragic Madness*. Princeton, NJ: Princeton University Press, 1995.

Painter, George D. *Marcel Proust: A Biography*. Vol. 2. New York: Vintage, 1978.

Pankejeff, Sergius. *The Wolf-Man: With the Case of the Wolf-Man*. New York: Basic Books, 1971.

Parker, Robert. *Miasma: Pollution and Purification in Early Greek Religion*. New York: Oxford University Press, 1996.

Payne, Michael. *Reading Theory: An Introduction to Lacan, Derrida and Kristeva*. Hoboken, NJ: Wiley-Blackwell, 1993.

Pozzi, Dora. "The Metaphor of Sacrifice in Sophocles' 'Antigone' 853–856." *Hermes* 117, no. 4 (1989): 500–505.

Proust, Marcel. *Contre Sainte Beuve*. Paris: Gallimard, 1954.

———. *Contre Sainte-Beuve*. Translated by P. Clarac and Y. Sandre. Paris: Gallimard, 1971.

———. "Filial Sentiments of a Parricide." Translated by Barbara Anderson. *Partisan Review* 15 (1948): 91–99.

———. *Finding Time Again*. Vol. 6 of *In Search of Lost Time*. Translated by Ian Patterson. New York: Penguin Classics, 2003.

———. *The Guermantes Way*. Vol. 3 of *In Search of Lost Time*. Translated by Mark Treharne. New York: Penguin Classics, 2005.

———. *In the Shadow of Young Girls in Flower*. Vol. 6 of *In Search of Lost Time*. Translated by James Grieve. New York: Penguin Classics, 2005.

———. *The Prisoner* and *The Fugitive*. Vol. 5 of *In Search of Lost Time*. Translated by Carol Clark and Peter Collier. New York: Penguin Classics, 2003.

———. *Remembrance of Things Past*. Translated by C. K. Scott Moncrieff and Terence Kilmartin. Vol. 1. New York: Random House, 1981.

———. *Selected Letters*. Vol. 2: *1904–1909*. Edited by Philip Kolb. Translated by Terence Kilmartin. New York: Oxford University Press, 1989.

———. "Sentiments Filiaux d'un Parricide." In *Contre Sainte-Beuve*, edited by P. Clarac and Y. Sandre, 150–59. Paris: Gallimard, 1971.

———. *Sodom and Gomorrah*. Vol. 4 of *In Search of Lost Time*. Translated by John Sturrock. New York: Penguin Classics, 2005.

———. *Swann's Way*. Translated by C. K. Scott Moncrieff and Terence Kilmartin. New York: Modern Library, 2004.

———. *Swann's Way*. Vol. 1 of *In Search of Lost Time*. Translated by Lydia Davis. New York: Penguin Classics, 2004.

———. *Within a Budding Grove*. Vol. 2 of *In Search of Lost Time*. Translated by C. K. Scott Moncrieff and Terence Kilmartin. New York: Modern Library, 1998.

Putnam, Michael C. J. *Tibullus: A Commentary*. Norman: University of Oklahoma Press, 1979.

Raab, Kelley A. *When Women Become Priests*. New York: Columbia University Press, 2000.

Rehm, Rush. *Marriage to Death: The Conflation of Wedding and Funeral Rituals in Greek Tragedy*. Princeton, NJ: Princeton University Press, 1996.

Reineke, Martha J. "After the Scapegoat: René Girard's Apocalyptic Vision and the Legacy of Mimetic Theory." *Philosophy Today*, 56, no. 2 (Summer 2012): 141–53.

———. "Not a Country for Old Men: Mimesis and Violence in Santa Varvara." In *Kristeva's Fiction*, edited by Benigno Trigo, 57–78. Binghampton: State University of New York Press, 2013.

———. *Sacrificed Lives: Kristeva on Women and Violence*. Bloomington: Indiana University Press, 1997.

Ricardou, Jean, and Erica Freiberg. "Proust: A Retrospective Reading." *Critical Inquiry* 8 (1982): 531–41.

Ricoeur, Paul. *The Symbolism of Evil*. Translated by Emerson Buchanan. Boston: Beacon Press, 1986.

Rike, Jennifer. "The Cycle of Violence and Feminist Construction of Selfhood." *Contagion* 3 (1996): 21–42.

Robertson, Noel. *Religion and Reconciliation in Greek Cities: The Sacred Laws of Selinus and Cyrene*. New York: Oxford University Press, 2009.

Rogers, Brian. "Proust's Narrator." In *The Cambridge Companion to Proust*, edited by Richard Bales, 85–99. Cambridge: Cambridge University Press, 2001.

Roith, Estelle. "Ishmael and Isaac: An Enduring Conflict." In *Sibling Relationships*, edited by Prophecy Coles, 49–73. London: Karnac Books, 2006.

Rosivach, Vincent. "The Two Worlds of the *Antigone*." *Illinois Classical Studies* 4 (1979): 16–26.

Ross, Suzanne. *The Wicked Truth about Love: The Tangles of Desire*. Glenview, IL: Doers Publishing, 2009.

Schmid, Marion, "The Birth and Development of *A la Recherche du Temps Perdu*." In *The Cambridge Companion to Proust*, edited by Richard Bales, 58–73. New York: Cambridge University Press, 2001.

Schwager, Raymund. *Must There Be Scapegoats?* Translated by Maria L. Assad. New York: Herder & Herder, 2000.

Scubla, Lucien. "The Christianity of René Girard and the Nature of Religion." Translated by Mark R. Anspach. In *Violence and Truth: On the Work of René Girard*, edited by Paul Dumouchel, 160–78. Stanford, CA: Stanford University Press, 1988.

Segal, Charles. *Interpreting Greek Tragedy: Myth, Poetry, Text*. Ithaca, NY: Cornell University Press, 1986.

———. "Spectator and Listener." In *The Greeks*, edited by Jean-Pierre Vernant, 184–217. Chicago: University of Chicago Press, 1995.

———. *Tragedy and Civilization: An Interpretation of Sophocles*. Cambridge: Harvard University Press, 1981.

Shattuck, Roger. *Proust*. London: Fontana Press, 1974.

Shea, Christine. "Victims on Violence: 'Different Voices' and Girard." In *Curing Violence*, edited by Mark I. Wallace, 252–65. Salem, OR: Polebridge Press, 1994.

Shepherdson, Charles. "Antigone: The Work of Literature and the History of Subjectivity." In *Bound by the City: Greek Tragedy, Sexual Difference, and the Formation of the Polis*, edited by Denise Eileen McCoskey and Emily Zakin, 47–80. Albany: State University of New York Press, 2009.

Sichère, Bernard. "Roman Noir et Temps Présent." *L'Infini* 37 (Spring 1992): 75–86.

Sjöholm, Cecilia. *The Antigone Complex: Ethics and the Invention of Feminine Desire*. Stanford, CA: Stanford University Press, 2004.

———. "Fear of Intimacy? Psychoanalysis and the Resistance to Commodification." In *Psychoanalysis, Aesthetics, and Politics in the Work of Julia Kristeva*, edited by Kelly Oliver and S. K. Keltner, 179–94. Albany: State University of New York Press, 2009.

Smith, Anna. *Julia Kristeva: Readings of Exile and Estrangement*. New York: Palgrave Macmillan, 1996.

Smith, Anne-Marie. *Julia Kristeva: Speaking the Unspeakable*. London: Pluto Press, 1998.

Solodow, Joseph B. *The World of Ovid's Metamorphoses*. Chapel Hill: University of North Carolina Press, 2002.

Sophocles. *Antigone, The Women of Trachis, Philoctetes, Oedipus at Colonus*. Loeb Classical Library. Cambridge, MA: Harvard University Press, 1994.

———. *Sophocles*. Translated by David Grene. Chicago: University of Chicago Press, 1991.

———. *Sophocles' "Antigone"*. Edited by Mark Griffith. New York: Cambridge University Press, 1999.

———. *Sophocles' "Oedipus at Colonus"*. Translated by Mary Whitlock Blundell. Focus Classical Library. Newburyport, MA: Focus, 1990.

Splitter, Randolph. *Proust's Recherche: A Psychoanalytic Interpretation*. Boston: Routledge & Kegan Paul, 1981.

Staniloae, Dumitru. *Orthodox Dogmatic Theology*. New York: Continuum International Publishing Group, 2002.

———. *Orthodox Spirituality: A Practical Guide for the Faithful and a Definitive Manual for the Scholar*. Translated by Archimandrite Jerome and Otilia Kloos. South Canaan, PA: St. Tikhon's Seminary Press, 2003.

Stein, Ruth. *For Love of the Father: A Psychoanalytic Study of Religious Terrorism*. Palo Alto, CA: Stanford University Press, 2009.

Steiner, George. *Antigones*. New Haven: Yale University Press, 1996.

Swartley, Willard M. *Covenant of Peace: The Missing Peace in New Testament Theology and Ethics*. Grand Rapids, MI: Eerdmans, 2006.

Tibullus, Albius. *The Poems of Tibullus*. Edited by E. M. Michael. Bloomington: Indiana University Press, 1968.

Tucker, David. "Snowbound." In *Late for Work*, 26. Boston: Houghton Mifflin, 2006.

Tyrrell, Wm. Blake, and Larry J. Bennett. *Recapturing Sophocles' "Antigone"*. Lanham, MD: Rowman & Littlefield, 1998.

———. "Sophocles' Enemy Sisters: Antigone and Ismene." *Contagion* 15–16 (2008–9): 1–18.

Van der Kolk, Bessie, and Onno Van der Hart. "The Intrusive Past: The Flexibility of Memory and the Engraving of Trauma." In *Trauma: Explorations in Memory*, edited by Cathy Caruth, 158–82. Baltimore: Johns Hopkins University Press, 1995.

Waller, Margaret. "Intertextuality and Literary Interpretation." In *Julia Kristeva Interviews*, edited by Ross Mitchell Guberman, 188–202. New York: Columbia University Press, 1996.

Webb, Eugene. *The Self Between: From Freud to the New Social Psychology of France*. Seattle: University of Washington Press, 1993.

Williams, James G. *The Bible, Violence, and the Sacred: Liberation from the Myth of Sanctioned Violence*. New York: HarperCollins, 1991.

Worthington, Everett L., et al. "Compassion and Forgiveness: Implications for Psychotherapy." In *Compassion: Conceptualisations, Research, and Use in Psychotherapy*, ed. Paul Gilbert, 168–92. New York: Routledge, 2005.

Zakin, Emily. "Marrying the City: Intimate Strangers and the Fury of Democracy." In *Bound by the City: Greek Tragedy, Sexual Difference, and the Formation of the Polis*, edited by Denise Eileen McCoskey and Emily Zakin, 177–96. Albany: State University of New York Press, 2009

Zeitlin, Froma I. "Thebes: Theater of Self and Society in Athenian Drama." In *Nothing to Do with Dionysos? Athenian Drama in Its Social Context*, edited by John J. Winkler and Froma I. Zeitlin, 130–67. Princeton, NJ: Princeton University Press, 1992.

Ziarek, Ewa. "At the Limits of Discourse: Heterogeneity, Alterity, and the Maternal Body in Kristeva's Thought." *Hypatia* 7, no. 2 (1992): 91–108.

———. "Kristeva and Levinas: Mourning, Ethics, and the Feminine." In *Ethics, Politics, and Difference in Julia Kristeva's Writing*, edited by Kelly Oliver, 62–78. New York: Routledge, 1993.

Index